Notes for Juicy Ghosts

Rudy Rucker

Including Notes
For the Short Stories
"Surfers at the End of Time"
"Juicy Ghost"
"Everything Is Everything"
"The Mean Carrot"
"Mary Mary" and
"Fibonacci's Humors"

Transreal Books
Los Gatos, California

SHORT CONTENTS

FULL CONTENTS

WRITING JOURNAL

October 18-24, 2018. Seeds for "Juicy Ghost."

This entry is drawn in part from my July 20-23, 2017 entry in the "Writing Journal" section of my volume, *Return to the Hollow Earth Notes*. But I keep editing this entry. I'm in the mode of what G. I. Gurdjieff called, "Wiseacreing for the Swing of Thought."

***

Cory Doctorow's 2017 *Walkaway* is so modern and relevant. I posted a big review of it on my blog. He does a lot of stuff with converting people into "sims" that live in the cloud as ghosts that are embodied on Earth via sensors and such effectors as drones. It's a move I introduced in my novel *Software*, some forty years ago, and by now it's acquired new twists. Why shouldn't I pick up that tune again? Call it, like, *Juicy Ghost*.

Certainly software immortality is a popular topic now. So I wouldn't be oversaturating the market even though Cory just wrote about it. I'm the old grandee, the master of the trope.

As Cory has it in *Walkaway*, the cloud sims have Earthly sensor/effector embodiment in that they can use very rich senses in our world—eyes, ears, tastes, smells, and even haptic touch probes. The sensing can be taps and bugs or indie drone-type things, like bundles called, um, *gnoses*. "The gnose peered at him, sniffing the currents of air, cocking its anterior knob to one side, and cleaning an antenna with a pincer." Gnose like gnostic. Better than *knose* like knows.

The gnoses can of course act as effectors as well. And the ghost's taps and bugs can use our machines and networks as effectors as well. In a broader sense individuals and cohorts of humans can become ghosts' effectors as well—either by *Freeware*-style leech-DIMs or via simple propaganda.

So I do the move of people becoming like ghosts, in the cloud, gloating over Earth, running in quantum computational strata, and then they notice there are "real" ghosts or god or animistic spirits there already.

The afterworld—Twas ever thus! Maybe the "real" ghosts have an issue we have to solve.

***

Another hit for me in 2017 was Chris Brown's *Tropic of Kansas*. I read it on my Kindle, it's very political, along the lines of *1984*. Posted on this one, too. Chris is a charming guy from Austin, TX, maybe 50 years old, a lawyer, author of numerous fantasy stories, and this is his first novel.

In July, 2017, we had dinner in SF with Chris, and Michael Blumlein, and Joseph & Rena of Tachyon Books, and my then Night Shade editor Jeremy Lassen

I told Chris my notion of having someone move their mind/soul into the cloud, and I remarked that chip-based computers wouldn't actually be powerful enough to do the necessary personality-maintaining crunch, and I explained that we'd be using matter-computers, that is, quantum computational chunks of (somehow) tamed matter. And I told Chris that when my character transfers to that platform, he or she senses that something else is in there, and it's a "real" ghost. Turns out all along people's ghosts have been migrating up into the hylozoic and panpsychic matrix of rich matter. Chris loved my book idea, he said only I could do it.

***

And I'll work in some politics. I'd like to step forward to help raise the nation's consciousness lest (or especially *if*) Trump is reelected in 2020. It's my civic duty, you could say. Reading the ongoing news about what our so-called President is doing, I feel amped up for protest. Bursting. I think would feel good to write a hard-core rabble-rousing political novel. A good time for it, historically speaking.

By the way, here's an image of my painting, "The Tyrant's Wife", from October, 2018, when Trump was pushing through the new Supreme Court justice Kavanaugh. Originally that mean guy on the right was inspired by Lindsay Graham, but as I worked on the painting, I tweaked it to be Trump.

On the other hand, current-events novels don't age well? Yet, look at *1984* and *Clockwork Orange* and *Man in the High Castle* and *The Trial*. Classics of political paranoia. Note that these books are deliberately somewhat removed from our

actual world. More fable-like. But to universalize it, things
have to be not too close to our world, I think.

Figure 1: *The Tyrant's Wife* (Painting of Trump)

Mathematicians in Love had a political flavor, as did the
Postsingular diptych, not that anyone especially noticed. Even
if I do politics, I don't like being sour and bitter. I like sunny
and sense-of-wonder. I've always wanted to see politics wither
away, rather than becoming even more central. So maybe I
invoke some ghosts that simply execute every single
Republican oppressor. Of course, the French-revolution-type
"off with their heads" strategy never ends well. It runs wild,
turns against the splinter groups within the revolutionary party,
and provokes Draconian retaliation from the enemies.

Could my juicy ghosts do something other than killing the
pigs? Dial up their empathy? Allay their fears? Give them
prophetic dreams? A new way out. Group hugs instead of the
guillotine.

***

Another thread: I'd like to work in some of the Gibson-
style time travel moves like from *The Peripheral*. My move

11

could be to have a Gibsonian weak embodiment of juicy ghosts into our physical world, across time, as peripherals. The juicy ghosts are sending signals back and forth between now and the future and the past, and embodying themselves as peripherals—which don't have to be machines. They could be bio things. Rabbits. Or social factions. Or, for that matter, bugs in our networks and machines.

Not sure if I'd like to have a character be living in the cloud as a juicy ghost, at least not long term. Being dead is basically boring, I fear.

I could have the main story for *Juicy Ghost* be in the future. *Or* have it be in a near future, and they hop to the far future, maybe I should hop to the 22nd century, not the 21st. This is suggested by a remark by William Gibson in an interview. He's, like, "In the old days everyone was dreaming about the 21st C. And now we're there, so why aren't people dreaming about the 22nd C?" Well, maybe we just haven't gotten around to it yet. But it's a good idea. They live in 2050, and they jump to 2150. A hundred years.

In Bruce Sterling's Oct 16, 2018, talk "How to Be Futuristic" he makes the point that, now that it's the 21st Century, we're not so interested in older SF novels that make (incorrect or jejune) speculations about the 21st C. Gives you more shelf life to set the book in 22nd C.

     ***

Should either the near future or far future world be a dystopia? Easy move is the near future is dystopia and the 22nd C world is a utopia, and that's a happy thing to think about, a hopeful prospect, and how do we get from here to there. And that way I'm not stuck in full dystopia all the time. If we know we will escape, we can even laugh at the down part a little. I'm tired of people writing "seriously" about dystopias. As I always say, I want *escape literature*. Fun stuff. So in the golden future, we're *past* the dystopia. Of course then, if we want a twist, the bottom of the future utopia falls out, or is about to fall out, and my heroes prevent that.

Or the other way around: the future fixes *us*.

Random idea: you could have a seamy underside to the future utopia. They have free energy magical subdimensional "twinklers." Only later do we learn the twinklers are enslaved juicy ghost souls. But, (someone might argue) isn't every type of matter a kind of slavery? Condemned to be a proton. Like working forty hours a week as a waitress, or on a car assembly line. When you'd rather be an angel. Or an aethereal vibration singing the Music of the Spheres.

October 25-26, 2018. Character.

So I've got some general ideas about things to put into the book. I went back and reread my review of Cory's *Walkaway*, which has a lot of good quotes from that novel. I don't think I could work up Cory's kind of chatty, revolutionary, young-people cast, much as I like that stuff. I'm too old and jaded and out of the loop.

So do *that* kind of character, that is, an old man. He risks all to assassinate an evil dictator, someone like our worst dreams of a guy like Donald Trump reading a full Hitlerian apotheosis. Call him Treadwell. Or maybe just the Moron. Or Treadle. Our hero has to kill Treadle, not only in our physical world, but in the cloud. Kind of a Terminator thing…it's not enough to kill him just *once*. Oh, and our hero gets killed by the Secret Service when he assassinates Treadle, but he's already backed up into the juicy-ghost-cloud.

My guy is fairly confident. His employer gives strong assurances.

[Perhaps the employer is someone from the future tells him that he *will* succeed. Closed causal loop—but that's perfectly okay. And if there could be a paradox, we undo it via magic healing and amnesia. Some of the time travel numbers done on the past are never publicly known. Secret miracles. But I don't think I want to muddy the waters with time travel here, it's not needed.]

Possible twist: the person who engages our guy to do the assassination of Treadle is in fact an agent of Treadle's party, who orchestrates this to make Treadle a martyr, and revivifies his party's fortunes.

***

And we need a woman. The hero's wife? His controller?

***

And even if the book is about a political assassination, I want it to be, in some dry sense, funny. Writing degree zero.

Language with a flat tire. He's kind of a transreal me, but how I'd be if I was taking some new kind of drug. Would be a nice virtual high for me, writing it.

Reality Clipping. High Vibrance. I think of Milgrim who was on Ativan in Gibson's *Spook Country*. Or of the "old writer who lived in a boxcar by the river" in Burroughs's *The Western Lands*. And, especially, Elmore Leonard's characters. It doesn't absolutely have to be chemical drugs my guy is taking. Software highs are cool too. Like make the world seem to run twice as fast or a hundred times slower. I'm working up some bogus tech in my "secret" Rucker X lab.

Might I include flying saucers? Well, maybe, but maybe they're really small. And they look like elves. Yes, elves are fresher than saucers. Rizing up from the subdimensions. They're used as Gibson *peripherals*, that is, gnostic "gnoses" being "driven" by minds in the biotech-based cloud. The people in that cloud can sense what's on Earth, and they can use elves from the subdimensions as their meaty little effectors. Thereby they're embodied.

To make it sweeter, I'll take another arrow from Gibson's quiver—the minds and the sensor/effectors might be in different temporal locations. Thanks to the cross-time communication channel of subdimensional subquantum wheenk. But, again, I'm leaning towards *not* doing time travel. The cloud afterlife, and the peripheral embodiment, and the biotech juicy ghost routines are enough.

All this is "breaking news" to me. That is, I made it up as I typed a blog post today, "The Old Writer Scheming.". And here's a premonition painting I did of some people who might be in the book.

A time travel idea I had today. A new way out of the old yes & no paradox...you go back in time and shoot yourself in the head from behind, and then do you die? Well, the way out is that the original organic you *does* die, but someone takes your splattered head and assembled a biotech kritter version of you, and installs a juicy ghost of you in the kritter, and the "you" that is the juicy-ghost-driven kritter somehow never notices it is fake, or is in denial about it, and this fake you is the version of the you that lives on, and eventually it does the trip to the past to kill the original organic you. So no paradox?

Figure 2: *People of the Red Saucer*

Well, no there's still a slight problem, which is that now it seems there's two new-yous, the one that traveled back in time, and the one that was created from the remains of the dead organic you, and this could iteratively make many of the fake yous. To nip this in the bud, we need for organic you to in fact destroy the new you from the future. They kill each other, and then the remains become the new you that goes into the future and comes back and kills the organic you, and then gets instantiated as a new you. The new you, in other words is a closed causal loop with a node at the death of the old organic you.

I could make this into an SF short story if I wanted to. I mean, it's logical. But would anyone want to read it? Well, that would be up to me—adding characterization, motivation, romance, etc. Have a trans thing too, maybe, with new you the opposite gender from you.

Whenever there's what might be a paradox, it turns up the universe has vitiated it via special effects. I've always *hated* branching time lines as a paradox solution. Only one timeline, but it's constructed all at once, holistically, and it has back loops, but any possible illogic is carefully tweaked away.

October 30, 2018 - Jan 7, 2019. "Surfers At the End of Time."

Oct 30, 2018.

Speaking of time travel, I'm temporarily detouring into a full-on time travel tale with Marc Laidlaw, another of our Surfin' SF Zep & Del stories. I'm going to develop my idea that the universe smoothest over time-travel paradoxes by miraculously healing over any heretofore-unknown depredations by future-to-past time travelers. And I guess there would have to be convenient amnesia as well, so that you don't remember that encounter with your next-week self.

Funny twist—we were at Rudy Jr's family Halloween party, complete with kid-organized haunted house in the basement, and I'm texting Marc L. about the story idea, saying Zep and Del should be living in a rented condo in a gray/beige building off the Great Highway by Ocean Beach. And then in kitchen I meet this long-haired friend of Penny & Rudy's and he's wearing a horned Viking helmet and his hair's partly in braids and he has a long beard, he's wiry and lively, and he tells me he's a big wave surfer and he lives in a condo on the Great Highway. Synchronicity! Thank you, Muse!

And I text Marc, and he texts back, "HE'S A TIME TRAVELLER, DUDE." And then I used that for my first scene. A guy who looks like that, but who is in fact the future Zep, comes and cuts Zep in half with his broad sword, and then he leaves, and Zep's body heals up, and Del and Zep temporarily forget about the encounter.

Want to have a couple of cute, feisty Time Police woman as well. I see them in old-school Pan-Am stewardess outfits.

A little worried that doing the story might "use up" some of the ideas I want for the novel. But I sort of want to do it.

Nov 2, 2018.

I wrote a 2,000 word start and sent it to Marc. The boys live in a condo off Ocean Beach. Future Zep shows up and kills now-Zep, who then heals over after Future Zep leaves. A couple of future women show up too. Marc's not sure what to do next, and we don't really have a plan for the whole story. I hope he just writes something, and we can go on from there. He wants to have a surfing contest in 2150, which sounds really boring to me. Maybe if it was somehow "time surfing" it could be interesting.

November 7, 2018

We're up to 6,000 words. I wrote an opening with future Zep splitting our Zep and Del in halves that regenerate. That way at the end, one pair will have gone off into the cosmos, and the other pair can still be surfing on grotty Ocean Beach. We have two women characters too, weird Sally and punk Gother. And possibly Gother's son Lars.

Marc wrote a section where they use a time machine that looks like a surfing handboard to hop to 2150. And, looking ahead, I'm imagining a final stop in the year one million. I think having an intermediate stop at year 10,000 would be too much. I want to get the story finished, and not have it bloat into a novel.

I see this as a double love story. And it has loop explanations of how the couples met, and of how the time machine came to be. Here's a hard-won diagram that explains it. I'm surprised how complicated it turned out, but that's where the logic leads. I had to draw it five times to get it even this tidy. By the way I marked successive instances of the love relations between the two couples, and I numbered these heart-throb moments from the women's point of view. And the notes below help clarify this.

To Do

* I'll insert an initial scene of Zep having a vision of a time travel technique. He has this vision while surfing alone by the standing waves of the Potato Patch near GG Bridge. We need it because otherwise, Zep and Del have no *agency*. They need to be *causing* this chain of events to happen.

* How does time travel with the handboard work? I'd like to make it crisper than having someone swim circles around you as you bob up and down. That's a good start, but we need

more. The natural move is a vortex that becomes a time tunnel. And this wormhole or time tunnel is an ER bridge like I've often described. Basically a 4D cylinder, that is, a stack of spheres. So along the way, Zep, Del, Gother, and Lars will be in a spherical cross-section of the tunnel, like in an observation bubble, and they'll see San Francisco growing over a century, like Marc wrote about.

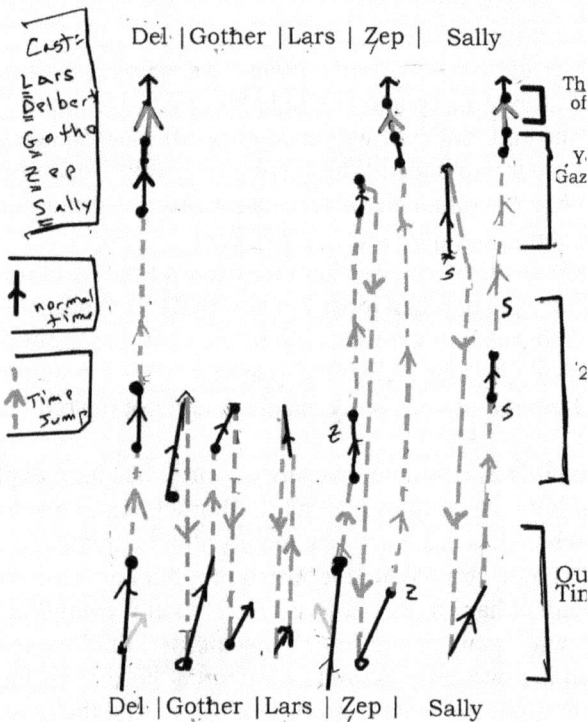

Figure 3: Early Draft of Time Lines for "Surfers at the End of Time"

* How do Viking Zep and Sally time travel back to the future *without* a handboard? Viking Zep can use his sword, and Sally can use an amulet hanging from her neck. Lars can use his beanie, by the way. I need more rubber science behind the time machine workings. Think of a double 4D rotation. Like a Necker cube. Inside/outside. Sally's amulet is a birefringent

crystal mirror with two images that do-si-do around each other, creating a real-space rotation that sets off the vortex that becomes the time tunnel. Lars's beanie does the same thing, reversing its direction in a dynamic-Necker-Cube-style Pulfrich Effect. The handboard cuts very sharp lines into the water in a peculiar Celtic knot that generates a vortex via autopoesis. Zep sweeps his Viking sword in oddly entangled space curves. (Like that thing where a performer holds a glass high on a tray, and then somehow brings the tray under his arm, and then out to the side.)

* When Gother meets Del in the hospital cafeteria, she says "Hello, stranger." Because they already fell in love in the future (which came earlier in Gother's timeline). Ditto, Sally has in fact met Zep before (relative to her own timeline). The two women haven't been in SF long at all. (Possibly Gother is in a futuristic tent on the beach.).

* When Del gets to 2150, Gother leads him to younger Gother (relative to Gother's personal timeline). She urges him on. The younger Gother doesn't know Del yet. But Del charms her, and they get a romance going. Del knows a little about Gother by now—like how Bill Murray in *Groundhog Day* woos a girl with past knowledge of her taste. Del charms Gother and moves in with her. Meanwhile the older Gother is around, but in the background.

* Meanwhile in 2150 SF, Zep is using his handboard in the bay, figuring out and improving the handboard time machine. Then he announces he's invented it. Acclaim.

*And then a younger Sally and the younger Gother steal the handboard and go back to give it to Zep in 2018. But, where did Sally come from in 2150? Well, she hopped there from year million, where she was born. So relative to her own timeline, it's a *younger* Sally that shows up in 2150. Anyway, younger Sally and younger Gother repossess Zep's handboard time machine and take it back to Ocean Beach where Zep and Del can get it.

* Then Gother jumps to 2150 with Z & D, sics Del on her earlier self, as described, and then her earlier self disappears (going back to 2018 with younger Sally) and our original Gother is the only Gother in 2150. And she has Del to herself in 2150. (For a little while there were two Gother women, but I

don't think they interacted much, but maybe they did.

* Now why did younger Sally jump to 2150 from year million? It's kind of similar to Gother's motives, that is, it's a love thing. Having left with Viking Zep in the first scene our Sally is in the far future, and younger Sally sees her and Zep, and falls in love with Zep. Hearing from the older Sally and from older Zep that there's a Zep in 2150 SF, younger Sally hops back there up so she can accompany younger Gother to 2018 Ocean Beacon and deliver the handboard.

*What's the motive for the hop from 2150 to the far future year million by Del, Gother and Zep? Well, while Sally was passing through on her way to 2018, she told them all to come to year million because it's so cool and the Sun is about to explode and the Earthlings are about to spread out into the galaxy. A real scene.

* Note that Lars has essentially no function in the plot, so we might cut him. But he's interesting and let's hope to find something for the lad to do. Marc had mentioned Gother's ex-husband, and we might use him as a villain, but maybe just explaining the whole timeline tangle is excitement enough. At one time I'd mentioned a stop in year 10,000 as well, but three stops are going to be more than enough. Keep it simple as a four-person love-farce, with the kicker about the extra Zep and Del in the final scene. Pare it down like a geometric figure. Note that the final Zep and Del were regenerated from their *butts*.

November 19, 2018

Marc has been working for about a week on his next addition to the story. Meanwhile we've exchanged over twenty emails about what he's doing, or planning to do, or planning to revise. At one level I wish he'd just do something and mail it to me. I don't like getting into a head-space where I imagine I'm tussling with him over the material, like two lepers fighting over an *obol* coin in the gutter, in Pynchon's phrase. Or like two dogs growling over a greasy bone. And I get anxious about finishing the story at all. This said, I *do* like hearing from Marc so often. His letters are always interesting, and he gives me something to think about, and I get to exercise my voice in writing my replies. And probably all the time he's putting into the story will make it better.

November 23, 2018

I got Marc's Version 4 and am working on a Version 5. That gnome-like Lars kid is now a murg and Marc has him selling Murgburgers which are supposedly made of ground-up murgs, but also seem to be made of those pillbugs that Sally gave Zep and Del. Marc didn't decide. I can't quite see the murg beings grinding themselves up for food. And if they did, wouldn't everyone already be infested in a year or two?

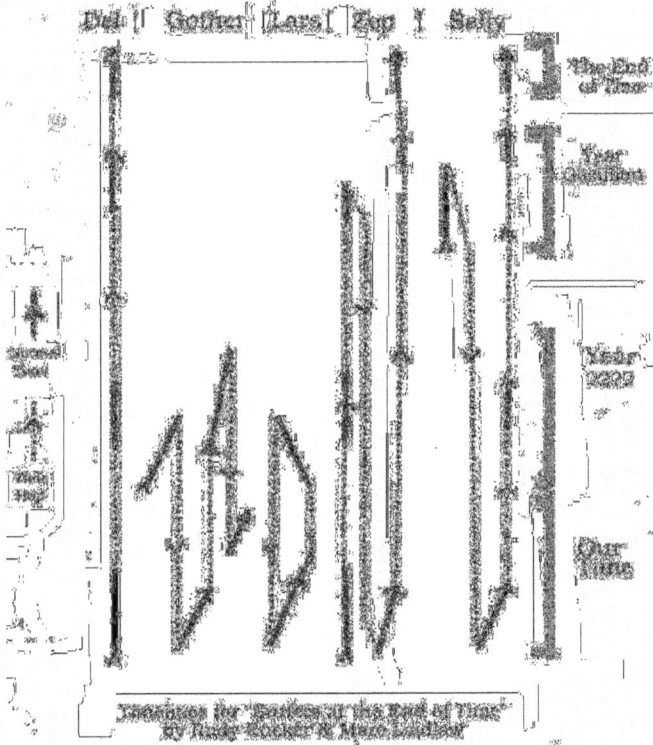

Figure 4: Final Image of Time Lines for "Surfers at the End of Time"

Why would the murgs want money? What kind of world do they live in? Why would you want to eat one?

Or what if a murgburger is a pupal form of a murg. It goes larva=pillbug, pupa=murgburger, adult=murg. And maybe they lay eggs in humans who then explode into clouds of larvae.

Possibly Zep and Del are infected with the pillbug and

they'll explode in the year million. "Righteous rush, man." We're free to kill Zep and Del, as the alternate "ass men" Zep and Del are still on Ocean Beach for their final scene.

There's a female murg named Sral who's after Lars, she wants to mate with him. Too many loose ends here. I'm paralyzed.

Dec 7, 2018

Meanwhile lots more back and forth on the story, we had all sorts of ideas. Marc's working on Ver 6. I'm hoping I can wrap it up with Ver 7. It's been fun to work together with him again, not on my own, and I like the story, but it's taking too long, and collaborating means I have to think about it more, and there's some interpersonal stress involved, although probably the tale ends up funnier. A lot of elements to balance by now, too many, and the time travel thing is tricky—you need to be careful not to impute foreknowledge of the abrupt, and effectively uncaused (by any normal links of causation) appearances of the time travelers.

Jan 7, 2019

We ploughed through 11 drafts and hit nearly 20,000 words. I think I probably did more work on it than Marc, but he made really essential contributions. I sent it off to Sheila Williams at *Asimov's*. The story is good, I think. I hope people can understand it. I need to make a cleaner drawing of my spacetime diagram of the characters' worldlines. I'll write my next few stories alone.

November 3, 2018. Quantum Tantra. Plot.

I spent yesterday with my old hippie physicist pal Nick Herbert. He's 82. A sage. We sat on his porch talking for a few hours, also took a little walk around his neighborhood. I can talk very openly to Nick, and more often than not he understands what I say.

I was feeling a little bummed when I got there as I'd had a slight squabble with Sylvia before leaving, and I'd written Marc Laidlaw a fairly bossy email about what I thought he should be doing on our story. And I got lost on the way to Nick's—and I was playing uptight mental tapes about Sylvia and about Marc the whole time. Then I had this classic koan-type conversation with Nick.

Rudy: "I wish I could stop being a fucking asshole."
Nick: "What would happen then? What would be the difference?"
Rudy: (pause) "Nothing."
Nick: (laughs for a long time)
And in that moment, the monk received enlightenment.

Figure 5: Nick Herbert

On the subject of science, Roshi Nick made the point that the "Planck length" doesn't necessarily imply granular space. I's just an artifact. There's a "Planck mass" which is a few hundred micrograms, about the size of a dose of LSD.

I asked Nick about my idea that the universe might be "self-healing," in the sense of automatically repairing any time-paradox damage (like having Zep's body grow back together after the future Zep chops him in half). He said there are things called "fictional forces." Example: the quantum mechanical "exclusion principle" that keeps two particles in the same state. Nick taps the table we're sitting at. "That what makes for solid matter. Fictional forces holding the atoms apart."

As we parted, Nick gave a fervent peroration about his longing to achieve quantum tantra, that is, a direct dialog between man and nature. I told him I'd write SF about this idea…but I'm not quite sure what the idea is, other than the things I already put into *Hylozoic*. "I want to make love to this tree!" said Nick, gesturing at a youngish redwood by my BMW.

    ***

I told Nick a little about a story lines from my still inchoate plans for *Juicy Ghost*. It always helps me clarify these things if I get to talk about them. But I hardly ever get to talk to anyone anymore.

* Chapter 1. *The Big Hit*. An old guy, call him R, has been hired to assassinate a guy like T. A tyrant. The only way it'll be possible is that R accepts that the Secret Service is going to kill R too. (Possibly the SS is in on plot, and will grant him access.) R knows this in advance, but that fact isn't revealed in the story until after the hit. Kind of a twist. R is gunned down. Black-out ending, in R's voice, "It looked like I was dead, but I wasn't. I was in the cloud. And now began the second part of my mission."

* Chapter 2 *How I Got Here*. The faction who hired R paid to get him that zottarich pigopolist immortality coding. He wasn't in great health anyway, and he was old, so it was reasonable for R to go for the gig. Also, he didn't like T either. After the assassination, R is slated to go up in to the cloud and assassinate the zottarich pigopolist emulation of T that's living up there. Short description of the immortality treatment.

* Chapter 3. *Heaven*. R is in a VR in the cloud, eliminating all traces of T. (I need to find a visual or experiential way to describe this. Like killing every ant in an anthill, maybe.) He'd doing well, but then there's a reverse and he's trapped and his emulation is about to die. Something saves him.

* Chapter 4. *Some Pig*. Enter the juicy ghosts, the first one,

I should put in a love interest, too. Maybe R's wife Mary. The faction paid for her to go into the cloud too, and a simulacrum of her us up there, even though she's still alive on

Earth. But maybe R falls in love with a juicy ghost who maybe *is* Mary. The astral plane dreamgirl is something I did in both *White Light* and in *Frek and the Elixir*. Maybe I come up with a fresh move?

I only told Nick the part about the double hit, that is, killing T and then killing his cloud emulation. I didn't get into the juicy ghost biocomputation angle although, in one-day-later retrospect, I probably should have. Juicy ghosts are, come to think of it, a quantum tantra thing.

***

But I did tell Nick about Gibson's "peripheral" time travel move. There's a server—somewhen/somewhere—that allows messaging between any two points in spacetime. It's a self-installing kind of message, in that you don't need futuristic hardware/software in the target device/organism. Suppose it uses quantum computation, which is ubiquitous (that is, any piece of matter can quantum-compute.)

In G's novel you can poltergeist into past devices with some kind of web access, and I guess something similar holds for the forward direction. The future things can of course be tuned for the channel, and respond very smoothly. But the past things can kind of klunk along…Bill doesn't really push this issue.

Nick wondered about using a past or future human as your peripheral, your meat-puppet. Or arranging a swap (like a house swap). You'd need to worry about the risk of your body being trashed by a temporary occupant—I feel like I've read a story about this, like the visitor in your body jumping off a cliff, and then bailing back home on the way down.

***

I don't actually see a place for the absolute continuum in *Juicy Ghost*…feels like one twist too many. But it could be useful as a Maguffin to justify the ubiquity of computational souls. Deeper than quantum computation. Subquantum computation, if you will.

November 18, 2018. Miami.

I was in Key West for three days, went snorkeling for day, then came to Miami for five nights.

I was in Miami to speak at the Miami Book Fair. A random

invite, via my 4D scholar friend Christopher White. My
appearance was underwhelming. I'd prepared slides, but didn't
have a really smooth talk, and I only had ten or fifteen minutes
to talk in. I did manage to get a few laughs. But they didn't let
me take questions until two other guys had talked as well.
Worst of all, the fair organizers had failed to get any of my
Also, *Return to the Hollow Earth* books to sell on the spot.
They said they'd expected me to *bring* the copies, as the book
is a lowly self-pub title. I'd thought they would ask me to *mail*
them some. And that they'd email be about that. Or that maybe
they'd *buy* some from Ingram. A very bitter pill for me to
watch my fellow panelists selling little stacks of their books,
providently laid in by the Fair organizers. Yet another of those
"What the eff am I doing here?" career moments.

My leg is hurting very much. Pain levels 8 and 9. As this
junket wears on, the leg is becoming something I think about a
lot, and it's affecting my moods in a bad way. None of my
painkillers really seem to fix it: aspirin, Tylenol, Aleve,
ibuprofen, Celebrex. Deep stabs of pain. I'm limping a lot of
time. When possible, I like to lean on a wall or a railing. I hate
to be like this around Sylvia.

I asked my hip replacement surgeon about it. He says it's
"end of stem pain." Wikipedia says the causes of end of stem
pain are "iatrogenic," that is, the cause is doctors. The titanium
spike that my guy hammered into my femur (accidentally
splitting the bone, *sigh*, which then grew together)—the spike
bends in a slightly different way than the bending of the old-
and-partly-regrown femur bone surrounding it, and this causes
bone pain. Differing moduli of elasticity. Microfractures.
Maybe in time my muscles will be strong enough to cushion
this? Maybe in time the bone will thicken up or revise itself
and become more rigid. It's been two years since the operation.

The staggering pain kicked in after Sylvia and I had three
glorious days of hiking in the Sierras near Carson Pass about a
month ago. At the time I was saying, "I'd thought I'd never be
able to hike in the mountain again. I'm so happy. But what a
price I'm paying."

When I sit, or lie in bed, the leg is fine. When I get out of
bed in the morning, I can't walk. I
have to lean on things or hop, or drag my leg or, at least

one morning, *crawl* to the bathroom.

***

I had an exciting snorkel outing off Islamorada Key, the second big key down from the top. I paid a guy $300 to boat me three miles out and essentially throw me overboard near a rusty, steel frame structure on a six-foot-deep shoal, the tower is called Alligator Lighthouse. Like a gangland hit, it was. All that was missing was the cement overshoes.

I'd only wanted to go one mile out, to the Cheeca Rocks, but the water was turbid, so he points out to this thing like a little oil derrick or an Eiffel Tower…barely visible on the horizon, and we plow out there. Saw stacks and stacks of fish, yaar. I was having trouble keeping it together as the sea was rough—three-foot waves. I was ready to puke from the ride out, and my heart was pounding really hard…I kind of thought I might die. But it was worth it, in a sad and lonely way. I missed Sylvia; I missed the cheerful South Sea Islands vibe. My last chance to snorkel, perhaps. Naturally the outing made my leg hurt even more.

***

I haven't thought about the next novel at all. If there is one. If anything, the things I'm seeing are going into my vision stash for "Surfers at the End of Time." We're supposed to have a long scene a hundred years from now, and another that's a million years from now.

Re. that story, I like the idea of really closely imagining the world a hundred years from now. Some of the things we've seen around Miami are very futuristic.

In the Design District we saw a parking garage for the Institute for Contemporary Art Museum, four stories high, covered with something like a Jim Woodring mural, made of embossed 3D parts, heavy pasted-on glyphs, and with huge rococo pillars at the bottom—not exactly pillars, more like the figures on ships. Insane. Very. 2150.

Maybe in 2150, instead of pecking at smart phones, people will have balls of light around your head, and you can't see in through the balls, but on the inside the balls the users are seeing augmented reality. The augmentation won't just be flat images on the inner surfaces of the balls, but, rather, holograms within the sphere.

In Wynwood district we saw really astounding murals. Some of them cover a whole house, some a whole building.

November 19, 2018. More on Juicy Ghost Plot.

I still don't have a better idea for my new novel than a story about an old man Rudy-stand-in assassinating an evil president. And then comes immortality as a sim in a biotech computed cloud. And then the kicker of biocomputed "ghosts" that have been there all along.

I need to make it have very human characters. I want the hero to be an old man who dies. Fab elevator pitch, that. Prospectively transreal, that is, I'll be envisioning my not-so-distant-future life. Originally, I wanted the main character in *Jim and the Flims* to be an old man— but then I flinched and went for a young guy, me imagining, I guess, that would help sales. But the book bombed anyway. And if my books are going to bomb, they might as well be about exactly the things I want/need to write. I like that book of Burroughs, what's the title, *Last Words*? Starts with his rap about the old writer who lives in a trailer by the river. I like the idea of writing about an old writer.

As for the immortality thing. I've of done that already, in *White Light*, and in *Jim and the Flims*. I'd need to make it new. Since boyhood I've loved Dante's *Divine Comedy*. But that really is what I already did in those other two novels.

The juicy ghosts move is something I already did in *Hylozoic*—with the difference that in *Hylozoic* the so-called silps (living and conscious souls in Nature) were independent agents. I didn't use the (corny?) idea that they were embodiment of dead humans. Like, oh, this rock is my dead father, or no it's Bill Burroughs. That could get very sentimental or gauche. Thin ice. Maybe the story is an echo of Peter Beagle's haunted-graveyard classic, *A Fine and Private Place*.

Other elements? How about scientific optimism. All of today's probs being solved by cool new inventions. Had some of that in *Saucer Wisdom*. What's the plot angle of a great new scientific fix? Some evil oil-monopoly-type capitalists trying to quash it—though that angle is paranoid and stale.

If this could in fact be my very last novel, it would make

sense to go out on a hylozoic immortality theme. Not entirely sure I'd want to go with an assassination—although certainly that gives the story some marketplace legs. But doing an assassination—it's so negative, so bitter, so resentful, so unenlightened. What if I do a twist on that, and my guy walks away from the assassination. Doesn't want to be that person. Kind of wimpy of him, makes him less of a hero. But then, second twist, gets gunned down anyway...perhaps by his controllers who were, perhaps, Treadle cadre all along. Later, a third twist, the natural world's juicy ghosts take down Prez Treadle after all. Or my guy orchestrates this. A mini ghost of turbulence enters T's blood stream and precipitates the Chief Moron's stroke that so many of us would like to see.

Changing my tack now. If this really were to be my last novel, I might want to put in some life experiences that I haven't gotten around to writing about, that is, my early childhood and mid childhood stuff. *Secret of Life* kicked in when I was about 17. I don't think I've ever had younger characters than that, other than the somewhat autistic kid in *Postsingular* and *Hylozoic*, and that kid wasn't really much like me. He was made-up. I did write about my childhood quite a bit in my memoir, *Nested Scrolls*—in particular I started with a series of stained-glass-windows-in-the-memory-chapel vignettes. But in terms of life experience, I've got sixteen years' worth to be transrelaized.

So maybe combine a book about an old man who dies with a book about a young boy. Kind of what I expected (on the basis of title) from Faulkner's *As I Lay Dying*—not that F's novel actually does take that approach—but I can imagine (and have surely read, somewhere along the line,) a book that flips between an old man's final experiences and his life-flashing-before-me early memories. Possible title: *I Didn't Die.*

Nov 19 - Dec 7, 2018. Wallace's Infinite Jest.

On another tack completely, I've been reading David Foster Wallace's magnum opus, *Infinite Jest*. So as not to have the small-font problem, I bought an ebook of the 20th Anniversary Edition from 2015. I read the novel when it came out, in 1995. And the next year I got sober, that is, in 1996, when I was 50. *Infinite Jest* made sobriety seem both feasible and cool to me. It really has the best descriptions of AA that I've ever seen. I might not have gotten off alcohol and pot without it. While reading the novel, I tend to skip some of the sections and focus on what I consider to be the "good stuff," that is, the parts about the recovering addict Don Gately.

Something I hadn't realized before—or had forgotten—is that Gately gets shot about 60% of the way through the book, and then he spends the rest of the book in slow recuperation, hallucinating in a hospital bed and having flashbacks of his earlier times. So there's this epic drug-using scene in the very last section, and I'd been thinking, "But I thought Gately got sober?" But that's a *flashback* scene, see. Wallace has this intensely alluring description of the effect of a drug called Sunshine. Everything is covered with yellowish gel.

I wrote a highly favorable <u>review</u> of Wallace's first novel *The Broom of the System* for The *Washington Post Book World* in 1987. I was really excited by his work, he seemed like the next generation of cool. A new Pynchon. He was sixteen years younger than me. I hoped he and I might eventually be friends, like I am with a number of SF writers and other underground types.

I liked a lot of Wallace's essays and stories, too. He developed a great and unique colloquial literary voice, this engaging, conversational modern style, which has in fact influenced me to some extent.

But I disliked his 2003 nonfiction book *Everything and More: A Compact History of Infinity*, which was about transfinite numbers—which is the field in which I got my Ph. D., and which I wrote my best-selling nonfiction *Infinity and the Mind* about, not to mention that infinity is the subject of my novel *White Light*.

I felt Wallace didn't do justice to the material, and that he spoke too slightingly of my hero Georg Cantor and my mentor Kurt Gödel. And when the book came out, I was annoyed at Wallace's editor. They guy had sent me a preprint, asking me for a blurb—and I found serious errors in the book and pointed them out to the editor, and the guy airily said it was too late to fix them. Wallace's pose was kind of self-aggrandizing in *Everything and More*, and he got some important math things wrong. I felt like he was an entitled hodad at a surf break that

I'd been riding for most of my life.

So when *Science* magazine asked me to comment on the book, I wrote a harsh <u>review</u>. The review was over-the-top, but in a way it was funny, and everything I wrote was factual, and the book really did suck. Of course five years later I felt guilty when Wallace killed himself. But I want to doubt that my review had any influence on his sad demise. To think that would probably be self-aggrandizement on my part.

When W. hung himself, he was 46. It's one of those suicides that are so hard to understand. Like Vincent van Gogh or Diane Arbus. A creative genius, at the peak of their career— and they can't take it.

December 7, 2018. Just Write a Story?

I'm still not up for starting a novel. Like I've mentioned, I'm still working on "Surfers at the End of Time" Marc Laidlaw, still not quite done, but done soon. When I get my next crack at it, I'm gonna finish it no matter what.

By now I'm in the mood to write a story or two or three on my own. Doing my own thing again. Ideas?

A simple idea would be to Just make the "Juicy Ghost" routine into a story or novelette. I have a feeling *Asimov's* might not go for it—too political. Maybe the Motherboard *Terraform* site would take it. They want 2,000 words. I used to sell to Claire Evans there, but I can't tell if she's still on the staff. I know a guy called Brian Merchant is still there. Or maybe I could sell it to *Lightspeed* if I want to make it longer.

Opening line which I'll never be able to use if I expect to publish it at all: "How did I get the point of assassinating the President?"

January 17, 2019. Starting "Juicy Ghost." Starting TEEP.

Here's an opener that I've been playing with since early December, and today I finally focused on it enough to bring it to life. (I didn't save the earlier versions, just kept overwriting them to get to today's version.) Anyway, here's what we have today, Jan 17, 2019. I could expand it, obviously, but for today I liked the idea of making it pretty fast and immediate. (And at least getting a scene done!)

[This scrap became the story "Juicy Ghost," which became a chapter of my novel *Juicy Ghosts* (originally called *Teep*), so today is when I started writing *Juicy Ghosts*—which I fished in March, 2021.]

I'll start the *Juicy Ghost* novel (or story) document as a separate file today, and move this frag over there and start endlessly revising it. It's just a seed, you understand. So I'll say that today, January 17, 2019 is when I actually started the novel, or story, or novelette or whatever the hell it turns out to be.

As I've been saying, the title *Juicy Ghost* has to do with the kicker that I have in mind.

(I think of this opening section as taking place in 2024 in some possible future history, but I won't say the date as that imposes a shelf-life.)

It was to be the day of Len Treadle's third inauguration. Treadle and his cabal had stolen the Presidency for good. The thronging protestors had an end-times air. The country was on the brink of revolution.

Starting at dawn, the rebels mounted a reverse procession down Pennsylvania Avenue, with the cheated candidate Sudah Mareek at their head. The protesters converged at on the Jefferson Memorial. The plan was to mount a symbolic counter-Inauguration—before Treadle's charade would take place. They'd swear in Mareek as the true President.

Naturally Treadle's aides deployed troops to the Jefferson Memorial. Young men and women armed with truncheons, water-cannons, tear-gas and loaded guns. But the soldiers had little sympathy for a Treadle autocracy. The revolutionaries had been laying their groundwork, and now they won the soldiers over. The troops drove their armored vehicles into the Potomac, spiked the muzzles of their guns, and joined in cheering Mareek as he swore his oath of office.

Treadle took the next step. Shortly before noon, gunship helicopters converged on the Jefferson Memorial and laid down withering fusillades of automatic weapons fire—massacring the rebels, the renegade troops, and Sudah Mareek.

Not all of us in our transbio faction had expected this. But I had. And that's why I was standing in the crowd on the grassy Mall, less than five hundred feet from the Capitol steps, waiting for Treadle to appear.

We needed a bold, exemplary act to spark the revolution. And I meant to be the spark.] Starting very early in the morning—I'm talking four am—I wormed and wheedled my way into the crowd of spectators on the Mall. It was essential that I be within two or three hundred feet of the speaker's armored rostrum. It helped that I looked so old and infirm. And of course I was wearing pro-Treadle regalia.

Soon Treadle was in full throat, spewing lies, self-adulation, and hate.

"Get him," said I, not very loud, but loud enough to matter. The wasp pupae in body heard me. Bumps and welts formed on my skin, splitting open, with bloody insects wriggling out, drying their wings, and taking flight.

I was like a seed-pod, a piñata of Turing wasps. Lethal biotech. I'd been a worker in the secret lab that created the wasps. Originally, I'd been a copy-writer for the group's social media jamming. But now as the final crisis arrived, I'd been shifted into lab work, even though I knew little about science. More of a literary man. A dissenter.

For the last six months I'd been, effectively, a janitor in the wasp lab. And then Treadle won, or stole, the election. It was time to act. I volunteered to be seeded with wasp eggs, to grow the larvae to term within my flesh, and to carry them to the Inauguration for the moment of the hatch.

Slammy and Leeta, of the transbio faction, thought it was a great idea. I was old. No great loss. Slammy, our faction's leader promised me I'd get life after death—and Leeta, our chief tech, said it was true.

So I said "Get him," and within seconds the wasps had taken out Treadle, his wife, four of his guards, the

Veep, and a bystander. Somewhere in the crowd, Leeta
threw back her head and chirped from the back of her
throat, sending a code that subdivided the wasps into a
fog of gnats who whirred away.

I learned these details later. But at that moment, I
was dying, spewing blood from my riddled flesh,
everything growing black. I faded out, filled with pride
and satisfaction at my completed task. And wondering
about my upcoming life in the cloud. I only hoped
Slammy and Leeta hadn't been scamming me? But
even if they were, I'd killed Treadle. Hurrah and
goodbye.

February 1-3, 2019. "Reculer Pour Mieux Sauter."

*(This entry caption's epigram means "Step back, the better
to leap.")*

I did a rewrite of my opening passage, but haven't been
able to get myself to work on it anymore. Somewhat reluctant
to get back into that metaphorical rowboat and do another
metaphorical crossing of another metaphorical ocean. So
fucking many details to do.

***

Like, I mean, what the hell is even my hero's name?
Victor, Hector, Baz, Junko, Wally, Frank, Rafaelo, Joe, Kurt.
Go with Kurt, for good old Gödel. Or, no, Curtis is better. Or
Kurtis? I like Curtis. Curtis Winch for now. And let's give the
evil President Treadle the annoying first name Ross.

In Curtis's Freal Treadle-assassination-action-group, I've
got Leeta as kind of a handler. And maybe there's a Slammy, a
hard guy, an organizer who is in fact a double agent working
for Treadle.

And eventually we'll need a tech genius who invented the
technique of uploading people into the cloud. Let's say he's a
good guy, a Freal too. His name is Weeble, or no, call him Gee
Willikers. That's a cool name. He could be yet another of my
John-Walker-clone-characters, I haven't used one of them
since *Spaceland*—but that paradigm is dated.

What if I model him on one of my best CS students, a guy
who's come to be a friend—a complex character who's had an
interesting career as a videogame designer. Call him Gee

Willikers, that's perfect, it's almost like something he'd say. Skinny and with short hair, from So Cal.

I'll need a love interest, a girlfriend. Might Curtis be a widower, and I'm doing another rescuing-Eurydice routine like in *Frek and the Elixir*? No, try something new. What if he had a girlfriend but they broke up and he wants to get her back? Like the lovers in that Polish movie *Cold War* which we saw last night. The heroine was Zula, short for Zuzanna. I'd love to write about my image of Zula—although, wait, I'm always warning tryos *not* to base their characters on real people and not on characters in books or films. Have I ever known any actual women who are in any way like Zula? Well...there's always Sylvia! And she could *look* like Zula.

***

I want to flesh out my initial frag with back story. Like how did my character Curtis Winch hook up with the biotech terrorists? And what's he like? How old is he?

Re. the "living in the cloud" idea—I noticed Charles Stross observing, in a Twitter post, that it would be bad to end up living in a cloud silo owned by, say, Facebook. I hadn't thought of that. If the cloud enclaves are specifically on various biz-owned computers, they could really suck. Like you might be a slave of some kind—running a sex-talk line, or driving a truck, or processing tax returns, or working a job teaching remedial math or introductory programming or English as a second language. Or working as a programmer. A whole virtual city of mostly tech jobs in the "cloud." So escaping your hi-tech sweatshop-type silo would be a plot element. With a transreal hook to the objective correlative of having a tech job in a veal-pen-type office in a glass-sheet-walled building like Sales Force Tower in SF.

This cyberspace of soul silos suggests a reprise of the vintage Bill Gibson images of cyberspace as a gauzy translucent Manhattan. But my guy doesn't see this right away, or maybe only for an initial flash before the vision fades. The silos use incompatible standards, and have security ice, and usually only a super sysop or powerful hacker can get a clear overview. It'll take a while till my guy Curtis can see it.

Initially his silo might as well be like a nightmare I had a few days ago. I'm in a huge crumbling old Vic house with junk

in the room, paintings leaning on the walls, and doors that
don't' properly close, Gravity is iffy. I have a crushing sense of
an omnipotent and essentially Satanic force nearby, like always
in the next room, watching me and prepared to do something
horrible to me— like maybe erase me or do some brutal
personality-destroying tweaks (akin to a lobotomy). Ripping
out the inessential subroutines and memories.

There are of course ways to find backdoors and tunnel your
info over into different databases or emulation engines. Cf. the
"fnoor holes" in *Hacker and the Ants*. Curtis has a friend who's
helping him, the friend looks like a rat. (Like Skungy in The
Big Aha.) And then he gets the Manhattan view, although there
are ack-ack-gun bursts of flak trying to take him down,
exploding in cartwheeling double-word-length strings of
opcodes. He sees the Twin Towers, which aren't *really* gone, it
seems.

***

Now let's talk about the "juicy ghosts" angle. Some, or
why not *all*, of the soul simulations are running on quantum
computing biomatter. I had this move in *Hylozoic* as I recall, or
even more so. In *Hylozoic*, as I recall, both a candle and a
dripping faucet were functioning as high-end universal
computers. (I ought to reread that novel, and *Neuromancer* as
well.).

The juicy-ghosts idea is that, as I've already mentioned in
these *Notes*, human "ghosts" have been living in natural spots
all along. Like animistic "spirits of place." I could be kind of
oracular about them, which is probably more "mersh" (Bruce
S.' old term for "commercial"). But if I want to play the
buffoon, at least some of the time, I might adopt a Sheckley-
esque tone for the juicy ghosts' utterances—like the way the
Sheck-man's ganzer egg talked like a New Jersey guy. Cf. also
the raven among the ghosts in Peter Beagle's *A Fine and
Private Place*. Or, for that matter, the talking objects in the
"Candy Hearts" chapter of my *White Light*. Well, a mix will be
best, some romantic, some comic.

***

Another story element can be that Ross Treadle is ensconced in the cloud already. Like the proverbial White House
fallout shelter deep underground. And my hero is going to have

to kill Treadle avatars again and again. At some point a Treadle (like the Sheck-man's ganzer egg) will make the move of getting Curtis to have empathy for him. And then of course Treadle will take advantage and deal Curtis a serious setback. And then, with the help of his companion, Curtis will *really* kill all the various Ross Treadles for once and for all. It's like killing the Terminator over and over again in the original movie. "It feels so good you can't do it just once."

    ***

And there ought to be a double-cross. Curtis's assassination of Treadle is a hoax, a set-up, a trick on Curtis and the Freals. Treadle's coterie orchestrated the event to make Treadle more popular, with the aura of a martyr. Also, they wanted to demonize the Freals. That's a Treadle *double* that Curtis kills. A meat puppet. A customized manta ray, rolled up and stuffed into a suit. A manta ray in drag. Orange.

And, as I mentioned a second ago, there's already a Treadle avatar in the cloud. Or he's already been there for a while. Maybe Curtis's so-called co-conspirators put the Treadle-ghost there with their new tech. And a Treadeloid virtual agent is in charge of the Gitmo-like haunted-devil-house where poor Curtis ends up.

    ***

In terms of restarting my work on the novel or novella, the easiest path is to just keep polishing the frag that I have. Turn it into Section 1, which ends when Curtis goes into the cloud. If it was old-school cloud, on the way he could get a glimpse of Gibson's old translucent cyberspace Manhattan. If it's cyberbio organic cloud, then the overview would look different. Like an overgrown hill, or like a reef. If Treadle's really juked Curtis, he tumbles down into a prison to the tune of demonic laughter.

Section 2 shows Curtis in the nightmare Satan house I dreamed about, with Ross Treadle nearby. Curtis cringes into a corner and thinks, "How did I get here?" Actually, I think it's too conventional-space to have him in something like a room.

And we get a flashback of how Curtis got into the Freal labs, and how Slammy and/or Leeta got tricked or co-opted into setting up the Treadle-hit. This line could in fact run through an alternating sequence of two or three flashback chapters.

Section 3 we're back to the virtual Gitmo with Curtis—and he meets a helper. A peripheral run by Gee Willikers, whom we won't see in person for a while. Initial thought is that I'd like the helper to be a rat, but I had a rat friend (named Skungy) in *The Big Aha*. And, I used a cockroach (named Franx) in *White Light*. I want some despised-vermin-type creature who reminds you of a fennish Silicon-Valley hacker.

I'm sorely tempted to have a talking pencil. I did have a talking pencil in my story "Jack and the Aktuals: Physical Applications of Transfinite Set Theory." But that was only a short story, and I love the talking pencil *so much*. Maybe I can use him. I saw the talking pencil in the Disney *Alice in Wonderland*, many years ago. He wore glasses, but maybe the one could wear contacts, hah! I could call him Scruffy. Well that's pretty elaborate, and maybe too jocular for the kind of spy thriller tone I'm edging towards. I'll keep the pencil in reserve for later, perhaps. He could be a peripheral for my legendary superhacker pal Bill Gosper, and the pencil might augment the Gosperesque conversational gambits by drawing insane, animated diagrams like Gosper creates.

But the helper can be a lively stick figure called Gee Willikers. A hyperactive skinny drawing like in the stories in the creepy old German children's book, *Struwelpeter*, like the character *Suppen Kasper* when he's nearly starved to death.
***

In my current version of Section 1, I have a thing with a helicopter knocking down the Washington Monument, and the Inauguration is then happening right near there on the Capitol steps anyway. I love the image of the falling Monument. But seems implausible they'd still have the ceremony? But maybe they would.

I did have a thought that maybe Curtis could realize the Washington Monument crash was a hallucination. But if he starts hallucinating so early in the book, it undermines the whole rest of the book. Hallucinations suck. We want a reliable narrator, at least in terms of what he *sees*. And I do want that falling Monument. So I have *heavy* first chapter. A first chapter that's like a chapter you'd see as the final climax of a novel. Movies do that sometimes, start out with the cataclysm right away.

Well, say the Monument really does fall down. And they *pause* the Inauguration ceremony but only until dusk. "We will not be intimidated!" Treadle's guys say this even though, in fact, it was *them* who knocked down the Monument, so really there was no intimidation, unless you mean the horde of largely peaceful Freal protestors, augmented by a fair number of National Guard deserters by now.

Maybe the Treadlers knocked down the Monument on purpose. Thereby setting up Treadle for an especially savage speech. And *then* when he's seemingly assassinated (as Treadle himself has planned), it really whips people up against the Freals.

And *then* the real, living, human, all-meat, stinky Ross Treadle pops up right away—and they redo the inauguration just to rub it in. Curtis "sees" this last bit from the cloud.

If I'm using a cyberbio cloud, Curtis could be inside that swarm of gnats. He was the wasps, and then he's the gnats.

February 2, 2019. Cyberbio in the Woods.

[I put most of this entry into the tail end of a Feb 4, 2019, blog post, "Rain, Art Show, Chaos."]

It's been raining for two or three days. I went up into the woods behind St Joseph's Hill, at the top of our street, and made my way partway up a creek bed that I like to explore. No real path along the edge, lots of rocks, branches, soft soil. I use two walking sticks, and wear boots.

Walking there with the stream full, I revelled in the physical chaos. The multiple-pendulum action of the waving branches. The intractably complex analog computations of the water's flow. The 3D fractal clouds above, the lichen on the trunks and stones below. The moss with its endlessly various detail. The banks of bubbles around the splash-pools at the bases of cataracts.

I looked for a while at one floating piles of cataract bubbles, the pile continually replenished by new bubbles entering it from beneath. As some of the smaller bubbles below pop, they add volume to larger bubbles above. The biggest bubble grows and grows—then pops. Some of the big guys manage to last a little longer by somehow managing to shrink just a bit...not sure how they do this move. Maybe the seeming shrinkage is an illusion, it's just that they ink a bit deeper into t pile of lesser bubbles below.

Groping for a metaphor about people in society here. The big bubbles the richer or more influential ones. The bubble also a bit like the cells in my body—although in the case of cells, there isn't that kind of growth phenomenon.

And the cataract, so…joyous. Rapidly, but without haste, it pours down, multi-stranded, grooved, stirring up the basin, making bubbles, utterly chaotic and unpredictable.

Someone might ask me: "What *is* this 'chaos' you're always talking about?" A non-random natural process, governed by natural law, but of sufficient complexity that its detailed behavior is wholly unpredictable by any computers we can conceive of building. What makes chaos different from brute randomness, is that, in a chaotic system, the overall behaviors and the general patterns are drawn from a limited repertoire, patterns familiar and known and expected. The wagging of the branches, the nodding of the clusters of leaves, the bubbles at the base of the waterfall, the bumpy flow lines on the surface of a rushing stream, the back-and-forth oscillation of a flow, the drifting of a cloud, and so on/

Human behavior has this same chaotic quality. The fine details are unpredictable. The moment-to-moment evolution of someone's moods—quite unfathomable. But a given individual's overall emotional climate becomes knowable, and the full range of human personalities is a gamut that everyone learns.

***

Regarding my current juicy-ghosts notion, what is the anima in a cataract "like"? She's not concerned with human things. Just splashing and making bubbles and wearing away bits of stone and mud. Enjoys more intense flows and higher octaves of oscillation. I really need to look at *Hylozoic* again and refresh my ideas about what I said there.

February 4, 2019. Overall Plot.

Where is *Juicy Ghost* going? What do I want from it? Why write it? I can think of three types of answers.

(Wish Fulfillment) Actualize a cool scenario I'd like to experience, some fantasy/thought-experiment I want to immerse myself in for the months and months that it takes to write the novel. An alternate world I want to live in and explore and create.

(Social Issues) Touch on topics or themes that are relevant to our human condition, either in general (e.g., "understand that everything is alive," as in *Hylozoic*), or in a specific relation to our time (e.g., "the President is an evil moron," as in *Mathematicians in Love*.)

(Personal History) Write transreally about some aspect of my personal life, or some aspect of my life as I wish it had been. These days I'm inclined to write about getting old and approaching death. I also long to write about the early years of my childhood, running from, perhaps, ages two to thirteen.
***

So what reasons can I find along any of those lines?

* I'm tempted to go into the afterworld, but that seems a little stale, given that I did that in both *White Light* and in *Frek and the Elixir*. Kind of pathetic to write longingly of the afterlife at my age.

* I want to fly like a bird and/or live in the bodies of animals. (i) I did learn how to fly in *Secret of Life* and *Master of Space and Time*, using something like antigravity. (ii) I had Andrea form her body into the shape of a pelican in Freeware. Cf. shapeshifting sorcerers who become animals. (iii) I entered the mind of a bluejay in *Hylozoic*. (iv) Could use a flying biodrone as a peripheral. (v) Would be cool of *lots* of animals had people or juicy ghosts looking out through their eyes. You "hop" into a handy animal. Don't really see where any of this goes in terms of a novel.

* A time traveler fantasy. I have a recurrent longing fantasy of smoking pot while standing in an open doorway at the back of a hall like the Filmore, near the stage at a Summer of Love concert while, let's say, Quicksilver Messenger Service plays variations on Bo Diddley's "Who Do You Love." Maybe I'm helping R. Crumb with *Zap Comix*. Later in our group house, a hot, musky woman lies atop me, pressing her pussy against my face, shuddering as she comes again and again—*mais oui*! Did I do a hippies-in-the-Haight thing in *Hylozoic*?

* Lift Gibson's time-travel-via-periphrerals-run-by-

tachyonic-reverse-causation-channel-antitelephones?
***

Random stab at three acts.

(Act I) The mad inventor who puts Curtis in the cloud could be a secondary character. Kind of a Fletcher and Harry setup. Fletcher is Curtis, and Harry is the scientist behind the Freals. Sent Curtis to eliminate the evil Treadwell faction from the juicy ghost cloud. Curtis kills Ross Treadle, goes into the cloud prison, makes his way through two or three cloud silos, breaks out into a natural computation, gets to know some juicy ghosts and then what? Well, I could stop there, if I were doing a novella, but by now I'm getting some momentum, so I'd like to come up with ride that'll last me a year.

(Act II) Animate everything like in *Hylozoic*. Ghost in everything, but there's a problem. Plenty of the ghosts are Treadwell bots. Almost like the guy is a virus who's infected reality but I totally don't want to take that route. Too facile and overwrought. Phil Dickian like *The Three Stigmata of Palmer Eldritch*, which is not a row I want to hoe. A big final battle in Act II Yawn. Dunno. Let's skip to Act III.

(Act III) We go up, up, up. Save the World with Science. The Freals fix the world's problems that relate to energy, pollution, war, hunger, and disease. The discover a new energy source, as in a trad Golden Age mad-inventor SF tale. "Dark matter = Ubiquitous cosmic consciousness" — Nick Herbert.

Really these are three separate stories, and not three acts along an arc. The third has nothing to do with the first two. Maybe I should just write the three stories.

Re. the third one, there's a current SF subgenre called solarpunk. See, for instance, "Solarpunk: Against a Shitty Future" by Rhys Williams. The idea is close to what I have in mind, that is, making a good eco world for ourselves, but it doesn't by default include my scientistic addition of some great new neo-Golden-Age tech discovery. We tend not to want to use the world utopia, as it historically ends up being dull or crackpot or authoritarian. How about EZ flo. Sunny Daze. Enlightenment. The Long Day. None of those work. I'll think of something.

February 7, 2019. Wading In. Uneasy.

The last few days I've been repeatedly rewriting the opening section of *Juicy Ghost*, going a little further in with each rewrite. Details are opening up; the texture is thickening.

I really am enjoying writing again, I've missed it. Don't know what to do with myself when I'm not writing. But, as I've said, I'm not 100% confident about the *Juicy Ghost* project.

And, flipside of enjoying the writing—I again have the dread and fear and anxiety about whether I'm doing it right, or whether I should be writing another novel at all.

***

I think it might work better to have Curtis already be sensing the presence of his cloud clone. The system is doing realtime backups. The cloud clone mind can apply massive extra computation and amplify his intelligence.

I'm still not sure about them shooting down the helicopter (wouldn't more and more of them come?). Also, not sure about toppling the Washington Monument, as that really upstages the impending wasp assassination scene. Maybe *later* in the chapter I can topple the Monument. Like maybe as a blackout ending. Bam. I'll try that. And maybe the fall of the Monument kills Sudah Mareek.

And how about a kicker where it wasn't really Treadle who Curtis killed. It was a giant orange rolled-up manta ray disguised as Treadle, and now the *real* Treadle comes out. And gets inaugurated.

Would be nice if Curtis saw these things. But if Curtis is lying on the ground dying, he can't see the monument's fall or see the manta ray switcheroo. And I do want him to drop down dying from ejecting the wasps—the self-sacrifice aspect is essential. I guess he could see the Monument fall, like right after Treadle takes the oath and right before he unleashes the wasps. And the manta ray switcheroo happens after he's in the cloud, and he sees it from up there. A gloating cloud Treadle shows it to him.

Well, I'll just have to jigger these things around till it feels right.

***

Terminology. I want the lingo to be simpler than it was in *Hylozoic*. I'd like a nice clear and simple word for the ghost copy of you that's in the cyberbio cloud. Why not just *call* it ghost!

Another point. Right now I'm talking about cyberbio and biocomputation right away. It's better if I start with the old-school cloud on chip-based. And then later shift over to the cyberbio computations, like I was saying before. And the cyberbio ones are the *juicy* ghosts.

Curtis is getting throttled down as a toy ghost in the chip cloud, and then he breaks through to the biocomputation zone. (Let's not get into quantum computation or in to hylozoic computation at all.)

Saying it again, Curtis starts as a fairly kludgy, shitty pixelated toy ghost. And he's getting weakened by Treadler clean-up bots. And then he breaks into analog cyberbio mode on some kind of host (who?). He's a juicy ghost. And he kicks ass.

February 9, 2019. Toy Ghost.

I was talking to Rudy Jr. today about where lo-res current-tech cloud ghosts would be hosted. I'm calling these things toy ghosts as they're not all that sophisticated. By *hosting* a ghost, I mean two things.

(Ram) Store and maintain a large data base (what I some-times call a lifebox) of the person, along with the code for a program that can use the data to emulate the personality.

(Crunch) Provide processing power to run a simple-ass data-intensive personality emulation code on the data base.

For a while I had a retrograde notion that some companies like Google or Facebook might host ghosts on enormous supercomputers. What I was calling silos. But that's an outdated way to think. Rudy pointed out that most storage and processing is distributed, with chunks of it scattered across a zillion nodes.

Rudy also made the point that there's always going to be limited space on the nodes—not enough to immortalize *everyone*— so a kind of fitness function determines who gets to have, and to keep, a toy ghost. That is, if a toy ghost is to continue to living in the internet cloud, people have to be looking at it and interacting with it. The system's automatic garbage removal will prune away all traces of a ghost that's rarely visited.

[This a bit like the author's perennial issue: Which books remain in print? Which books continue being stocked in libraries? Which books remain readily accessible online? And pirated editions are better than none!]

It may be that an internet toy ghost is designed with an "instinct for self-preservation," so it'll promote itself. Similar to the old meaning of "meme," a sticky, catchy, useful thought that impels people to pass it on to others, thus reproducing itself. These days a "meme" just means something like a phrase or image that people repost. *Cat* pictures, for Christ's sake. The zillion node older notion of meme kind of presupposes that the meme as some heavy intellectual content.

A toy ghost might say, "I seem to be a meme. Kan I has cheezeburger?"

I'm sure Treadle and his boys would like to remove the Curtis Winch ghost from the cloud. For that matter Curtis and the freals would like to remove Treadle,

How do you kill a toy ghost that lives on the internet?

(a) We might invoke the notion of a smart malware bot that finds and erases all scraps of info relating to that toy ghost. But in practice I'm not sure if/how that would work. The scraps could disguise themselves. It's hard or impossible to search the whole web and remove all traces of something. And the ghost cold be continually redistributing and coding and re-encrypting itself. And it sounds kind of boring to read about.

(b) Or the oppressor makes sure the targeted toy ghost doesn't show up in common search engines. (Eyeball kick: an online program that searches for specific toy ghosts might be called "The Book of the Dead.") If you can hack the search engines you can make a given ghost be effectively invisible. And by reducing its registered hits you make it likelier to be pruned.

[Like if the magazines refuse to review your books, you're more likely to go out of print.]

(c) Another way to lower the effectiveness of a ghost, it to make sure that whenever the ghost *is* accessed, a shitty stupid parasite shows up with it. Like an unshakable troll commenter or spammy-ad link. Degrading the ghosts' reputation, making it be treated as malware or as spam.

[Re. spammy viral ad clutter, I'm thinking of the meme/photo of blackface-guy-and-KKK-guy that has this week been attached to the VA Dem pro-abortion governor. A confluence of issues. On the one hand there's the ensuing zero-tolerance hair-trigger universal-denouncement-by-liberal-politicians-and-media. On the other hand, there's the fact that the photo was unearthed and distributed by an ultra-right-wing anti-abortion media-gaming site called Big League Politics. Troll farms exploiting our Puritanism.]

February 10-11, 2019. Juicy vs. Toy Ghost. Novella.

In the previous entry, I was talking about ways to mess up an internet toy ghost. And I was working my way around to the idea that a bio-based *juicy* ghost would be more resistant to attack.

That is, I want to say that a ghost can be more autonomous and robust if it's a biocomputation than if it's an internet chip-based and system-moderated computation. So, escaping from the digital to the analog would greatly empower a ghost. And being juicy or biological makes a ghost safe.

I need this as a plot point. When Curtis Winch turns juicy it's a climax.

Let's say a bit more on why juicy ghosts are more robust. If you're juicy, you're "in the wild" and not living on a human-built net by the sufferance of the internet operating systems and protocols. You aren't subject to the ravages of the mindless internet pruning bots.

This said, one of those bad-reputation troll-parasites *could* follow you into the bioweb, no? But, at least for the upbeat short term, we can suppose that the trick of converting a toy ghost to a juicy ghost is something that only the freal lab people have mastered.

A freal programmer called Gee Willikers found the trick of ghost migration while they were designing the weaponized wasps.

By the way, I still think it might be nice to call *those* critters "Turing wasps."

***

Let's interrupt this interesting and pleasant discussion for an attack of despair and existential panic. Why am I even trying to write *Juicy Ghost*? Isn't it just a rehash of worn old Rudy ideas? Maybe I should give it up. I'm seventy-two. I'm feeling hopeless about the novel. I can't face droning on at such great length.

So…it's time to switch to my fallback plan. To hell with a laborious novel, I'll write a novella instead, or novelette or story (depending how long it runs), and I'm banishing any cringing, greedy thought of making it a novel. [Totally sick anxiety-spasm notion: what if I end up pruning the tale down to, like, 3K words? Or to one page? To a 300-word short-short? Eek. Please, god, let it be at least 10K words after all this *Sturm und Drang*.]

Doing a story instead of a novel changes my eventual distribution plan. With a novel, I can try to sell it, and if I can't sell it, I self-pub it with a Kickstarter. If I can't sell a novella/story, what do I do? I can give it away to slobbering freaks via something like the *Mondo 2000* site. Or, better, I can give it away to slobbering freaks via my old *Flurb* site, which still has some residual cachet. And I'd rather not delve into the intricacies of doing a mini-Kickstarter thing with Patreon.

But first I'll try and sell "Juicy Ghost" to an SF zine or, (fat chance) a mainstream zine. And if I can't find a one, I'll go to *Flurb*. Maybe even do a whole new issue…drum up a few contributors like I used to.

Re. a commercial sale, I do see a potential problem if my tale hinges on the assassination of a Trump-like President. I think I'd need to water down that aspect—e.g., don't say that Treadle is *orange*, or that his palace guard is made of *Russians*, but he could remain a ranting, venal, right-wing, faux populist.

And in any case, at this point in time, the public and the publishers might in fact *be* receptive to a tale about the bumping-off (or co-opting) of a Bullying Moron.

***

If I'm dropping down to novella length, I have to keep things simple. Deploy only a very small number of my bogosity-generator, rubber-science Maguffins. Let me make a list of what I need to have in.

I NEED

An existing internet-based toy ghost technology, marketed as digital immortality. These are thin, pixelated constructs with cardboard personalities. Curtis and Leeta have them.

Toy ghosts have wireless contact with Earth peripherals. Curtis's toy ghost talks to him on the phone. Like a type of smart cloud storage. Leeta's toy ghost helps her with finding her way through the crowd, like Google Maps would do.

The weaponized gene-tweaked Turing wasps mature in Curtis's flesh and crawl out to sting Treadle.

Curtis's existing toy ghost program blooms inside Treadle as a juicy ghost. It kind of helps that the meat Curtis is dead.

I DON'T NEED

Minds in waterfalls and candle flames like in *Hylozoic*.
Wasps dissolving into clouds of gnats.
Stuff about erasing toy ghosts from the web.
The soul-in-a-prison rap.
Treadle's stand-in is a rolled-up manta ray.
***

How do toy ghosts work?
They're common. Like cloud storage. With a lifebox data base and an AI program and a self-symbol so they can emulate consciousness, Damasio style. Kind of like a really good and personalized Google Assistant.

How do juicy ghosts work?
In the process of their biohacking, the freals learn to program living organisms. (I had a lot of this happening in Bangalore in *Freeware*.) The organism runs a program on its neurons, in its hormone flows, in its DNA, its quantum computations, whatever. It's tricky to port a block of info as large as a toy ghost onto an organism. The organism has to be temporarily paralyzed, like with curare. Not even breathing. Numbed with cone-shell toxin.

A bio-hosted ghost is a juicy ghost, much richer than a toy ghost. The *vis viva* is, in effect, real. Thanks to the usable richness of structure and function in living cells.

Who or what is the bio thing hosting Curtis at the end of the story?

It might as well be Treadle. Yah, mon. The wasps didn't kill Treadle, they paralyzed him. And they streamed in Curtis's toy ghost program. And then it woke up as Curtis.

February 12, 2019. Leeta's Switcheroo.

The freal cell members think the wasps in Curtis's body will kill Treadle.

But they find out that Leeta has changed the plan in a fashion as yet unknown to them. Slammy tries to warn Curtis, but Leeta kills him with a shock star.

I'd thought that perhaps Leeta has sold out, warned Treadle, that Treadle will have a meat-puppet stand-in to be assassinated in his place, and that the failed assassination will then be used as fodder to elevate Treadle's status and to instigate a yet sterner crackdown on the freals. But now I want to do something different.

Leeta has tailored the wasps so that the wasps will temporarily paralyze Treadle, and inoculate him with Curtis's personality, starting a juicy ghost of Curtis in Treadle's body and brain.

The physical Curtis Winch dies. His feeble toy ghost enters Treadle's body and—wakes up.

Perhaps, for fun, Curtis finds a juicy ghost helper inside Treadle with him. It's Gee Willikers, a freal programmer. He'll teach Curtis how to run Treadle.

February 16, 2019. Finished a Section.

So I got kind of stoked about working on the story or section or chapter or whatever it is. 3,300 words now. I've been working fitfully, always having difficulty in starting, but then when I start, I'm fiendishly grinning, and having fun. I *do* love to write.

And it's a profound source of catharsis to be writing about assassinating the President.

But at the same time, I've been wondering off and on if I'm going crazy, or having a breakdown. I get so irritated about small things. So obsessed with the political news. Drift so deeply into reminiscences of my youth. Have trouble doing various simple things like putting on a coat, or making love. Last time we tried I couldn't get it up, and now I'm scared to try again, and we're falling out of love. I can easily sit around doing nothing for hours.

On the outdoorsy side of things, I've been really happy about the interesting clouds, and the heavy rainfall, and the wonderful computational richness of the cataracts in the creeks and, most recently, the glorious roaring overflow below the Lexington and Vasona reservoirs dams.

***

Curtis Winch sics the wasps on Treadle, dies in a hail of bullets from Secret Service agents but now his toy ghost will enter Treadle's paralyzed (not dead after all) meat via one of the wasps—and the toy ghost will bloom to a juicy ghost, and Treadle will wake up, and Curtis will be living inside him as a biocomputation. Like the flu.

Possibly Gee Willikers will have a juicy ghost of himself in Treadle too, just so Curtis has someone to talk to.

So now I need to detail (at least in my mind) the process of becoming a juicy ghost. And what it's then like to be one. I could have Curtis and Gee be in that devil-house scenario I dreamed about a while back. At first Curtis doesn't even realize he's living inside Treadle. Gee has to tell him.

And then what? Do they "drive Treadle around like a car?" Function like "an inner voice of conscience?" I think it's awfully icky to be inside Treadle, so maybe by the end of the second section they have gotten out of him. Maybe T really does die by then, or he's resigned. Or I do the cornball thing of Curtis and Gee understanding the "poor man" and help him to reform, sheesh.

To make it a marketable story it does still need another twist, and 6 or 7 thousand words would be better than 3.

Once I figure out Curtis's wake-up scene, maybe I just do a hard jump cut to that, and then I can have a reveal from Gee Willakers that they *are* juicy ghosts now.

February 17, 2019. Depressed.

Working on this "Juicy Ghost" story is making me de-pressed. It's just so ugly and discouraging to be thinking about goddamn Trump, and about assassinating him, and about his war on our people. I woke up this morning and I felt utterly hopeless. More and more I feel like a powerless pawn. And now I'm sandbagged by that old feeling of wishing wish I was dead.

"I wish I was dead." As I think I mention in my *Journals*, this is a phrase I've said to myself for decades whenever I'm down: I used to say it nearly every day when I was drinking and getting high, back when I'd wake up with a pounding headache in the wee AM, plagued by fear and remorse. I'd say those words like a prayer almost.

When I say this phrase, it's not exactly suicidal ideation, in that I don't (usually) have a concrete plan for doing myself in. Although, yes, in the worst days, in the early 1980s, I did visualize the flat lethal L of a 45 automatic like you used to see in tiny black-and-white ads in the paper. And later, in California, I'd sometimes visualize taking a leap off the bench of the big eucalyptus tree outside our bedroom window, a leap with a hangman's noose around my neck.

But since I got sober in 1986, I rarely think that phrase, and when I do, I'm not thinking about actually killing myself. Usually, if I'm down, I might water down the old antiprayer from "I want to die," to just "I want a shot of heroin," not that I ever took heroin, but it has a certain mythic status in my cosmos, a reputation as being a quick trigger for a way out.

"Wanting to push the button," as I say in recovery meetings, when describing my perennial and resurgent and vehement-at-the-time longing for a quick way out of my current emotional state. Although by now, I know it's always enough to just wait a few hours or at most a couple of days. My emotional weather is always in flux. But I also know that, more than just waiting, it's good idea to do so something to promote the change of gears. Go outside, do something creative, open my heart to a fellow human being.

***

So…what to do? I need to wrap up this story and move on. I'm thinking maybe a thousand more words could do it if I can find a clean wrap. But I *do* want to finish it and not abandon it. I want to reach a finish line after putting over a month's effort into this story—I wrote the first words of it on January 17, 2019. I don't want it to be for naught. Even if I can't sell it, I'll put it out in some form.

***

At this point, I'd like to interject some bitter, self-indulgent wheenking—which is always uplifting. So here are some other reasons I've been depressed.

* Some Bitcoin-type blockchain guys called IOHK (Input Output Hong Kong) invited me to give a talk in Miami Beach. I bargained them up to paying me $7,500 plus all my expenses. But the more I read about cryptocurrency, the less I want to meet people involved with it. Bitcoin mining in particular seems so stupid and slobbering and missing the point of even having computers. I'm tempted to cancel. Or maybe just go out for the one day and get the money. But will they actually pay? Now I see they tweeted that I'm coming, and I'm seeing they have lots of stuff on the web, I guess it'll work out.

*Got invited to the BayCon SF convention in May. I really don't want to go, but I have this fantasy that going my help my launch for *Million Mile Road Trip*. When I went to my last con, Worldcon in San Jose this summer, it was horrible. The organizers treated me like I'd never written anything in my life. They put me on a ridiculous panel about spy in science-fiction, with no signings, no readings, etc. When I went to the Book Fair in Miami, not a single person had read me, and the organizers had none of my books in stock to sell, and I got zero understanding or feedback from the sparse audience at the panel I was on. Cons depress the shit out of me.

*My left femur hurts all day long, some weird problem called "end of stem pain." From that botched five-operation hip replacement a couple of years ago. Not clear if it will ever go away. I saw two joint surgeons and they said I'm more or less stuck with this.

*Valentine's Day the rain flooded our bedroom, soaking the edges of the rugs, making the room smell like mold. And my hoped-for tryst with Sylvia that morning didn't work out. I wasn't up for it. So now I'm obsessively worrying about that.

February 18, 2019. New Ending.

I'm better today. I "closed the deal" with my fair lady this morning. And did some home repairs. Unpacked my 25 paintings that I brought home from the 3-week show in Borderlands Cafe. Picked him up yesterday afternoon after Sylvia and I went to the SF Ballet and had a fancy brunch beforehand. Things actually aren't all that bad.

By th way, from the car, on Hayes or Franklin Street, we actually *did* see a guy taking a shot of heroin, shooting it into his calf or shin, leaning way over, in a bus shelter. Looked horrible, not like fun at all. Cosmos was saying, therewith: "A message to you, Rudy. You've done enough wheenking for now."

***

I'll finish my frikking story any old how, and maybe I should get on the stick and plan a trip to Guanajuato in Mexico for my birthday next month like we've been talking about. That would be something good to look forward to. My week in Guanajuato in November, 2015, was one of the happiest times of my life. It was right before the series of hip operations that sent me into a year-long slough of pain and despair, capped off by another stent operation.

Yes, I want to return to that prelapsarian Eden, and bring my fertile Eve with me.

***

I think what was bumming me the most about my story was the idea of Curtis (and perhaps Gee) living inside Treadle. Fuck that. Let's keep it simple. The wasps kill Treadle and his vice-president.

We don't particularly *need* that juicy ghost thing for the story, all that much, but I'll work it anyway, given that I've talked about it so much. I'll say Curtis's juicy ghost is a biocomputation in his meat. Doesn't matter that technically he's dead. The meat still has some kick in it for a while.

He awakes in that same hallucination of being the juicy ghost in the abandoned house. And his toy ghost is newscasting to him, or Gee Willikers is talking to him, telling him that Treadle is dead, and that the remains of the troops and freals are leading Sudah Mareek to the Capitol steps. Treadle didn't manage to shoot her after all.

And the Secret Service agents have all flipped to Sudah's side. Leeta is with them on the dias. And Sudah gives a great speech, and the country if free. People cheer for dead Curtis. They carry his broken body to the rostrum. His resolution is decreasing. Leeta lays her hand on him.

"You can room with me!"

So the plan was *not* changed. That's not what Slammy was there to talk about. He was trying to finger or double-cross Curtis. Maybe the SS knew about Curtis's approach, but they let him come and let him launch the wasps because they too wanted Treadle to die.

I'll try and rewrite it this way and see if I can tighten up the Slammy scene.

February 22-23, 2019. Revising the First Draft.

I finished the first draft the other day, it's pretty good. But the end feels tacked on.

I got some comments back from Marc Laidlaw and from Christopher Brown, shown below. Very useful. On the other hand, I can't be *too* influenced by their suggestions. I need to stick to my own vision and get this done pretty economically.

One recurrent thought—I'm not really using the juicy ghosts all that much in this story. Maybe I shouldn't even have them in here? And then I could use them better in a different story? Though probably it would be better to use the idea a bit *more*. Always good to have *two* SF kicks in a tale, not just one.

And I can always use my beloved juicy ghosts again, in a more up-beat tale.

Here's some action points that I might try now, in the light of Marc and Chris's comments.

- Leeta is a bodyguard. Gee Willikers is the cloud programmer. Slammy raises funds and organizes. Curtis is the bioprogrammer. He invented the wasps
- There's a big swarm of wasps, hundreds, and they sting Treadle to death.
- Dying Curtis has his viewpoint travel with a wasp, and he sees Treadle die. That one particular wasp has a wireless antenna? It's a biodrone.
- A few more lines on Sudah's inauguration. "This wasn't an act. This was real."
- One or two more cameos of the Treadlers, making them realer. Just a sentence or two. Ugly, touching.
- It's confusing to talk about toy ghosts vs. juicy ghosts. Say chatbot instead of toy ghost. Most people know,

more or less, what that is. Networked chatbot assistant. I can use the phrase "toy ghost" once, but only when I introduce the "juicy ghost" term.

- Point to make: As a soul in a living body, you are *precisely* a juicy ghost. A biocomputation.

***

MARC LAIDLAW COMMENTS

It's funny and exciting and seems like just the right length for the idea. I feel like a little more about how juicy ghosts figure into all this would be good, instead of that being a somewhat disconnected bit of exposition at the end. More central to it somehow? Maybe he keeps hearing Gee gibbering about it subliminally right from the start but he's not sure what it means until the end.

I like the wasps but is there some reason that this narrator was the ideal choice for them? When Gee tells him he's parasitizing his own dead form, I flashed on the wasps and the way they lay their eggs parasitically...I was expecting the narrator himself to be more the wasp instead of simply hatching them.

I'd like a paragraph that actually describes the inauguration of the alternate real president...like, you mention the Lincoln Bible and set up the event but we don't get to see it. Something visual to contrast with the event of the Treadle inauguration.

The crowd pushes over some kind of armored vehicle...and takes off the gas cap and sets it on fire. I have to think that these military vehicles are too well designed to make any of that possible. How about if with the cooperation of the deserting soldiers, they figure out a better way to destroy the vehicles.

And at the very start I thought the explanation of the word "freal" came too soon.

CHRISTOPHER BROWN COMMENTS

This is a pretty fucking awesome story. Thanks for writing it, and sharing it with me. Of course I love a story like this. Using Sf to express insurgent political energy, charged with urgency, violent revolutionary impulse. Biting into the copper wire in a way most similar efforts shy away from.

My comment would be that there's room in here to dial up the feeling. It's all there on the page, but you kind of tell the reader how the POV character and his fellows feel, rather than show it. And there's so much to work with in there that could easily have that feeling drawn out with some judicious dollops of sensory and emotional descriptors. If you want to "do the hit and get out," you might as well let us feel the kick running through the veins and lighting up the neural net. Let us really feel the anger, the hatred of the Prez and his supporters (who are all pretty thinly characterized—it would be so easy to show us one fucked up hate-provoking thing the Prez did, maybe destroyed something wild and cherished by the Freals), the certainty that assassination is the only solution, the feeling of being a suicide bomber, the feeling of shooting back at the cops, the feeling of that emergence of the Hymenoptera, the witnessing of what actually happens when the Prez is attacked (that's the real hit you want, right—the liberatory release of regicide), the feeling of being a toy ghost (does it assuage the anger over immediate political events?), the feeling of being a dog (what's that smell? Treadlers?).

Also, I wondered if you could give this more punch if you didn't foretell or prefigure that the assassin will survive as a toy ghost. What would it be like if he didn't know? How would it read if he's loaded with eggs and ready to have them burst from his body to do the only act that makes life worth living, even at the presumed cost of ending his own? Watching through his eyes the hatchlings do their job, feeling the ruptures in his body, then going into the ghost land and finding he's been preserved by Freal hackery.

February 25, 2019. Sent it Off. Fear of Persecution.

I spent a day doing the revisions. At first it seemed too hard to start. But then, as usual, I just went ahead and started, without any really specific plan, marking up the latest printout by hand, typing in my changes, revising them on the screen an adding more, making a fresh printout, and doing the cycle again.

It's cooler now. Our guy jumps into a wasp, stings Treadle, then flies to a neighborhood and jumps into a dog. A rough bit is that I elide how upset the Treadlers might be with the chopper attack and crash having already taken place…I have them doing tailgate-type picnics. Ought to move that to before the chopper attack, Curt can see it via his chatbot.

Marc gave me the "private" submission address for *Lightspeed* (which is currently closed to open submissions), and I sent them the story.

***

I'm having second thoughts about what might happen if/when the story appears. On the one hand, a few months back, the *New York Times* Sunday book section ran a couple of pages of short-short fantasias about the end of Trump, and one of them depicted, in an approving way, an assassination scenario. So one feels it's open season. And it feels brave and noble to stand up against our oppressor.

On the other hand, my story is vitriolic and detailed, and it could raise hackles. It could be that the FBI or CIA starts tracking me or, worse, I somehow get onto a Trump enemies list and they harass me with IRS audits and the like or, even worse, some freelance right-wingers launch a vendetta against me via social media or, worst of all, some loner wingnut sets out to personally attack me or my family or our house.

Thoughts of this nature may well go through the mind of the *Lightspeed* editor, and he might reject the story out of hand. Or ask me to tone it down. The British zine *Interzone* might take it, but why bother, would take a year to come out, and nobody reads it. Or, as I mentioned earlier, I could just put it out as a *Flurb* special. I had the *Flurb* process streamlined pretty well, and I think I could do it again. Or just frikkin put it up as a blog post.

In any case, I'm seriously thinking that, however it appears, I might use a pseudonymous author name, like the cognomen I put on my "Wheelie Willie" cartoons in the Rutgers daily Targum, back in 1971 or so. Rubber. v. B. Tire. With a disclaimer about how a guy mailed me this story.

It *would* be cool to get a few more Trumpian SF stories for the *Flurb* if I could. Of course I'm the official editor of *Flurb*, so those repression worries would still apply, so, duh, *Flurb* isn't really a cover after all. But if I run it under a pseudonym in *Flurb*, I at least have a fig leaf. And if I got some others in there, I'd be thinking, "In Unity is Strength."

***

Another idea…which maybe seems silly after my worries about persecution…this story rounds out very nicely, but it has some intriguing loose ends, and it really could be the first chapter of the novel I was thinking about in the first place. And somehow if the chapter was part of a novel, it might be less of an affront. Well, let's see what *Lightspeed* says, and take it from there.

Tempest in a teapot. The tininess of my self-centered concerns.

February 27-28, 2019. What is Blockchain.

I've straightened things out for our trip to Guanajuato, March 17-23, and for our trip to Miami Beach, April 16-21. Made a bunch of reservations, and hassled for advance payment by the IOHK blockchain guys behind the Miami Beach con. They're going to send it, but I had to sign an online contract with them. It says they get to see a draft of my talk 2 weeks early, and that I should incorporate whatever (moronic) suggestions they make. Never had that in a speaking contract before.

I do keep worrying about what I can say about blockchain that' interesting and, more to the point, if I can work into an SF scenario. Marc Laidlaw had the good idea that blockchain might have a role if you're doing time hops and loops, with, perhaps, possibilities of forking time lines. Or, in a more mundane way, in the structure of my memory, as Wolfram seems to have casually suggested in his half-serious blog post. Some of my study notes:

Blockchain is in a way like a doubly-linked list. But instead of a pointer to a memory location for the previous block A, a successor block B has a data triple {hashcode, timestamp, none} that lets you *recognize* the previous block A. That is, it has a timestamp, a nonce number, and a hashcode for the structure consisting of {block A, B's timecode, B's nonce). If you have an accessible pool of all existing blocks, you can plow through them, and find the A that generates the hashcode in B when hashed with the timecode and nonce in B. Finding A needn't take long, as in practice, you need only look at old blocks whose personal timestamps are in a shortish interval of time before block B's timestamp. So B can find A. Conversely A can find its one or more successors B, using the same process. Note that an A can have several successors. But in practice a B can have only one predecessor as hash collisions via SHA-256 are so rare, like 1 in 10^25 times. The way to break the security of a blockchain is to generate and distribute one successor, and have a secret alternate successor. The proof-of-work idea makes it hard to generate the next block very fast, so by the time you create one, everyone learns it before you have time to make another. The alternate proof-of-stake seems to lead to oligarchy.

Drone, drone, drone. Who cares?
After writing that note, I got a better angle on it from the famous urtext white paper on Bitcoin by the mysterious Satoshi Nakamoto I like his emphasis on proof of work as giving you the right to record a block and mint a new Bitcoin. I still think the IOHK proof of stake Cardano cryptocurrency seems less secure. But they don't want me to say that, thus, perhaps, the "preview" clause in my contract. Whatever. No need to delve into it, especially since I don't especially know what I'm talking about.
Last night I woke up at four am worrying about my talk.
I don't really want to talk about the blockchain bullshit, and I don't want to be "playing catch-up ball." Better I talk

about what I know. I'll send them a slightly tweaked version of my Louisville Ideafest talk for the lecture, and I thing I have a *Lifebox* era PowerPoint slide-set for the workshop.

And I will, as window-dressing, tack on some generalities about, as Wolfram says, computational incompressibility and proof of work.

March 6, 2019. "The Mean Carrot." Uses for Blockchain.

Feeling at loose ends again. Too rainy to paint. In limbo on "Juicy Ghost" story, waiting to hear from *Lightspeed*…if they'll respond at all.

I killed a few days doing the taxes and (for my own purposes) my "annual report" of Transreal Books income from Kickstarters and sales. I've made about $70K over six or seven years.

***

In the background, I'm still groping toward that happy UFO 1950s transreal early autobio story I want to write. Or toward, really, any kind of story about my early childhood. In the evenings, before going to sleep, or in the mornings still in bed, I sometimes go into my memory bank and "walk around" our 620 Rudy Lane house, and around the back and front yards, with memories going off like landmines, or rather, memories opening up like the window flaps on an Advent calendar.

A problem here is the shadow of my brother's unpleasant-ness towards me as a boy I do not want to make that the main thing, don't want to build it up, don't want it to be the center of the story, but I do have to acknowledge it, or deal with it in some fashion—otherwise I won't be able to write the story at all. It's like when I wrote *Turing & Burroughs*, I had to write about Bill shooting his wife Joan, even though I didn't want to.

Various options. Future Rudy goes back and warns 6-year-old Rudy to, like, make himself scarce whenever his big brother Oscar is supposed to baby sit. Or the brother-thing is an alien, like in PKD's "The Father Thing," or in *Invasion of the Body Snatchers*. Or we're a bit into the future, and the "brother" is some kind of tank-grown not-quite-human creature. A talking carrot! Long and bumpy. Wanting to push his dirty root into the young Rudy's flesh, but the boy having the good sense and the force of will to rebuff the carrot's overtures.

And all those horrible boys picking on me at Louisville Country Day. Some of them were carrot-things too. Peter Lyons with his little Butch-waxed flipped-up piece of hair at the front of his buzz-cut. Chanting ugly things to me in Music Class. He called me Suck. "Suck's a big boy now." Couldn't I have punched him in the face? But I was small and weak and timid. It would be nice to have the Peter Lyons character die. Parasitically drained down to a smelly husk by a proboscis from the living UFO. With that tiny wedge of burr-cut pompadour on the husk. Rudy steps on the husk, cracking it. UFO larvae wriggle out.

Transreally speaking, I feel like my liberation from my early down-trodden Louisville days came when, a week before my 13th birthday, I went off to boarding school in Königsfeld, Germany. And perhaps I could transrealize this into young Rudy getting aboard a spaceship as a member of the crew. I remember when I was about to start *Jim and the Flims*, I had an image of a dinghy-like small spaceship coming to ferry a boy to the mother ship. This was inspired by a ship and motor launch that Sylvia and I saw in Balestrand, Norway. It's in the Notes for *Jim and the Flims*. Along with that great stuff about Weena Wesson living in a piece of cow liver. "*Muuur.*"

***

I made up a pair of illustrated webpages to serve, eventually, as the texts of my two scheduled talks at the IOHK Summit in Miami Beach on April 18. "Your Cyberpunk Future" and "Everything is a Gnarly Computation." They're adapted from, respectively, my Louisville Ideafest talk, and an article I wrote for Asimov's SF magazine.

It took me a whole morning just to figure out the work flow. What I'm now doing is to edit them as HTML pages in the Word Press interface for my blog. I uploaded a stash of likely images to use, and I stick those into the two pages with *img* HTML tags. And I do to my usual blog post move of never going more than a half page without an illo. I'll post the files to the public on the day before my talks, and when I give the talk, I'll show just the images via Powerpoint, with at most one or two text slides, and mainly I'll extemporize the words along the lines of what I wrote in advance.

The talks look pretty good to me, and I can fantasize laughter and applause from an admiring crowd, but to really sell them, I do need some fantasies about future uses for blockchain. Really a short-short story would be the best. I could read it there, and then sell it to *Terraform*.

I just reread Bill Gibson's 1996 *Idoru*. Such a great book. He has this real knack for presenting internet/cloud things as sensual images. Doesn't worry one tiny bit about the tech or code. I need to do that with blockchain and the blocks. The code is boring as shit in any case.

One ongong issue for me is that even now, I really and truly *don't see the fucking point* of blockchain. Like this month someone turned their house into a "token" in the cloud, and someone bought it with, I guess, cryptocurrency. And presumably the transaction is a smart contract that's automated to plug the right things into the government's data bases. But why is this in any way better than just filing a paper at the courthouse?

And crypto currency—I mean, why use it except for buying cocaine, or hookers, or gangland hits on your enemies? It's so much trouble. And the fact that it's *not* backed by a government makes it, to my mind, *less* stable.

And publishing my blog posts and my ebooks—it seems easier to just put them publicly online, with or without buy links. And it's fucking *obvious* that I wrote them. We don't need crypto for that, do we? Why would I put my writings up inside blocks? The proof of work is that I spent time writing them, and I've been talking about them all along.

I guess, okay, there's this loser pulp-magazine fantasy of a secret mad scientist working on something, and he doesn't want to "tell anyone till it's done" so he puts up secret, slobbering posts about in in crypto, and those go into a blockchain to get a date stamp onto them. But it's my experience that guys who want to do that are self-aggrandizing crackpots, and their "thuper thecwet thience thtuff" is junk. If you have something real, you can post it in clear.

But it's not helpful for me to be pointlessly snotty.

We want a web where you aren't beholden to your local ISP. And where there can't be system-wide internet filters to evaluate your posts. Another possible choke point is the browser used by you and your users to, respectively, post and access your material.

Now get imagistic on this. A butterfly or a paper airplane flies out of my laptop, with writing on its wings. It dips and curves, tracing a chaotic space curve, sniffing out a spot to land, then launches from there, hop scotching, as if on stepping stones. When it finds a piece of blockchain, it fastens itself on.

I wake up in the cloud. I'm immortal. But there's another Rudy who claims he's the real me, and he has the rights to my estate, which will be used to pay for his software support. Blockchain says I'm the real Rudy. But he has a certificate too.

I found a really useful article by Emily Su, "Use Cases for Blockchain."

(a) Asset Tokenization. Sell off 0.01% of your house to a thousand people. Or do this with a painting. If the house is sold, I guess the thousand people split the profit, and ditto for the rent. Can apply to a work of art, too.

(b) Bruce's old arphid thing, of having an ID on an object and blockchaining each step of its supply chain.

(c) Medical records. So lots of people can see them, and edit them, but they don't "belong" to anyone who might data mine it.

(d) Energy market. Letting individual sell their extra windmill or solar energy. Making an open exchange.

(e) Digital ID. So people without credit cards or bank accounts can have IDs for online transactions. And again, the central companies don't monetize. Or you can control what people do with your ID.

March 7, 2019. Blockchain a Scam? Use Cases?

So I tweeted out a link to that Emily Su article, "Use Cases for Block Chain." And one of my 7,500 Twitter followers came back with a link to an article that goes a long way towards scuttling the validity of those use cases. See Kai Stinchcombe, "Blockchain is not only crappy technology but a bad vision for the future." I tweeted this link too, and got a bit more feedback. Stinchcombe himself lives in Atlanta and runs a business that advises seniors about not getting scammed, so who knows if even should believe his opinions. Oh, and here's yet another article, by Jimmy Song, '<u>Why Blockchain is Hard</u>," where he makes the point that for most use cases—like supply chain or health records—blockchain is too slow and kludgy to use. In most cases you can't readily wipe out the centralized aspect of the database, and if you do manage a full blockchain solution, it becomes inefficiently slow.

***

If I do write one or more short-short SF stories about blockchain (or, rather, about a more effective and hylozoic distributed data base technology), I think I'd probably have the first one be about a really brutal scam. Like, a woman is in the digital afterworld, and she loses your body-simulation—or, rather, she loses her juicy-ghost organic peripheral—and she accept an incarnation as a light-bulb switch. Or she has to work as an NPC (non-player character) in a videogame. And then, (John Shirley's suggestion) she runs a drone herding sheep in New Zealand, but she gets aced out of that, and then she becomes a little cascade in a creek.

In other words, instead of doing upbeat product-flogging "use cases" I could do "misuse cases." And that's legit, too, for the purposes of a talk at the IOHK con. Gaming out flaw scenarios is something that futurists do. I could even call the story "Use Cases." Yeah. Now I'm getting somewhere.

***

Meanwhile IOHK still haven't sent me the travel + 50% honorarium money, even though I've requested it three times. I should phone the guy today. I think he's in London. Oops, he didn't give me a phone number. Meanwhile I got an email from the guy saying he'd wired the money, but he hadn't wired it after all, and then I got an email asking for me to reformat and resubmit my invoice. So I did that and now I'm waiting again. Slow, time-lagged communication channel as Hong Kong is on the other side of the world.

I wonder if they're scammers. I mean…a cryptocurrency and blockchain consortium in Hong Kong? Paging William Gibson. Is someone in the company is having second thoughts about inviting me? Or have my doubting, ill-informed tweets about blockchain convinced them I'm not a team player? And I wonder if I can possibly say anything intelligent about blockchain? And I'm paranoid about having to submit my talks early to IOHK—and then perhaps being vetoed at the last minute?

Very hard to communicate with the IOHK guys, as we're 8 hours out of synch. I'm so sick of waking up worrying about this every morning. I'd frikkin bail on this project right now, but it'd be hard to get back the airfare I paid, and the room I reserved for the last two days at Miami Beach is nonrefundable. But who knows, it may yet work out.

March 12, 2019. IOHK Talk: "Cyberpunk Use Cases."

As I say, I've been feeling like I'm going crazy without a book or story to write. I'm in such an unsettled frame of mind these days. Frantic. The constant rain and no painting, worrying about my and Sylvia's health, the pains in my hip and my tooth, fretting about our rashly booked trips to Guanajuato and Miami Beach, loneliness. Did a blog post about this, "Adrift."

***

Yesterday it got a little better. The sun came out and I worked on a painting about spring, but with the "goddess of Spring" wearing a haz-mat suit. Because of COVID. I was inspired by seeing my young neighbor lady working on her yard and wearing a facemask.

And this morning, IOHK, the con organizers, wired me $4,600 which covers my airfare and half my honorarium. On Friday, March 8, I'd written a really angry email to them, saying I was going to bail on Friday, and by now, Tuesday, March 12, I was going to bail…cancelling my plane tix etc. And I was glad about that, happy to be off the hook, welcoming the surcease of pain. But then of course the money came through. The payment paranoia has been an example of those blockchain-candidate processes where one is dealing with "untrusted" people…such as a cryptocurrency consortium in Hong Kong.

IOHK also said they want the talks to be just a half hour long, so I'm thinking of ways to trim my talks down. Will get to have some Q&A I hope.

Rather than getting too far into what I (don't) know about blockchain. I'll focus on three or four SFnal cyberfreak "use cases." Give the audience something to think about. I see the use cases as short-short stories,

Figure 6: *Hazmat Spring*

By the way, Could I make "The Mean Carrot" into a use-case story? Well, I think that's probably something else. Unless I need a walk-on villain, like an evil hacker bully, and maybe then the mean carrot can have his say.

In my "Your Cyberpunk Future" talk I can have three far future scenarios at the end. Illustrating these points.

Goodies	Drawback	Old Fix	New Fix
Web Search	Ads, Data Mining	Ad-blockers, VPN	Search dots
Telepathy	Mental Spam	Filters	Recommendations
Digital Immortality	Impersonation	ID	Memory thread

SEARCH.

Use a superchip instead of Google. Or, go quantum computer. The device could be very small. Call it a crystal ball. I think of. Borges' story, "The Alef." Now, of course Google has giant banks of computers worldwide. But we do a Moore's Law move. In ten years, you can fit all of Google's current info and processing into your phone. The power of a search engine like Google stems from the users' need to employ search as an index or catalog of the web. A company like Google is doing massive updates daily or hourly. Suppose everyone has a crystal ball. We enrich our crystal ball's history automatically as we surf the web. And we share our updates peer to peer. It's like Wikipedia. A blockchain element akin to the Wikipedia edit tracker to prevent spam updates.

TELEPATHY

First we get rid of the kludgy haptic interfaces like keys, voice, and mouse. We get what I call an "uvvy" patch to put on the backs of our necks. A soft piezoplastic slug.

Then comes telepathy. It's more than a silent videophone conversation. The level after that is to link to thought patterns in the neurons. It's like, instead of sending someone a JPG image, you send them a link to the image on the web. Instead of talking to someone about your idea and having them construct a model of your thought, you send them a link to the thought pattern in your brain.

A new medium. Every new medium attracts porn, scams, and ads. Hucksters want to invade your dreams and daydreams. They want to overlay AR ads on your sensations and even on your thoughts. Use ad filters? Need something stronger. You have to personally recognize the caller. Or how about requiring an input to carry with it a link to a trusted agent or a trusted page. Like a letter of introduction. "Rudy sent me." I use block chain to have a non-hackable provenance history.

DIGITAL IMMORTALITY

I've been thinking of a story along these lines that I was calling "Mary Falls." Blockchain aspects: Continuity of personality is a blockchain thing. Each successive state has a pointer to the previous state. The crypto element is the richness of detail, which is a "proof of work" thing. This comes into play if the ghost is supposed to be a writer. Each story or novel has echoes of the ones before. It's a block chain thing as the references are subtle. The thread of consciousness is a block chain. A non-hackable, non-forgeable record of my thoughts.

But in reality, I probably won't use block-chain in my SF stories. Too hard to understand. I'd instead use some more hand-waving kind of thing. "Quantum lock."

March 15, 2019. In SF. My IOHK Webpages.

I'm sitting outside the Caffe Rulli in Union Square in SF. Cool but sunny. A large Green New Deal rally of high-schoolers. They're enthusiasm and idealism. "The Dinosaurs Said They Had Plenty of Time Too." Would be great if the movement really catches on. Another sign. "It's Time to Change All the Rules." Indeed.

I worked for two days solid editing the webpage with my IOHK talk, now called "Cyberpunk Use Case," although "Cyberpunk Crypto Use Case" might be better. I only have a half hour for the talk, like at the TedX in Brussels, so I need to keep editing it down. 2,000 words of text would be good.

<Geek Alert> I don't know if I mentioned that I've been editing it inside my blog maintenance software, I think it's called WordPress. The editor is a little like the Dreamweaver editor, in that I can flip back and forth between the "Text" and the "Visual" modes. Text mode is close to being raw HTML without the bother of <p> tags. Visual is live online, so I can see an image as soon as put an appropriate <img> tag into the Text-mode window. Another win in this editing mode is that the file is online, so I can move between laptop and desktop without having to copy the file. And WordPress lets me post it onto my web site in a "Password Protected" mode. So, I was able to send the link and the password to my contacts and IOHK, so now they can see I've got my talk together, and they c can get off my back about previewing it. </Geek Alert.>

I'm stupid to be looking at my laptop here in Union Square. So much to see and hear. Relax, Rudy, and turn off the machine.

March 17, 2019. Flying to Guanajuato.

On the plane. Our original flight got cancelled, so we have

to fly a weird route, San Jose - Chicago - Dallas - Leon. Looking forward to a week down there in Guanajuato, a pretty town, lots of color. I went in October, 2016, three years ago, right before my left hip woes began, the four operations in a row. That hip's still hurting, thanks to the doctor's bungling. A new development this fall is "end of stem pain," which is officially considered to be "iatrogenic," that is, doctor-caused. He put too wide of a replacement spike into my femur and cracked it. This new pain flared up again this week, right before our trip, so I brought a crutch and my walking canes along. Kind of sad to bring those on a vacation. But happy to be on a vacation at all. Actually, yesterday afternoon— after I finished the last of the little tasks that had been hanging over me—the pain went down a bit. Wheenk, wheenk, wheenk. I need this vacation.

Thinking about that "Mary Falls" story...maybe I could use it as Chapter 2 of a *Juicy Ghost* novel. Like in the three "Bridge Trilogy" Wm. Gibson novels I just read: *Virtual Light, Idoru, and All Tomorrow's Parties*, where you have alternating chapters of close-in mind-reading-type POV of different characters, and at the start they seem to have nothing to do with each other, but eventually they knit together. I've done that too sometimes, like *Freeware* or Hylozoic or *Million Mile Road Trip*.

Speaking of those Gibson novels, I think I like *Idoru* the best, and *All Tomorrow's Parties* is great too. Masterpieces. *Virtual Light* doesn't have a good plot, and the chracters are a little corny, so naive, oppressed, and noble. They draw you in, and you root for them, but they're kind of 2D.

Back to *Juicy Ghost*, were it to be a novel made of stories, *Accelerando* style. I could have Curt Winch thread, and possibly have the Mary thread and maybe another thread, like a Gee Willikers thread or a Leeta thread. I'd say that, as a rule, you don't want more than three threads, and really two threads is best.

If Mary's gonna carry a thread to novel length, or even story length, she'd have to be more interesting than she is right now. And I still need a twist. And that old desideratum for our lead character Mary: *agency*. Don't have it yet. And if she sticks around for novel-length, I might have her mutate to look younger so that the readers would care about her. And I'd want her to encounter Gee Willikers in the course of her body hops.

Re. POV, Curt Winch is 1st person present-tense, and I see Mary as 3rd person past tense. Could I blend those two? Seems to me like when novels to that, the first-person present tense thread is for some undead ghost or psycho killer or spirit of place. Multiple 1st person threads too confusing.

***

Time for a nap. Sleep about ten mins and an announcement wakes me. We got up at 5 am. I totally bungled the airport check-in process, ended up just walking to the gate with our suitcases and the preprinted boarding passes I made last night, and we barely made the plane at 7 am. They let us gate-check the bags, a relief.

The flight wears on. So boring. When I booked this alternate route, I didn't quite realize how long it would be. I paid extra so we'd have slightly more comfortable seats. We forgot to bring food. I bought yet another Gibson e-book to read, but this is from his "Blue Ant" trilogy series which I now remember I don't like. It isn't really SF at all. And a lot of it is about having jet-lag and staying in fancy hotels—which was, I imagine, a big part of Bill's life by then. We're lancing in Chi now. At last.

***

Now over the Great Plains or MidWest, or whatever. Irregular checkers of beige and brown fields, lifeless, dull, awaiting the vivifying force of Spring. Bands and copses of dark green trees, all the images attenuated by the thin mist the perfuses the air. I guess we're one or two miles high, maybe three. On our way to Dallas/Fort Worth. They used to have a good local BBQ place on the lower level there, undecorated, all business, greasy and weathered, metal, glass and plastic.

Bends of a river below, oxbows, dragon-spikes along the curves, attempted new branches like fat spikes, pinched-off islands in the hearts of the old folds.

Sylvia asleep next to me. Something always so emphatic and *sincere* about her closed eye, the curve of the closed lid, makes me want to shout and laugh, gloating, as always, at her presence beside me.

Just spent a half hour reading the first chapter and a half of

Sigmund Freud's *Dream Psychology*. I found it amid the
clutter that has accumulated in the backwaters of my Kindle
over the years. "Free download! I'll read it someday." Glad I
finally got to Freud's dream stuff. Very meaty. He makes
interesting points right away. The underlying "dream thoughts"
are folded into the "dream events." Usually, the more
significant nodes are the smaller, less central events. Usually,
several unrelated dream thoughts are overlaid to make a single
dream event. You discover them by free-associating from your
memory of the dream events.

Let's try an example. Last night I briefly dreamed I was
with Sylvia and we were eating fried foot out of a pair of pans,
it was a sort of game, trying to guess what you were eating,
with your eyes closed. There was a pair of fried eggs in one
pan, a pair of thin hamburger patties on the other. Greasy. Hot,
with some danger of burning my mouth. I peeked and could
see. A crowded place.

Relates to our dinner at Andale last night, we had identical
oval plates, she had two enchiladas, I had chicken fajitas. Her
food looked better than mine. I got a stomach ache from the
heavy, spicy meal, and I was angry we'd gone out. The pairs
might be testicles, breasts, buttocks, or two people. Closed eyes
suggest being in our bed together. Sylvia was in bed before me,
and wanted the lights out. Various sexual activities come to
mind. And the other day I burned a plastic spatula by leaving it
an omelet pan and forgetting to turn off the gas. Eyes closed.
Two days ago, we watched a TV doc about a graphic designer
Paula something, who'd once done a records album cover with
two fried eggs. Hmm.
***

Now it's dark and we're on the last leg of this absurdly
long trip. We left our house at 6 am, and we'll be in
Guanajuato at, I don't know, about 9 pm our time. Fifteen
hours. As bad as flying to Europe.

I wasn't at all hungry in Dallas/Fort Worth, as I'd eaten a
huge sandwich in Chicago, but we had over an hour to kill, and
I saw an outlet of my fave TX BBQ chain, Cousin's. So I got
half a pound of BBQed brisket, half lean, half fat. The lean is
wonderful. Firm, like an artificial substance, then crumbling as
you bite. Smoky like other foods *say* they're smoky. *Cousin's*

has an actual wood-fired smoker in each of its outlets. Marvellous coleslaw and sweet ranch beans. And the BBQ sauce…exquisite. Eat we must. A gastric kamikaze run.

Reading some more of Freud on dreams. Wonderful stuff. The dream work is about converting the dream thoughts into dream events. You compress several thoughts into one event and, conversely, several events may refer to the same thought. There's absolutely no logic. *Or* becomes *and*. Disdain becomes absurdity. He thinks that in a typical night of dreaming, all the dreams are representations of the same constellation of thoughts. He says it's common to have an initial dream that is, so to say, the *conclusion*, and later have the set-up dream that is the *hypothesis*.

Note that Freud's theories are still not universally accepted. Indeed, his popularity is less than it was when I was growing up. To me, this makes his theories that more attractive. If it's possible they might be *wrong* then, in an odd way, it gives weight to the possibility that they might be *right*.

I've always wanted to write an SF story about dreams. "Dream Work." Thinking this, I feel like I'm starting in on my vacation already!

March 22, 2019. 73rd Birthday. "Teep." IOHK Slides.

We're on our last day in Guanajuato now, leaving tomorrow. It's been great. The colors, the colors, the colors. Here's a painting of it that I did when I got home.

This morning I took a rather long hike up through the jumbled streetless neighborhood on the hill behind our hotel, going up for half a mile, dwellings cobbled together from stone and wood and stucco, completely irregular, not exactly hovels or shacks, but formless, like a reef, with the shapes evolved to fit into the hill's topography, all Mexicans in there, goes without saying, established in their niches, poor but not destitute. Generally, they were friendly to me if I greeted them.

Everyone paints their house in some different wild color. Magenta, baby pink and baby blue, chartreuse, sour lime, deep cinnabar red, traffic orange, rich buttery yellow, pale citron. Often they paint "frame" rectangles around their windows.

Figure 7: *Mexico*

I was happy to be able to walk up there, not collapsing from heart failure, and getting along well enough on my still-bad hip by dint of wielding a crutch in my right hand, one of those fancy forearm-band crutches I got two years ago. I'm so used to the crutch that it doesn't feel like much of a burden, although whenever I go to sit down and lean it somewhere, it falls down with a clatter, and then once it's stashed, when I leave, half the time I forget it, as I don't totally need it…it's more like if I'm doing a long haul, using the crutch means I don't get as much of a post-outing pain flare-up in the bad hip.

Mom was an invalid by 73, and she died at 74. Pop had a mild stroke at 78, then a worse one, and then he died at 79, But he was still in decent shape when he was 74. Maybe I'm in slightly better shape, hard to say. One hopes.

While writing this about my parents, I delved into my *Journals* book for ten minutes, reading the parts about their deaths, and then reading some other entries, like about the start of writing *The Hacker and the Ants*. My *Journals* really are very clean and polished. I went over them a lot. Yet another of my curiously ignored masterpieces.

Talked on the phone to my Mexican author/cartoonist friend Bef (Bernando Fernandez) the other day. He'd hoped to connect with us in Guanajuato, but can't get out of Mexico City. And he said something nice: "I tell everyone that Rudy Rucker is the most under-recognized American author. You're as good as Pynchon, but you're ignored. It's very strange." *I'll* say!

I took a nice selfie of myself, looking hale and lucid, and posted it on FB and Twitter with a birthday announcement, that is, a request for greetings. Big score. Got over 400 likes on FB, along with over 200 replies. And lots of replies on Twitter too. A soothing, pleasant activity, scrolling through the replies, "liking" them, enjoying what they say.

Sylvia was nice to me all day. Kept saying "It's your birthday," when any choice had to be made. Although, by the evening, she began pointing out that my time was running out.

I made a bad choice for our dinner restaurant. (a) As we wanted to go see some classical music at the Teatro Principal at 8:30, I felt we should eat at 7:30, and the restaurant was stone cold empty. Mexicans *never* have summer before 8. (b) I ordered something called Mar y Ter, like a Mexican surf n' turf, but it was, as Sylvia put it, more like beef n' beet. Served as a tower, with two small flat rounds of tough gray steak, interleaved with two massive disks of firm, cooked, purple beet. And a single butterflied prawn on top. Nearly inedible, but we laughed. I didn't care. It was funny. Sylvia had gotten chipotle shrimp, which I also tasted, and it was so hot it removed all sensation from the diner's tongue. "What tongue?" said Sylvia.

Actually, some of the best meals on this trip were our free hotel breakfast buffets, a little different every day. And once I managed to get a really great enchilada/quesadilla (the distinction seemed less clear here than at home).

Meanwhile, as I disassembled my birthday beef n' beet, outside in the triangular main square, visible through the dining-room's two open, street-level doors, the Friday night festivities were raging, and augmented by a student group of troubadours at University of Guanajuato. They dress in 16th C type garb, like puffy dark sleeves with slit folds that are gold fabric inside. Seven of them will sing in front of the San Diego church, gather a following of tourists, and lead them around the old town, singing all the while. They did the "Ay, ya, yi, yi" song, I Googled it and it's called "Cielito Lindo," which is "My pretty little sky [or pretty darling]."

    ***

I've been noticing over the last year or two, and especially on this vacation in Guanajuato, how much people, especially tourists, use their phone. Shot gunning the area with photo clicks as they walk into a square. And endlessly, I mean endlessly, taking each other's pictures, doing selfies, and doing group selfies.

Our room looks over an open spot at the corner, cobblestones, not really a square, but an area where people can mill around a little, and I watched a group of Chinese tourists, students probably, selfie-shooting for easily half an hour. Posing, laughing, rushing to look at the shot, doing another, over and over, and intermittently messaging the shots out to the cloud.

Yesterday S and I had lunch at a kind of bogus tourist-oriented cafe in a strip of four or five similar joints, in a cobblestoned square with big trees, breezy, pleasant, and the food not as bad as I'd expected, and I noticed two Japanese girls at the table next to us. Both very thin, possibly anorexic. They ordered four or five large dishes, and left after only nibbling a few bites. One of them wandered over to another cafe to bring back a coffee, and while her friend was alone, she was relentlessly selfying herself, striking fashion-model poses, her head at varying angles, her facial expressions flipping through shades of ennui, jadedness, madness, lust, and inaccessibility. Very rote and by the book, you understand.

And I'm thinking about how much the smart camera phone has affected what people do.

And then I flash on *teep*. What if the girl's smart phone was a telepathy transmitter? It might, initially, just capture "single frames." A few layers of moods, a few dozen associations, plus the sensory inputs at the moment. Sight, sound, smell, taste, touch, proprioception. That last one is a complex of inputs. People are sending and receiving them. Need a name for them. Poses, shots, freezes, eggs, rooms, suits, mes, me-me, meemie. Meemie is pretty good. Like selfie and like meme and like "Me, me!".

There's an old slang expression, *screaming memes*. I found an etymology post that says there was a German rocket shell they called a screaming meemie because it made a sound like meeeeem, and the phrase was used for a condition of shell shock brought on by battle fatigue. Later it was used to mean drunkenness or the DTs. Sometimes "heebie-jeebies" was used for "DTs" too.

This doesn't mean I can't use meemie for a teep shot. But I'd need to mention the older meaning, maybe even retrofit and re-introduce it.

Anyway, my point is that I had a vision fo a novel called *Teep* [later named *Juicy Ghosts*] about the coming of the teep technology, I've been writing about teep, off and on, for at least ten years. Starting maybe with *Saucer Wisdom*.

Years ago, I read a vintage SF book which I need to find now. It was about the coming of telepathy. And there was a religion based on it, and our narrator goes to a service, and he's pulled into a teep vision, sees himself walking down the aisle, notices his wearing a sharkskin suit, hardly his normal wear, and up at the altar is a woman and she says she loves him and she means this in a very physical and enjoyable way. And, maybe in the same book, a woman gets teep and is upset to teep the men lusting for her. I remember the phrase: "Bounce, bounce, bounce. Nice." When I get home, I can check the online *Encyclopedia of SF*.

I have a sense, possibly mistaken, that nobody's done a modern-tech, witty, satirical, Rudy-style novel about the coming of commercial telepathy.

I feel like I got a hot tip from the Muse. The zap I'd been waiting for. She always shows up, but in her own time.

***

My contact guy at IOHK is bugging me by email that he wants a copy of "my presentation" by March 25. I'd had the impression I took care of that with the web page I posted, and sent him a link to? I guess he wants a PowerPoint of the slides, that's what a "presentation" is to a certain kind of tiny, business-schooled mind. Well, okay I can snap the slide set together from my web page draft in a couple of hours when we get home.

I'll have the "crystal ball" private Google search engines, the "coming of teep," and the "lifebox / digital immortality" raps. That's plenty Will whittle it down to make sure that I'm not having to rush. And I'll flesh out the remarks on teep.

The private personal Google chip system evades having you being individual stalked and data-siloed and ad-profiled by a big company. And—ad tailoring aside—it reduces your exposure to bad, spammy paid-for links. A downside is that an indie content-generator seems to lose the ease of being automatically visible, that is, search-locatable, by everyone. Promoting your offerings becomes more of a word-of-mouth thing, hopping from crystal all to friends' crystal balls. And of course you can submit it to curated lists or, for that matter, put your post on public centralized Google. It really only needs to be your browsing that's not done via central Google.

I'm groping for how to connect this with Wikipedia, which seems to have a good central/peer-to-peer dynamic. And, far as I know, Wikipedia doesn't track you.

By the way, my IOHK "workshop" (whatever that means) is supposed to last an hour. So I'll add a little more material to that talk than I had. I can use some of the old slides from existing PowerPoint talks I gave when I was promoting the *Lifebox* tome.

March 23, 2019. Mummies / God Disk. Redo "Juicy Ghost."

We're on the flight home now, a four-hour direct flight, thank god, not like the twelve-hour two-intermediate-stops-marathon it took to get from San Jose to Mexico.

Day before yesterday in Guanajuato, I took Sylvia to the Museo los Momias, that is, the museum of the mummies. I'd visited it with Bef a few years ago.

Guanajuato is very dry, at an altitude of six thousand feet, and of course hot in the summers. Bodies were buried either in the hardpan, white, alkaline soil, or sealed in crypts. If the descendants didn't keep paying the annual plot-rental fee for someone, the cemetery owners would dig up the body and put it on display in their Mummy Museum, which remains to this day.

The bodies still have their skin, flesh, teeth, and even wisps of hair. Leathery, dried-out, twisted from the contraction of the tendons, the distorted mouths open as if in the hideous screams of the damned—in every respect like undead, eyeless, zombies. Truly horrible—although from time to time a viewer's terror flips over into anxious mirth.

There was one guy in particular, with a big jaw and his mouth wide open and quite a few teeth missing, but with a kind of Hell's Angel biker energy to him, an undead hick out for a good time, and the curators had, for whatever reason, left a grayed-out pair of pants on him, the waistline very low, Pachuco style, or like he might even be on the point of dropping-trou exposing himself to you.

And near him was a woman with her mouth an open O, turned a bit to one side, as if wailing in woe, some teeth in there, her nose dried down to little more than skully nostrils, and somehow I saw her as the date of the Hell's Angel.

Sylvia was groping for the *mot juste* to describe how she felt about the displays. Discomfited, dismayed, discombobulated. "I could have lived without seeing this," she said. But, having heard about it from me, she *did* want to see it, at least to some extent and, charming though Guanajuato is, there are not a surfeit of cultural venues to explore.

That evening, after regrouping in our room, we had dinner downtown at a fancy Italian restaurant on the triangular square, and on the walk home we passed the big yellow basilica or cathedral of Guanajuato. We'd wanted to check it out before, but that day there'd been a funeral with an adult-sized white coffin, and a hundred mourners on the steps, and some mariachis playing away, and the mourners heading off down the cobblestone street behind the hearse.

The day of the mummies, as if in counterposition to the theme of death and decay, the cathedral doors was wide open, with the place lit up like no church I've ever seen. Intensely bright white-light bulbs festooned in over twenty elaborate chandeliers, and bright pale-blue LED bulbs arrayed in vertical strings along the edges of the columns.

Sylvia and I went in, some kind of service taking place, we slipped into a rear pew. The space was filled with resonant chanting, wonderful music, and the increasingly fevered ringing of bells. The priest's voice up there, very soothing, a couple of hundred worshippers closer to the altar. Was it okay for us to be here?

Well, too late for that, here comes the priest, in his white cassock, and four or five assistants, also robed, some of them are women, a couple of thurifers are swinging these billowing incense burners, the priest is moving in a cloud, he's holding something up, shaped like a hand-mirror, a disk with a handle, the flat disk has glass on front and back, with a wide silver band around the disk's edge, like a frame, the disk might be a couple of feet across. The music and chanting continue, and the bells, the ringing, the sound is rising to a crescendo, rattling, frenetic, unsystematic, getting into my head. The smell of the incise is mild and pleasant. The priest has come all the way down to the end of the aisle, people are reaching out toward him, at first, I don't get what the people are doing, but now the priest is right by us, and I see they're touching the priest's raised disk with their two open hands. I can see through the glass, a big white circle is inside, maybe four inches across, it's a communion wafer, what they call the Host, it's sealed between the two layers of glass with the silver frame around the rim. The glass and silver holder is what they call a pyx, I recall, and, yes, that big round white flat shape inside the pyx—it's *God*! Of course God is a white disk. Like the Sun. The priest is bringing God down to us, and even a poor mean wretch like I can touch God, or at least touch the pyx that God's riding in. Sylvia reaches out first, and touches the silver band of the pyx with the fingers of her two open hands, and now I do it too, with the smoke all around, and the frenetic rattle of the bells inside my head. I glimpse the priest's face— humble, good, calm, he's not looking at me, he's absorbed in his work. I feel vast, unknown forces moving within my body and my soul—I'm filled with joy in the bright white church. A religious experience, wow. Sylvia and I are quite overwhelmed, nearly in tears.

The beautiful music is playing on, the heavenly glow of the lights continues, the congregation is chanting. People are drifting up the aisle, following the priest, massing in the church's apse. Will they be taking communion? Not wanting the exulted moment to end, Sylvia and I go along.

The white-robed priest fits God and his pyx into a cabinet

on the wall above the altar. God's house. Rather than offering communion, the priest extends a simpler blessing. He has an ewer of holy water. Over and over the dips in a religious instrument, a little like a ladle or a pestle, then makes a flinging gesture which sends drops flying down onto us. Sylvia and I feel a few on our faces and hands. All right!

"Those Catholics," she says to me when we're back out in the square. "You've got to hand it to them. They really know how to do religion. The *theatre* of it."

March 24-25, 2019. Revise "Juicy Ghost." Revise IOHK.

By the way, my story "Juicy Ghost" got rejected by John Joseph Adams at *Lightspeed*. He said the politics was fine with him, but the story didn't quite convince him. When I get time, I'll do a light rewrite…one thing bothering me is that after the battle at the Washington Monument, I don't show a very strong reaction on the part of the Treadler crowd.

And after I rewrite, I'll try it on Sheila at *Asimov's*.
***

IOHK did a second money transfer to my bank account; they sent me the full $8,350 I asked for. Unbelievable. Maybe it wasn't such a bad idea to write them that crazed, angry email saying I wouldn't come at all if they didn't pay me now. A lesson learned from Robert Anton Wilson.

I want to revise my IOHK workshop talk now, I'll call it "Lifebox for Telepathy and Immortality." This way it'll expand upon what I briefly say on these topics at the end of my main talk, "Cyberpunk Use Cases." I'll try and do that tomorrow.

Still pretty tired today, from that big trip with miles of walking each day. I did a little yoga this morning, and my hip hardly hurts at all. Lying around with the *Sunday Times* today.

March 26, 2019. Workshop Talk.

This Kerry De Jong character at IOHK, turns out she's a young Scots woman, not the Belgian functionary I'd been imagining in my mental arguments with her. When I added her to my phone contacts, her image popped up, who knows how.

Anyway, I did my PowerPoint for the talk yesterday, and today I need to put together a slideshow for the workshop. To start with, I'll revise the web page version of the talk. I'm rooting around in my old essays, and my *Lifebox* tome. The new idea I have is that your lifebox could be used as an intelligent assistant to filter out spam. Also, the lifebox could be used as background context tool to make your teep comprehensible. Also, your personal "crystal ball" Google could be used to develop AI via deep neural net learning. Hope this isn't too ambitious. I was just going to do a rote description of gnarly computation and Wolfram's NKS. But then in Guanajuato I had this vision of a bigger picture of teep.

March 29, 2019. Moving On.

So finally I finished my PowerPoints and the accompanying web pages for the IOHK summit—crazy that I put so much time into this, I'm so compulsive. But I'd like to think I gleaned some SF ideas from this exercise. Mostly relating to the *Teep* novel [later named *Juicy Ghosts*]. Not that, even now, I feel like diving into a big fiction frenzy.

Near term I'll do the following. I'll come back to this spot and asterisk the ones that I get done.

To Do

- * A blog post on Guanajuato.
- * Finish my *Moonrise* painting.
- * Do a rewrite on the "Juicy Ghost" assassination story and send it to Sheila at *Asimov's*.
- * Get my own ebook of *Ware Tetralogy* into distribution.
- * Make an ebook for *Million Mile Road Trip*.
- * Launch Kickstarter for *Million Mile Road Trip*. Rewards: ebook, Night Shade hb with color bookplate, color pb of *Notes for Million Mile Roadtrip*. Shoot for $7K.
- * Do the trip from April 16-21 to Miami Beach.

Here's the *Moonrise* painting by the way.

Figure 8: *Moonrise*

Will things ever settle down? I'm ready for another blank phase. At least that's what I *say*. But in fact, I'm not happy when my schedule is blank.

I'm just starting in one of those wintertime congested colds I get. Often they last a month or six weeks. My left leg's hurting a lot, ever since our active time in Guanajuato. Some of the time I use a crutch to walk.

Oh—some great news—*Publisher's Weekly* published a starred review of *Million Mile Road Trip*, very positive. I think they didn't review my last four novels at all.

"Tipping his hat to Thomas Pynchon, Jack Kerouac, and Douglas Adams, Rucker immerses readers in a fantastical roadtrip adventure that's **a wild ride of unmitigated joy**."

"Rucker populates this story with **boldly surreal**, humorous personalities and environments and **moves** it **at a frenzied, ever-increasing pace**."

"He ties everything together with internal consistency, playful use of language that keeps his ideas alien yet accessible, and a solid grounding in fourth-dimensional math. **This wacky adventure is a geeky reader's delight**."

Thank you.
***

Now we're at Cruz. Nice to see the ocean, and be on the quietly busy little main street. Pacific Ave. Like being on vacation. As I said, just now I have desire to start writing anything.

I've been feeling really tired since we got back from Guanajuato. All the walking. And that four-day push I did on the IOHK talks. I haven't been sleeping very well. And the cold. Ready to go back to Los Gatos and nap on the couch.

April 4, 2019, Kickstarter for *Million Mile Road Trip.*

So I rewrote my "Juicy Ghost" story. As I mentioned, the *Lightspeed* said the story was basically okay, but it didn't quite convince him. And one of the friends I showed it to said it ought to be published, and that in the earlier days, SF had political stories like this all the time.

I marked it up from beginning to end, fixing the logic and making it flow. This time I wasn't "trembling with emotion," and that helped a lot. I had it under control. Treating it simply as an SF story that had to entertain and make sense. It was good to be away from a month and let it cool.

Now I think it's really good and solid. So I sent it off to Sheila at Asimov's. We'll see.
***

Sean Wallace at Prime Books agreed to take down his Prime Books ebook of *The Ware Tetralogy*. I made a new cover. I kept Sean's text, but changed the image. I used a photo of me making my acceptance speech at my P. K. Dick award ceremony for Software in NYC, and to make it cyber, I ran the image through the Photoshop Pixelize | Crystallize filter, turning me into a mosaic of triangles, looks pretty cool. My look at that time was very Elvis Costello. I bought a fresh ISBN, tweaked the book's credits page and used most of Sean's EPUB, changing the default justification to "Left" and the default font to "Georgia." Put it on Amazon, Barnes & Noble, and (via D2D) Apple. $8.95 price now. Still need to do Google Play.

One remaining hangup is that Amazon is still listing the old version at $2.99, as being published by them—I think it's some fuckup involving my Quixotic choice to make a free Creative Commons version of *The Ware Tetralogy* years ago. Cory Doctorow convinced me that was a good idea at the time. I wrote Amazon a complaint, usually they're pretty good about these things.

***

Now I need to make an ebook of *Million Mile Road Trip* before it comes out in hardback and paperback on May 5, 2019. And make a color paperback of *Notes for Million Mile Road Trip*, just make the PDF from the DOC file, and publish it on Amazon. Use the higher-quality paper to make it pretty. I don't think I'll bother with the Lightning hardback of the *Notes* this time.

I'm a little embarrassed to do a Kickstarter for a book that's coming out from a mainstream publisher. Seems a little greedy. But, dammit, Night Shade only paid me $5K for the ten books, and I feel I ought to score a little more. And they agreed that I *could* do the Kickstarter. Collector's edition!

Also doing the Kickstarter seems almost like too much trouble. And I'm bone tired. But it *is* a type of promo.

Re. *Million Mile Road Trip*, I have a number of versions of the "final" manuscript. The copy editor on the book was a stuffy, overbearing, clueless individual, and I had to roll back the bulk of this person's *two thousand* changes. And I have a lingering worry that I let too many of the changes stand. On the other hand, there were some good changes in there, like I did a number of small, suggested rewrites that improved the logic and the flow. So, no, I won't go back there. I'll use the final version that Night Shade used, which I have in PDF form, and that includes a few more proofreading changes.

I'll make the ebook and the InDesign for the *Notes*, and then worry about the Kickstarter. If I ship the prizes on May 5, I still have a month, will be a little tight.

April 16, 2019. Kickstarted.

So I did all those things on my March 29 post's. list. A lot of them in the last week, that is, the ebook of the *Notes for Million Mile Road Trip* and the Kickstarter, plus a home page for MMRT. For the Kickstarter I made a video, which is always hard. First I have to do a decent performance and have it in focus, which takes about five tries. I tape the sound separately on my little Sony recorder with the good mic. Then I go into Pinnacle Studio 21 and wrestle with it. Lots of issues— I describe them in my ongoing publishing journal document and *aide memoire* called *Notes for Transreal Books*.

One thing worth mentioning is that I put in about six hours clipping out pauses and instances of *uh, and then*, and *so now*. I need to clip the video in synch with the audio, so that means the video is jumpy, but that's kind of the fashion anyway.

I went live with the Kickstarter campaign three days ago, on April 13, and I've already raised $4,500 of the modest $7,000 that I set as my target. Keep in mind that, with a Kickstarter, if you don't raise as much money as your preset goal, then you don't get any money at all. So you need to be modest in your demands. This said, in my five (!) previous Kickstarters, I always made it to my goal and then about 25% to 50% more. So I have a decent chance of making it to $10K.

It helped that almost right away I sold to big rewards to a pair of whales who've been around before. One bought the marked up final manuscript ($600), the other went for the pen sketches of my diagrams made while working on the novel notes ($700). I'm also trying to sell off some of the remaining eight paintings for the book, $800 each, with Ebook Cornucopia and Collector's Set included—so far, no dice on that.

It's the Collector's Set that should be the biggest money-maker. That's $180 for the Night Shade hardback of MMRT, plus my Lighting-printed color hardback of the Notes, edition limited to however many rewards I need, plus maybe five more. No real point leaving that book on the market as nobody ever buys the *Notes* books. Let it be a true limited edition. Like something Virginia and Leonard Woolf printed up for their Hogarth Press. Harrumph.

The most popular (if not particularly remunerative for me) reward class is the $25 Ebook Cornucopia award, where they get about five of my ebook editions. This time I didn't include any ebooks of the nine titles that Night Shade Books is reprinting this year, as I don't want to undercut Night Shade, also I want to sell some of those ebooks at my new price point of $8.95 each.

A plus is that I was able to add to the Cornucopia the ebook of the *Ware Tetralogy*. My all-time fiction best seller. I got the rights for it back from Prime Books two weeks ago. Then I figured out that the $2.99 Kindle of it on Amazon was in fact a pirated edition, simply a copy of the free CC version I (foolishly, extravagantly, heedlessly) released about ten years ago, with a pirated copy of the Prime Books paperback cover on the free CC version. At first Amazon didn't want to believe that I own the commercial eBook rights, but I kept after them, and now I 've got my own edition reigning, with that $8.95 price tag I now like, an amount which, kind of surprisingly to me, is now at the low end of the *de facto* standard for ebooks. I've been noticing myself paging this much, or even $13.95, for ebooks of late. Used to be you practically gave them away. But somehow the public has lost sight of the fact that it costs *nothing* to make a copy of an ebook (as opposed to printed it and mailing it). And more and more people just prefer ebooks.

Converting my new Night Shade reprint editions to the updated commercial ebooks I sell will take some work. The only one I've converted is *Million Mile Road Trip*.

I'll describe the process. In general, I only have the published PDF version from Night Shade. Nowadays Adobe Acrobat Pro will in fact save a DOC version of a PDF (it didn't used to have that capability). My typical method for making an EPUB from a DOC is to crossload the DOC into InDesign and export the EPUB from there. This is time consuming. But it ought to be easier for the nine backlist books of mine, which are already in InDesign. Presumably I can user Word to compare my existing DOCs for those titles to the newer DOCs from the Night Shade editions—all of which have undergone a bit of editing, copy editing, and proofreading, making them cleaner.

Nobody but me would be interested in the minutia that I'm annotating here, but I find it pleasant to jot this stuff down.

Worked like a madman Sunday and Monday, with Sylvia out of town for a one-day trip to Vegas to meet up with her brother. In AA people sometimes mention the duality between workaholism and alcoholism, and for sure it's true. Obsessively going off into some psychic cul de sac. Back in Lynchburg, I'd stay blasted for days when S would go off as a guide for her students on a European trip. The kids didn't like it. Now I go nuts with a bloodlust hacking frenzy.

Another thing I did while Sylvia was gone was to watch the two-and-a-half-hour masterpiece, David Lynch's *Mulholland Drive*—and read about it online, and think about it, and watch some Criterion Channel backup docs relating to the film. Somehow I managed to stay up till quarter to two doing this. Just like being up late getting high! I'd been hacking till nine on the video, the new MMRT webpage, etc.

I got a friend at *Boing Boing* to post about my Kickstarter, and I massaged five years of records into a vast thousand-entry long mailing list (previous KS backers, purchasers of my ebooks direct from Transreal Books, and owners of my paintings). I wasn't sure if the list would work, but it did. I had all the names in the blind copy BCC field so as not to *totally* alert the spam filters—although the paranoid servers at Yahoo blocked it. But got a lot of feedback.

***

On the "Juicy Ghost" front, it was turned down by Sheila at Asimov's, she liked it, but it was too "topical" for the zine, and I do understand that. They've got a loyal subscriber list, and can't afford to alienate some percentage of them. So I'm gonna do another *Flurb*, it'll be *Flurb* #14. I wrote some of my friends on a cyberpunk mail list, and I think I'll get about five or six tales to add to mine. I was telling them deadline is June 7, but, hell, I could push the deadline back to end of June and publish in July.

April 21, 2019. IOHK Summit Rundown.

The IOHK Summit went well. As I mentioned, I feared the attendees might be sinister Bitcoin whales, Russian Mafiya, pyramid-scheming con-men, coke dealers, sex workers, blackmailers, kidnappers, gunrunners, pornographers, hired assassins, and extortionists. Surely there were some of those in attendance, but the overall vibe was sunny and even idealistic.

The ebullient and likeable head of IOHK, Charles Hoskinson, described his dream of a free internet with financial services and trusted registrars for all manner of things. In countries with disorganized and venal governments, like in parts of the third world, blockchain could serve as a reliable way for people to have credit and banking, to register the ownership of real estate, and to register the validity of academic credential they might have. Blockchain could also serve as a tool for honest elections.

One of his employees spoke to me about "liquid democracy," a catchy phrase. It suggests that you need to distinguish between cryptocurrency and the notion of blockchain as shared public ledger.

On the one hand, speculators, criminals and tax-evaders seem like the most likely people to use cryptocurrency. Rich people are always looking for ways to hide their money. And nobody likes to mention the criminals, but the local Miami crypto people did speak elliptically of party people and pretty ladies.

On the other hand, there's that non-centralized public info thing. It bugs me that Google knows everything about me. And Amazon has a chokehold on all my paths to publication—not only their listings, but their publishing tools: Kindle, CreateSpace, and Kickstarter.

I was talking to Aggelos Kiayias, the chief scientist at IOHK, a smart, worldly, younger Greek man living in Scotland. He spoke of the asymmetry between Google and their users. I mentioned how well Wikipedia works—although it's a centralized server, it seems like the users keep each other in balance as the IOHK scientist Aggelos Kiayias said to me in Miami Beach: "But what if the owners of Wikipedia were not neutral? What if they chose to slant it? And we have no way to know. Certainly Google isn't neutral. Certainly it promotes its advertisers."

Indeed, in my IOHK talk, I spoke of the possibility of individual users running their own web crawling software (instead of Google). This could be feasible in less than ten years. The actual text content of all the webpages on the internet, although a bit hard to quantify, is perhaps as low as ten terabytes.

Probably I'll get some SF ideas from the things I heard at the con. Stephen Wolfram in particular said some useful things. He spoke of our future "smart contracts" having a fairly high level of AI, so they can understand the natural language that humans uses. And he had the notion of these kinds of AIs evolving as a race in parallel to ours.

And Wolfram made some key points about his Principle of Universal Computation. This says that any nontrivial natural process can be viewed as a universal computation that is, in principle, capable of emulating any other computation at all. Now consider the computations inherent in our vaunted smart brains. There may be equally rich computations inherent in the weather system, or the ecology of a forest, or the flow of a waterfall, or in the flames of a fire. So even our smartness doesn't make us unique. Nothing about humanity is unique. And looking for extraterrestrial aliens is a quixotic endeavor. We've got zillions of "alien intelligences" inherent in the natural processes all around us here on Earth.

To really make his idea hit home, Wolfram said something like this. "Suppose that we find ways to encode human minds in software. These coded processes are like souls. And perhaps at the end of time, there will be a box with ten trillion human souls in it. Now suppose someone looks at the box from the outside. There's really on objective difference between this box, and a box with turbulent water in it, or a box that's simply a block of stone, with the atoms vibrating and endlessly interacting."

The high point for me was taping a 50-minute podcast with Stephen Wolfram, the two of us in some random room in the Miami Beach Convention Center, an exceedingly large empty box with massive air-conditioning. Windowless, forty-foot-high ceiling, and some fifty by seventy feet in size.

Thank god my recorder and mic worked as expected. I started work on processing the tape in our hotel room in South Beach, using Audacity to remove the steady noise of the AC, and to uniformize the volume levels of our voices—I talk a bit louder. Listening to the tape, I feel sorry for myself—how eager and relieved my voice is at the start. And, towards the end, I hear my undertone of sadness at how rare it is to talk to anyone as smart like Wolfram. He's someone who continually *gets* what I'm talking about. Like it was during those golden hours when I met with Kurt Gödel in my twenties.

One of the speakers filled me with real loathing. He was, I think, a stockbroker. Three times he referred to his activities as cyberpunk. As if. He liked the idea of crypto making it possible for anyone to invest in anything. With no government oversight. No slow-downs on scams. And the possibility for "investors" to buy up interests in the activities of any individual (such as a sandwich-shop owner or an indie writer like me) and to then, if you think it through, control and monitor this no-longer-free person's activities. Like a protection racket. What got my goat was how this guy got choked-up and almost tearful while showing us a slide of Iranian stockbrokers going ape on the day after the US bombed Baghdad. The traders are frantically buying and selling interests, groping for ways to profit off the unfolding human tragedies. And somehow, in the stockbrokers' mind, this seemed like a noble, "the show must go on" activity.

My "Cyberpunk Use Cases" talk was well received. Afterwards several beautiful young women pressed up to me, befriending me, wanting selfies and video. Like I was cool.

A young Chinese programmer guy from Shanghai, Lei Hao, told me that my science fiction is very popular in China. I'd never heard about this. "Your novel *Postsingular*," said Lei. "The programmers took turns translating of it into Chinese, working on it in their spare time." "Pirated?" I said. "You said it was Creative Commons for free use," countered Lei. "And we're all reading it." So that's good. I might send him the CC version of one of my other CC novels.

Although IOHK stands for "Input Output Hong Kong," the base is in fact in Colorado, and some of their tech division is in Edinburgh, Scotland. Oddly none of those techs had heard of Charles Stross, nor of his notion of a population of AI biz bots called "Business 2.0." In Stross's *Accelerando*, Business 2.0 destroys the global economies. "We put Hong Kong in the name because we thought we'd have a lot of business in Asia," Charles Hoskinson told me. They seem currently to be focused on business in Africa, Mongolia, and Wyoming.

What is their business exactly? I still don't quite get it. They have several interlocking software platforms or code suites: Emrugo, Ada, Cardano, Daedalus, Ethereum, and, now, Atala. My guess is that they're presently in "burn mode," that is, spending money on developing their system and evangelizing for wide adoption. This Summit in Miami Beach was a lavish event—and I was grateful to get some scraps from the table. Perhaps the likeliest way to score big money from this would be an eventual IPO. It's reminiscent of the 1990s boom companies. I remember going to an Autodesk party where they'd rented the San Francisco Museum of Natural History for their venue. Those were the days. Could be that crypto and block chain are the new web.

A figure or cabal named Satoshi is inventor of Bitcoin, and the concomitant technique of blockchain. Nobody is sure who Satoshi was, although there are a handful of commonly mentioned candidates. At the opening speech by Charles Hoskinson, I sat next to a taciturn young Swedish hacker. Later in the con, after my talk, he came up to me. His expression was one of wild surmise. "Is it true you are descended from Hegel?" he asked. "Yes, he's my great-great-great-grandfather." Long pause. The boy staring at me wide-eyed. "Satoshi was very interested in the ideas of Hegel." Fever pitch on intense staring. It clicks. "No, I'm not him," I said, and walked off. But who knows if he believed my denial.

Re. Satoshi, I heard an interesting theory of who Satoshi was. We might suppose that he was a highly computer-literate individual who wanted to leave a nest egg for his family. And he come up with the notion of Bitcoin, as described in his famous white paper. As the inventor of the system, Satoshi was at the very apex of what is, many would say, a very successful pyramid scheme. Satoshi might well have accumulated the Bitcoin equivalent of several billion dollars from his operation. Now suppose that he died and left the money to his wife and children. So, if he's dead, why does Satoshi's identify remain secret? Why can't his true name be emblazoned in glory? Tax and inheritance issues! The IRS would want a hefty cut of Satoshi's earnings and of his estate. But—and this is the whole point of the Bitcoin technology—Satoshi's crypto nest egg is invisible to them.

No Bitcoin for me, *sigh*. But, yes, pass the liquid democracy.

May 31, 2019. Post Launch. Absolute Continuum Story?

I finished the launch for *Million Mile Road Trip*. Made a

book trailer, did some email interviews, made the web page, posted the ebook on distributors hither and yon, and fulfilled the Kickstarter rewards, mailing out about 110 books. Then we did a trip to visit Georgia & Co in Madison. Finished a painting of Guanajuato. Did a blog post about my recent activities. Now what?

- Blog post on the IOHK con.
- Blog post incorporating my email interview text, especially the one in the *B&N Sci Fi & Fantasy Blog*, which was a good one.
- Blog post on the Absolute Continuum, using some stuff from that new preface. Unless I already did this?
- Do a mailing about submissions for that proposed *Flurb* #14 issue with my assassination story, and start assembling the issue in a temporarily "hidden" page online.

And, someday, start writing fiction again. No ideas for anything just yet. Kind of fried after all the pushing. The reviews for *MMRT* are excellent, thus far. Possibly this would be a good place to stop. Quit while I'm ahead. Or, of course, I could write a sequel, though we'd want to see if the books actually sell copies before I get into petitioning Night Shade to do that.

Another short story would be the thing, for now. I do miss, somewhat, having a piece of live fiction to be working on and thinking about. Don't miss it *that* much yet, though. Going to the beach at Cruz today.

Maybe the best is to write a story about the Absolute Continuum—based on that preface I wrote for the new edition of *Infinity and the Mind*. I feel happy and high whenever I think about that idea. My body, right here and now, is precisely as large as the cosmos. As is a rock or a leaf or a scrap of paper. No more yearning towards the far reaches of the Space (erroneously quantified as having 10^{80} particles) or the abysses or primordial Time.

Okay, fine, but what's the *story*? Our hero or heroine talks to God? Finds a way to scale-shift? The talking to God thing feels stale to me just now—also, in an Absolute Continuum there might not be a "top" level that is *the* God. Every iota is God. And jumping scale shades into a multiple-universe story, and I find those uncompelling for my usual reason: if you can live in many worlds, nothing matters in this world. But maybe I could do a fan-out-then-fan-in move. So then the story ends with, like, Dorothy of Oz back in her own back yard. *Meh.*

Well. what if I make the story more techie? Golden Age kind of thing, a story about a new device. A Silicon Valley start-up. Mad scientist is monetizing the Absolute Continuum. Making some practical tech out of it. Energy source? The devices run amok, natch, and we have an ending like the ending of the movie, *The Incredible Shrinking Man*, where my character drifts out through the window screen into the All. They came unglued. They're a radical on the lam, taking shelter in the mad scientist's lab. "They'll never catch me now." Have the character be a woman, and the mad scientist is a man.

June 1, 2019. Sober 23 Years. Teep + Absolute Continuum.

Today is the twenty-third anniversary of my sobriety. I'd been trying to quit for about six months, and going to some AA meetings, but still not quite getting there. The turning point was a night I spent in a tent in Big Sur, near Vicente Flats, down the coast near Santa Lucia. I let go and accepted that everything is the cosmic One, all of it, all around me, all the time. And accepted that I can pray to it for help, and that this move works.

Getting sober was one of the best things I ever did. I'm so much happier than I would be otherwise. Thank you, God.

***

You know, I was talking about doing a teep novel...what if I fold in the absolute continuum move as the kicker to my novel? You'd need something like teep to "see" down into the subdimensions anyway. I need the thing that goes wrong to be quite concrete. Paul Di Filippo had a gymnasium full of goo in his recent *Aeon*. But I want something more down to earth. Could I put the "Mean Carrot" into this story, too? Or some of the "Mary Falls" stuff?

I need some concrete surreal images for a start. I got hold of two small canvases at Palace Arts in Santa Cruz yesterday…maybe I'll make a diptych pair of paintings I can paint fast, using acrylic this time instead of oil. Like a Yin/Yang pair.

June 3, 2019. Loafing.

I've been reading Somerset Maugham's *The Razor's Edge.* Kind of a proto-beat/hippie book, from the 30s. After WWI a guy comes back from the Great War and doesn't want to do any work. "What are you going to do?" they ask. "Loaf," says he. The word is used over and over, kind of fun to see it. You start to think about a crusty French bread. And it reminds me of a guy who loves to lie down beneath a tree and chew on an ostentatiously chosen halm of grass. Found the book at random in the Library Bookstore where Sylvia sometimes volunteers.

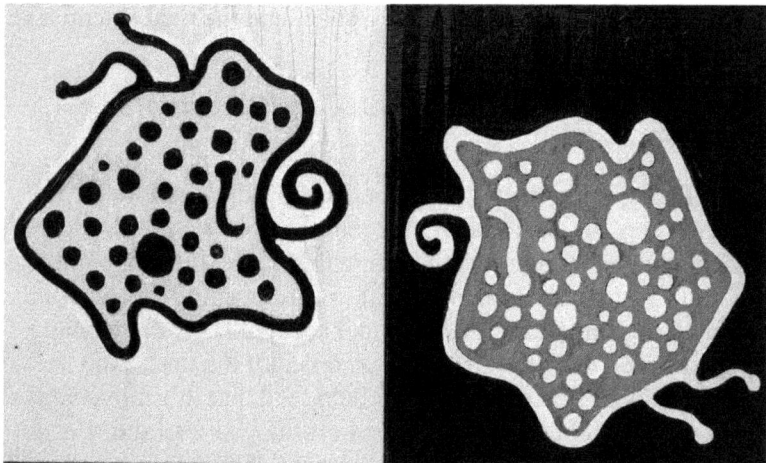

Figure 9: *Meet Cute*

I got started on the paintings, made one canvas whitish, one blackish. Can't believe I've sunk this low. Painting a black and a white canvas. I found a cool pattern online, generated by Hele-Shaw ferrohydrodynamics, see the video. I'll do a white on the black and a black on the white. Motel art…eek! I'll have to funk it up with some little critters in full color.

Last night I woke at 3 am, and to pass the time I was trying to count how many kinds of alien critters there are in *Million Mile Road Trip.* About thirty, I think, and if you include the ones glimpsed in the stratocast-powered hundred-basin run, the total might be fifty. Seething.

I still can't get it up to think about actually writing a story, let alone a novel. So many steps involved.

Soon I might move forward on *Flurb* #14.

July 6, 2019. Samizdat "Juicy Ghost." Novel? To Maine.

Early in June, I decided I couldn't deal with putting out a new *Flurb*. I didn't have enough stories, and they weren't very strong, and I was paranoid about publishing "Juicy Ghost." And I happened to go into Borderlands Books, and they didn't have any of my Night Shade titles in stock, not even *Million Mile Road Trip*, and somehow this totally knocked the wind out of my sails, and I was like, fuck it. So I told the guys who'd sent me stories for *Flurb #14* that I wasn't going to do it.

(The only one who complained much was John Shirley. To make it up to him, I spent several days, maybe twelve hours, rewriting the story he'd sent me, "Porris in Wunperland." I felt it wasn't logical enough, as an SF story. I thought he'd be grateful for the "script doctor" move, but he didn't say anything at all. Then then about month later he told me he didn't like what I'd done. I shouldn't have bothered.)

Anyway, once I'd shed the *Flurb* idea, I realized I could publish "Juicy Ghost" directly, both as a blog post, and as an addition to my *Complete Stories* page and ebook, and my *Complete Stories Vol II*. And this might be slightly less high-profile. Kind of a samizdat thing, I kept thinking.

I did after all want to put the story out. I just didn't want to do a *Flurb*. The news about Trump wanting to have a political rally during the annual 4th of July show on the Mall in DC— that got to me, and more than ever I wanted to speak up. And it seemed like a good match between Trump at the Lincoln Memorial, and "Juicy Ghost" starting out with a rally there.

So then I went ahead and rewrote "Juicy Ghost" about five times, and I made it a lot better. Not quite so hateful and rough. And with a better plot line about a coup. So I put it up on my blog with a bunch of cool photos, and a few people read it, not all that many. It was a good excuse for updating my various editions of *Complete Stories*, which was a certain amount of work…I have two print editions, two ebook editions, and an HTML edition, plus the blog edition of the story, with a single-story PDF of the story online as well.

And then while I was at it, I taped myself reading it and put it up as a podcast, knowing that Cory Doctorow likes listening to podcasts. So he went for it, and he posted about it on *Boing Boing*, and I got about a thousand hits in a day. And a few supportive comments by email.

The one response from the government: an ad for the Donald J. Trump Re-Election campaign popped up in my Facebook feed. Probably just a bot that's keying on the fact that I'd mentioned politics when I mentioned the story in an FB post. Reminds me a little of when I gave detailed instructions for building a terrorist A-bomb in *The Sex Sphere*, and never heard a peep. I'm so far underground, I'm invisible, it seems. I hope it stays that way.

Anyway, at this point, in my head, the story has kind of normalized its status, it's just an SF tale, and there's plenty of vicious political SF stories and movies out there. "Juicy Ghost" could easily be an episode of the *Black Mirror* series on Netflix—in fact I suggested that to my film agent. Or think of *The Manchurian Candidate*.

And I'm kind of thinking maybe "Juicy Ghost" could be the opening chapter of a novel. Looking back, that was my intention all along. But I got distracted. I could see a chapter of Curt being a dog, a whole chapter almost, and then he encounters another juicy-ghost animal. Possibly Treadle has been preserved—maybe Gee Willikers had a deal with Treadle and made a psidot of him. But, on the whole, I'd rather not go back to Treadle, at least not till many chapters later.

I often think or talk about discovering a new law of physics, and there could be some connection with that. Juicy ghosts in the quantum computations in rocks. The book could just have that one really strong coup/assassination opening chapter, and then go into the kind of juicy-ghosts novel I'd been thinking about all along. But with a Return of Treadle kicker near the end of the book. Like in the first *Terminator*…he keeps coming back.

If I don't want to do a novel, I could just write another story. Or I could split the difference and have it be a completely different story on that same theme of juicy ghosts. I remember I had an idea for one called "Mary Falls."

***

Anyway, now we're on a plane to Boston where we'll rent a car and drive up to Boothbay Harbor, for a massive Rucker family reunion. Brother Embry and I, and our wives, and all our children, and all of their spouses but one, and all of the grandchildren but one. Twenty of us, I think. Because my parents had a cabin in Boothbay Harbor for ten or twelve years, and we used to gather there… several times it was Sylvia and me with my parents, and with our children and Embry's children. Then Pop stopped coming, as he'd left Mom, and then Sylvia and I moved off the California, with not much likelihood of coming back in the summers, and they sold the place, and then Mom had a stroke, and the Boothbay Harbor years were over. But the five kids have been talking for years about the reunion, and they basically organized it.

***

We rented several houses on the same road where Mom and Pop's cabin was, Crooked Pine Road in Sprucewold by Linekin Bay, a mile outside of downtown Boothbay Harbor. I'm uneasy about Sylvia and me sharing a cabin with brother Embry and his newish wife Joanie. More on this below.

July 9-12, 2019, In the Thick of It.

In our Maine cabin now, two days down, five to go. It's almost dreamlike, being in these familiar-looking fancy log cabins, so similar to the one that Mom & Pop owned. Georgia made up a little booklet of old photos…I contributed about half of them. Everyone so beloved. And the wildly excited pack of cousins, squealing, chanting, thundering around. Eight of them, ages 7, 11, 11, 11, 12, 14, 14, 16. Our three kids, two with spouses along. Embry's two kids, with one spouse in tow. And us four geezers. Twenty in all.

It's very quiet here in the woods on Spruce Point. Lacking that ceaseless, omnipresent drone of freeway traffic that we have in the SF Bay Area. Don't exactly know what to do with myself. I don't happen to have a book that I'm reading, and I'm not working on any story or book just now. And I don't have the *oomph* to start a new story.

Wonderful to be with the children. In downtown Boothbay Harbor, we were all sitting around an outdoor table at a pub called the Tugboat for a while, a raised location, nice view of the harbor. Me, Sylvia, Embry III, his wife Leslie, Isabel, Rudy Jr., Penny, Georgia, Courtney, and Siofra. So many of us. Rudy Jr. laughing, so happy and relaxed, having fun with his cousin E III. I said, "I'm really happy. Im not usually this happy." Beaming at them. All of us amazed and aware of how rare a moment this was.

And early this morning I dove off the Crooked Pine dock and swam in the wonderfully cold water with daughters Georgia and Isabel. "You're the light of my life," I told them, after the dive.

On the last evening we were talking about my parents, Mom and Pop. It's been 25 years since Pop died, and 27 since Mom died. Pop would be 105 if he were alive, and Mom would be 103. They're *really* gone. So naturally, *mutatis mutandis*, I think about our kids doing a Maine reunion when they're in their seventies and I've been dead for something like 20 years, and the grandkids are in their forties, and there's a fourth generation rising up.

Dizzying. It's so inexorable, the turning of the vast wheel of time.

July 18, 2019. New York. "Chestnuts from the Gloaming."

Sylvia and I were in New York for five nights, and now we're on the plane home. We did a lot of fun things.

As is by now traditional I had lunch with my agent John Silbersack at his downtown club, the Century Association. We talked a little about my books. He's always very non-directive, doesn't suggest what I should do next, and tends not to answer at all if I propose something that might be unreasonable. Re. foreign book sales, he says the Japanese book market has cratered, and many of the European countries now have their own native F & SF writers, so are in less need of translated imports. His European subagent is a friend of Georgia's, her name is something like Molly Tanzer. He mentioned trying to get a review in the *Post* from Michael Dirda, whom I worked with thirty-five years ago. I'll get in touch with Dirda, mail him the print *MMRT* and the *Notes*.

The Met was running a production of Mozart's *The Magic Flute*, and at the Morgan Museum we saw Maurice Sendak's designs for a Houston production of that very opera from some years back—and it crossed my mind that *Million Mile Road Trip* might hold an analogous role in my career, that is, it might be my wondrous final work. And next year they'll bury me, unheralded, in a sheet, in a pauper's grave? Well, maybe not *that*, but maybe I won't write another novel. Maybe *MMRT* is a good place to quit. I'd be proud to have it as a final novel.

In all accuracy, I should recall that *MMRT* is *not* in fact my most recent (and potentially final) novel. I wrote *Return to the Hollow Earth* after *MMRT*. I finished writing *HE2* about a year ago, as I recall. But somehow *MMRT* seems like a closer fit to being "my" *Magic Flute*.

All I've written since then is two short stories—"Surfers at the End of Time" and "Juicy Ghost." I do still want to write more. More stories, certainly.

***

And maybe that little book of teachings that I've thought of off and on, short chapters summarizing the deep or arcane things I've learned, a lifetime's wisdom, pearls from my swine trough, loaves from my granary, orchids from my hothouse, slices of the ham I Am.

I was trying to pitch this idea to Silbersack, and he was non-committal. I was babbling, feeling giddy from my dessert of pear poached in Burgundy with whipped cream. The pitch needs a hook, John felt, a unifying twist. And he was anything but encouraging about where we might sell it. Princeton University Press? Dover Books? Why bother. Well, he's being realistic: those are the most recent two companies to publish nonfiction books by me. I tell him *I'm* dreaming of—a best-seller non-book mass market inspiration-for-pinheads market. And Silbersack is, like, "Well, if you say the book's about how to be happy, and then there's a chapter about chaos theory…" His voice trails off. Then, "Do some work on it, and then we'll see if it's a book."

Actually I did write a book something like this before, complete with grandiose subtitle, *The Lifebox, the Seashell, and the Soul: What Gnarly Computation Taught Me About*

Ultimate Reality, the Meaning of Life, and How to be Happy,
That book was 182K words! And it didn't get much traction in
the pop sci market. I'd want this one to be really short, like
60K.

I'd be recycling stuff from *GR&4D*, *The Fourth Dimension*, *Infinity and the Mind*, *Mind Tools*, and the *Lifebox* tome. I
might literally copy excerpts like for a *Best Of* or *Portable*
compilation. But that seems dull and uncreative—and wouldn't
make for a product that's attractive to my existing readers. I
might *start* with a compilation of excerpts, using them as a
draft, and then warp and hone.

I'd also be repeating some material from my autobio,
Nested Scrolls. And from my *Journals*, too. I could reread all
these sources and mark the passages to do. Or, in a perfect
world, snip them out with long scissors, letting a drift of clips
gather at my feet.

That "How to be Happy" list at the very end of the *Lifebox*
tome might be a useful framework. Here it is. It's based on my
stairway-to-heaven organizing principle of stacking up
Computer Science, Physics, Biology, Psychology, Sociology,
and Philosophy as a six-step ziggurat

- **Computation**, *Turn off the machine.* Yes, we can
  compare nature to computer simulations. But this
  doesn't mean that that virtual reality is as good as reality. Far from it. The natural world is incalculably more
  powerful and interesting than our odd flickering devices. I try not to let them run my life.
- **Physics**. *See the gnarl.* The air is a gnarly ocean; the
  leaves dance on the trees. I've always enjoyed watching clouds and water. The computations they're carrying out are fully as complex as anything in any book I
  might read. Each flickering shadow is a reminder of
  the world's unsolvable and unpredictable richness.
- **Biology**. *Feel your body.* There's always something
  interesting to feel in this wonderful meat computation
  that I'm privileged to inhabit. It's fun sometimes to
  think of my body as being very large—like an im-
  mense starship that I'm inside. I can focus on the inputs from all the different parts. Meanwhile my breath

and heartbeat are gently chaotic. I need to remember not spend more time upgrading my computers than I do in exercising my bod.

- **Psychology**. *Release your thoughts.* Underneath the wanting and worrying is the great river of thought. I don't control much of the world, and things rarely turn out as I predict, so why waste my time in focusing on fears, desires, and expectations? And why invest all my energy in logic which, as we now know, only goes so far? I can watch my mind like fireworks above a wavy sea.
- **Sociology**. *Open your heart.* People are the most interesting and beautiful entities I'll ever see. Society isn't about the news and the leaders. It's about the people I run into every day.
- **Philosophy**. *Be amazed.* Our studies of computation teach us that none of our theories will ever get very far. Not everything can be explained, nor even expressed in words. We're fully immersed in the incomprehensible. Life is a mystery; it's good to savor this.

Great. But…yawn. Finger-wagging. And, Rudy, you already wrote this! Is there really a need for this new book? I'd have to make it fresh. Turn each topic into an SF story? Boring, predictable, Sunday-school-lesson stories. Aesop's Fables. And I already did *that* in the *Lifebox* tome, too, using short SF stories as chapter separators. But nobody ever seemed to pick up on how cool that was.

Really, I could cook all this down to a series of minifictions. Didactic SF tales I never wrote. Would be fun to compile that list. Or make it an essay.

A *Chestnuts from the Gloaming* type book should be really concise. Each section should cook down to a single two- or three-word phrase. Aphorisms. And to make it worth doing, I'd need to find a higher synthesis. A gift, once again, from the Muse. First figure out what my main teachings are—and then, without forcing it too much, find a couple of unifying strands. That's the missing piece of the puzzle.

Title? *Last Words*? Wait…didn't Burroughs use that title when he was in his 80s? Maybe too early for me to be doing.

Final Tour. Going Out of Business. What I Found. "Found" is more fun than "Learned." *What I Saw.* "Saw" is even better. Less didactic. And then I can include more observational kinds of things. Word-sketches of cool things. Lifting these from my novels, even. So reread all of those and scissor out more excerpts.

Chestnuts from the Gloaming. I think "gloaming" means dusk, and of course chestnuts are road-apples, or well-polished old adages. Maybe this project needs to wait till I'm eighty.

A last-resort genre. The *Portable Rudy* mode. Yeecch. Let someone else do it after I'm dead. Or not.

As I mentioned, the one saving thing here would be if I could find a core insight to my life's ruminations. But, wait, that's what I fucking *did* in the *Lifebox* book. Auto Cryptomnesia much? The whole *point* of *Lifebox* was that the core notion is gnarly computation. Doh!

So let it go and move on.

July 22, 2019. Seed for "Everything is Everything"

What to do? *Nescio.* That's Latin for "I don't know," son. Don't know what I'll write next, don't know if I'll ever write again. Keep writing these notes, anyway.

***

Sometimes, as I'm falling asleep, in a liminal state, bobbing up and down beneath the surface of sleep, I'll feel myself sliding into a dream situation that seems familiar. A background is in place, with familiar scenery, and established characters, and a situation, and I have a sense of knowing a history of what's going on. What would be the word for this? Not déjà vu. Déjà revé.

At this point I may drift back towards the surface, and then I sleepily wonder what's the cause of my déjà revé. I see two options.

Illusion. In one fell swoop my dream-mind has created a new stage setting, *including* a sense of having seen it before.

Recurrence. The setting is a fragment of a recent dream. The setting was latently present in my subconscious, and it seems familiar because it *is* familiar.

The *Recurrence* option feels more accurate, as I do at these times have such a clear sense of the scenario having a history, and that I've been in the scene before, and it seems like wouldn't "have time" to invent all that background on the spot. This said, the *Illusion* option is viable. Sometimes my busy mental dream machine fills in fake histories along with its fake scenes. Why not? I don't see any easy way to decide which is the case.

This said, there *are* cases of repeated dreams, like portentous nightmares in a pulp novel, and this kind of dream is something that you remember and brood over when a you're awake, But the dreams I'm talking about aren't particularly important or epic dreams, and you don't especially remember them when you're awake. And it could well be that my fabulating mind does endow them with a sense of history.

In a recent one, I'm living in a rooming-house and working as a salesman—and I know things about the other tenants.

I see an F & SF type story here. The guy (or woman) realizes that they're doing work in their dreams, like as a spammer or telemarketer or focus group or image-recognizer. It might be nice, if possible, to connect this to the psidot tech I invented for "Juicy Ghost."

I started out calling it "Dream Work." Later its name was "Everything is Everything." POV is the wife of the guy. He's bewildered after his naps. The way I was after my 45-minute nap on the Santa Cruz Beach today, a nap which, by the way, started with a familiar-feeling sensation of returning to a rooming house where I've been working long hours of late. I woke unrested. I was tired the rest of the day.

How did Carrot (my proposed name for Amazon/Apple/Google/Microsoft-type dream-work exploiters) get their hook into our character?

A psidot that acts as a hearing aid. He had one of those hearing aids with little bristles, and he didn't like it, but he got the psidot. It works great, but even so he doesn't like to wear it, and she's always scolding him to use it—and he keeps forgetting to take it off when he sleeps. And then she'll feel guiltily later on when she realizes the psidot hearing aid was enslaving him to Carrot.

I *could* call the story, "The Hearing Aid," but maybe that's a bit too squarely in the Fiction for Seniors camp. So "Dream Work" or, come to think of it, *this* one could be "The Mean

Carrot," and that carrot who gets in bed with our man could be one of his psidot visions.

***

Who knows, I could end up with a volume of related psidot stores and *voilà*—they might jigsaw into something like a novel. Don't write a straight follow-on to "Juicy Ghost," at least not yet. Start a completely different thread. And then a third thread. And then braid them.

Looking back, I recall that I also wanted to write about my new kick: we live in an Absolute Continuum. That could be the third strand. I mined this rich vein of ore "Jack and the Aktuals." But in that story, I didn't go the whole hog, as I do in my new preface to the fifth edition of *Infinity and the Mind*— that is, in my story I didn't think of fanatically insisting that our actual, waking-life cosmos is an Absolute Continuum. It would be cool if, by a roundabout way, the angels of the Absolute Continuum were working their way into our lives via the psidot.

Key fact: nobody invented the psidot. Like the time-machine hand-board in "Surfers at the End of Time." Some guy just found one and learned how to copy it. The psidots are, like, spores from the nod-nod bush, or eggs from the rambumpus.

And, who *is* that hacker guy, Gee Willikers? An alef-two space squid, naturally.

August 1, 2019. Weird Sync.

Yesterday I got a good start on my story "Dream Work," a.k.a "Everything is Everything."

And right about then I got an odd letter email from a guy, Eric David Cowan writing as Kahoosh@protonmail.com. Protonmail is a private, encrypted mail service. His mail was kind of freaky.

> "So, back in 2013, my older brother found a journal of our deceased fathers that had hand written notes in it, styled in a way you'd expect something like a military psychological experiment. This got us thinking about the idea of making a hyperreal intelligence agency that track and deconstruction synchronicity.,

My friend Trevor became a house mate around this time and joined in with the project. We were both into the idea of cut ups, beat generation type stuff, imagined ourselves as continuing on with that type of energy. It's a long story, but things started to unravel and very quickly became like a detective/spy novel, living intrigue. For example, we ended up get a trim job from this woman who happened to know Billy Burroughs, had this far out story about her grandfather being an ex-Nazi neuroscientist who sent her to the same camp as Billy in Florida, which she claimed was covertly being used for medical experiments on problematic children from military families. And things just progressively went in that type of direction for a while to the point where it was difficult to tell what was going on. Anyways, we called ourselves at the time, the Nameless Syndicated Archives, and the point was to sort of mirror the NSA as, almost like a token of sympathetic magic I guess you could say.

Recently I moved to Florida to be near my parents who are retired here and getting to the age where I want to get more time with them and be able to help out with things. My girlfriend found us an apartment in a town called Fort Meade. It took a while for it to dawn on me how funny that was and ended up taking it as a signal to re approach the ideas we had been working with in the NSA. I started toying with it all again. I got a job at local state prison as a librarian. Very much of a learning experience. One of the good things that came out of it was reading one of your books there while in down time, "The Hacker and the Ants". Enjoyed it a lot and found it inspirational to my own creative work. Anyways// One of the original "members" of the NSA, unofficially, mostly me just bugging him, was Jay Lee Jaroslav, a conceptual artist. Without explaining the whole damn situation, he's been off the radar for over a while now. The other day I was looking up videos of you on YouTube and came across a talk you did in Gloucester that tied a lot of stuff together and low and behold, at 46 mins in, during question and answer,

Jaroslav starts talking from the audience about something with MIT lol, the timing was just really funny because… well, it's just such a long story. The point is, you really hacked it, dude. You hacked into it. Thanks for doing it."

Makes me a little paranoid even, what with him using a private encrypted email server Protonmail, and mentioning the NSA, and he's surveilled my online presence so closely as to notice something at minute 46 of a years-old tape, and the fact he's working as a prison guard. A little rich for my blood. I even wondered if he might be a Secret Service agent trying to inveigle me into saying something criminal.

But I did like his last three sentences a lot. And at some level I think I know what he meant. There is indeed a certain non-logical synchronistic Muse-related quality to writing far-out transreal cyberpunk.

And meanwhile I'm working on an interview with a guy called Cliff Jones, who runs a website called Dreampunk. And last night, for kicks, I let it all hang out in my original answer to Cliff's last question, viz:

Q 6. What are you working on right now?

A 6. People always ask that question. And I'm like, well, did you read my last two novels? *Return to the Hollow Earth* and *Million Mile Road Trip*? The supreme masterpieces of my career? So why be asking for more already? And I'm defensive like this because I don't fully know what I'll write next. And I worry I'll never write again. I've been faking all along, you see. Lifelong imposter syndrome, right? Last month I wrote a heavily political story called "Juicy Ghost," and I published it online, and I'm a little paranoid about that. Today I got an email, seemingly friendly, but very spacy, from a guy with the handle Kahoon, who could, theoretically, be an agent meaning to entrap me. How do I ever know? And for that matter, "Cliff Jones," why are *you* hassling me for a dreampunk interview? The mode of thought that I'm into right here, that's a mode I'd be interested in writing a story about. A place where dream and reality are merging, and maybe not in a good way. But it's hard to do that right. If you get too far into it, then the narrator is batshit crazy, and nothing they say or do matters, and the readers don't care enough to finish the story. You have to use SF conventions to ballast the story, so that maybe it's true, and so there can be an interesting plot with a hook. So, I'm thinking about an angle where a guy recognizes that a certain recurrent part of his dreams, is in fact infested by, like, Facebook or the NSA or some alef-seven-dimensional alien space-squid mind parasites. And those sinister controllers are getting our hero to do a certain type of work them in the course of his dreams. He's like doing pattern recognition for them, or personality simulations. Maybe running some characters in a game. Freud uses the phrase "dream work" for what you're doing in the night. So this guy is doing dream work. And I like "Dream Work" as a title for the story. So, getting back to the paranoia, I've been thinking about this story, Cliff, and here you come and say you're into *dreampunk*, and that you want to interview me, and that's almost too synchronistic. And then this other guy, "Kahoon," today he writes me an email about synchronicity and he mentions the NSA and he refers to some question that a guy asked me at minute 46 of a video of a talk I gave about four years ago in Gloucester, Mass. And maybe this is more synchronicity than I can handle. But I've been here before, way out on the edge. It's something that happens when I get really plugged into a writing project. The real world starts leaking into my story in progress. I'm hoping it's a matter of the So, Muse blessing me, and that the universe is dancing with me, the way it's done before. And maybe you and Kahoon are good guys. You're Professor Rucker's oddball new pals. But one false step, and it could turn all sinister and PKDickian on my ass. My only way out is to keep working on the new story. Follow the tightrope. Dream the rest of the dream. Finish the story, and fill it with love. Help us, dear Muse, in this our hour of need. We ask this in the name of Thutmosis.

Today I dialed back that answer somewhat. And I wrote Kahoon/Cowan that, although I appreciated his interesting letter, I wasn't going to have an ongoing correspondence with him. Sent him a *Million Mile Road Trip* ebook just to be friendly. Probably he's harmless. I attract some odd people as fans, that's for sure.

And Kahoon wrote back that he'd supported my Kickstarter for MMRT, so in a weak moment, I sent him a link to "Juicy Ghost," and told him I was paranoid about it, and he wrote me back a letter where he obliquely referred to assassination twice, and I got super-duper paranoid, like maybe he was an agent trying to entrap me, so I blacklisted his email address. Even though probably is just a fan. But he could be pretending!

August 6-8, 2019. Working on "Everything is Everything."

So I'm working on this story I was calling "Dream Work." I might connect it to "Juicy Ghost," although that might add too many constraints. I haven't found the plot yet at all.

It's 3rd person, and I might do a dual 3rd person, the kaleidoscope thing where I flip between the two characters' points of views. It's an old woman and old man, although maybe I shouldn't have them be old, as that's supposedly not good for the market. Basically, it's Sylvia and me, from when I took a nap on the beach last week, and she woke me up because of the wind, and we went and sat on the bluff.

I had this idea the guy is *working* in his dream, and it's one of those recurrent dreams I was talking about, and he's just noticing that.

How is he connected to the cloud, or to the dream world? Maybe he has a psidot? I wrote some stuff to make this work.

But now, believe it or not, Wick had gotten a consulting gig as a napper. For a new cloud AI company called Mean Carrot, Wick wore this brain wifi antenna on the back of his neck. It was a tiny disk of plastic called a psidot. Psidots were very hot right now, because the guy who'd assassinated the out-of-control President Treadle last winter had been wearing a psidot. Curtis Winch.

The Secret Service had gunned down Winch, and he'd become a folk hero because pretty much everyone was glad Treadle was gone. Some people said Curtis Winch was still alive, even though everyone had seen his dead body on video. But maybe he was alive in the cloud, maybe. Like Jesus, not that Vi would put it that way.

In any case getting a shot at the possibly mythical Curtis-Winch-type software immortality was a good reason to want a psidot. But you couldn't just buy one. They weren't in commercial production. So Wick had been super excited when a contact of his at Mean Carrot and set him up with one. Wick had a lot of connections in the Valley. He'd worked as a CS prof, as a programmer, and as an SF writer. But now he was more or less retired. And Carrot was paying to watch his naps. ...

... "What *are* you doing in these Carrot dreams?" asked Vi. "Programming?"

"It's more like I'm inventing puzzles." said Wick. "Those quizzes you see when you sign onto some websites? The quizzes are called captchas?"

"Like gotchas? Like, *ha-ha you're wrong*?"

"Different from that," said Wick, very intent and scholarly. "Captcha is a geek word. It stands for *completely automated public Turing test to tell computers and humans apart*. A captcha is for checking that the user isn't a bot. A puzzle that requires some kind of typically human skill to solve. Captchas used to be, like: Which of these pictures has a bus in it? Which two faces are the same person? Is this a picture of Sacramento? But now the bots can solve all those captchas, and Carrot is raising the level. They're mining my thoughts for captcha puzzles. At least that's what Carrot claims they're doing. But I think really they want to make a bot version of me like they did for Curtis Winch, which might be a good thing." Wick broke off with a laugh. "I just remembered the captcha I gave them just now." …

… "It's good to get some money," said Wick. "And I like being in on something big. And epochal change. Like when they discovered DNA, or when they built the hydrogen bomb."

"I wouldn't like it, wearing a psidot," said Vi.

"Right," said Wick. "The Carrot bots and programmer and administrators are in my head. I call my manager Pigling Bland. He knows this. It's hard to cover up anything in brain-to-brain conversation. It just comes out. He's Pigling Bland and he's a rah-rah middle-management greed-head with no mind. He calls me Space Case." Wick bent over, closed the umbrella and packed it into its case. Wadded his towel into his knapsack. Not entirely happy about his gig.

***

It's not bad, but I decided not to use it. The psidot is much higher tech than I want ot have in this story. In any case, I want to have this tale be in a different world than "Juicy Ghost." Maybe later I'll write a sequel to "Juicy Ghost," but this isn't going to be it. I need something new.

So, okay, how is the dream work thing going to be organized? I'm going tearing it free of computer tech to have it be magical. That's more interesting to me just now. No tech, no digital hoo-haw, no cloud, no wireless. Just the weirdness of dreams. Like in a high fantasy story. Some external force from dreamland or higher-dee reality is reaching our guy through his dreams.

The guy is a mathematician, and not a computer scientist. A set theorist.

We still have the repeating dream, and the guy is doing something, but what? What is his dream work? When I was in the CS mode, I thought it could be something like solving captcha puzzles, or acting as a bot, or doing pattern recognition, or tagging things, or getting his personality copied—but I now I want something more fantastical. Like talking to the dead, or to aliens, or to critters from alef-seven, or opening the door to the Absolute Continuum. Something crazy. Like in a fairy tale.

Maybe they're using his dreaming mind as some kind of *amplifier*. Maybe humans dream, and this is rare (vintage SF trope here, I think), and the "othern" are using us dreamers to "see" or notice stuff they can't quite resolve. Like we're electron microscopes or stethoscopes or infrared film or X-ray plates.

Starting with the Absolute Continuum as the end result, I can reason backwards to find out the nature of our man's dream work. The end result will be an egg that the entitled prick (EP) in the Mercedes hands to Wick or Vi. Possibly the EP is an alien. The EP unlocks his trunk, and Vi takes out the egg. A misty ball that they bring home and tend to. Or no, not a misty ball, it has a hard shell like a chicken egg or, better, a leathery shell like a turtle egg, or maybe a jellied covering like a frog egg. Maybe the shell has galaxies on/in it, like the rocks on the mountain ridges in MMRT. And it hatches after they get it home and set it on a pillow in the kitchen. Ta da! *Glorp*.

Today I want to call this story "The Egg." (But, again, it will eventually be "Everything is Everything.")

***

What's in the egg? The Absolute Continuum. It oozes out. Sparkle-goo. And we have a section of dealing with that. And then at the close, Vi and Wick are back on the beach. And Wick has a still higher dream that accesses something yet higher. The othern are using him like a terminal, or a switchpoint, or a railroad station. Because (a) as a human he can dream and (b) he knows the mathematics of infinity.

Upshot? Vi and Wick nullify some potential threat from the Absolute Continuum (AC). And they normalize our relations to the One/Many civilizations of the AC.

Meanwhile I'm working on a 30" x 24" acrylic-on-canvas painting with five eggs in it. They are, I might now recklessly claim, an objective correlative for the object in my story. I *could* have my egg have a branching fractal Russian Doll sequence of smaller eggs in it. But again, that's too digital and discrete. Better: It's all five of my eggs at once, overlaid on each other. The eggs contain, respectively an elephant, a snake, a gnome, sick yolky ylem, and a metaquark. Or, for the last two, how about an anthill, and a congeries of math symbols. Or a squawky bird instead of the symbols. I want a sparkly, gooey Absolute Continuum. I can hardly wait to imagine and describe our world after the sparkle-goo comes out. Also I'm anxious that I won't be able to do it.

Either way, I have something new to be excited about. A prerequisite for a story if I'm actually going to write it.

August 10, 2019. Paul Simon. "Everything Is Everything."

I'm slightly worried that "The Egg" ("Everything Is Everything") will be a lot like "Jack and the Aktuals" and "The Knobby Giraffe." Oh well, at least I'm aware of this, and can steer away from it a bit.

Sylvia and I went to see Paul Simon at the huge 1920s Fox Theater in Oakland last night. Wonderful concert, very inspiring. "Angels in the architecture" he says in one song. The bright, highly saturated colored stage lights pointing at us some of the time, blinking on and off.

Day before yesterday I dreamed someone like Nick Herbert was giving me a new psychedelic drug, bit the tab or pill was mixed in with a batch of about twenty other pills, dumped on the sofa cushion next to me, and I was too thirsty to get them down, some of the pills nearly the size of pool-cue-chalk blocks, and pale blue. Like a daily dose of AIDS meds. Then inside the dream I saw, in a small pop-up screen in the corner of a news-show, I saw a sidebar type item on the drug I was supposed to be getting, it was called "Buddha Slime," and it was a slick gel presented beneath a layer of transparent plastic, like on those old mood ring thingies. I woke up, drank a lot of water, laid down to go back to sleep and earnestly hoped I could return to the same dream and get my Buddha Slime, but didn't get there.

Back to Paul Simon. He spoke of us being in hard times, and that we'd win. That kind of made me want to finish the "Juicy Ghost" start. Get up to novella length, anyway. How does the tale work if Trump wins the next election? If he loses?

Back to Paul Simon. The beauty of music. My egg in "The Egg," maybe it's like a blue robin's egg in a little nest. A bird comes out? Or better to have sparkle-goo? Vi describes the interregnum when we're all in an Absolute Continuum frame of mind. And then something happens. It condenses back into discreteness.

If there was a bird in the egg, that can be the being from the AC who wanted to come here. Why did it come? To take over? Why would it bother? What do we have that they want?

Again, for lack of a better idea, I propose that they appreciate our skill/ability to dream. Readers like an angle like this, makes them feel smart and proud for having, just as they are, an ability that the AC othern yearn for.

Vi has to do something to save the day. Maybe a lizard in the egg is better. Slightly unexpected. The guy driving the Mercedes is a lizard and so is his girlfriend.

What happens to the Mercedes after Vi takes the egg? It turns into a cloud of sparkle goo, leaving a hyperreal zone. With angels in the architecture.

***

On an up note I just now came across this uplifting bit of hip-hop scripture by Lauryn Hill, a very cool (you need to watch it at least twice, and I've actually watched it four or five times now, and will watch it more times) video for her 1998 song "Everything Is Everything," which naturally I'd never heard of, or no, the song is from an album I owned, but didn't listen to enough, *The Miseducation of Lauryn Hill*. Anyway, I heard it in an Urban Outfitter store in Berkeley today, and at the time I was kind of mentally dismissing it, not realizing how heavy it was, but also thinking this could be a good title for my story as, in the Absolute Continuum, everything really *is* everything. "After winter must come spring."

The video https://www.youtube.com/watch?v=i3_dOWYHS7I uses a cool gimmick of showing a giant old turntable-type tone-arm dragging a needle along the streets of NYC, playing the track of the street. The record is rotating around the Empire State Building.

So I'll use "Everything Is Everything" for the title of my story. "The Egg" is too specific, and gives too much attention to the egg from the trunk of the Mercedes. The egg is just a means, and not the end. The *end* is flooding our reality with the Absolute Continuum—which *was*, however—reveal!— always already here. Because Everything is Everything.

So, um, if the sparkle goo was always here, what is the change brought about by the egg's contents?

Well, maybe it is always here, but it's only for a little while, during the story, that we *notice* it. Here's a kicker: our normal waking state is *itself* a type of dream. And if it's only if we *really* wake up that we can perceive the AC. The othern are fully awake, they can handle the blaze of info and noise and live. We're, like on the nod most of the time, and then we go even deeper on the nod and sleep and have states that even we realize are dreams. But, again, even our waking states are dreams.

Figure 10: *Five Eggs*

August 12, 2019. Inching on "E is E." Entitled Pricks.

I'm writing only a few hundred words a day, if that. Repeatedly revising, trying to find a flow. Today they got the egg away from the EP couple. (EP is for "entitled prick" because I think that's funny.) And now I'll have the EPs' Mercedes disappear, and then Vi will drive them back to Los Gatos.

On the drive back, Wick can be like I was on Memorial Day, 1970, when I'd taken acid on the Livingston campus of Rutgers, and Sylvia was driving us a mile or two back to our apartment at 43 Adelaide Avenue in Highland Park, with ten-month-old Georgia in my lap…and I thought *I was the one driving*. Telling this to Sylvia. So Wick will think he's driving the car back to Los Gatos, even though Vi is driving.

I finished another painting today, "Five Eggs," and in some off-center way it's an image of the egg in the story or, rather, an inspirational previsualization. Nice painting.

***

Line I'm not going to use:

> The EP woman's plaint was rising in volume and pitch. Like a Chinese soap opera video, played in fast reverse. The EP guy was laughing, kind of. Or maybe he was singing. Vi and Wick scrambled into their car, with Vi at the wheel. She got the engine roaring, and squealed the tires on the way out. Wick was cradling his giant frog egg in his lap.
> He had his dick out, and it was stiff. He was fucking the alien egg.
> "Oh, Wick."

August 16, 2019. Get Loose. PKD's "War With The Fnools."

I wrote 800 words today on "Everything Is Everything." The best writing day I've had about two months. Pushing it and pushing it, like a car stuck in the snow, not letting up, rocking it, pushing some more. And throwing in some weird crazy shit that seems like fun. Here's an email note to Nathaniel

Hellerstein about where the story is right now.

> "I'm working on a story where this guy keeps dreaming of being at a math seminar on the top floor of the math building at Berkeley. The speaker is a large sea anemone with a head at the end of each tentacle. And they guy can never quite understand the talk, but finally he naps long enough to get it, after twenty tires. And then a man and woman with no faces (just smooth lumpy skin) show up and give him a gelatinous egg, said to be a bud off the anemone. He puts it into his chicken coop at home to hatch. Goes to sleep. When he awakes it's the next morning, and two of the chickens have become real estate agents and are knocking at his door. Also…his space has become Absolutely Continuous. Waiting now to see what happens next…

I love the idea of chickens as realtors. This is a move I'm lifting from a 1964 P. K. Dick's tale called "The War With The Fnools." Wanting to check PKD's wording, which I could *almost* remember, I found the story on a Russian pirate site called "sickmyduck." See http://sickmyduck.narod.ru/pkd105-0.html

> "Good morning, sir," the Fnool piped. "Care to look at some choice lots, all with unobstructed views? Can be subdivided into —" …
> "As long as you're here," the first of the remaining Fnools said to Lightfoot, "why don't you put a small deposit down on some valuable unimproved land we've got a listing for? I'll be glad to run you out to have a look at it. Water and electricity available at a slight additional cost."

August 19-20, 2019. "Everything Is Everything," Ver 1.

So I put in the chickens as realtors routine, and it's great. Like maybe the aliens are switching wick and Vi's world into plenum mode as a real estate gambit. We don't know.

After the chickens showed up, I was able to end the story

pretty abruptly. I'd reached maximum weirdness, so exit on that not of comedy and heaviness and deep meaningfulness.

I was thinking I need a word for using your brain as a special sense organ that sees the world as an absolutely continuous plenum, not just in dreams, but while you're awake. A verb. How about seering? Well, that seemed a bit corny. And, come to think of it, I can get by without a word for this as they're not going to discuss it that much.

So basically the story's done, although I've rewritten the ending about four times, and may polish it once more tomorrow, and polish the opening maybe one more time as well. And then I'll send it to Sheila Williams at Asimov's. She wouldn't buy "Juicy Ghost," perhaps reasonably not, but she said she'd still like my next story, and when she buys it, she does it pretty fast, so it would be nice to just have that done.

As always, I'd thought my story might "amount to more," but usually they don't. It's kind of allusive, and more like fantasy than SF, or like a philosophical parable, but it seems light and fun and engaging, so maybe I can sell it.

I read a version to Sylvia yesterday, and she was grumbling that it was too transreal, and that my Wick and Vi characters are too much like me and her. So I made some minor changes to it's not quite so much like Sylvia.

I really enjoyed the (relatively short) amount of time when I was really *writing* on the story (as opposed to worrying about it). I'd like to score some more of that kind of time. Might as well start another story. Maybe gear this one to be more like 5K or even 10K words, so I can wallow in it a bit longer.

I still can't see starting another novel. Last night I was thinking maybe I really am done with being a novelist. I mean—I'm 73. Ageism is real. People tend not to care what I do, even if it's good. And Age is real as well, that is, my powers are fading. At this point I'm sometimes repeating myself.

Novels take so long, and they're so hard for me to sell anymore. This said, I would like to write that sequel to *Frek and the Elixir*. With the whale ships. But when I wrote a sequel to *The Hollow Earth*, it went over like a lead balloon, in that I had to self-pub it with a Kickstarter. But I did have fun writing HE2, and I did put it out, and it's there for the ages. Well, I need to wait a bit to see if Night Shade will be up for more titles. I did get to mention the project to my new editor there.

Anyway, for now, just write another story. Let me examine, yet again, the ideas for stories that I had thus far in these notes. Jump to my Story Bank

August 22-23, 2019. Idea for "The Mean Carrot."

So I'm going to write this story that I once discussed with Richard Kadrey. If he wants to come in on it, that's great, and if not, I'll write it anyway. It takes a while to get in touch with Richard, so I'm gonna start anyway. I was going to call it "Diorama," but eventually I called it "The Mean Carrot." I put some preliminary notes for it up in the Story Bank section.

Rather than recopying the Story Bank notes in the upcoming entries, I'll keep them in mind, but in this entry I'll basically start fresh. It's set in the near future, and a guy hires prostitutes to set up marks with a certain as-yet-untested deliriant so he can monitor the effects for political, criminal, and/or commercial application.

Problem: writing about a pimp hiring female prostitutes is very iffy, in terms of not enraging women. I think it's safer to write the story as a first-person narrative of some person who can then, I hope, absorb most of the flak for whatever perceived slurs are inadvertently made. And have this person come to a bad end.

So, okay, I'll have my POV character be the op who's running the project. His name is Chick Chixper. Actually, instead of working for NSA or CIA, it's fresher if he works for a large high-tech company called, say One Wow. (Just checked, and that's not an existing name.)

And it'll be better to go somewhat non-binary. The sex workers can be of both sexes, as can the marks. And maybe the pimp/researcher could be a woman instead of a man? But then the parasex between Chix and the Mean Carrot wouldn't have the right quality. It would be too degrading if it were a woman having sex with the Mean Carrot. If it' sa man, no big deal, men do things like that all the time.

So Chick is a man, very repressed, kind of asexual, but leaning towards gay. And his sex with the carrot is like the preacher with the dildo named Dr. Jerry Falwell in *Freeware*.

Chick carries the Mean Carrot around in a slender duffel bag, like a piece of sports equipment or a musical instrument, and we don't get to see it or awhile, but in the reveal, we see it's the Mean Carrot, four feet long, stout, exactly like an orange carrot with warts and wrinkles that make features, plus a shock of green, leafy hair, and the carrot's dog-dick-like tip oozes out drops of smeel when the carrot is aroused. In a swoon, Chick licks the drops off the Mean Carrot, trembling with joy, blushing in shame.

The project can be, as it was in the Sixties, a matter of hiring sex workers to give experimental psychotomimetic treatments to unwitting partners, and to let Chick Chixper observe the outcomes.

Rather than being an old-school pharmaceutical, the treatment is a brain-stim patch, electronic in nature. Call it a stimple. Or a stimble? Either pimple/simple, or thimble/stumble/stable. I gues I like stimble better, as it's more awkward, and the near-homonyms are richer.

Probably cooler if the stimble is bio. Like a shelf fungus on a tree. It doesn't go away. It digs its hyphae into your brain mass. Where on the head is it? Replaces an eyebrow? Behind an ear like a kludgy hearing aid. Tearing one off would be hideously painful, one assumes, a full brain zap leading to a full-body clonic seizure, perhaps lethal.

The effect of wearing a stimble is extreme empathy and bonding and fixation and obsession and imprinting. The mark wears the stimble, but the target doesn't have to. In other words, the agents don't have to wear stimbles, and they don't want to. Possibly they *pretend* to, wearing dummy shelf mushrooms behind their ears. Just to jolly along the mark. The mark wearing a stimble falls in love with any woman or man he or she has sex with, and wants to marry them or, at the very least, serve them like a slave. Useful for spy ops, for recruiting the head of a rival movement, or (used en masse) for propaganda, and for general advertising.

On second thought, I'll call it a stumble instead of a stimble. Simpler for the reader.

***

Reread the notes. Maybe it's better if one of the sex workers, say her name is Molly, has the carrot in a duffel bag.

She kind of knows what it is. It's an alien transmitter that sends select oddball human types to the Wax Museum in Studio B…located in the Twilight Zone, which is another word for the subdimensions.

And she'll send Chick Chaxper there.

August 30-31, 2019. "The Mean Carrot," Part 1.

I'm moving along on the story. It's fun to write. Deeply fun. It's the core of my being. Easier to do a story than a novel, yes, but even so it's hard. You keep hitting blank spots and having to think of What's Next.

I'm making it pretty funny. But with a tragic touch. My hero Molly is, after all, close to being a junkie hooker. Why does she have this job of flirty-fishing johns into having stumble sessions? Why is she herself hooked on the stumble? I want some reason that's not trite and pat.

I introduced the Mean Carrot already. I'd imagined he was an alien, but now it seems like he's a new biotech product. Mobile oversized intelligent vegetables. MOIVs. What are they for? Bodyguards? Certainly if you put your wallet into the Mean Carrot's mouth, it'll be safe. He's quite hard, like plastic or wood or like a carrot that is, however resistant to a knife blade. And the Mean Carrot isn't with Molly, he's with her mark, Anselm.

I think I'll have Rhoda and her date get into the sleigh as well. Maybe we'll drop Thuy as a third-party girl or, better, Thuy can be Rhoda's date. Or maybe it's better if Rhoda's date is a default goob tech bro, and I can mock him. Low road, but easy. He could even be a sales guy or middle manager and not a programmer. Let's say he doesn't know Anselm.

Synchronicity note. I was calling the other party girl Rhonda, but yesterday decided Rhoda is better, and today the actress Valerie Harper who played Rhoda on TV died. Like her vibe passed through me on her way out. But now maybe I can't use the name Rhoda? Respect for the dead. I'll call her Ramona. If I have Ramona and her mark in the sleigh we can have more conversation, and more exposition done that way.

Looking ahead, what's the payoff gonna be? I had this idea of one of the characters being an alien who pulls them into a stasis diorama for an alien human-types museum. But we've got enough weird shit already with the sleigh, the Mean Carrot, and the stumble. Aliens would be overkill, unless they're incorporeal aliens maybe, and you see them in stumble space, which is, it occurs to me a bit like the DMT experience with the baffling hallucinations of religious personages. I happened to be reading my journal entry about DMT in Sept 12, 1992, today because R. U. Sirius, having notice my journal online, posted about this excerpt, so I reread it, and it's useful for thinking about the stumble experience. The Muse/Cosmos dancing with me once again.

I started getting into this thing of having it be a Christmas story, since Anselm now has, instead of a car, a hacker-type pirate sleight that rides the streetcar rails, so it seemed funny to put Santa jokes. And I can have Christmas happy ending of Anselm saving Molly from her drab life. But, *ennnnh,* Christmas stories are kind of niche and corny, aren't they? I *did* write that one Christmas story I liked, about the golden goose. But if this is a Christmas story that kind of overwhelms and floods out the other themes. Should Anselm say, "I am not Santa. Anyway, in Finland, this personage is the Christmas Goat." But if I say that, my Google-research is showing, and it's not freely invented, and it's weak.

Sept 2, 2019. Reminiscing: My First Job.

On Labor Day, we had some people over for a picnic, and Sylvia had the idea that we should sit in a circle, and each of us should tell about their oddest job. She talked about being a sign painter in Lynchburg, Virginia, and I talked about my early day of teaching Computer Science at SJSU when I didn't know anything about the subject at all. But later I thought of a better story I could have told.

My oddest job was working in the summer at a house-construction site by my parents' house in Alexandria, VA, I was eighteen, it was 1964. They were building a subdivision of about twenty houses all at once, and the roads weren't in, just dusty tracks.

My job was to drive around a watering truck to keep the dust down so it didn't stick to the fresh paint on the houses. The truck was just a pickup and the tank was some big metal thing that didn't especially fit the truck, and didn't have a very big hole on top for filling it. I'd drive around dripping water, one issue was that I couldn't stop moving or I made a puddle. Once I did that, and the head boss, a little guy named Mr. Keene, screamed at me really hard. And every half hour I'd drive to this certain fire hydrant to refill the tank.

I had a special pentagonal wrench for turning the valve on top. And the water would gush wildly out of the canvas fire hose. And they'd told me I couldn't just turn the flow on partway because if I did that for some reason the fire hydrant would leak underground and undermine the road.

My big issue was that the metal rim at the end of the hose didn't fit into the hole in the tank, so the hose would be lying on the ground when I turned on the blast, and then it was a bitch to climb up onto the truck, holding the hose with its wild-anaconda rocket-like giant stream of water. Sometimes it would throw me off the truck, and always it would soak me from head to toe. But the temperature was over ninety degrees, so getting we didn't really matter.

And I think I used the accumulated pay to buy a ticket to fly to Geneva to visit Sylvia

Sept 4, 2019. "The Mean Carrot," Part 2.

It's going pretty well, I feel like I've finished Part 1.

I got Molly, Anselm, Ramona, Noah, and the Mean Carrot to 5th and Market, near the apartment that Molly and Ramona share. Ready for a stumble party. Possibly Yack and a woman will show up later on. I see the woman as an analogue of the wealthy arts-patron socialite DeDe Wilsey.

Not sure what happens in Part 2. Can't just be a blow-by-blow of Anselm and Molly getting high. Any events that happen in VR are, ipso facto, boring. Like dreams. A cream can't carry the action. You can run one for half a page, like as an illo, but not much more. To keep them awake, something needs to go badly wrong, almost as soon as the stumble trip starts.

Who throws in the monkey wrench? Maybe Anselm isn't what he seems. He's a troll, a garden gnome. Dancing wildly, "Garden gnome, garden gnome." Shells of light around him.

I don't see dull Noah as doing much. He's just a sacrificial lamb. Or possibly he's working for Anselm.

Having Yack show up with a Shiva-the-destroyer for Part 2 is not good either. Better to hinge the plot on the characters we have from the start. I could drop Yack. Or if I use him, have him show up hilariously late, like in Part 3 when Anselm and Molly are out in the street and Anselm has saved Molly.

Anyway, we need a fiasco in Part 2. Some interlocking transplanetary deal with One Wow and Chick Chaxper. A Nova Gang burn. Soft Willy, the Heavy Metal Kid.

I was thinking of rotating the POV from Molly in Part 1 to Anselm in Part 2 to the Mean Carrot or Chick Chaxper in Part 3. But that's too baroque. This is just a short story. I rotated in "Everything is Everything," but this time I'd like to get through the story in one person's mind. It's meant to be a kind of salvation-for-Molly tale anyway, so better to stay in her mind.

I do wonder what it's like in the Mean Carrot's mind, though. Maybe Molly can teep into him. Like guide him to the apartment after, say, Noah nearly kills Anselm. Noah isn't a good name; I keep forgetting it. I'll go with Burbage. Willy the Shake's best actor. Or it could be Kemp, Willy's clown.

Still don't have much of a role for Chick Chaxper either. I'm changing his name to Chex Chapster. And I'll have him be reading the Wall Street Journal all the time instead of drinking vermouth. I have to be careful not to overdo the drugs & alcohol, as I am so prone to doing.

Sept 5-18, 2019. Finishing "The Mean Carrot."

By now I've changed the story's name from "Diorama" to "The Mean Carrot." The title I always wanted to use. I don't know if I'll even get to that "humans in an alien diorama" routine.

Infodump chunk that I disassembled and shuffled in:

Stumblespace is kind of like the internet cloud, except that it's based on biocomputation and on people's latent powers of telepathy. The telepathy angle will mean big bucks for One Wow if they tame the stumble. It'll be, like: Wear a live phone!

But the stumble zonks you out. And it's addictive. And, as far as messaging goes, the stumbles don't forward messages from their human hosts. All they talk

about is heterothallic fungal mating. Wha? A guy from
One Wow ame in and told us about it. All the stumbles
care about is contacting other stumbles, and exchang-
ing explicit sexual details about—the info in their
genetic codes. They build a copy of the other stumble's
code, fold it together with a copy of their own code,
and wrap it up as a spore. All based on messages in
stumblespace. Not like meeting up all clammy and
personal.

So now I'm rewriting the growing tip of the story again,
something I've been doing daily for over a week, just like in
the old novel-writing days. I'm repeatedly editing the following
list as I go along. I * asterisk a point when I've resolved it.

To Do

- * Drop the Yack character.
- * Drop all references to Christmas. Set it in October.
- * The way I've written Chex is too despised and 2D.
  Boring. A knock-him-down Bozo clown. I'll round
  him out and have him be in love with Molly, and have
  him save her near the end by shoving Burbage off the
  fire escape? Him and Ramona together. Instead of *Wall
  Street Journal*, I'll give him a more contemporary toy?
  Maybe he's a gamer or a day-trader. The day-trading
  tool is an N-D maze. Nah, I like the *WSJ*. Keep it simple
- * Burbage was (unknown to Molly, but maybe known
  to Anselm) tasked by One Wow (or a splinter faction
  thereof) to crush the stumbles while the others are tripping and thus to find out whether this induces telepathy. Chex is in on it.
- * Who crushes Burbage's stumble? Chex. Burbage has
  paid Chex off to help.
- * If Burbage knew this was going to be dangerous,
  why would *he* put on a stumble? He's stupid, and he
  doesn't grasp what was happening. He is *not* a techie.
  He's a for-hire industrial spy, working on contract basis. Calls himself a free-lance researcher.

- * The stumble-kill process leaves the user with telepathy for a time. But there's a lethal side-effect: the mycelium enters a phase of explosive growth, and fungus threads boil out of a subject's ears, mouth, nostrils, and eye sockets and he/she drops dead.
- * We want this to happen to Burbage, but not to the others. We need a fungus-explosion-fix? I was thinking of using Anselm's "garden gnome" chant, but, although fun for me, that's illogical and a bit silly. Not satisfying for the reader. Let's say Anselm is fading, and it's Molly and Ramona who carry out the fix? But what is the fix? Oh, I know, we have the fix come from the Mean Carrot—thus justifying the use of his name as the story title. He scrubs you down with his taproot, sending it right into your skull.
- * But who is the Mean Carrot? He's Professor Broadbent! *Craaack*, he splits open the carapace (like a molting lobster) and expands to his own right size.
- * That thing about the Hungarian chess grandmaster who programmed huffy is funny, but it has nothing to do with the story. Let's say the guy's name is Professor Broadbent, and he's English. Anselm knows him from some time he spent in Cambridge. Both the stumble and the huffy infection were invented by Broadbent. Both species use mycelium threads that are very much like neural dendrites and axons.
- * What about the little chessmen that huffy sufferers were supposed to cough out? That's a great Surreal image, but it's (a) nauseating and (b) too much of a distraction. *Maybe* they could be tiny carrots? Or maybe just hard little green lumps and we leave it to the reader to think they might be carrots.
- * Anselm found out about One Wow via Broadbent, who works for both One Wow and to Finn Junker.
- * The Mean Carrot *is* Professor Broadbent. In disguise. He saves Anselm, Molly, and Ramona. Then removes his disguise. The guy likes carrots a *lot*. Rübezahl.
- * Ramona and Molly go to Finland with Anselm, happy ending. Chex stays in SF.

- * I don't like using the name Burbage for a bad guy. Burbage was Shakespeare's best actor. Don't defile the man's name. Call the bad guy Loftus instead. I've always found it disturbing for a surname to end in "us." Saw that name in the paper yesterday.
- * Ramona is presently zero. She needs some quirks, a physical appearance, and a few more lines.
- * Instead of calling Anselm's friend Professor Broadbent, let's call him Lev Broadbent. A bit of a clash between the names, but that's fine. And more likeable and less parodistic.

***

I cut this next paragraph. I loved how surreal it was, but it didn't fit.

As part of the gig, Ramona used huffy every day for seven weeks. And she came down with a condition akin to whooping cough. During her fits, tiny, perfectly-formed ivory and dark-red chessmen would fly out of her mouth and skitter across the floor. Spore-laden lumps of fungus. Why chessmen? No explanation was forthcoming from the huffy project's chief wetware engineer, a shadowy European contractor called Bent.

Not using this next line either. Dialect is always a drag, though I personally like it. "Naturally Anselm pronounces One Wow like *Vun Vaow*."

***

I did numerous more revisions, and mailed it off to *Asimov's* on Sept, 18, 2019. I had the inspiration of putting a little man inside the Mean Carrot, and he pairs up with Ramona. I decided Chex is gay. Put in a few lines to indicate that Molly had a bit of a personal transformation while doing teep, which will make it easier for her to kick her stumble addiction.

I saved the sheaf of all my revisions to give to the PKD Award Committee as a "prize" they might auction off to get money for the annual reward.

Sept 19, 2018. On "Surfers at the End of Time."

I wrote this blog post for the Asimov's SF magazine blog; it's to appear with our story.

"Surfers at the End of Time" is the seventh story that Marc Laidlaw and I have collaborated on. All but one of the tales are SF surfing stories that feature two guys called Zep and Del.

Often when I collaborate, I'll do what I call a *transreal* move, that is, I'll have the story be about two people, and one of the characters is somewhat like me, and the other is like my co-author. To some extent Zep is like me, and Del is like Marc. This said, we often ventriloquize each other's characters, in that Marc might write Zep scenes and I might write Del.

Figure 11: Rudy and Marc Laidlaw in Kauai

This time out, we wanted to do a time-travel story. We'd talked about this for a few years. At first we were focused on the notion of flooded cities, with the sea-level half-way up on the sky-scrapers. This theme was featured in the excellent 2001 Brian Aldiss inspired movie, *A.I. Artificial Intelligence*, and there's a touch of it in *Tomorrowland* too. Marc had imagined surf contests amid the buildings. But in 2017, just as we were ready to start, Kim Stanley Robinson pretty much used up the trope with his *New York 2140*. Marc and I *did* write some nice flooded-San-Francisco scenes, but we needed more.

Marc was enthused about the H. G. Wells novel *The Time Machine*—and about the 1960 movie version directed by George Pal. I watched the movie online, and I dug it. We wanted to use Wells's classic scene where the Time Traveler goes so far into the future that the sun is bloated and the Earth is nearly lifeless. Thus our title: "Surfers at the End of Time." I like to pronounce the last word like I'm in an echo chamber: "*Tiyiyiyiyiiiiiimmmme.*" *You* know.

Figure 12: Hand Board Time Machine

Since Marc and I both know Ocean Beach in San Francisco pretty well, we decided to start our story there. A significant research element was William Finnegan's memoir *Barbarian*

Days: A Surfing Life. The book has a long section about Mark "Doc" Renneker surfing the intensely cold and gnarly waves at the SF beach—you can read it <u>online</u> in the *New Yorker*.

We felt the time machine should be in some sense a surfboard, and I spotted a cool-looking little "hand board" in the wee Santa Cruz Museum of Surfing which is inside a diminutive lighthouse by Steamers Lane. Marc had the idea of having the boys activate the time machine by scribing an intricate mandala-like sigil upon the face of the sea.

I expanded on the notion of a time sigil by imagining an intricate, arabesque spacetime diagram of our boys' worldlines. I redrew the figure ten times while we were working on the story. I'm a little surprised how complicated it turned out, but that's where the logic leads. I kept sending the successive diagrams to Marc, but he wasn't all that into trying to decipher them. The dude wasn't a math major!

The diagram helped *me* a lot in terms of planning the complex plot of the story. Time travel is a bitch. Like, you need to be careful not to imagine that the characters can predict the abrupt and non-causal appearances of time travelers. And, as I'll discuss below, there's the matter of time paradoxes.

In the diagram, you'll notice five names at the top, and these names correspond to the five worldlines below. Gother and Sally are women that Zep and Del meet, and Lars is kind of gnome called a murg. As I'll discuss shortly, he has a closed-loop worldline.

In time travel stories you always have to deal with the issue of possible time paradoxes. There are two main types of problems.

(1) *Closed Causal Loop.* A creature like Lars the murg appears at time and place X with a handboard time machine. You hang out with him for a while, making your way forward in time. And once you and Lars are in the future, he uses his time machine to hop back to the time and place X. Who produced the murg? Who invented the time machine? They produced themselves. Their worldlines are loops. Is this a problem? Not really. There's no real *contradiction* in a Closed Causal Loop. It's just odd. But we can live with odd. Especially in a Zep & Del surfin' SF story!

(2) *Yes and No.* Your future self comes back in time and

chops you and your friend in half with a broadsword. If you die, then your future self doesn't exist, so he doesn't kill you, so then your future self exists, so he does come back and kill you. A contradictory situation. A standard journeyman SF-writer solution is to say that, when you travel back in time, you don't actually go back into your own timeline. You go into the past of a parallel world. I don't like this solution; I think it's facile and dull. My deeper problem is that, if there a zillion parallel worlds, then everything happens. An if everything happens, then nothing matters. And then cares what happens to your characters?

Once in a while, sure, I'll invoke an alternate world—like if I need a world whose physics is wildly different from ours—like if I want a world with infinitely high mountains, or with an endlessly wide plain. But it seems cheap to invoke parallel worlds just to avoid a piddling little yes-and-no time travel paradox. Like using an H-bomb to light a joint. There's always gonna be a tricky way out of any seeming paradox, if you think hard enough.

In "Surfers at the End of Time" our characters Zep and Del travel up and down the timeline, and they do, at times, encounter past or future versions of themselves. So how do we avoid Yes and No paradoxes without invoking alternate worlds? As the great logician Kurt Gödel once suggested to me, "Let's suppose that the world always arranges itself so that these paradoxes do not occur. If something is logically impossible, then it doesn't happen. *A priori* logic is very powerful."

As I've already hinted, in the opening sections of our story, it appears as if a Viking-like Zep from the future comes back and slices both the original Zep and the original Del in half. Ye and No paradox? Well, it doesn't have to be—*if our boys don't die*. But how do they survive being chopped in half across their waists by a huge broadsword? Well, not to give too much away, let's just suppose that the boys' severed halves are treated with some special futuristic biomedicine... Like good old Kurt Gödel says: "The a priori is very powerful!"

By the way, I got the idea of future Zep being like a Viking when my wife and I went to our son Rudy's family Halloween party in San Francisco. And in the kitchen I met a guy named

John Bowling, wearing a horned Viking helmet, and with his long hair's partly in braids, and he had a long beard. He was wiry and lively, and he tells me he's a big wave surfer and that he lives in a condo on the so-called Great Highway by San Francisco's Ocean Beach—exactly where Marc and I wanted Zep and Del to live. I texted Marc a photo of the Viking surfer dude, and Marc texts back, "HE'S A TIME TRAVELLER, DUDE." Synchronicity! Times like this I feel like I'm dancing with the Muse.

Figure 13: My Viking Friend

It was fun to work with Marc Laidlaw again, and not by writing on my own. Collaborating takes longer than writing alone, and at times it's a little stressful to iron out the necessary shared decisions. But and I end up thinking about the story more deeply. And I think when I collaborate, the story ends up being funnier. I'm not necessarily *trying* to write funny stories—I'd hate to be called an SF humorist—but I like it if a story makes people smile or even laugh out loud. And it's even better if it's kind of sad and tragic at the same time. Like life itself.

Sept 21-23, 2019. Patreon?

So I mailed off "The Juicy Carrot." That's my third story in six months. I could probably do a story every two months. Wouldn't want to push for one a month. I'm starting to wonder about Patreon. Richard Kadrey, Tim Pratt, and Kameron Hurley are all doing it. You can publish your Patreon stories via WordPress, using a plug-in so only your patrons can see them.

It's not clear to me whether you can turn around and sell a story to, like, *Asimov's* or *Lightspeed* if you've posted it on Patreon. If I was getting money and readers via Patreon, it would be kind of relaxing. I could run a *Rudyzine* that people effectively subscribe to via Patreon, and then go public three months after their first on *Rudyzine*.

I'm interested in this because just writing story after story and having to keep selling them all is kind of paralyzing. The writing is okay, it's the marketing that I can't take. I *can* just give them away, like I did with "Juicy Ghost," but people don't value what they get for free…and it would feel stupid to be giving away my full output.
    ***

I went and made a draft Patreon page, but doing it, I realized I'd be committing to something like an extra blog. And, after asking around I found that once you show a story to your closed circle of Patreon subscribers, the story is deemed already published by most outlets. It's the same as if you'd published the story in a small ezine. Some commercial magazines will take such a story as a "reprint," but I don't totally like havin to do that.

Although, come to think of it, my "Juicy Ghost" is appearing as a 'reprint' in *Big Echo* because I self-pubbed it on my blog.

Long story short, I don't want to bother doing a Patreon. It's not like the Kickstarter was for publishing my novels. It's more like me being an old man begging in the street. Don't want to do that. And later, if I want, I *could* in fact do a Kickstarter edition of my next round of stories. Perhaps I'd hold back on putting them live in *Complete Stories* right away.

A non-obvious reason for me wanting to the Patreon was so that I'd be making a public promise to finish a story every six weeks or so for a year. But, why add that stress to my life? Just go ahead and write stories, if I can.

Sept 24-30, 2019. "Starship Lauch" + Hvalship.

What story next? As I think I've mentioned, I *could* do that "Mary Falls" story, which is pretty clearly outlined. But it's a about the decline of a lost old woman, and the thought of writing it makes me sad. So maybe no.

That little "Starship Launch" scrap about the hovering starship and the "lighters" ferrying people in—I do like that one. It's almost a novelistic idea. Would be interesting to squash a novel down to less than ten thousand words. Kind of a new approach for me. Yeah, why not try that. Something fresh and "outdoorsy"—as opposed to all that in-my-head stuff about dreams, telepathy, and virtual avatars. Wholesome, hale, wind-blown, Scandinavian space travel!

And Arf can come too.

***

Would be kind of cool to collapse a galactic epic novel down to, like 20,000 words, like "The Lost Plateau of Leng" or "Surfers at the End of Time."

Figure 14: *Seven Dragons*

We start with the Starship Launch routine… really that's

just a couple of pages. And then we probably have the trip use hyperdrive so we can get it over in a few pages. My main character meets two figures on the ride, one good, one bad. The character is a teen, similar to Zoe Snapp of *Million Mile Road Trip*, and she will soon meet a boy who is in fact Frek from *Frek and the Elixir*, but I'll hold back from saying a whole lot about Frek's background.

Zoe's in the (living) spaceship, and she arrives in the locale I wanted to use for the *Frek* sequel I dreamed of. Maybe I won't ever write the booklength sequel, but this tale can be segment of it that can stand on its own, or which perhaps I might expand into a full sequel someday.

I have this locale very clear in my mind, it's a misty, rainy, jungly spot in an archipelago of islands. I'm thinking of the northern end of the southern half of New Zealand. They have full biotech like in Frek and the Elixir, that is, every device or vehicle is an organism and not a machine. And they have fishing ships that go out from the islands. And these ships are living beings, adapted from whales, just as the "elephruk" vehicles are evolved from elephants. Call the ships hvalships.

My Zoe-type character befriends and falls in love with Frek. There's some specific thing that they're supposed to do aboard on the hvalships.

Now—here's a twist. If the starship brings the girl to the Earth of 3333, which is where Frek lives, where did she come from? Is she an alien? Or perhaps a colony-world person. The latter is the simpler option.

***

On Sept 23, 2019, I sent "The Mean Carrot" to Asimov's. And now I'm starting to miss writing again. Most of this week I was working on a painting called *Seven Dragons*.

So okay, what to write? I can't quite get it up to do that *Frek* world mini-space-opera thing, I *did* think of a working title for that one: "Starship and Hvalship." Or drop the starship part and just set it in the Frek world of year 3000, and don't worry about taking a starship to get there. The character could be someone who wasn't even in the *Frek* novel. So it's a story in that universe. But that's a big ramp-up for me just now. Maybe later.

October 25, 2019. Home from Italy.

We were in Italy for two weeks. Great trip. I gave a talk at the "Internet Festival" in Pisa, we spent seven nights there. We also spent a day in Lucca, three nights in Florence, and three nights in Genoa.

Meanwhile *Asimov's* rejected "Everything Is Everything," Sheila said the ending is "too open," and I can understand that. I kind of like the open ending but maybe I was being lazy. I'll take another look at it, and then I'll probably send it to *Lightspeed.*

Asimov's still has "The Mean Carrot," and I think there's good odds they'll take it. They're printing the Zep & Del Laidlaw collab novelette "Surfers at the End of Time" in the Nov-Dec, 2019, issue.

I was going to write a story about Fibonacci from the year 1200 with Bruce Sterling, whom I enjoyably saw in Pisa. The guys in Pisa wanted us to do the story for an antho in the man's honor (Fibonacci was born there). I can't face the project, though. No good ideas for the story, and hashing out a tale with Bruce can be stressful. I might do a different story with him in 2020 if we can think of a better idea than Fib.

Figure 15: Futurism In Pisa. Sylvia, Rudy, Jasmina, Bruce.

I am jonesing to write something now. Which brings us back to "Mary Falls."

Or maybe I make "Starship and Hvalship" into a novella and pitch it to Jonathan Strahan, who, according to Laidlaw, buys standalone novellas for Tor. The hvalship story would be in the Frek and the Elixir world. And, weary geezer that I am, I'd rather make it novella than a fat novel.

On the other hand—waffle, waffle—"Mary Falls" could be the novella, and if Strahan doesn't take it, I try it on *Asimov's*, and meanwhile I'd have "Starship and Hvalship" on deck in the batter's circle, subliminally percolating. I don't presently have the plot for the hvalship story, and the plot for "Mary Falls" is almost ready to go. I'll tweak my entry on this a little more.

October 28, 2019. Rolling Blackout.

Meanwhile PG&E has turned off our power for our region because it's very dry and there might be some high winds that could fell lines, produce sparks, and start fires. An enormous fire is raging north of here, and there's one near LA. In our third day of no power now. The hardest thing is not having wireless, and having to recharge our devices from the cigarette lighter of my BMW while I let it idle. You can get internet via the phones, but of course the screens are very small and there's no keyboard.

At night we get in bed about 8 pm...it gets old sitting in candlelight and darkness; it turns dark at 6:45 pm. In the morning, we're so glad when the sun finally comes up at 7:30 am. And now this is, as people are saying, the new normal. The climate crash we've been talking about, it's here. We'll put a bag of ice in the fridge today to cool it a bit. Sylvia is upset, although at times it seems fun...candle light is generally cheering.

They're calling this a "rolling black out" but I don't see anything *rolling* about it. It just sits here. I thought a rolling black out was when a black out was moving across the state as transformers blew out, producing satellite-view Zhabotinsky scrolls of light and dark.

***

Meanwhile Bruce keeps emailing me more ideas for our Fibonacci story, so now I'm thinking we can do it after all. Bruce insists he doesn't want to try and write a Clifton Fadiman Math-Is-Fun Educational story about Fibonacci that's actually set in 1200 AD. Current plan is that we've got two heavyweight cybercriminals, the North Korean guy who stole over $2 billon from banks for his country, and a Texas guy who did something like Silk Road or a cryptocurrency scam,

I want some kind of superscience kicker ending. I'm now leaning towards a scale-ship type trip, as in my first novel, *Spacetime Donuts*. Only here they don't wrap around, instead they drop through into a flat comic strip. Or they turn into a dust mote that one of the Silk Road guy's pals duplicates and includes in all shipments of coke for the next month so that our heroes "live on"

Have the North Korean be a woman?
***

As I type this, I want to Google some background facts, but, um, I don't have wireless. There's a similar but more muscle-memory error I'm making. I keep automatically tripping light switches. Last night I was carrying a candle, coming out of the bathroom, heading for the bedroom, and, as it's light in the bathroom (from my candle), I reflexively tap the light switch…to turn off the woman? light.

Nov 11-Dec 31, 2019. Fibonacci Story with Bruce.

Nov 11, 2019

So I wrote a 2.000 word opener for that Fibonacci story with Bruce Sterling after all. Thought about it a lot before being able to write it. Now I sent it to him, anticipating cuts.

The angle for our new story is that there's a simple-as-arithmetic method for decoding what other people are thinking. So I gave it the silly working title: "Algorism of the Humors." *Algorism* is an old word that precisely means what Fibonacci taught in his *Liber Abaci*, that is, the exponentially faster method of using positional notation and grade-school arithmetic algorithms instead of tally system or abacuses or Roman numerals. And the four humors are, of course, the ancient Greek notion about the make-up of our personalities.
***

Meanwhile I'd like to have something else to write on, as it could be week before Bruce gets back to me. So I'd like to get started on "Mary Falls."
***

Bruce did indeed make cuts on my Fibonacci Ver 1. I ranted at him via email, as is customary, then I worked for a week or ten days on my Ver 3. I restored a lot of things he'd removed, integrated his new stuff, and wrote a bunch more. It still could be a good story, although Fibonacci's role is dwindling. It's now a post-disaster story in Austin, Texas. We'll see what Bruce does in Ver 4.
***

A week went by; Bruce has had family in town. He did manage send an email to the effect that everything I've done is wrong, and that he'll fix it soon, when the spirit took him. And then I got Bruce's Ver 4. Despite my pleas for moderation, he's once again rewritten every single word, as if I'd told him the story verbally over the phone, and he's writing down his version of it.

I lost my temper and wrote him that I'm bailing.

He Bruce wrote back that it doesn't matter that he changed my writing, because nobody cares about my style or his style anyway. He said I needed to work harder at the story—this from the guy who with each revision destroys all the work I've already done, throws my plot and characters out the window, and expects me to start over from the beginning.

As my idea of a compromise, I told Bruce I'd base my Ver 5 on my Ver 3, folding in whatever useful new bits by him that I can find in his Ver 4. I said I'd find a plot and write Ver 5 through to the end, and he could do some final touches for a Ver 6 we could sell.

No word back from him as yet.

***

Dec 9, 2019.

I got a few stories rejected, and I started thinking the one story that I *might* be able to sell to *Asimov's* right now would be that Fib collab with Bruce. So I'm starting a fix-up process on it. So like I planned, I took the good bits out of his Ver 4 and pasted them into a new Ver 5. And I am in fact doing some of the cuts that Bruce wanted to do; he was actually right about some of the cuts he made on Ver 3.

The big problem is still, as Bruce points out, that the story doesn't have a conflict, a goal, a plot, or any hint of how to put in a twist at the end. So I'm racking my brain. So painful, this process.

***

December 31, 2019.

Returning to thoughts of Fib after a few weeks off, I realize I still haven't thought of a plot fix. And this time the collaboration isn't much fun. Maybe it was a misguided snap decision to do this story, so I'll set it aside, at least for now. For the next stage of this slow progress, jump to where it resumes at my entry <u>May 30-June 2, 2020. "Fibonacci's Humors" Ver 6</u>.

Nov 23, 2019. Revise "Everything is Everything."

I still can't quite get going on "Mary Falls," so I went back and had another look at "Everything Is Everything." The first version is very drifty and gauzy, like a dream or a hallucination. Actually, rereading it, I felt uneasy…kind of wondering if I'm having bouts of insanity. But yet when I wrote the story, I felt normal, and like I was writing really well. I was thinking the story was a subtle, allusive, poetic, surreal masterpiece.

Oh well! Though I do still like the first version, if I'm ever going to get it published, I'll need to, sigh, make it more logical, and give it a plot, and a twist that makes sense.

My basic idea for the story is to show a world that undergoes a transition to seeing that physical space is a transfinitely divisible absolute continuum. So now I'm going over it, revising it, and we'll see what big structural changes I come up with.

December 1-7, 2019. "Everything Is Everything," Ver 2.

Rather than going crazy worrying about my story with Bruce, I got going on "Everything Is Everything" again. I hope to make it clear what happens—clear both to the reader and, more crucially, *clear to me*. As if. At this point I don't actually know at all.

Backing up, the basic idea is that space is everywhere absolutely continuous. In some zones the residents notice this, in some zones they don't. Some envoys from an enlightened zone come to enlighten humankind—for reasons as yet to me unknown.

The enlightenment process involves simply spilling out some "smeel" that spreads through our level of space, knocking the scales from our eyes. So here are some thoughts and issues.

- I wrote the first draft so that when the EPs' car disappears at the beach, it seems to clarify space and to make it be absolutely continuous. But later at Wick's house, after the chickens peck open the egg, it clarifies space again. This shouldn't happen twice. Need to rewrite the first passage. Maybe the car grows to cosmic size, and Wick feels a whiff of clarity as the shell passes through him.

- Where do the EPs live? Let's say the EPs share our space like an overlay—but we unenlightened folks don't know about them. There's "room" for the EPs between the atoms and above the galaxies. They could be much smaller than us, or much larger. Let's say larger, which fits with them being entitled pricks. And thus, yes, they are a kind of overlay.

- Why do they want to bother us? Is it, like, an investigation like turning over rocks on the seashore? Or do they have some evangelical motive, like a zealot going out to preach to trees? Nah. They're selfish EPs, out for themselves. They're not doing science or religion. Well, do they want to *eat* us? Nah, that's stale. Do they want to collect us like trophies…like maybe a coarse human body is like a quaintly pixelized mosaic, or a person's mind is like an African mask, fascinatingly primitive and expressive. A collectible. Nah, that's stale too.

- So what *is* it that the EPs want from us? They want to settle in our location on the size scale. The EPs are sinister realtors. Or, more precisely, they're *developers*. Wick and the rest of humanity isn't going to *move* in the sense of changing location—we'll be moving down the size scale! The EPs live at a larger scale, and they want to expand their domain to include our lowly size scale—and they're going to push us down a level in size. Like yuppies gentrifying the Mission district of San Francisco and sending the occupants off to scuzzy blue-collar burbs, or to trailer parks, or to hick towns in the Central Valley.

- The two EPs will now be wearing the faces of Wick and Vi. They're ready to move in. Wick and Vi's house will be their base office.

- What does the smeel do, exactly? Basically I want it to let Wick and Vi slide down to the subatomic level and find an undeveloped Earth-like planet there. Or maybe it's more like they're shoved down, or lured near the edge and then shoved. And then the smeel is gone and they're stuck.

- How exactly does the smeel work? Maybe some bullshit about gauge theory and fractal spacetime? There's actually a book about "scale relativity" that uses fractal spacetime. Maybe the passage is like riding a taxi in Tokyo, and you keep turning into smaller and smaller streets, going faster and faster, and you pop past 1/alef-null and into a new level at 1/alef-one. Don't stress the fractal quality. Focus on acceleration.
- Is the *whole* Earth being retrofitted? Maybe just some areas, that would be funnier, and closer to the satirical intent. In fact, I'll have it just be Los Gatos. And then the new EPs are moving into Los Gatos, and they blend in, and we don't even know they're replacements. Like pod people.
- Kicker: Our heroes' fate will be to act as pioneers of the sub atomic level, creating a bustling civilization down there, with the knowledge that eventually the realtor/developer EPs will come and take that over and boot us down the size scale again. We'll be like the artist colony forever being pushed out by Mammon. Because everything is everything.

Title? I do still like "Everything is Everything," and it doesn't telegraph the plot, and it has an oblique twist. I mean the woman EP might pitch this as a slogan. And later Wick and Vi might say that to each other with bittersweet irony when they're in Nowheresville at the end.

Other title options: "Redevelopment." "Redev. "Retrofit." Vintage Charm." "Urban Renewal."

I saw Vintage Charm used in an article about old SRO hotels or cheap apts being turned into luxury apartments near the lake in Chicago. Article's title: "When Housing for the poor is remodeled as luxury studios." Urban Renewal is more of a 50s concept, involving the razing of neighborhoods, as opposed to co-opting them. Redev is peppy. There is a company called ReDev Properties in Canada. There's a contracting company called Redevelopment Services. There's a Redev Group in Indianapolis. So I think redev is fair game as a generic word. Retrofit doesn't quite fit. Probably I stick with "Everything is

Everything."

December 9. Third Rejection.

Today Sheila rejected "The Mean Carrot" for *Asimov's*. That's my third rejection in a row from *Asimov's*. First for "Juicy Ghost," and then for the first draft of "Everything Is Everything." Those first two I can kind of understand—"JG" is so political, and the first draft of "E Is E" was gauzy. But "Mean Carrot" is about as good a story as I can write.

Getting a little uneasy here.

I offloaded "Juicy Ghost" to an online freezine called *Big Echo*. And I did an email submission of "Carrot" to John Joseph Adams at *Lightspeed Magazine*. They published my "Knobby Giraffe" a couple of years ago.

Not sure where I can send "E is E" now. *F&SF* never buys a story from me. Marc says Ellen Datlow isn't currently looking at stories for *Tor.com*. I'll rewrite the story some more and then decide.

December 12, 2019. "Everything Is Everything," Ver 3.

I got my eyes fixed and now I'm puttering around, wanting to finish "Everything Is Everything." Can't quite get it up to do the ending. Maybe there should be a Part 3 of the story, from Vi's point of view. If they both go down to the "underworld" of Earth Alef-Two, it's sad. If just Wick goes down, it's maybe even sadder. And why should Wick be punished so horribly? Like what did he ever do that was bad? I'd have to set it up so the trip would be something he'd want to do. But if the higher EPs are in fact doing a redev on Los Gatos, seems like they'd be sure to send Vi down too.

I drafted a pushed-down ending, and I don't like it.

> Later that day, they packed up some stuff to go. Vi was going to phone their two kids to ask if they wanted to come along, but it didn't seem likely they'd want to. They were just starting out. And, come to think of it, the EP versions of Wick and Vi would be there for them.

The EPs ordered in a special Mercedes, driven by an anemone. It ferried them down the scale to Earth Alef-one. A winding road, with tricky turns.

Nobody much lived on Earth Alef-one yet, but more people from Los Gatos came trickling in, and then some people from other cute towns. They got a new civilization going. And eventually more EPs would show up and boot them down the scale again. But there'd always be more room.

Everything is everything.

They have to save themselves. Kicker: Vi could convince the EPs to be plants and animals instead of replacing people. Chickens or crows.

Or some kind of twist, like in those groove-dog "The Devil and Daniel Webster" type stories where the character outsmarts the devil, often on the basis of some semantic or logical twist...although I don't want a cheap trick. Maybe if I had some kind of nested regress gimmick.

Another point is that maybe the EPs aren't human beings. They're imitating them for most of the story, but they might be, who knows, electrons or quarks or neutron stars or space squid or misprints. What if we got them to want to be characters in a comic book? Wick has a big stack of *Donald Duck* reprints. Or ants! Or squirrels in the tree. That would be nice.

The shape of the "Mercedes" changes to that of an aethereal UFO when it leaves in Act I. It was never a car at all.

Re. not replacing Vi and Wick, note that the EPs don't need a particular body, per se, as they make their own bodies. What they need is a *niche*. They can be the whole ant colony, be a queen or, maybe better, all the ants. Or a wasp hive, like the one in the ground at the bottom of my bamboo patch.

Another bit I'm dropping:

"Have a taste of that egg's skin," said the redev man, extending his hand, palm up. He held something like two damp scraps of fruit leather.

Against his better judgment, Wick took a piece and chewed it. Delicious.

I got a good ending, did two or three more rewrites, and, what the fuck, sent it off to *Analog* on December 16, 2019, including a few last-minute fixes inspired by comments Marc Laidlaw made on the next-to-last draft. If they bounce it, I'll try *F&SF*.

December 31, 2019. Reset.

Can't believe tomorrow will be 2020. That's when I set my novel *Software*—2020 seemed a date fantastically far in the future, relative to 1979. I saw a four-year-old kid today and said "Happy New Year" to him and his mother. Imagine being four in 2020! He could live to 2100. His whole future so wildly different from the time-segment I've traversed.

The whole family's been here for Xmas, and we're not quite done yet. Tonight it's just me and S, we're going over to some neighbors who kindly invited us to dinner at the last minute. Relaxing now with my laptop…it's been over two weeks. Ready to write something again. Cancelled the Fib collab plans. Ready for "Mary Falls."

March 15, 2019 - Jan 24, 2020. "Mary Mary" Notes.

All along I was going to call this story "Mary Falls," but then I changed to "Mary Mary." Not sure the woman will end up simulated by a waterfall, also the "Mary Mary" title works in that there are several versions of Mary in play.

The following is a bunch of notes run together. The very first bit is from something like March 15, 2019, and then a lot of the rest is from December, 2019, and early January, 2020, and then I revised it some more towards the end of January, 2020, over and over, marking it up and typing in changes, and eventually I actually started Tonight, writing the story.
***

Mary is a nice old woman. She dies and migrates into the digital afterworld under the auspices of a company called Juicy Ghost. And then she has problems getting control of a physical peripheral.

Arc: Mary becomes a powerful agent on her own behalf. And we have a tech twist at the end.

They create a cloud-based lifebox-style sim of her by using an uvvy or lifebox type device called a psidot. And they equip her with a physical world peripheral. The sim plus peripheral is called a juicy ghost.

The gold standard for a peripheral is a tank-grown human body, ideally a youthful clone of your original body. A Mary-2. Mary can't afford to grow one, but Juicy Ghost offers her a "free trial" of a cloned copy of herself. Six weeks. From the cloud, Mary sees through Mary-2's eyes. And she controls what Mary-2 does. And then time's up and she's evicted from Mary-2 by a pushy EP (entitled prick), a wealthy one-percenter who's registered a cloud-based mind.

Juicy Ghost does this maneuver—of offering free trials of clone peripherals—as a way of training or breaking-in the clones. And naturally the original mind that matched the clone is the perfect trainer.

Juicy Ghost Inc. is within their rights to reassign occupancy of the clone. As an alternative, they give Mary a gig-worker job running a biobot ball walker.

Even in this body, the awkward and unworldly Mary has to give it to a richer or pushier sim. As a consolation, they give Mary an ambient naturally-occurring "peripheral" which is simply a physical chaotic computation. She becomes the spirit of place in the waving leaves of a forest glen, or in a cascade. Call it Mary Falls.

In the summer, the falls dry up. By now Mary has mastered the control of natural computations. She migrates into the slow computation of the shifting of the crystals in the cascade's sedimentary stone. But now she doesn't have much agency. She finds an out?

***

We're in the world of my June, 2019, story "Juicy Ghost." "Mary Mary" is a bit further into the future. In the long run maybe I can write a cycle of juicy-ghost stories. For context, here's a quote from the initial "Juicy Ghost" tale.

> While I'm still alive, I'm continually updating my psidot. The device itself is a wireless antenna and a brainwave transducer. A shiny piezoplastic disk the size of a freckle, on the back of my neck. Like a paste-on beauty mark, except it's smart and it can crawl around a little bit.

My psidot captures whatever I experience and stores it in the cloud. Works the other way too. My psidot feeds me info. And, better than that, it uses heavy cloud-based processing to munge my data stream, and if I ask, it'll suggest what I might do next.

…you can live inside your psidot, as long as it's leeched onto a person or an animal or even an insect. As long as you're leeching, you're a juicy ghost.

I want to have the psidots be biotech. Maybe I ought to weave back and make that clear in the first "Juicy Ghost." Or let's say the old psidots were materials-tech, and mention that now they're bio.

Ought to mention commercial teep somewhere along the line. When did it kick in?

***

I see Mary as being a little like my Mom. It would be nice to give Mom's life a happier ending. I'll write it in third person, close-in to Mary, essentially writing her POV. Need to avoid heavy bathos, going light on the lonely-old-person thing. Mary is odd, spunky, a tough old bird, unpredictable, a little nuts.

Mary has a younger friend in her 30s, Kayla—a popular name these days. Kayla and Mary live in Boulder Creek so I can do a scene at the falls in Big Basin Park. Also, this hamlet is a place I know well. I'll give Boulder Creek the name I used for it in *Saucer Wisdom*, that is, San Lorenzo.

On Dec 30, 2019, we went to see a bluegrass group called the Goat Hill Girls, at our local coffee shop —Izzy, her husband Gus, Georgia, Sylvia, and me. Something very cozy and lovely about seeing ordinary humans make music. Twinkling Christmas lights. I'd like to write about people like that. Let's say my two women characters play bluegrass together. Mary is the mandolin player, and Kayla the fiddle player. Mary might look like an older Irish woman I know, thin, jumpy, hair dyed black, raucous, devil-may care.

We're far into biotech—cars or phones are biobots. The psidots are fully biotech. And for package delivery they use *walker balls*. A walker ball is a rubbery sphere, with a slit-like mouth, and two dot eyes, like a happy face, and it has a kind of bulge underneath with two jointed legs like ostrich legs. They can kick hard enough to be lethal.

Figure 16: Ball Walkers

Mary is in her 70s. She works in the Boulder Creek YouYou. Evolved from UPS and USPS. You2You. She wrangles the ball walkers who pick up and deliver mail in the back roads around Boulder Creek. They ball walkers live in a barn. Mary feeds them, and instructs them. The ball walkers interact with elephruks that shuttle packages between Boulder Creek and the main center in San Jose. Maybe there's a boss ball walker that's a bit smarter than the others.

Why would Mary's young friend Kayla be in Boulder Creek if she's from San Francisco? She was born in 2010, like our grandchildren. She moved into the mountains to be organic, and to get away from the hideous city heat. Kayla is a biofabber, growing parts for people's broken biodevices. Like replacing organs. It's analogous to 3D printing, but it's *not* printing, but more like "assembling" in the nanotech sense. She's also a musician. And she has artistic aspirations. She wants to grow some weird biofab things of her own, like maybe living musical instruments. Angel harps.

Kayla lives with Carson, a work-obsessed engineer who's always leeched into his psidot. She feels stalled. Midlife crisis. She's in her thirties, with a young daughter. Carter works for Juicy Ghost in San Jose. They specialize in software immortality lifebox sims, psidot-recorded while the user is alive, then posthumously animated in the cloud, and, for the upper tiers of customers, connected to biological peripherals which are then called juicy ghosts.

Most days Carson doesn't physically commute, he lolls, gently twitching, in a life-support hammock, like a pupa supported by strands of insect-spun silk. He's bald, pale, and soft. Curiously like the newborn baby. Model the pupa on the veebie from the "Fib" story.

Kayla and Mary happen to be neighbors, and they play bluegrass music together. Mary plays mandolin, and Kayla plays fiddle. Kayla is seen from Mary's slightly ironic point of view. Mary is in a crumbly place, a shack, a grown home, like Frank Shook's house or, more accurately, Nick Herbert's house. Kayla's in something a bit better, a stick-built house with two floors, a cobbled together thing from the 80s, with some grown-home add-ons, like a balcony and a tower.

Mary falls ill—with cancer, I guess. I have enough stuff in the story, and don't really want to get into future plagues. Ordinary cancer, and maybe there's a pricey cure, but for less money you can try to get immortality via software lifebox upload. Kayla's husband Carter gives Mary a spare psidot that he as at home. Last year's model. And she gets a trial Juicy Ghost account. It cheers Mary up, going around in her yard talking to her psidot—like I did with Grandpa Ned in *Saucer Wisdom*.

The psidot and Carter (in person) keep pressuring Mary to enroll for higher service levels, and she funnels her savings to Juicy Ghost. Carter is maneuvering to get Mary's house. He makes a deal where he'll grow her a clone peripheral for the house. Soon comes an Elena's-death-bed scene with Kayla reading from Rumi. Touching her psidot as she fades, Mary feels confident.

***

Mary has the meat-body Mary-2 for six months. She's

going wild in San Francisco. Doing what? But then, um, she has to *renew* the contract and pay a high semi-annual bill. And she hasn't made any money. And her house is Carter's. And Carter didn't even buy her a five-year contract, which is customary. He embezzled some of the house money for himself turning it over to Juicy Ghost. He wanted a better pupa. He's fucking his new pupa, matter of fact. Kayla is breaking up with him. Kayla is living in Mary's old house.

Mary now is a cloud-based sim, and she learns that her subscriber level doesn't qualify her for an independent peripheral. Juicy Ghost's best offer to Mary is that she can have a gig-worker job being the team leader of the ball walker crew at the Boulder Creek Country Store. They'll be eliminating the human wrangler job for a dead-gig-worker. Mary slightly enjoys the job, it's better than being in the cloud, but she wants out. Kayla feels guilty about Mary's raw deal.

Kayla has the idea of putting Mary's database and AI interface into stone, like a fancy funereal tomb-stone...remember that Mary is a 3D fabber. Like one of the chaldrons in Lethem's *Chronic City* Maybe it's more like a bowl, a singing bowl? Or, no, stick with a stone log. It can be in a little graveyard in Boulder Creek.

***

While I was in Pisa, Italy, doing my talk, and then being taped in 3D for a VR clip, I worked out a good routine for one of the final scenes in "Mary Mary."

This story's twist is based on the computer architecture issues around using a psidot to parasitize an animal to live as a juicy ghost. The problem is that you're depending on a massive cloud company like Juicy Ghost to run the database and back end for your psidot. You're much better off if the psidot's back-end data base is stored in some object that you fully own

For the back end I'd like to take advantage of natural computation, in particular we store a person's lifebox ghost as a pattern in the octillion interwingled atoms of a stone. For visuals, we might have this be a gravestone. Like in the cemetery in Saratoga where Sylvia and I walked—I remember a monument shaped like a stone log. Mary's soul is in there.

And whenever Mary isn't embodied as a juicy ghost, she's waiting in the stone for some person or, less problematically, some animal to chance past. And she can do a surgical, cyberknife-type, tight-beam narrowcast of her code into the brain (and the muscles!) of an animal. And then she lives in the animal for a while as a juicy ghost. A crow. He circles up into the air, a rising gyre.

In explaining this in that interview, I made a theatrical, swirling, upward gesture with my hand, with a Tim-Leary-type pitchman's smile on my face, faking ecstasy for the camera.

The stone log there in the graveyard, lurking. Story title could be "Mary's Gravestone."

***

Can Mary spawn multiple Marys? A flock of Mary-crows? Seems like she could. "Stinging" a crow a day. Kayla scatters cracked corn to draw them.

Unused opener:

> Mary ended up with a strange job. She was in charge of a barn of ball walkers in the mountain town of San Lorenzo, California. YouYou had more or less replaced the US Mail, UPS, and FedEx. Ball walker were meter-wide, rubbery, slit-mouthed, smiley heads with ostrich legs. Mail and packages went inside the heads. The ball walkers roamed the villages around San Lorenzo, delivering and picking up. And an elephruk ferried loads between San Lorenzo and the city of San Jose.

Repeatedly thinking over the fan of options, I see many variations, too many. I'll need to prune down.

- *Master lifebox is where?* Either the master lifebox lives on the proprietary Juicy Ghost cloud. or it lives on a privately owned cloud that you maintain, or it lives as a natural computation in an organism or in a biobot or in a piece of brute matter—any of which might function as a cloud. Note that we could simplify things by simply saying the lifebox lives *inside* the psidot.
- *Psidot as modem.* Master lifebox <—> psidot leech <—> host. Two-way channel. *Uploading*: While you are programming your master lifebox, the psidot com-

municates between you and the master lifebox in the cloud. *Downloading*: Mobile parasitic psidot is an "controller" interface between your master cloud lifebox and one of your peripherals. You may get lag issues with this—what VR programmers call delta-t's. So you embed as much of the lifebox in the peripheral as you can.

- *Fully embedded lifebox via psidot.* Psidot is used as an "infection vector," and your personality is like a disease. In other words, the psidot is like a tiny rat that darts over and "bites" the intended host, implanting the lifebox ware, and then the rat darts back to live like a tick on the lifebox owner's body (if they're alive), or to live under, like, a stone log. The embedding takes a few seconds—it's like copying, decompressing, and installing a ZIP file for an app. Note that the master lifebox code might live either in some kind of cloud or simply inside the psidot. Psidot would need to hang on for dear life to the bucking host until the "ZIP download" and "network handshake between peripheral and master lifebox" are done. Optionally, the infected peripheral might stay in occasional contact with the master lifebox, which might be, as mentioned before, in a proprietary cloud, in a private cloud—perhaps inside the psidot), or, in an organism, or in a naturally computing chunk of matter. Over time the peripheral's embedded lifebox could get occasional updates and instructions from the master lifebox which, so long as you're alive, might be updated by you.

- *Fully embedded lifebox via wireless.* Lifebox code *could* be downloaded directly into animal host and it runs there. Could do this without a psidot if have "projective teep." But, really, why bother. Being bitten by a psidot is so much easier to imagine. In any case, even if you have wireless of some kind, then you might still use a psidot for initially recording and uploading your lifebox personality info to wherever the master lifebox is going to live.

January 22-24, 2020. Starting "Mary Mary"

I started actively writing the story around January 15, 2020, very slowly at first, sometimes just a sentence a day. I'm writing it in the present tense, with Mary's POV. By January 22, it was past 2,000 words, and starting to come alive.

I'm still not exactly sure about the sequencing of events; I'm feeling my way; I'm groping for a plot. The stuff in my hulking NOTES entry is, by now, scattered and vague and unwieldy, and with a ramifying tree of branching case options. Even now I continue revising it, but I want to have this fresh entry as well. A clear spot where I can stand.

Not quite sure what kinds of bodies Mary gets. Mary clone, Miss Max ball walker, a bluejay, a flower, a waterfall. Actually it'll be better to have a stranger in Miss Max, so Mary can react to that, and then have Mary herself end up in a ranger drone in Big Basin Park like I was talking about a long time ago.

Mary's at her retirement party, she's due to die in a couple of months, Kayla's husband Carson has offered her a free Juicy Ghost psidot.

Carson and Kayla would like to buy Mary's house. In return, Carson might offer her a cloned-peripheral contract with Juicy Ghost. And the right to continue living in her house as a rent-free "granny cottage." And he'll also promise to "jailbreak" Mary's lifebox out of the JG cloud, and migrate her into an indie cloud, or into an embedding.

Here's the Juicy Ghost fee schedule.

Fees can be waived or reduced for gig workers.

Lifebox Storage	Cost per year
JG Cloud	$2K
Indie network	Not offered.
Embedded in peripheral	Not offered.
Peripheral Access	**Cost per year**
Human clone	$10M
Biobot	$50 - 200K
Animal	$5-10K
Natural computation	Not offered

You have to pay for lifebox storage/simulation in the Juicy

Ghost cloud. If you agree to doing gig work in the cloud—as something like a spambot or a researcher— then the lifebox storage fee can be reduced or waived.

You have to pay extra to JG if you want a peripheral: a human clone, a biobot, or an animal. In the crude JG architecture, each of these is remotely controlled by your Juicy Ghost cloud-based lifebox via a psidot that sits on the peripheral in question. If you agree to do some type of gig work with the peripheral, your fees are, again, reduced or even waived. Prostitution, crime, construction, delivery, consulting, tech work, etc.

Carson has a plan to change this. What is his project called? Free Ghost (Lame), Ubiquity (Name of a retirement funds manager), Everywhen (Name of a Norwegian SF movie? *Dirt Psych*. The last one is punk and cool. It means, like, you can even embed your mind into dirt, if you want to. That's how ubiquitous it can me. But it's a stupid name. Need a better one.

Here are some types of lifebox immortality. (I heavily revised this part as recently as Feb 5, 2020.)

- (Level 1) **Lifebox in Cloud.** Lifebox communicates with a psidot that sits on a body and controls the body, using its sensors and effectors. The computation is enhanced by the fact that the body is physical and, even more, alive. The lifebox uses psidots to link to host peripherals. Key consideration: is the cloud independently owned, or does it belong to a corporation. **1-indie** vs. **1-mersh**. In Level 1-indie, your master lifebox is stored on something you own. In 1-mersh, the cloud belongs to something like Google/Apple/Microsoft/Adobe/Facebook. We'll call our company Juicy Ghost.
- (Level 2) **Lifebox in Psidot**. Store a copy of the full lifebox in the psidot so you don't need wireless hookup. The lifebox-loaded psidot perches on a peripheral and runs it like someone driving a car. Might still use wireless for cloud info searches.
- (Level 3) **Embedded Lifebox.** Embed your lifebox personality directly into each living rich peripheral— whether human, biobot, animal, or plant. No psidot

needed. To instantiate, perhaps a flying psidot acts as a vector, infecting bodies and then perhaps flying away.

- (Level 4) **Natural Computation**. Embed your lifebox into a natural computation such as, rocks, flames, water, air currents, or even molecules.

The first Gee Willikers juicy ghosts were 1-indie. A company took over, and called themselves Juicy Ghost. Their product is 1-mersh. Carson has raised the option of supporting *non* 1-mersh architectures, but the Juicy Ghost techs and managers, oppose them, as (a) 1-mersh is easily monetized, and (b) 1-mersh supports data mining and slavery.

There's also the issue of whether levels 2 and above are technically achievable.

The lifebox was invented by Gee Willikers. It uses what's called the GeeWill architecture and a language that Gee called Spork. He's a guy like Bill Gosper. He's still alive, or at least he's an active 1-indie juicy ghost, supported by private servers he's somehow hidden.

But the GeeWill + Spork hack was taken over by, let's say, Leeta and Slammy. They founded Juicy Ghost.

(Biohackers use a language called Fweedle. Programming a natural process or object is even more intractable—there's research on a language called Leibniz-Keks.)

You'd *think* a localized psidot (as in 2) or, even more, an animal embedding (as in 3) might in fact be able to support the running of a lifebox without any cloud back-end. That is, you shouldn't *need* to run the lifebox emulation in the cloud.

Come to think of it, option (1) makes *exactly* the same mistake I made in in *Software*, forty years ago, in 1980—where I had the brain-ware running in the Mister Frostee freezer truck hulking mainframe machine that followed the emulated humans around.

[Retroactive questions. Did the Little Kidders run on Mr. Frostee too? I guess they did. Why didn't the Moon boppers need hulking giant computers? Oh, right, they had computers in their bodies.]

This said, the transition from (1) to (2) is a little hard because the Spork code and the GeeWill lifebox architecture are first-gen-kludge ware, stiff, quirky and perhaps heavily dependent on searching through, huge data bases.

Carson's project has the ultimate goal of embedding lifeboxes into the natural computations of anything at all. We'll say Mary and Kayla contribute. First they'll do step (1), that is, run a lifebox on an indie network. Then they'll do step (2) embedding in a clone, a biobot, and an animal. And then (3) they'll embed into natural objects.

***

Re. Carson, in the beginning I was having fun writing him as a stoned idiot, and making him thoroughly despicable. A cartoon chauvinist pig. But, for the sake of the story, I'm going to turn this around. He is in fact a genius, and he is in fact thinking useful deep thoughts in his pupa. He's breaking with Juicy Ghost, quarrelling, and resigning and—we still need some bad guys—Juicy Ghost thugs and lawyers will try to take him down.

Ultimately it might be nice to add on a second plot, something about the superduper embedded minds discovering subquantum Absolute Continuum life, a pet topic of mine these days. This could be the third story in the *Juicy Ghost* cycle. Possibly this story could be a repurposed and revised version of the thus-far-unsold "Everything is Everything." Hell, maybe even "The Mean Carrot" could eventually fit in.

January 27-28, 2020. Mary's Next Steps.

Okay, I've got Mary with her personality uploaded to a Juicy Ghost lifebox in their skyhive. Things to do next.

- Carson grows Mary a meat clone body in exchange for her house. Deal is that she can keep her clone living in her house.
- Die. Mary snaps awake in the clone with Carson is fucking her, *ew*, she recalls the interlude of being a soulless lifebox in Skyhive.
- Mary helps Carson and Kayla undermine Juicy Ghost, Inc. Goal: liberate lifeboxes.
- Mary loses clone body. Maybe Carson double crosses her? He wants to have her house all his own? Or maybe Juicy Ghost security murders her clone.
- Carson jailbreaks her lifebox from Juicy Ghost to a

stone.

- Comes back as a ball walker or a drone. Goes to hassle Carson.

And then more stuff. That's more enough to chew on for now. I like the idea of having a tecnho thriller / industrial espionage thing. Would be nice to have one or two of the characters Curtis Winch, Gee Willikers, and/or Leeta turn up, from the story "Juicy Ghost."

On Feb 4, I finally reread that story to remind myself how those characters end up (unspecified), and whether the Juicy Ghost company exists yet in the context of that story (it doesn't). I'd especially like to bring back Gee Willikers. And then Curtis Winch might show up in a later story. He's still on a 1-indie network, not 1-mersh.

***.

You know, I *did* write my *Turing & Burroughs* novel by first writing a couple of loosely related stories. Maybe the new stories could stick together and grow. Basically I'd prefer to be working on a novel again. Makes me feel like a lost, over-the-hill geezer to just be doing stories. "The guy has lost his shit."

I felt that way at Michael Blumlein's memorial service this weekend, seeing other writers, and saying, "Well, I'm writing some stories." And they're like, "Oh, that's nice." Not that, in fact, they're actually judging me. They don't really care, and why should they? Hell, I don't care what *they're* doing. And I'm 73, alright? Nothing I do matters much anymore. But *I* still care. It still feels like writing is what I *do*.

In terms of making the stories into a novel, it might be useful to list all the diverse juicy-ghosts kinds of story ideas I can think of. Keep in mind that I started doing this forty years ago, with the *Wares*. Cory Doctorow had a lot of upload gimmicks in *Walkaway*. I should reread that one. I can use some of his moves, and find different ones.

- (Cory) Keep testing your lifebox ware to destruction. It crashes, you reboot.
- Dual gig-worker notion—as e-worker in cloud, and as physical worker in peripheral.

- Animals (or biobots) as peripherals. (See *Freeware.*)
- Natural computations as peripherals. (See *Hylozoic.*)
- Instantiate as flock (see *Saucer Wisdom.*)
- Subscale travel. Project self into an amoeba. Into subquantum foam.

January 30, 2020. "Mean Carrot" for Evergreen Review.

Turns out my ghosts' former editor/publisher John Oakes (Four Walls Eight Windows) is now, improbably, the owner of *Evergreen Review* (online only, about one issue per year). That's one of my oldest ambitions, to sell a story to *Evergreen Review*, the Beatnik Valhalla. John says if I send him a story he might run it.

Just after I heard from Oakes, John Joseph Adams rejected "The Mean Carrot" for his SF ezine *Lightspeed*. His turndown was word-for-word the same "failed to convince me" note as for "Everything Is Everything," so this time I didn't take the words especially seriously. Just a paste-in.

And now *ta-da* I'll send the story to *Evergreen Review*, that is, to Oakes, my man inside. Always remember that H. P. Lovecraft couldn't sell "At the Mountains of Madness" for five years.

So today I'm doing a light revision of "The Mean Carrot." I'd showed it to Marc Laidlaw, and he gave me a few suggestions too. Like obliterate all sex-worker talk, now that we're post #metoo. Sure, why not. And the plot wasn't perfectly clear—mainly because I made it up as I went along, and hadn't adequately prefigured the ending. And lots of little blips.

Kind of freaky how whenever I go back and reread something after even a month, I see so many things to fix. Why didn't I notice them before? If I kept revising on and on, would it ever stabilize? Like sanding and sanding...does the object finally disappear? Just before that, it's three perfect words.

Another blot: in "The Mean Carrot" I had a passage written in Shakespearian English, like Sheckley did in *Mind Swap*, because I thought it was funny, and because I'd just reread

Hamlet. But now I decided the pastiche is a bad idea. The story is confusing enough already. Here's a ripe bit of Shakey-talk that I cut.

> "Well said, sirrah! how is it you freed our locked powers of thought-speech?"

"Stumbles scramble our signals with scuzz from a sixty-bit shift register," says Anselm. "Took me about ten seconds to crack *that*. Only a fungus would use something so dumb. Come away with me to the saunas, Molly! I'll help you kick your stumble habit."

> "Mayhap I shall—if this eve's alarms and affinities are as augured."

Ew.

Finished fixing it, working all through the evening. Another constant is how often I feel in despair because a plot seems too screwy and confusing—I fret and fret, and then the fix comes to me. The Muse whispers it in my ear. And now I've mailed it to Oakes. Not that, by any stretch of the imagination, it's at all that likely the NYC coterie of *Evergreen's* actual staff will run it. Another lottery. "Nobody ever jumped off a bridge with an Irish Sweepstakes ticket in their pocket."

Rethinking it, maybe they would have been more likely to buy "Juicy Ghost" (modulo the fact that it was in *Big Echo*).

February 3, 2030. Methods of Telepathy.

A bit of cryptomnesia here. Of late, I'd been thinking: "Okay, I'll call my new story cycle collection or novel *Teep.* Have it be about the coming of commercial mass-market telepathy, pervasive as smart phones…and the fallout thereof. So rad! Great idea. High concept, J.B."

The cryptomnesia aspect of this is that mersh teep was my key idea for *The Big Aha* (2014). Doh!

Oh well, I'll kick it up a notch and do it anyway.

And, looking back, I think teep was in a golden age novel I read in high-school. Had a playful title, can't quite remember it. The title was maybe something like The Big Spree or The Full Cup (though those aren't it at all.) Scene: A guy in a sharkskin suit walks up an aisle (in his head he does this) to the woman preacher and she "shows him Love" in the sense of a heavy sex. Can't remember the title. Not Heinlein.

Found it: *The Big Ball of Wax*, by Shepherd Mead (1954). Some of the teep methods I've used.

Quantum wetware. *Big Aha.* Oscillate at will between merged and discrete states.

Alien vibrations. "Everything is Everything"

Fungal wireless. "The Mean Carrot."

Psidot wireless. "Juicy Ghost" and "Mary Mary."

Exact physical map. *Postsingular* and *Hylozoic*. Need to check this one.

Quantum entanglement. "Panpsychism Proved," a story about telepathy with a stone.

I was wondering if others have used the word "teep," I found that David Gerrold used it in his *War Against the Chtorr* series. He has a "Teep Corps" of people telepathically linked by implanted chips. They sometimes control each other's bodies, and sometimes act as hive minds.

In "Juicy Ghost" the teep is via psidot, and it's pictures and voices in your head. Doesn't seem to be commercially available in that story…the only ones using it are, I think, Curtis and Gee Willikers.

So maybe part of "Mary Mary" is that the psidot is a teep phone. The lifebox backup might be an add-on feature.

Checked the telepathy entry in the *Encyclopedia of Science Fiction*. They suggest that with smartphones in use, people don't lust for telepathy as much anymore. It doesn't seem so "modern" now. It was a popular theme during the ESP craze of the late 40s and early 50s.

February 5, 2020. Indie vs. Mersh. Psidot Lifebox?

As I keep saying, there's a way in which "Mary Mary," "Everything is Everything," "The Mean Carrot," and "Juicy Ghost" are all part of one narrative. They all have to do with lifeboxes, telepathy and body swapping. Is a fix-up in the offing?

One of those creation-tales where the humble author says "I had no idea that I was working on it." Would make me feel good…as these stories are all I've been working on (other than the magisterial "Surfers at the End of Time") since April, 2018, which is nearly two years ago now.

Oh, well. As long as I'm writing. And maybe edging bass-ackwards into something bigger than a single story.

***

I've been working to fix a slight discrepancy between "Juicy Ghost" and "Mary Mary." And in the course of repeatedly revising my recent "Mary Mary" entries in these writing-notes, I've been studying and lightly tweaking my older story "Juicy Ghost."

* In "Juicy Ghost," which predates "Mary Mary" in my future history, they were using the Level 1-indie architecture. The stored the full lifebox in the cloud, and a psidot could run any organism it sat upon, interfacing between lifebox and peripheral. The lifebox is in a secure dark-net secret-server cloud created and maintained by Gee Willikers.

* In "Mary Mary" the peripheral body also wears a psidot to link it to Mary's lifebox which lives in the cloud, but this time it's the corporate Juicy Ghost skyhive cloud. This is the Level 1-mersh architecture. Juicy Ghost Inc revels in "owning" many lifeboxes.

Carter wants to move back to Level 1-indie. And maybe, longer term, move forward to Level 2, where a user's lifebox would be fully in their psidot. As always, the psidot would run a peripheral body like a driver in a car.

Eventually, in a different story, Carter or someone else will proceed to Level 3, embedding the lifebox into the peripheral and letting the psidot wither away.

There's some worth-mentioning history of the corporate machinations that moved from 1-indie to 1-mersh. A missing story. Cf. Heinlein's (never actually written) "The Stone Pillow." The indie-to-mersh process mirrors what's happened to our internet in the last couple of decades. Big companies inveigling you to keep your wares and your data and your projects in silos in their proprietary clouds. I might just call this story "Psidot."

***

Don't forget juicy!

I claimed in my story "Juicy Ghost" that only by linking

with a living being did the psidot lifebox personality (somewhat magically) become living. It gets quantum aha from the organism. A lifebox on its own in the cloud, a too-poor-to-hire-a-peripheral lifebox in the Juicy Ghost skyhive—it's more like a really good chatbot. It has no *soul*, in the bluesy sense of the word. It's robotic. Even though it might *say* that it's alive, it's isn't *funky*. It's a Spork-language cloud-based data-base-mining computational architecture with no real mind.

Juiciness is an appealing mysto-steam SF idea to use.

So Skyhive stores *unembodied* lifeboxes—as well as juicy lifeboxes. In a way it's like an orphanage of orphan children hoping for adoption. So again, those Skyhive ghosts with no biological bodies are *not* juicy. The full juicy ghost body service is a luxury add-on. Many people might want a Skyhive version of their ancestor, but very definitely *not* want a meddling juicy ghost body around. I recall, in passing, that the *Terminator* robot was made by Cyberdyne and Skynet. My name Skyhive echoes Skynet.

* Note that a ball walker is an organism too, so a psidot/lifebox on a ball walker can have soul. A ball walker can make you juicy. Can, like, a stone's natural computation make you juicy? Later down the road, I might say, yes, it does, but not yet in "Mary Mary." Don't put every idea into the one story.

* In "Mary Mary," I'm initially putting the lifebox in separate (commercial) cloud storage, and just using the psidot as a controller.

* I should dramatize the moment when Mary's lifebox hooks into her clone body. At that point she "wakes up" and remembers being the shadow lifebox in the Skyhive.

* Even with the peripheral, Mary might feel like there's glass between her and her clone. Like a diaphragm or a condom.

February 12, 2020. Lifeboxes, Psidots, Hosts. Mary Dies.

I've been working on the story a lot. Not even printing it out so often, just opening it up and going through and revising. Mary is getting interesting as a character.

Not sure how long the story will get. I can see 10-15K

words at least, and possibly it grows into a novel with, like I've said, the "Juicy Ghost" story as an earlier chapter. And maybe a chapter about Curtis Winch as a dog.

If I go for a longer narrative, it would be interesting if Carson's free-the-lifeboxes plan fails, at least the first time around, and we have Mary with no body, living in the Skyhive cliff-city. Interacting with the other listless lifeboxes there, trying to organize a revolution, the storks like prison guards. She takes gig work as a drone operator.

And I might bring in the man who went on the Palau dive trip with Mary when she was fifty. The love of her life. Maybe he ended up as a lifebox in the Skyhive too, and Mary meets him there. The bump into each other when she and the guy both have Skyhive gig worker jobs running, like, drones. The groovy old-*Dumbo*-movie-type stork carrying them down in a shared sling.

***

I don't have Carson's jailbreak scenario clear at all. Somehow Mary's clone body is involved, and somehow the attempt fails. I do *not* want Mary to be playing a seductress. Something feminist. Chief engineer, maybe. Keep in mind that the Skyhive brass would know who Mary is. So how does she get the job?

The only career I've sketched for Mary is low jobs. I ought to put in some kind of background.

Building on whatever that is, say Carson overclocks Mary's lifebox and makes her a genius? Overclocks it and adds a huge amount of RAM. Objective correlative for being on performance-enhancing drugs.

There's some danger to Mary's sanity, and to the integrity of her peripheral clone body. And ultimately the body has a heart attack or a seizure which is brought on, let's say, by a skeevy move by one of the Skyhive execs, such as Slammy.

Keep in mind that we *do* want the body to die so Mary can end up marooned as a low-ranking lifebox on the Skyhive cliff.

So for a while, Mary is ultrasmart, working in the inner lab of Skyhive, with Leeta and Slammy, and she's juggling some bizarre coding practice, maybe some blockchain kind of thing, secretly moving some lifeboxes into rocks. Like getting immigrants out of their internment camps and finding them safe havens in sanctuary cities.

But won't Skyhive have backups on the moved lifeboxes?
***

Backstory. Skyhive was founded by Leeta. In "Juicy
Ghost," Leeta walked off, and Slammy was "the money guy."
She was a fanatic, but maybe not so trustworthy. Let's say that
Leeta and Slammy founded Skyhive. Leeta used to be
idealistic, but Slammy turned her. Maybe they made a deal
with Sudah Mareek.

I just clarified "Juicy Ghost" again to say that Gee Willikers is the man who invented the psidot. The psidots don't
belong to Skyhive. In "Mary Mary," Gee runs the psidot
company. The psidot company, is called what? Just plain *Teep
Inc.* The way that "Google" is both a noun (the company) and a
verb (to use the company's product).

Gee Willikers is consulting and doing business with
Skyhive, helping them to connect to his psidot teep phones,
even though he thinks Skyhive is wrong to be enslaving the
lifeboxes. Maybe he recruited Carson to get him onboard. He
gave Carson the "mute patch" for the psidot.
***

In "Mary Mary," I've been saying the psidots are alive.
Like leeches. So I put that assertion into "Juicy Ghost" as well.

Question: Can a lifebox with a psidot get juicy off the
psidot if the psidot isn't even on a bio host—like if the psidot is
just sitting on a shelf? Well, I guess I have to say yes. But then,
wouldn't lifebox Mary have had juice even after old Mary
died—given that Miu Miu is still functioning? But I want to
say that new Mary's memories of being disembodied lifebox
Mary are kind of faint.

It works if I say that the psidot "passed out" or "went into a
coma" when it didn't have a body for a while. And then lifebox
Mary wouldn't have juice.

Why did the psidot go dormant? This is because a psidot is
really like a leech, in that it sucks nutrients from the bio host.
Possibly the bio host's body also acts as a kind of antenna
enhancement for the psidot. (In this case you might need a host
that has a nervous system.)

Because they're leeches, psidots feel great urgency about
finding a host. If there's no host available, the psidot goes

dormant in less than an hour. And it only revives up when it's placed on a host. By the way, a second reason why both the lifebox and the psidot want a bio body is so that without one, they have not meaningful effectors. On its own a psidot can't really do jack, and again, it can only stay conscious for about an hour. A psidot is designed to be a parasite on a bio host.

Re. the parasitism of psidots, this is an objective correlative for the addictive nature of smart phones.
***

The So, sequence of Mary dying goes like this.

- Mary dies on the blanket in Carson's backyard.
- Her psidot is signaling lifebox Mary that it needs a new body soon.
- The psidot isn't all that mobile—it plans to leech onto baby Daia, who's nearby.
- Sensing this, Kayla pinches the psidot. She and Carson put the psidot in a jar.
- The psidot falls into a coma.
- They cremate Mary's body and put the ashes in a pot in her house. (Too gross to cut it up and brain-map it and repurpose its other organs like in *Software*.)
- With no functioning psidot, lifebox Mary is out of touch, and she has no juice.
- A day later, Carson walks the grown clone over to Mary's house and put the psidot on the clone.
- Lifebox Mary is, like, *roar*. She jumps Carson, rips his clothes off, and fucks him.
- It takes a couple of minutes for the real Mary emulation to come into focus on the lifebox.

February 13, 2020. Skyhive and Gee's Lifebox Servers?

Two questions.

First, what is Skyhive is using for servers? I'd been instinctively thinking of Google data centers, buildings with stacks and stacks of machines that are chips in a box? But this is kind of retro. Everything else in the story seems biotech and biobot and post-silicon. So the servers really ought to be biocomputational.

Second, what does Gee Willikers use for servers? It should be slightly cooler than what Skyhive uses. (I considered bringing in the veebie fungus from the abandoned Fibonacci story to be Gee's server, but I don't want to have a server that's too smart—otherwise the hosted lifebox won't need to reach out though a psidot to some host organism. Save the veebie for another story where it can star.)

In answering these two questions, let's catalog a few of the possible server options. And the first, more thoroughly described, option is the one I plan to adopt.

(1) BIOCOMPUTATION.

Have your lifebox server be some kind of biocomputer. This is the path I'm going to take.

Problem: this seems to undermine my current projected juicy ghost architecture which says: *Lifebox software lives on dead server, and gains soul by using a teep psidot to connect to a living body.* I've had this architecture in mind for over a year, and I used it when I wrote "Juicy Ghost" story and I won't give it up.

But if the server is already alive, seems like you don't *need* to hook into a live body to get soul. You'd be able to get your juice from the live biocomputing server itself. So then all the lifeboxes would automatically be juicy. And there's no story left at all. *Ouch.* Can't have this. What do I do?

I'll say the bio computers are programmed in a boring Von Neumann architecture-type way, like with LISP or Spork or Java, and they don't have soul. There are differences in the quality of "soul" you might get from different organisms. Skyhive uses stupid mats of yeast for its servers. Or dough. Not intrinsically high-bio enough to have any soul action in there, that is, no juice.

And Gee is subject to this ex-post-facto constraints as well. Okay, his server will be *slightly* more interesting than yeast mats. Like a redwood tree. Or a smelly bucket of piss (with lots of microorganisms in it). But for my story to work, even Gee's server biocomputers have to lack the requisite high-weirdness biocrunch to foster juiciness. Both Skynet's and Gee's lifeboxes need the psidot/live-host connection.

Absolute law: to get juicy a lifebox has to do teep with a living animal body via psidot. You don't get that juicy bio soul until you're hooked into a real animal or insect body. Why is this? Wal, you glom onto those way-sick natural computations in a holistic body, with its mitochondria and ribosomes and quantum entanglement and all that fine shit.

As an aside, even if your lifebox *was* alive and juicy on the server, you would still need the body so you have a peripheral with sensors and effectors in the physical world. A disembodied juicy ghost (if such a thing were possible) would feel lonely and second-rate. But we're not going to settle for this weaker justification for the psidot-to-animal glom move.

(2) ANIMALS.

Why can't I just host my lifebox directly inside an animal. Or even inside another living person. This would be akin to demonic possession. So here we wouldn't be using the whole architecture I'm talking about. So at least for now, we'll say that for some rubber-science reason it's not feasible to dump a lifebox program directly into an animal. You have to rasterize (as it were) the lifebox onto a trad-code Spork server, and then the psidot knows how to take *that* kind of code and link it to an animal body, and even then the code isn't *in* the animal. The code is just "driving" the animal. And nobody knows how to put non-mediated lifebox data directly into an animal.

But using plants as hosts might be okay. Plants might support Spork. And they don't complicate things by making the hosted lifeboxes be juicy.

And, later, if we want, maybe we can do a direct hop into another person's body via a psidot-to-psidot link. That could be another bad thing that happens to Mary later on.

(3) BRUTE MATTER

Using brute matter is a variant on using computer chips. But without having to build a computer.

I'd entertained the notion that Gee uses a granite river rock as his server, I've often talked about the quantum computations in brute matter (see *Hylozoic*). I like the idea of my server being a nice rock, let's say the rounded stones from creeks and rivers, or like boulders you see sitting around in forests. (I think these are mostly granite. The solid black rocks from rivers are basalt, and the layered ones are schist.) A soul-server rock doesn't have be all that big, as any old rock has an octillion atoms. Maybe you can even carry your server rock in your pocket.

But, you know, all of a sudden server rocks seem kind of silly to me. Better to just accept that the servers can be low-level biodevices without enough oomph to make a hosted lifebox be juicy. I did the living rock thing in *Hylozoic*, why do it again.

(4) DISTRIBUTED LIFEBOX

In a less outré mode, Rudy Jr. was talking to me about distributed storage. Each of his MonkeyBrains customer antennas has a few megabytes of extra storage on it. You could split up your lifebox and have the pieces hopping around on network storage devices. This could be done even if the devices were biocomputing fungus lumps. This might be another alternative that Gee might use instead of big Skyhive-type yeast mats. Here, a hosted lifebox doesn't have a fixed physical server location, so it's not really possible to erase it. Distributed biocomputation.

Pushing it, think of an anthill or a disease.

(5) CHAOTIC PROCESSES.

Very early on, I was talking about Mary's server being a waterfall. Back when I wanted to call the story "Mary Falls." The notion of natural processes being usable computers is in *Postsingular* and *Hylozoic*—as is the notion of computing rocks—but I think I could make something new of the computing natural processes. See the sketch in the next two paragraphs.

I was walking in the woods yesterday, and looking at a tastily chaotic bunch of wind-waved branches, and thinking about how, wherever I am, I always look around for something chaotic to, like, feed my mind. And I was thinking that it would be nice if, at some future point in the narrative, a person's lifebox storage hops from one natural process to another. It not hosted on a yeast mat or in a redwood tree or in a computing river stone. It hops around. The lifebox mind is like a person using stepping stones to walk across water. Always have an eye out for the next vortex of natural chaos that you can be hosted on.

A soul like this would still need a body for doing stuff. But it would be a body whose mind lives on in the waving of the branches in the trees. That's cool. Objective correlative: that's my life in a nutshell.

Maybe Gee—or Mary on her own—gets to this point.

February 16-17, 2020. Next Plot Twist.

So now Carson wants to soup up Mary's lifebox so she can work as a wetware engineer at the Skyhive lab. And the plan is that she'll infect the Skyhive yeast mat servers with some new Gee Willikers software called Fweedle B, and supposedly that'll open the prison doors of the Skyhive cliff city, and the captive lifeboxes can move into Gee Willkers's servers which happen to be a pair of redwood trees.

Supposedly Carson will stream new skills into Mary's lifebox, and add some computational power.

But we're not going to let this happen. It makes Mary be too much a of a "thing," or a slave, or a puppet. We want her to have agency. If she sabotages Skyhive, she'll do it her own way. But before she does that, she'll put in some time as a gig-worker slave for Skyhive.

So how do we get from here to there. Mary is walking home alone with Gee Willikers, and he's going to propose some different plan from what Carson wants. And that's going to blow up, and Carson will lose his job, and Mary will be a slave, and Gee will disappear for a while.

Then Mary is a slave on the cliff.

And then maybe a dog shows up. The dog being Curtis Winch.

And maybe there's some high-level political thing in-volved, like with Sudah Mareek, and the sullen, viscous, remains of the Treadle party.

Maybe I start with Mary and Gee visiting his redwoods. And then a Skyhive drone attacks? The ball walkers should get in on it too. Gee seems to be killed, but of course he won't be.

Some of those buzzing flies in the Pot O' Gold could be

Skyhive biodrones piloted by lifebox gig workers. Can you make a psidot really small? Oh, probably.

***

I'm uneasy about the scene of Mary having sex with Carson as soon as she gets her new body. I was thinking Mary was into it, but I'm worried today's PC readers will go #metoo on my ass. And maybe I *am* being sexist if I include this scene? I mean, maybe she was a little bewildered in her new body and Carson is in effect raping her? And even if she has initiative, must a risen-from-the-dead woman's superpowers include being promiscuous? Would you expect that for a man? Sigh.

So I just now (Feb 17) went and changed it from a fuck to a make out session, with Mary clearly doing this as a tease, and leaving Carson begging for more. I think this is more like a scenario a woman might approve of. Not that I ever really know.

What actually put me off doing the sex scene in "Mary Mary" was reading the 1954 Shepherd Mead novel, *The Big Ball of Wax*, narrated by an ad-man type who encounters XP (which might stand for "extended perception," though the book only says "Variety coined the name.") I remembered reading a hot scene in this book when I was a horny thirteen-year-old, but now coming back to the book, it seems like fairly lame semi-porn. Slavering yet prudish descriptions of experiencing orgies via XP. Nah.

***

If I *was* going to make this be novella length, I'd want to have a conclusion in mind by now. What might that be? An obvious goal is freeing Skyhive lifeboxes.

By what's so great about that? Why would rich dead people "deserve" to have biobot bodies running around? I mean, they ruled for their whole lives, maybe they should bow out. Fuck them!

What about if, at the conclusion Mary learns to accept death. What if, *doh*, merging into matter and natural processes, that is, becoming hosted by a brute-computation-natural-matter-and-chaotic-process landscape—what if that's what's been happening all along anyway when you die. Ta da! (What Bruce Sterling dismissively calls "the transcendence move.")

And then—nothing? Well, what if after you merge into the

landscape there's a growing sense of freedom and air, and you go into a *real* afterworld. (Like I was hoping for when I first read Robert Sheckley's *Immortality Incorporated.*) Would get us back into the zone of *White Light* and *Jim and the Flims*, where they visit an afterworld. In both those novels it's a guy going for a visit, like Aeneas or Dante in Hell, and then coming back. I'm not sure if Mary would come back or not.

***

So I'm circling around, vamping, and I still don't know what's in the next scene. I had some ideas, but then I began overthinking them, wanting to undermine and complicate.

Mary and Gee ride a couple of ball walkers deep into the woods, where Gee has a shack by his two redwoods.

Gee teaches Fweedle B to Mary, and then turns her psidot off. Mary snaps back into being lifebox Mary. She finds a dog door in her condo wall. Crawls through it. She's inside the percolating fluids of the redwood.

February 19, 2020. Leaving San Lorenzo with Gee.

I was going to have the ball walkers grow wings and fly Gee and Mary to Gee's hidden redwood server. But that's too much trouble. And then I was going to bring in an elephruk from *Frek and the Elixir*, but have its ears be wings. Or maybe I'll make up some new kind of biobot, that's more fun.

Maybe Gee and Mary can fly on Gee's dagon (without an "r," as suggested in a tweet by Richard Kadrey). He looks like a fifth-degree Julia set? I don't know what he'd be made of then. I just see electrical fields—and how can you sit on them? That dagon could be a 3D Zhabotinsky scroll made of slime mold. But how does that fly?

What was that flying thing in *Return to the Hollow Earth*? The thing that fetched Mason and Seela from the sinking *Purple Whale*? Oh, right, a nautilus. So maybe an ultrasnail with buoyant shell. Awfully similar to the nautilus. I rode a big bird in *Million Mile Road Trip* just now. Had a manta ray in *Hylozoic*. A bat might be good.

Or recycle the angelwings from *Frek*. But make them more like happy cloaks. Boneless. Wizard cloaks. Sails on the breeze. Well, maybe later on we'll have some flying. Maybe they'll use those flexing wings to get from Gee's redwood tree camp to the Skyhive yeast dough barn up by the SF Bay. If I do that, would be nice to have the ball walkers in on it somehow. Maybe their heads get enormous?

Oh, fuck it, for now forget flying and ride inside a large, fast-crawling banana slug? Something like a bus. And that's how Gee got to San Lorenzo, he took that same bus. He lives in the woods on the Lost Coast. Ordinarily there wouldn't be a bus, but Gee does an info hack makes the bus-service run one whenever he needs. The bus route has some stupid bogus name. Outof Service. "It's not *Out of Service*, Mary. It's the *Outof Service* line. For me. The out of it guy. Mr. Outoff Itt."

Lost Coast is too far. I'll just put Gee in Big Basin Park.

Okay. So they get to the redwood, and Gee coaches Mary. He's going to turn off Mary's psidot and her clone will be in a coma. And Mary snaps to being lifebox Mary in the cliff city. Maybe Gee fakes clone Mary's death so the Skyhive just sets clone Mary to work like regular unclaimed lifebox.

I did a compressed time passage in—was it *Postsingular*? Where a VR person lives through eighty years in ten minutes of real time. So Mary might feel she's on the cliff for quite a long time.

Still need the details of the Fweedle B hack. Maybe it's a physical intervention on a physical warehouse of yeast mats? The warehouse is run by pot growers.

Upshot: Mary gets her lifebox into the redwood Not sure about her body.

And in a later scene/chapter/story, Skynet burns the redwood, but Gee has set up a server in a cataract. And then Mary does the transcendence move, i.e., she realizes she would have ended up in something like a cataract anyway, without going all around Robin Hood's barn.

February 20-22, 2020. Let It Rain. Looking Ahead.

I should do a little bit of a climate change thing, and have it be raining really a lot in "Mary Mary." I didn't have any rain in "Juicy Ghost," but if I want to weave back the weather change, then in "Juicy Ghost" I might mention that *for once* it's sunny on the Inauguration Day, and that *usually* it's raining, and that the Potomac is swollen, and permanently in a state of flood.

But in "Mary Mary" I'll definitely have it be raining a lot.

Very cyberpunk, right. And the rain will explain why it's common to have vehicles that run on legs, such as Bernardo the thudhumper who's carrying Gee back and forth from his secret grove by Gazos Creek in the Butano State Park at the edge of Big Basin Park, although though I won't say exactly this is where it is.

So on Feb 20, I did put in some rain, starting with the first two days of Mary's posthumous life in her clone. And later I'll add some rain to the first part of the story, but don't want to get hung up just now on revising that part yet again.

Next thing is that Mary gets into Bernardo the thudhumper (like a legged van) and rides cross country to Gee's lair with him and Glory and Miss Max. And as I say, I'll have Gee's server redwood by a cataract in Gazos Creek, so that later on, when Skyhive shock troops torch the redwood, the lifebox codes can migrate from the burning wood into the smoke and thence into the natural computations of the chaotic hydrody-namic flows of the cataract which, in these rainy times, is permanently seething.

And that last move can be where I wrap up this novella, if that's what it is. And if it ends like this, then I could in fact call the tale "Mary Falls" after all, as Mary will be living in a waterfall, like I'd once thought she would.

***

Looking ahead, if I want "Juicy Ghost" and "Mary Mary" to be episodes of a novel-like assemblage (the gold standard here is, of course, Charlie Stross's *Accelerando*), then I have a slight prob with the fact that in "Juicy Ghost" they're using gasoline powered military vehicles, but in "Mary Mary," I'm mostly using biotech. I don't want to over-edit "Juicy Ghost," though. What if in "JG" I mention that it's only military vehicles that use gasoline engines anymore? That would be kind of good.

And the guns? Maybe the guns are just with government people too? No way people would ever let that happen. Only possibility would if all the guns were to go. In fact, maybe by "Mary Mary," guns pretty much aren't around. It's SF, right? Dare to dream the impossible. Time span between "JG" and "MM" could be twenty years.

It would take a separate story to describe getting rid of

guns entirely. It would be some biohack thing, some smart fungus, it goes out and ruins all the guns and ammo in the world—plugs up the barrels, fouls the trigger action, degrades the gunpowder, punctures the shells. That would be fun for a story, or for part of a story. Call it "No Guns.". Maybe Gee Willikers and/or Curtis Winch do that. A Gee Willikers P.O.V. story that happens during the time between So, "JG" and "MM." About Gee teaming up with Curtis the dog. And this could also include something about the birth of Teep Inc and Skyhive. That "early days of commercial telepathy" period that I keep talking about.

But getting rid of the guns that way is more of a biotech thing, which is somewhat (but not entirely) distinct from teep. I mean the gungobbler fungus *could* use teep find the locations of guns, but this would make teep seem like a tool of oppression and government meddling which, I guess, it would be. Alternately the gungobbler mold could literally sniff out guns. But, again, that has nothing to do with teep.

In terms of adding bulk to my collection, I could include "The Mean Carrot," with Gee in the background of this tale. Gee could take the place of that midget inside the carrot. Lev Broadbent. Would be great. Slight problem here is that we have psidots in "JG" and in "MM," but in "MC," we're testing "stumble" fungi, which in fact don't work. So you'd kind of want "MC" to come first. Well, that could be okay, though I *was* liking the idea of starting the book with a real bang in terms of "JG." But, hell, if I can pick up "MC" as an opening chapter, then why not. Need words!

MC -- JG -- NG -- MM

I'm starting to see "MM" as being 20K words long.

Looking at the lengths of "MC", "JG," and "MM" I'd get:

$5,600 + 4,700 + 20K = \sim 30K$.

And that would be about a third of a novel-length book. We'll see.

For the record, here are the official SFWA fiction categories by word length.

Category	Word Count
short story	up to 7.5K
novelette	7.5K to 17.5K

novella	17.5K to 40K
novel	over 40K.

***

My initial idea for the Fweedle B exploit goes like this. They go and put a literal physical capsule of Fweedle B biocode into a yeast mat barn. Mary has to have some "agency" in this scene—she charms someone or does something clever, or uses the ball walkers in an interesting way. And I don't want it just to be that she's flirting with a guard, that's too obvious, and she's got to be able to do more than be sexy.

What *skills* does Mary have? Well, I've mentioned that she's a musician who plays a mandolin. And she's good at managing the ball walkers. How does that get her past the yeast mat barn guards?

Maybe she's playing music at a Friday afternoon Beer Bust at Skyhive. And two other musicians are clones as well. Or the other musicians are the ball walkers, but they're grown hands? Naw.

Kukla, Fran, and Ollie.

After they plant the Fweedle B pod in the yeast mat barn they almost get busted, thanks to Miss Max doing something bad?

February 23-24, 2020. Dough Blimp.

So now I've got Mary in Gee's secret cave by his server redwood up in a canyon off Gazos Creek about twenty miles north of Santa Cruz. The ball walkers Glory and Miss Max are there too, as Gee insisted on bringing them. Gee should have a butler living in the cave, by the way. Mary's asleep. And now she'll wake up and I'll do the yeast mat barn scene. And after the yeast mat barn I have a relatively brief scene of Mary in the Skyhive cliff city for a bit to free herself.

***

What does the yeast mat barn look like, and where is it? In a cabin, in a mall-type building, in one of the two old Moffat Field blimp hangars, in the cube atop Mount Umunhum? I like the blimp hangar. Instead of being a mat, the yeast could be puffy and wrinkled and humped like an irregular cumulus cloud of dough. A lump, a hump.

No longer the *yeast mat barn* (much as I love that triple of monosyllables), but now, hmm, the *yeast hump hanger?* Awkward. I'd like to call it the dough blimp, but I doubt it could float. More like a deflated blimp. Blimp mound, dough pile, rising dough, dough barn. I guess I'll go with dough mound, or sometimes rising dough. Go back and change the name throughout in the story (but leave yeast mat barn in my writing notes before today).

Huge pale object in the blimp hangar, a lumpy mund of dough, and it's puffy and almost lighter than air, but not quite. Like a tired party balloon, or even like a deflated blimp. The tweaked computational yeast in there emits, say, a slight fizz of hydrogen. I'd *prefer* helium, but there are no chemical processes that produce helium. I'll also specify that the blimp is fairly warm, and the hot air in its bubbles adds some lift. The dough is always rising, collapsing, rising some more. There would be an issue around the extreme flammability of hydrogen, so I won't have *much* of that in there. (Skyhive wouldn't be so stupid as it have it full of hydrogen all the time. It would be too predictable to have a dough blimp go up in Hindenburg flames.) If we ever do want it to fly off, we'll load it up with helium. Maybe forget about having the thing float, don't want to go off on a tangent.

I drop hydrogen, as it entails huge worries about fire.

What about the ball walkers? I brought the ball walkers along on impulse because I like them, and wanted to have them reappear from the early part of the story. I thought Gee might somehow use them to raid the dough mound's hanger. So how does that work? Either Gee and Mary plan to *ride* in on the ball walkers, or they plan to send in the ball walkers as *remotes*.

Ride (Unused). Gee could make the ball walkers grow to be about 25 feet tall so they can carry him and Mary in their mouths. But everyone would notice the giant ball walkers, so this would be a terrible move for a covert mission. And they could just as easily ride a thudhumper. And why go to Gee's cave and grow the ball walkers *there*. Well, the cave is close (overland) to the yeast blimp, which is, as I said in one of the old blimp hangars at Moffat Field. But why just ride the ball walkers? They'd drop Gee and Mary by the blimp hangar and wait while they do the mission and then they ride the ball walkers to escape. This is completely boring and impractical. Forget it. But maybe later I can use the "riding in the head of a giant ball walker" in some other scene.

Remotes. Mary and Gee use, respectively, Glory and Miss Max as peripherals. Gee initially sees this as a suicide mission, and would be content to let the ball walkers charge in like kamikazes and puff the Fweedle B spores into the huge yeasty dough mound in the hanger and then get slaughtered. But Mary has pity on the ball walkers and makes an alternate plan. Which actually makes tactical sense—as Gee admits—for then Skyhive won't instantly know they've been hacked.

The ball walkers pretend to be delivering food and drink, as they are used to doing. They're certified as food service workers. They trot into the blimp hangar in the morning during coffee break time. Gee has forged an authorized order for a gift gross of Psycho Donuts for the blimp hangar crew, with the stipulation that he'll meet the delivery ball walkers, take over the goods, and deliver the food himself—to the techs and laborers at the rising-dough hanger. In their ball walker form, Mary and Gee distract the crowd with acrobatic routines, singing bluegrass, and knocking their heads together in a musical way. I originally had that last bit in an earlier scene.

> Glory and Miss Max are playing a game—they're bonking their heads together to make hollow sounds that they modulate by changing the shapes of their open mouths. It sounds like the old folk song, "The Times They Are a Changin." (Or some such.)

At the climax, Gee/Miss-Max spits a dose of Fweedle B in through the door to the dough mound.

Then they leave, acting casual, cadging tips, and moving slowly slowly, and once they're out sight, they run like hell, up through the fields, over the summit, and into the woods.

Along the way—or when they reach the cave—Gee takes Mary's psidot off of Glory, and Mary snaps back into being non-juicy lifebox Mary in the cliff city. She finds the dog door or, maybe better, sees Gee's head pop out of a flaw in the virtual Skyhive-cliff space, and she makes her way to Gee's redwood server.

And then comes the revenge of Skyhive, and the burning of the redwood, and Mary's migration into the cataract, and her pleased and surprised realization that lots of other souls are already in there. 'Twas ever thus.

February 25, 2020. Skyhive Cliff.

I decided I ought to back up and write an initial lifebox-Mary-in-the-Skyhive-cliff-city scene, and put it into the gap between Mary's death and her awakening *in media res* and *flagrante delicto* with Carson.

I see Mary bumming around the cliff city, like an eager yet lonely American tourist on the hills of Lisbon. And maybe she's supposed to go to an orientation meeting where, like, a recording of Leeta lectures them? Naw, skip the lecture, that's just infodump. I can weave in any exposition I need, via lifebox Mary rubbing elbows with others.

March 1, 2020. Final Push?

I think maybe I could finish "Mary Mary" this coming week. If I push. This said, I'm a little tired of pushing on the writing. Feels, then, like I have no life. Also…maybe I don't want to be done.

Evergreen Review rejected "The Mean Carrot," so I went and placed it with the free online zine *Big Echo*, which is a little like my old zine *Flurb*. He accepted it in one day. Yay. They'll put it out in Fall, 2020. At the last minute I tweaked the story one more time, replacing Lev Broadbent by Gee Willikers so it fits into the *Juicy Ghost* cycle.

I still want to do a story about what happens to that guy from "Juicy Ghost" after he turns into a dog. "I Am a Dog."

Backing up, when I say I might finish "Mary Mary," I'm still talking about having Skyhive—or someone else?—destroy Gee's redwood server.

Now, that could be kind of a blackout, or rather, *whiteout* ending, and "the rest is silence." But, in the vein that I'm into these days, there's never a real *need* to stop piling Pelion upon Ossa—and the Matterhorn and K2 on that. That is, I could start a new chapter "Heaven On Earth" after Mary is fully into the *Hylozoic* thing of being a spirit of place, like that stream god that was arguing with Thuy's boyfriend, whatever *his* name was.

Could all this somehow connect to "Everything is Every-thing"? But now that I reread that story, it doesn't actually even have telepathy in it, or lifeboxes. It would be a bit much to drag in the EP aliens and the Absolute Continuum. "Thus vitiating the plausibility of the entire construct." So drop that story from the fix-up.

The fix-up game's goal is connecting the three freely concocted story-inkblots I made. And adding a couple more. Maybe I could do a painting of all that. A canvas with scenes reflecting Mean Carrot, Juicy Ghost, Mary Mary. And the one or two more, "I Am a Dog" and "Heaven on Earth."

I do want to write the dog story. Why can't I remember that guy's name from "Juicy Ghost?" Cliff? Clint? *Curtis Winch.* Kind of a stupid name. Maybe it's okay that it's stupid. And Winch itself means clockwork. Curtis not quite right. Curt is okay though, you've got Kurt Gödel in there, and I like that "curt" can mean "rudely succinct." As a boy I saw Curtiss Saf-T-Pop lollipops with a loop of string instead of a hard stick so you could eat them in the car without putting out your sister's eye—or you could fall on your Saf-T-Pop, if you're a toddler.

***

More than usual, these days I wonder if I'm losing my mind. But then I relax and get into doing something and forget to worry.

I've had a couple of acquaintances or friends die in the last few months. In church today I was really getting into the reality of that. No phone to look at. In the pew in front of us was a lady whose husband of 59 years died this month. Always there were two of them, and now there's one. Internalizing the reality that this will happen with Sylvia and me.

I've had a mysterious intense pain in the back of my head all week. A tumor? I'm about to drop dead? The web says it might be an "arthritis headache." Aleve or Celebrex don't seem to improve it much. So distracting, day after day. Yoga maybe helps a little bit. If it was from eyestrain, it would probably be more in the front of my head. Possibly it's from typing on my laptop a lot.

Last week, my granddaughter was singing "My Grandfa-ther's Clock," with the closing line, "And it stopped. Short.

Never to run again, when the old man died." I sang that song in gradeschool. Somehow the last line struck me back then as slightly amusing. "Surprise, Grandpa!"

March 7, 2020. Being a Ghost.

The story's been going really well, I'm having fun, getting totally loose, putting in odd lists of things, making it colloquial, allowing sentence fragments, goofing around. My recent lack of success in selling any of my stories is, in a way, liberating, in that, since I won't be able to sell it anyway, I might as well write what I really like.

And now I'm nearly at the end—although possibly there could be another story after this one. Right now, I've gotten this far:

> "I'm gone," says Mary. By now she fully under-stands what Gee wants her to do. It's something she too has thought about, off and on, for many years. Move to the next level. The astral plane, the spirit world. Become a ghost. Abandon your flesh body and the computer simulations, and move into—
> Thin air.

Now what? I need a nice end.

I just looked back at my very first entry in these writing notes, October 18-24, 2018. Seeds for "Juicy Ghost." In there I suggest that I'd like to end up by blending my lifebox ghosts into the traditional afterworld. I keep flinching away from doing that. It's technically tricky, and there's a risk of corn, bathos, and flop. But I want to go for it. It's fresh, and it can give me a *wow* for the end of "Mary Mary," and set me up for, as I say, a story after that.

Going back to that Oct, 2018, note, here's an edited passage describing what I want to do.

> For our ghosts, we'll use natural processes based on chaos and naturally occurring quantum computation. When Mary migrates to that platform, she senses that other, similar, beings are present—and these are in fact traditional ghosts. All along people's ghosts have been

migrating into the hylozoic/panpsychic matrix of matter.

So Mary becomes a real ghost. An ambient natural computation that requires no server. She's, like, a tangle of vortices in the air currents.

Maybe air currents are too evanescent? The reason I'd been thinking of a *waterfall* as a host is that a waterfall pattern is a somewhat stable chaotic attractor that stays located in a specific place. This said, consider the turbulence in the "wind shadow" of a tree in a spot where there's a steady or at least recurrent breeze. Like a cataract pool, such a spot would host a stable chaotic attractor, a nest of dynamical gnarl that tend to have a generally consistent configuration.

Water or air, however, I can't easily see a pattern of turbulence moving back and forth all around the Bay Area like I'd like ghost Mary to be able to do. This said, remember the trope of someone feeling a chilly air current just as a ghost appears.

Getting away from using a mundane fluid-flow-chaotic-attractor lifebox host, I could sling the BS and talk about some rubber physics. I'll just have to mull it over.

- Ectoplasm.
- Knotted patterns of aethereal vibrations.
- Wormholes in Hilbert space.
- Quintessence, kessence (cf. *Frek*), dark energy, dark matter.
- Quantum entanglement, quantum foam.
- The transfinitely detailed absolute continuum. (Fits with "Everything is Everything.")

First thought, best thought: call it ectoplasm. And postpone or skip explaining what that stuff is.

One sometimes thinks of ghosts as being hungry, and wanting to latch onto people. This fits in with the juicy angle. Maybe a ghost needs a host to be fully functional. Juicy ghost.

So we'll give ghost Mary the ability to run a peripheral physical body. Akin to the So, Skyhive setup where a lifebox runs a peripheral via a psidot.

The ghost Mary "lifebox" is ambient and requires no server. But does ghost Mary need to use a psidot to control her clone or a biobot?

GHOST DOES POSSESSION

Ghost Mary doesn't bother with the psidot. She wafts into Gee's cave and settles onto clone Mary like a flesh-eating jellyfish on her prey. Possibly she's aided by the Spork code that she remembers from being a lifebox. But she doesn't bother with Miu Miu.

It's only an ectoplasm ghost who's been a lifebox that can easily do possession. That Spork code stands them in good stead. It's almost like they have a built-in psidot.

Note that we don't see *lifeboxes* possessing people without using a psidot. I'm saying the real ghosts are more powerful than lifeboxes, thanks to being made of ectoplasm.

Note that we don't see *old-time ghosts* possessing people very often, if ever. Reported cases are from marginal or mentally ill people, and it's not at all a daily event. I'm saying the old-time ghosts can't do possession because they don't know Spork.

OR – GHOST USES LIFEBOX?

Nah. Awkward. To start with, we'd have the issue of how the ghost connects to the psidot itself. If you're inside the Skyhive server or Gee's redwood server, then the lifebox-to-psidot channel is built in, based on the Spork language. But if you're a cloud of ectoplasm, the connection is up to you. Well, perhaps if you're a lifebox *before* you become a true ghost, you bring the Spork capability with you and thus, a fortiori, the ability to communicate with a psidot. And maybe a psidot is easier for the ghost to influence than a person's mind. But why bother with the detour. Note that if you *can* possess a person, then you could possess the psidot too. But it's better to pick the one channel and stick to it—and that channel would be old-school possession.

POLTERGEISTS

Can the ghost move objects? Spiritualists say that ghosts can do things like rap on tables. Or we could go all the way to having poltergeists. Breaking glasses, like that. If Mary can do possession, why not do poltergeist. Like the one in Sheckley's *Immortality Inc.*

***

Loose metaphor: relative to a lifebox, a psidot functions like a Ouija board, in terms of letting the lifebox mind manage a biological peripheral.

***

Can I use a variant on the "Everything Is Everything" scenario in a story after "Mary Mary"? If we have real ghosts, then we might have disembodied aliens. But, as I think I said before, this might be a bridge too far. Seems like I have enough balls in the air by now, with material for a couple more stories if we want.

But maybe. If I do the alien ghosts thing, it would be a later story in the collection. The role model for such overweening ambition is always Charles Stross' *Accelerando*, where he kept on doubling and redoubling the strange.

March 8, 2020. Redwood Vulva.

This morning I woke up with an image for the scene where Mary exits the redwood in the form of a standalone ghost. The redwood puffs ghost Mary out of a hole, in the form of ectoplasm. Like when, years ago, a billboard on Times Square would blow smoke rings of steam. Visually the ectoplasm ghost will look more like a mushroom cap or a jellyfish 3D Zhabo scroll than like a smoke ring. A vortex ring in either case. The tweaked redwood does a particle accelerator or quantum computation thing along the hole's rim to form this ghostly sheet.

What is the hole like? Redwoods often have hollowed out "hermit shelters" in the bottom parts of their trunks. I can use one of those. The ghost comes out of such a hole, urged on by tingling bioelectricity along the labial arch of the ridge or scar that surrounds the roughly isosceles triangle of the opening. We even have a bit of a rim at the base of the hole. It's totally a vulva. Initially I visualized a broken-off branch, a hollow stub, a penile cannon, but a vulva is much better for birth, and for fitting with the fact that Mary's a woman.

And if Mary is a traditional ectoplasmic ghost who knows

Spork, then she doesn't need to use a psidot. Fuck the psidot. She settles onto clone Mary like a shroud, sinks into that tasty young-woman flesh, and *wah-la*! Our holy Mary is fully alive again, in a twenty-something bod. Happy ending.

A hint of further developments at the end. She *can* leave her body and travel around as an ectoplasm ghost. Therefore, she's now like a powerful witch. A concern: leaving your body untended is risky, as another ghost might slip in and occupy your perch. "Be careful, Mary!" Perhaps she can learn to split her attention and keep a low-level watch going in her body while she's out flitting around.

Oh, one more thing: Mary should notice very soon that there are plenty of naturally arising ectoplasm ghosts around. Maybe she glimpses one in the clearing almost right away, but it darts off. (Who would it be? Oscar?) I did the other-ghosts routine in *White Light*, come to think of it. But, due to Mary's unnatural origin, she'll be a bit different from the old-school ectoplasmic ghosts. A bit sprightlier. Juicier, because she has that connection with her meat body. *And* she knows Spork.

And I need to address the question of whether there will be more "souls" making the journey from the Skyhive lifebox to Gee's redwood and then on to incarnation as an ectoplasmic ghost.

Maybe just the twelve other lifeboxes who broke out from Skyhive. Mary's apostles. All women.

Well, there's also the hundred or so old friends of Gee who are in the redwood.

Maybe at the end, there's an attack on the redwood and it goes up in flames, and Mary is milling around with the newly incarnated ectoplasmic ghosts from Gee's server, and there's a struggle to come. It ends with Mary saying somethin brave or accepting, a "To Be Continued" moment that can also be read as closing things off.

***

Loose ends. What about Carson? Better to kill him off—not sure how. Don't want Mary to do it directly. Maybe Gee does it. Or, I've got it, the thudhumper driver Bernardo. And who gets Mary's house? Kayla would back out of the contract.

Will the ectoplasmic ghost business take hold and grow? Probably Leeta would want to be in on it.

March 12, 2020. "Mary Mary," Ver 1.

I pushed hard on the story for a few more days and I got it done. I started on Jan 22, so it took six weeks. Feels like longer, as I've been focusing on it so intently. 15K words, which seems just right. I'll send it to Sheila at *Asimov's* once I give it a full read-through. I thought about her a number of times while writing it.

Has a happy ending, Mary and Gee hook up. At the end, Gee doesn't actually kill his present body, he'll just turn his lifebox into an ectoplasm ghost and put it into a clone, so there will be two of him.

I sent it to Marc Laidlaw. He said he liked the characters and that it flowed, with "something always going on." He said should trim down the infodumps, the mini-lectures to Mary, and I'll do that.

What happens sometimes is that when I'm figuring out what comes next, I start "vamping," that is, have my characters going on at length about the emerging and as yet inchoate plan. Once I've actually written the scene I'm leading up to, *then* I have to go and trim down the prefiguring. Another point is that, if the reader can just read the scene and see it happen, then I don't really need to describe it in advance all that much. The average reader doesn't want to read all that much explanation anyway. That's just the author being like a hen cackling over her egg. Before she lays it.

I can totally see more *Juicy Ghost* stories. I want one about Curtis Winch being a dog after he kills Treadle. Maybe he bites someone. And Leeta and Gee starting Skyhive. Or more ectoplasm ghost scenes. Would probably want to think of some overarching problem to carry from story to story. Like Annalee Newitz did in *History of an Alternate Timeline*, which was kind of like a fix-up or mosaic of stories.

There may yet be a place for "Everything is Everything." Or I could expand it.

March 15, 2020. "Mary Mary," Ver 2.

It's taking me a few days. Like revising a chapter of a novel, which often takes a week. Eventually I'll need to go over the "Juicy Ghost" story again to tighten the fit.

One issue I see is that in "Juicy Ghost" I had Gee Willikers as more of a 2D figure, characterized by his incessant compulsive giggle. And I can't have him do this in "Mary Mary" as he's 3D here, and mutates into a male lead. So at some point I need to balance out the giggling. "Mary Mary" is five or ten or fifteen years later, so we could suppose that he's learned to giggle less.

I'll put a *little* giggling into "Mary Mary," and I include a passage like this, with Gee talking at the start:

"Sorry about the giggle. It's an old neurotic tic. From growing up on the spectrum. I'm better at socializing now. Somewhat better." He giggles.

March 18, 2020. "Teep" as a Mosaic Novel.

So I finished the revision…it took almost a week, like revising a chapter of a novel. I got the plot threads and motivations all straightened out, including a slowly developing romance between Mary and Gee…which I hadn't initially seen coming, but that's good. Sylvia's reading it now, and she likes it, and I'm glad about that. She likes that Mary is "feisty." A believable woman character, I hope.

Like I said, I'll send it to Sheila at *Asimov's*, although with NYC on shelter-in-place or lockdown, it may be a while till she processes it. Hoping for a break, I'll send it to her in person as well as to the *Asimov's* submission portal (!). Maybe she'll have spare time, and will quickly read it, for the hell of it, and say yes.

***

I noticed yesterday that Bruce Sterling self (?) published a story on the no-filter high-visibility *Medium* site…not a bad idea. I might do that with my next orphan story. I have to wonder if *Analog* is ever going to read "Everything Is Everything." I'm not real familiar with what they're like these days. When I met the editor Trevor Quachi at a con a couple of years ago, he assured me that he'd like something by me. Just now I looked at their page online, and maybe I could fit in there. They have stuff by Benford, and the story titles sound cool. I'll wait another couple of months and see.

On the publishing front, *Big Echo* decided to publish "The Mean Carrot" in a special Quarantine Issue, which came out just the other day. He used my new painting *Pandemic #1: Infection* for the front illo for the ezine. And, hooray, he took my advice on the site design, making the prose easier to read. Before the contrast was too low, and the background page was translucent, forever showing a crescent moon underneath.

***

What do I write next? The obvious move is to return to my notion of a novel that's a mosaic of stories. I'm interested in Mary and Gee, and I could try and write another whole story about them,

At times I've said the novel might be called *Juicy Ghosts*, but I think I'll leave that for that one story title, and call the novel *Teep* [later I named it *Juicy Ghosts*].

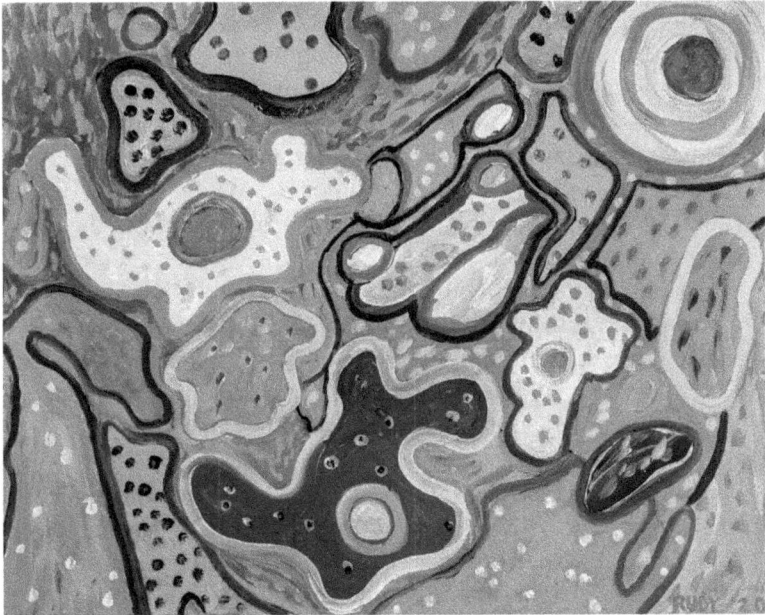

Figure 17: *Pandemic #1: Infection*

Certainly there's a lot of options in the situation that we reached by the end of "Mary Mary." The ghosts, etc.

On the other hand, I'm so glad to have finished that story and "gotten out of the joint in time," that I don't want to venture back in there.

***

I'd had the idea that "Everything is Everything" could be a later story in the contemplated collection. I could tweak it to work as a "sequel" to "Mary Mary." Push it farther into the future. Alternately, I could have it been an early story in the collection, kind of laying groundwork for a later outburst, and then circle back to it later. Once we have ectoplasmic ghosts, it wouldn't be that much of a stretch to bring in aethereal aliens from the Absolute Continuum. Would that be overdoing it?

I'll reread "E is E," and see if that leads anywhere, I could run it after "Mary Mary," and totally change the story to be in the future, possibly publishing the original in its present form.

***

I kind of wanted to do a story about Curtis Winch as a dog. Possibly this could be from the point of view of a kid in the family that "owns" the Arfie-type dog whom Curtis Winch is now using as a biobot remote, via the psidot that Curtis put onto the skin on the underside of the dog's earflap. Have the kid be a girl…naturally I think of Georgia and Isabel. Call her Emma? If I could swing it, would be nice to have her be Black. (2020 style guides for black vs. Black are mixed these days, safer to go with Black.)

What would happen in this story? I'd need a story arc with a problem, a resolution, and a twist. And I'd want to advance the action/world-building of the over-all mosaic novel.

Yawn, Losing interest in the dog story and, for that matter, the mosaic novel. But I'll circle back to it soon.

***

A pandemic story would be apropos just now. Seems kind of superficial to write about anything else. But it'll be a mob scene, all the writers at once. Wouldn't want to do it in an overly literal way, not "hitting the nail on the head," not "ripped from today's headlines." Something oblique and allusive.

***

Or maybe, on the surface at least, turn my back on all this bullshit and write something completely escapist or transreal with, no doubt, the pandemic subtext nonetheless.

March 23-24. 2020. I'm 73. Hvalship?

March 22 was my 74th birthday. Two times 37.

I was 37 in 1983—a time of renewal, a year after I'd lost my teaching job at Randolph-Macon, and after Sylvia and I had patched up our marriage. I'd embarked on a hot run of writing books on my Selectric typewriter, working in the office I'd rented in an abandoned building on Church St. in downtown Lynchburg.

I used to bring the typewriter home in my car every evening so the bums (who occasionally broke in) wouldn't steal it. In March, 1983, I was finishing my big book, *The Fourth Dimension*, and that summer I started *Master of Space and Time*. Half a lifetime ago. I wrote six books in four years, 1982-1986. One of the high points of my life, that period, though I didn't quite realize it at the time.

Anyway, here at the end of my second 37 years, Sylvia phoned up seven of our nearby neighbors, and they gathered on the street outside our front door, everyone staying six feet apart, and when Sylvia led me out, semi-unsuspecting, they sang *Happy Birthday*, with my neighbor Gerault and his son playing trumpet and trombone. So touching. Sylvia managed to video it on her phone, and her singing makes my heart brim over, a bit off-key, but the pure tone of her high, heartfelt voice on the first iteration of the words "to you"—*oh*. Dear Sylvia. My lover, my twin.

***

These days we're under "house arrest," that is a "shelter in place" order— thanks to the coronavirus We go out to buy food about twice a week, and we try and take a walk every day, sometimes driving to a park. You can order take-out food as well, but no movie theaters, no coffee shops, no library. In terms of my habits, there's *especially* no place outside the house where I can write on my laptop—at least until the unpredictable (like me) March weather clears up, and then I might sit on a bench to write in the little Los Gatos park by the post office.

The virus is so global, very strange. I don't like pandemic novels, and now I'm in one. I've done a *Pandemic #2* painting now. Very ab-ex, and with beautiful colors and fun passages of rough impasto brushwork. I might do a third, and have it represent people being cooped up.

Figure 18: *Pandemic #2: Panic*

***

As for my next story, how about that flash for a story that I had a zillion years ago, "Starship and Hvalship"? Though back then I spelled it Vaalship. I'll print out that note and look at it while I wait for my car to get a smog check. I'm driving out for that right now, a great adventure!

Okay, I do still like the start, with the starship and the lighter—this is the concrete part that I've worked out. But it's so close to being a replay of *Frek and the Elixir*.

They go to Mistport and my character works on a hvalship. Maybe he or she catches something like a sea cucumber, and brings the creature home, or a piece of it like the pineal gland.

Again, there's the matter of finding a story arc. Problem, reversal, lover, enemy, growth, the grail…all that. Doesn't have to be "he," I might as well make it a "she."

March 25-April 1, 2020. Hvalship and Krake. (Abandoned.)

Simplify the "Hvalship" story. Keep it on one planet. The pickup vehicle is like a local flying thing, and the people in it might be what they used to call a press gang in the 1850s, from "pressing into service." The abductors were also called *crimps* (great word).

The planet could be future Earth or, I think better, for a change, a completely alien world. For now, let's call it Boongo. Or, no, let's make it Boone. Simpler, less distracting.

Of course, to some extent, a future Earth *can* be as alien as we might need. Because biotech. Cf. *Frek and the Elixir*, which was in year 3003. But if it's an alien world, I'm completely free of any constraints, which would be fun. I think of Ursula Leguin's *Left Hand of Darkness*, although she does have a human main character for the POV in that one. And her natives are humanoid…indeed maybe they're part of a human-sparked interstellar empire, don't exactly remember.

An all-aliens story would be kind of new for me, a hard-core SF thing. I think even when I've had alien worlds, I've always had humans involved, but I just as soon do without the humans for once. It might enrich the alien world. Re. alien worlds, I've done a ton of them, but often they're quite sketchy, more like stops on picaresque journeys, as in *Frek* and *MMRT* and *Mathematicians in Love*. And I had alien characters in a couple of my very early Sheckley-inspired stories like "Jumpin' Jack Flash" and "The Facts of Life."

Of course, if your characters are totally alien, readers tend not to care about them. That's where the galactic civilization move comes handy. But doing true aliens…that could be fun, for a story or novelette. Hard to carry it through a novel length.
***

So the jolly, but not really all that friendly, crimps recruit our character. A girl or a boy?

Could be a girl like one of my daughters and/or grand-daughters. Izzy, Georgia, Althea, Zimry, Jasper. Could call her

Zee or Z-bomb, Z-bert. or Zeedie.

But I've done quite a few female main characters of late so why not relax and make it easy and use a boy modeled on myself. A transreal 13-year-old Rudy...I don't think I've written much SF about that part of my life. Going from Louisville to that boarding school in the Black Forest for nearly a year, and the boys at Louisville Country Day picking on me and ostracizing me, that's rich material. High school is mostly in *Secret of Life* already. I have a table about all this in one of my various novel's *Notes* documents, but I don't feel like looking for it today.

I do know that I have written about Frek Huggins, who was, I think 12, and Scud & Villy Antwerpen in *MMRT*, who were about 15 and 18. And Chu in *Hylozoic* was about 14. But what if I drop way down and have the boy be 10...that's an age I really haven't written about. Might be easier for me to write about that part of my life if the "boy" and his family and everyone else is an alien. Call him Ruggles. Yes.

The craft is a blobble. A bit like a lighter-than-air jellyfish. Should Ruggles bring a pet along? Okay, but I can't have a pet dog *again*. And not a cat. Some animalcule that's small, and it can talk, a little bit, little words like "if" and "it." Maybe in insubstantial thing that lives in Ruggles's body, or, visually more interesting, *on* his body, like a tattoo or a leech. A bit like a Happy Cloak, or like those Flatsie critters in *MMMRT*. It could perhaps be shaped like a silhouette of a dog, and it moves around on Ruggles's skin, like the tattoos on the woman in Gibson's *Agency*.

The crimps take Ruggles to Mistport, which, if this were on planet Earth, rather than being the planet Boone, would be somewhere near where (the now-melted) Antarctica used to be. Down on the tip of some continent, or on a biggish island. I want to walk the streets of Mistport.

The ship itself is akin to a biotweaked whale. And if, again, we were on Earth, rather than on Boone, it would have been developed by Danes and Norwegians, whose word for "whale" is "hval," and that's why it's a hvalship.

Basic plot idea is that Ruggles gets hold of some prize and brings it back home and in some fashion ameliorates the situation in his home and his village.

***

The hvalship is, as I say, something like a sperm whale but with a basin on the top where the passengers/sailors have their lodgings. Same general design as an elephruk. It's hunting for something like giant squid. A prey that we use for food, or perhaps for some subtle essence

And so the primeval foes—whale and giant squid—continue their unending fictional combat, which is a rich analog for the human battle of the sexes, although said battle is probably not one of Ruggles's concerns, although, yes there may be trouble between his parents.

We might suppose the krakes are highly intelligent but are viewed by the humanoid characters as malevolent enemies, and certain sailors even feel a righteous zeal in killing krakes.

It may be that Ruggles finds a creature called yeeyee that seems to be distinct from the krakes that they're fishing for. And the yeeyee will somehow cure a problem that's presented at the outset. (As in a Myth of the Hero!) Kicker: when Ruggles brings the yeeyee home, it indeed accomplishes some needed fix, but it presents a new, greater problem, which Ruggles solves.

The yeeyee will be, as it turns out, a larval stage of a krake. They find it in the krake's flesh, and they initially suppose it's a distinct creature that the krake had swallowed, or possibly a parasite that's lodged within the krake. Like a tiny oyster crab. But really it's a larva. Or maybe I should do it the other way around, yeah. They think it's a larva but it's a parasite, and something quite different.

***

But, you know, the "Hvalship" story idea isn't doing it for me. I mean, it's a huge galumphing epic with mongo world-building involved. I want something simple and light. A low-effort story for pinheads, and written by a pinhead. A story that centers around something that I care about. Also I want to see a cool wish-fulfillment scene or device at my story's core. Also I want something that isn't so cryptomnesic, that is, so close to things I've done before although I've half-forgotten that I did them.

A kid bringing home a squid parasite from an alien Antarctic Sea? I don't think so. Too *Hollow Earth*, too *Frek*.

I need a simpler story idea.

April 2, 2020. Golden Age Goodie. The Flickit.

I keep thinking, off and on, that there will be a big new physics discovery before too long. A new force, a new technique. Something as big as transistors, or the computer, or biotech.

Would it be at some unprecedented small size scale? Well, I did something like that in my recent "Everything is Everything," in one of my "Six Thought Experiments in the Philosophy of Computation" (that is, in "Experiment Six: Hello, Infinity"), and in "Jack and the Aktuals," This time around I'd like to steer clear of infinity, quantum mechanics, and psychic phenomena.

So, okay, stay at or normal size scale, and stay awake. Or like walking around a town in a weird way and finding a new layer of reality, like in *Jim and the Flims*, although *not* actually that. By the way I got the street-maze-portal-to hidden-world move from Robert Sheckley.

Something *new*. Possibly an unusual yoga position could to it. Forming your body into a multiply connected surface or a knot, although here's there's a whiff of my story "Inside Out." And there's a different topological MacGuffin in Martin Gardner's, "A Subway Named Mobius."

Something more like peeling off a decal and seeing a steel (or gold!) surface underneath.

Or maybe draw on the fourth dimension, as in "The Captured Cross-Section" or the lesser-known "Willows Island." Lots of 4D stuff in my *Spaceland*, of course. And in *The Sex Sphere* and in *Realware* and in *MMRT*. Maybe there's still a trick I missed?

I'm thinking in terms of the Golden Age story trope where a huge new scientific breakthrough is made by an eccentric and relatively uneducated man. This character is a stand-in for a member of the SF-writer's target audience.

My friend Nathaniel Hellerstein likes to imagine there being some kind of simple invention that we've all overlooked. A "simple tool" as fundamental and obvious as the wheel, the lever, the screw, or the inclined plane. He calls his tool the flickit. I kind of see it as small pry-bar, angled up at one end.

You step on the angled part and the flickit spins into the air. And, um, then what?

April 9-10, 2019. *"Everything is Everything"* Addition

I've been corresponding with Jim Buckmaster, a fiftyish guy who's CEO of Craig's List. He just bought two of my paintings, *Mexico* and *Gubs and Wormholes*. He is, naturally, an intelligent man, and is interested in some of the same things as me. He mentioned that he wished "E is E" was a novel. I'm getting just about zero feedback on my fiction these days, so this comment was enough to get me to reread the story (as I'd been talking about doing), and decide that, yes, more scenes in this world would be fun.

I don't know a novel, and it wouldn't necessarily have to be a second story, even. I might just make the present story longer. And maybe, just maybe, it could come to life and become a novel.

Maybe I'll abandon any Procrustean notion of shoe-horning the "E is E" sequel into the *Teep* novel (currently just a story cycle). That cycle can stop at three for now, that is, "Mean Carrot," "Juicy Ghost," "Mary Mary." And maybe another story there, someday, but for now I'll go off on a different path. I'd like the "E is E" world to be a separate timeline of its own.

So I'll do some light revisions on "E is E" to get going on it again, and then add a scene.

What I'll do is to remove the telegraphing remark that the EPs can switch to living in crows after the wasp hives die down in the winter. Instead, I'll show that happening, that is, show the wasps dying off and the EPs coming to Wick and Vi and saying they want some help in getting new bodies.

By the way, I ought to have names for the EPs. Something kind of alien and abstract. Spa and Fon would be a natural— that's a pair of words from a golden age comic frame that is a talisman among comix cognoscenti. From EC Comics, *Weird Fantasy*. R. Crumb quoted the "spa" "fon" exchange them in his *Head Comix*. A comics fanzine used the words as a title, and there was even a student/indie movie with the title *Item 72-D: The Adventures of Spa and Fon*. I could use them yet again, although the names are too jokey and sunny. I'd want something a little darker and more alien for the names of the EPs. Let's go with Qoph and Fon. Qoph has that Kabala and transfinite set theory vibe, so it's good. And the Fon for good luck.

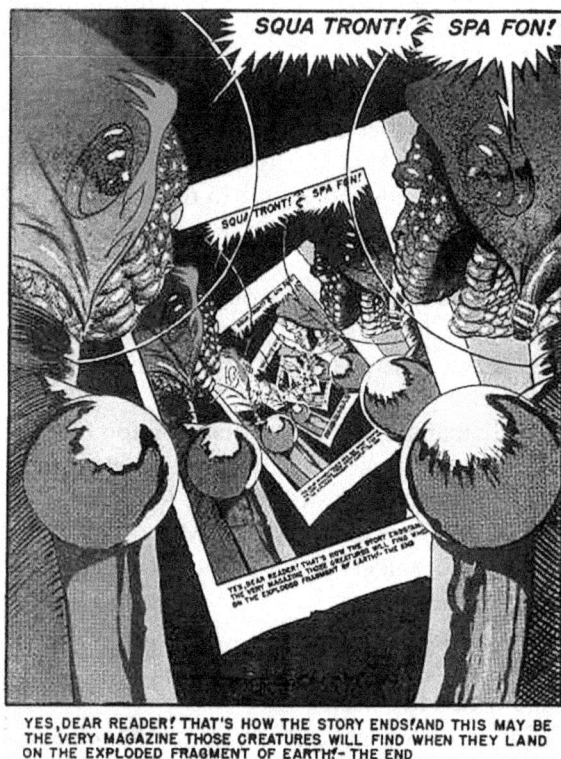

YES, DEAR READER! THAT'S HOW THE STORY ENDS! AND THIS MAY BE THE VERY MAGAZINE THOSE CREATURES WILL FIND WHEN THEY LAND ON THE EXPLODED FRAGMENT OF EARTH!- THE END

Figure 19: Classic "Spa Fon" Illo from EC Comics

Another thing about "qoph" (a letter of the Hebrew alphabet) is that a couple of days ago I was obsessing about the 2-letter pangram: "Zing! Vext cwm fly jabs Kurd qoph." And I made up this bogus explication of it:

"Zing: Cosmic birth, astral big bang. Vext: Torn by life's duality. Cwm: Circular world navel. Fly: Above material plane. Jabs: First act, free will. Kurd: Shepherd of secret religion. Qoph: Monogrammaton encodes All."

Was worth tweeting this, I thought…and turned out to be

my most popular tweet this month.

In "EisE2," before the winter die-off kicks in, and while still being wasps, the two alien EPs will have found some human EPs they'd care to dispossess. It's a couple who live, on the huge white house we see up on the crest of mountain behind us, I think it's on Aztec Road.

(I always imagine that the wife in the house is that Olympic ice-skating star, Peggy Fleming, who lives in Los Gatos. I've seen her, when she had a shop selling wine from her own estate up there; I don't know how they'd have enough grapes. I don't think she really does live in that white house, it's just what I like to imagine. I believe she married her teenage sweetheart who is now a well-off (I imagine) dermatologist, and they have children and grandchildren.)

But the woman in the house won't be Peggy Fleming. She'll be a big-time realtor, and her husband will be an SV billionaire, maybe not a creative one like Woz, more like a VC hedge-funders. Or what if he's a virus-vaccine scammer or trader. What to call them? I always loved the names of the local gentry, Hunk and Moo Anderson. Have mine be Barn and Sox Whitsitt. So annoyingly Anglo-Saxon.

And the wasp-embodied ET aliens have scoped out Barn and Sox, and they've decided they should move in on them. And they want Wick and Vi to help smooth the way. For plot purposes, I'll suppose that an EP plenum-dweller can't displace you unless you agree to it. Like making a deal with the devil.

Quibble: what about the wasps, did they get permission to replace the wasps? Oh, sure, why not. The wasps are, you understand, intelligent in their own way (more on this in my note of April 20, 2020).

They *could* have just outright murdered the former wasp queen, just as they *could* have murdered Wick and Vi, or *could* murder Barn and Sox, but that's considered bad form and declassé and is also, for intricate reasons, karmically dangerous, and in a very literal way (details later, after I invent them).

I pause to wonder if of maybe the EP aliens could go into being crows instead of wasps. I had a person turn into a wasp in "Juicy Ghost," already. But, nah, leave it that way. Having the EPs go and be wasps for a few months makes them seem so inhuman. And, who knows, maybe there could eventually be some connection between the "JG" and the "E is E" wasps.

April 13-16, 2020. Revising "Complete Stories."

I added "Surfers at the End of Time," "The Mean Carrot," and my updated version of "Juicy Ghost" to my *Complete Stories* antho. And it was time to move a few stories from the print Vol 2 to the print Vol 1, so as to keep the volumes at about the same size. So I had to update the two print covers to reflect the change in contents.

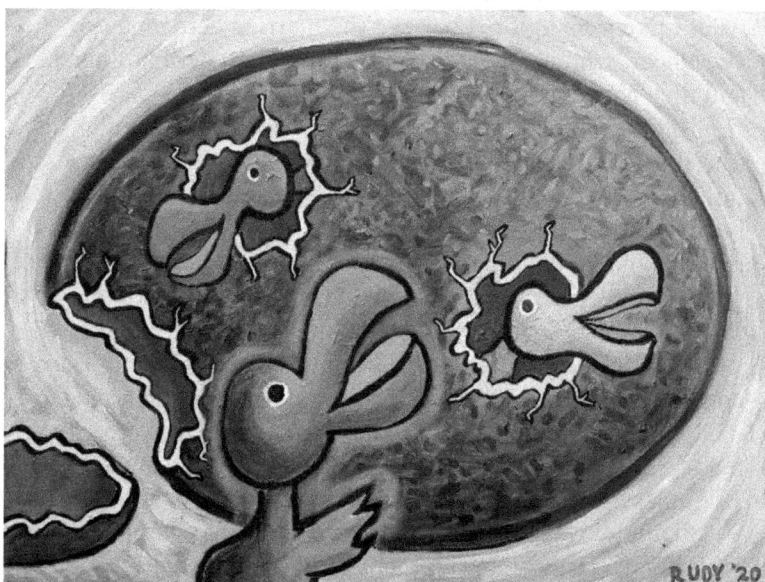

Figure 20: *Happy Egg*

What makes this a fairly taxing job is that there are so many channels involved. The free webpage, the two print volumes for Amazon and for Lightning, and the ebook editions for Amazon, Draft2Digital and e-Junkie. I make a DOC of the new stories, with newly written story notes, then I emplace that into the InDesign file, save that that file as a PDF for the print editions, also export the InDesign file as an EPUB for the ebook editions, then extract the HTML-formatted stories from the EPUB code and paste it into the HTML for the free online edition.

Meanwhile I've started a new painting called *Happy Egg*. Finished it on April 20, 2020.

I ended up giving it to granddaughter Zimry when she and son Rudy were here on Sunday, May 17. 2020. screwing struts on the underside of our porch deck.

April 20, 2020. "E is E" Extension? Wolfram Science Project.

So, *analog* rejected "E is E." A little over their heads, I guess. Or too surreal. So that leaves me free to work on it some more. I'll try and start that work tomorrow or maybe even tonight.

The story was already rejected by *Asimov's* and *Lightspeed*, who are the only pro places where I've published in the last few years. I'm still hoping *Asimov's* takes "Mary Mary," and if not, maybe I put that story into the underground free ezine *Big Echo*, so that all three *Juicy Ghost* stories are in there. So I won't send anything else to *Big Echo* till I know whether "Mary Mary" will need a home. And if *Asimov's* does take "Mary Mary," then I could always put "E is E" into *Big Echo* this summer or fall.

But for now, I might as well try "E is E" on *Evergreen Review*. John Oakes was semi-encouraging when he rejected "The Mean Carrot." Possibly that story was a bit un-PC, what with the heroine working a job that's similar to prostitution—although she *isn't* in fact a prostitute at all. But, still.

I'll do a quick revision on "E is E" and send that off to Oakes tomorrow or the next day—in accord with the freelancer's precept, "Keep it bounding." I'll say that it's surreal contemporary social satire, like George Saunders and Kate Folk's stories in the *New Yorker*.

And soon maybe I'll manage to start on a second scene for "E is E". I have a new Maguffin I might use. *Rulial space*. Although, really, the Absolute Continuum is enough—if I do rulial space, that probably ought to be a completely different story. Or, yet again, maybe I should swap in rulial, and drop

Absolute Continuum, as I've written about it before. Well, have them both, but have rulial the whole time so it's different. from "Jack and the Aktuals," which was my earlier Absolute Infinite story.

***

What is rulial space?

Well, there's this new fundamental theory of physics that Stephen Wolfram has come up with. He has some intriguing lines towards the end of his shortish popular sketch of the theory online.

He starts with the idea that a simple set of graph-rewriting rules can be seeded with some minimal starting pattern like two dots, and then, if recursively reapplied to its successive outputs, the rules will generate interestingly complex and gnarly patterns. It's a standard Wolfram move—like fractals, or CAs, or chaotic systems. And this might be how our universe arises. Nothing new.

But then, being Wolfram, he kicks it up a level and another level and another. He considers the option of running several sets of rules from the rule set, and seeing what you get. A multiway rule, as it were. And then he escalates to the idea of using *all* possible sets of rules. And somehow there emerges a single over-arching "world." And in this world, each viewer "sees" through the filter of their own particular update rules that they regard as the "laws of nature." Wolfram calls this congeries of world-views "**rulial** space."

Here's two quotes.

> I've always assumed that any entity that exists in our universe must at least "experience the same physics as us". But now I realize that this isn't true. There's actually an almost infinite diversity of different ways to describe and experience our universe, or in effect an almost infinite diversity of different "planes of existence" for entities in the universe— corresponding to different possible reference frames in rulial space, all ultimately connected by universal computation and rule-space relativity.
>
> ***

But there is something perhaps more bizarre that is possible. While we view our universe—and reality—through our particular type of description language, there are endless other possible description languages which can lead to descriptions of reality that will seem coherent (and even in some appropriate definition "meaningful") within themselves, but which will seem to us to correspond to utterly incoherent and meaningless aspects of our universe.

This line of speculation segues into my ongoing SF obsession with describing thoughts of stars, wasps, atoms, plants, stones, etc. I worked on this in my novels *Postsingular* and *Hylozoic*. But there's hints of new ideas in Wolfram's words. I like the beings who see some things as coherent and meaningful—even though we see them as incoherent and meaningless.

I gloat & chuckle over Wolfram's remark (edited): "some world-description languages lead to accounts of reality that seem coherent and meaningful within themselves, but which we see as describing utterly incoherent and meaningless aspects of our universe." Sports, art, politics, economics?

Politics & econ are utterly incoherent & meaningless. But I go higher, weirder. Strewn filth in an alley, sneezes in a crowd, patterns of flowers in fields, air currents, bird songs, your nightly torrent of dreams. Pohl/Kornbluth wrote about folk watching water come to a boil.

I always come back to the chaotic wobbling of the little green plant I once noticed on the bank of a stream at Pfeiffer Beach in Big Sur. The plant is moved by the air currents, but it's "saying something" via the persistent shape of its particular chaotic attractor. I can't get what dance *means*—but the plant knows. To the plant, I'm as inscrutable as a cloud, or as a car accident.

And Wolfram keeps hammering on the point that, given that pretty much *every* process is a universal computation, and none of them has pride of place.

April 30 - May 17, 2020. Not Writing.

April 7, 2020.

Thinking of that line in Zappa's song, "Stinkfoot." *A week went by, and now it's July...*

Although in the present case, ten days went by and now it's (almost) May.

Yesterday I noticed that I'd reached a point of not even worrying about writing. Which kind of feels like a relief.

I'm working on another painting, *Bird of Paradise*, a small landscape with some flowers. Possibly I'll put an eye on the side of the bird of paradise plant. I cut a bloom from our garden and I've been setting it on my painting table in the back yard. I've done about five revisions on this canvas, even though it's small, 20" x 24". No rush to finish.

I can still visualize a second scene for "E is E," but I'm sapped by a strong sense of "Why bother?" As Susan Protter once said to Marc Laidlaw (and he still stings from this), "Why would you write a sequel to a flop?"

I Kindle-read the first two of Patricia Highsmith's "Ripley" novels. Kind of repetitious, kind of inane, like a tourist's travel notes, but readable. I guess I'll read the third. By way of putting down Hemingway, someone, I don't remember who, said, "Fundamentally he was a tourist."

In a similar vein, one might call Highsmith a professional expat. Her character Ripley's castrato quality is tiring—I don't think he ever actually has sex at any point in the two volumes I've read. He's generally repelled by women, though he drools over some of the men. But he never gets down.

But who am I to chide Patricia Highsmith? At least she writes books...

***

May 7, 2020.

Working on my painting *Night Bird of Paradise* (I put stars in the dark blue sky), I got more into the idea that bird of paradise flowers are live aliens. Their messy petals, like the rucked-up hair of a homeless old man. Their sharp beak. The alert pair of "donkey ear" petals in front.

Yesterday I rode my mountain bike south along the bluffs near Three Mile Beach to Strawberry Beach, a completely isolated land-that-time-forgot locale where I go every year or so. I was looking at a little kelp bulb and thinking it could be an alien character too.

Figure 21: *Night Bird of Paradise*

I had my new Fujifilm x100v camera with me, and took a few pix. As always, I had to tweak them Lightroom, trying to reproduce my memory of how the scenes *looked* to me—in my rulial space. Imagine software that lets me see the viewpoint of a plant.

Don't present rulial space as a separate idea in "E id E," just have it be part of how the beings are.

***

May 12, 2020

Finished painting "Astral Travel," yesterday. A brain in an open cube, hovering over a landscape of fields, presumably the surface of an agricultural asteroid.

It was inspired by a sad iron box we saw on Mount Hamilton near the observatory. We weren't really allowed to stop and walk around, thanks to frikkin COVID, but I did get out for a minute.

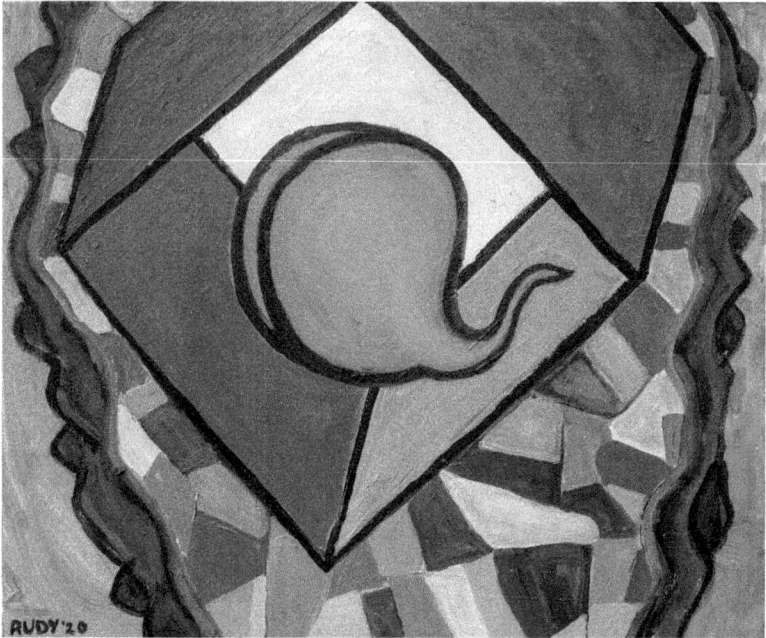

Figure 22: *Astral Travel*

Now that I'm not writing anymore, it feels natural to get out the paints and work with them every day. As if I really *am* a painter—twinge of imposter syndrome. Started a new one while I was at it, with eleven hovering spheres.

***

May 13, 2020

Started work on a painting of cells eating molecules. *Cells Eat Viruses.* [After about five sessions it came out well.]

This is my image of the COVID-vaccine-enhanced cells killing off those viruses.

***

May 22, 2020

Nearly done painting for now. I only have one blank canvas left. Need to order more. I did seven so far since the end of March when the pandemic shelter-in-place regimen kicked in.

Recently I spent about a week porting my old suitcase-sized desktop computer to a new Intel NUC 10 that's the size of two packs of cigarettes.

Figure 23: Sad Iron Box

Went hiking on the bluffs in Santa Cruz twice. Spent a day in Monterey and Pacific Grove with Sylvia.

I've been thinking a lot about the way I like to see chaos everywhere. I did a long blog post about it, "High on Gnarl and Chaos."

Looking back over these writing notes for the first time in about a month, I revised them a little, and I think I see a line into the second "E is E" story.

May 23, 2020. "Everything is Everything," Section Two.

The two aliens Qoph and Fon get tired of being wasps; also their colonies are dying off. So they turn up on Wick and Vi's deck. They now look like a couple of yuppies.

Figure 24: *Cells Eat Viruses*

Turns out they're shaped like a rich couple they plan to replace. They want Wick and Vi to introduce them and smooth the way. The aliens can't displace a person unless that person agrees to it. Like making a deal with the devil.

The rich people are on Aztec ridge, high above Los Gatos, in that big white house. He's a virus-vaccine trader. She's a venture capitalist. They're called Barn and Sox Whitsitt. In wasp form, Qoph and Fon have scoped them out.

Rejected idea. As I mentioned earlier, I was wondering if I should dial back on the Absolute Continuum (AC) thing in Section 2. I already did some of that routine in "Jack and the Aktuals." Maybe here the AC is just a line the aliens were using on Wick, because he cares about math, and they'll be running a different line of bullshit on Barn and Sox? Well, no, bailing like that would be a waste, after I went to the trouble of setting up such a complicated and unfamiliar SF Maguffin in Section 1. I think I'm only flinching about sticking with AC because it feels hard. And, like I said before, I could, if I like, move to an overarching thing of *rulial space* further on in the story. Both/and, not either/or. Or save rulial space for a totally different story.

***

What are Qoph and Fon actually doing here? Well, again, this is something I already solved. They're realtors in a sense, or rental agents, selling mind-slots.

But I had a moment of wanting to flinch from that when my college friend Rob Lewine was talking to me about how he'd worked for some years as a stock photographer. That is, he'd hire actor/models and get costumes and sets and have them all act like, say, doctors and nurses for a week, and accumulate a bunch of those types of photos that businesses might use in their ads.

Maybe Qoph and Fon are doing something like this as well?

May 30-June 2, 2020. "Fibonacci's Humors" Ver 6.

For the lead-up to this titanic task, jump to where it begins at my entry Nov 11-Dec 31, 2019. Fibonacci Story with Bruce.

Figure 25: With Daniele Brolli in Pisa

Believe it or not, I'm working on the Bruce Sterling collab

story about Fibonacci again. I'm calling this version 6. Version 5 was a merging stage that I never finished, and Version 6 is more of a fresh start. Current title is "Fibonacci's Humors."

What got me started again is that last week my Italian translator and dear friend Daniele Brolli wrote me that the University of Pisa does indeed want to put out their small book of Fib stories this year, in Italian, and they'd pay 300 Euro for a story. In Pisa I'd told Fabio I would write such a story with Bruce, with the plan that he'd translate it for the Italian antho. And then we were having problems, but now I'll get it done.

I told Bruce I was working on the story again. He hadn't heard from Daniele Brolli yet. So I told him I hope to finish it in one prolonged push, and that I'm cutting the long backstory, and the Korea stuff. And I said I'll show it to him before I send it to Brolli. And that I don't want heavy revisions from him, but would welcome tweaks and grace notes, so that it's not just *my* voice.

That's more or less how we finished our last two collabs, "Totem Poles" and "Kraken and Sage." At some point Bruce and I get tired of arguing, and I mail in what I consider to be a finished version of the story, and they buy it.

***

Collaboration strategies aside, what about the story itself? I'm leaning all the way into my original idea: there could be an exponential speedup for reading people's personalities—on a par with the speedup you get by using positional notation for arithmetic.

The challenge is to make this idea seem real. Not a joke, not a dippy New Age self-delusion.

Tim Leary actually wrote something like an expanded theory of humors, and Robert Anton Wilson popularized it in his *Prometheus Rising*, which I bought in ebook. Wilson and Leary talk in terms of seven or eight "circuits" by which they mean "mental subsystems." 1 is approach/avoid, 2 is dominate/submit, 3 is manual/mental, 4 is sex/society, and the higher circuits get into the nebulous acidhead zone.

Wilson points out that you can get the four humors from the four possible combinations of lo and hi on the first two circuits. He should then have noticed that you can get eight humors if you bifurcate on the lo/hi options for manual/mental, but he doesn't. I considered this path, but it gets too hairy.

The traditional humors are blood, yellow bile, black bile, phlegm. And the personality system where these are the talks elements includes Sanguine, Choleric, Melancholy, Phlegmatic. Getting intricate personalities from so few basics is a bit like creating additive RGB screen colors. Or CMYK print hues where, by the way, K is black.

Would be interesting if there were more than four humors in Fib's system. Maybe seven? Like the 7-shade Roy. G. Biv spectrum. And then when Cee Cee the veebie does her analysis, we get about twenty more humors; rare ones, like new particles. Tau neutrinos, mesons, like that.

No, no, no—keep it simple. I'll stick with the four humors being kind of primitives on their own, and for jollies I'll add a fifth humor, smeel, which relates to Joy. And of course smeel is a made-up SF word of mine that I've used in three or four or five other contexts by now. An old friend.

***

A point I could make is that the craft of humors relates to reading micro-expressions.

For the SF eyeball kicks, I would like to have a visual thing you see when looking at a person while using the Fibonacci Humors. I wrote a scene where it involves seeing something like a "Transparent Man" of image of a guy's head, with five colors braided together. But I need something stronger for the image. Something like a vintage *Mad Magazine* Basil Wolverton drawing, edging into cubist territory.

We'll do something with the voices too…like a Fourier series decomposition, but into certain humor tones, like a sawtooth, a square wave, a creak, a whine. Okay, this can be spectacular—if I can get my writing smeel together.

***

Regarding POV, I'll strictly alternate sections between our characters Jane and Link, with mostly Jane. Gender balanced. I want Jane to be quite strong. I was even thinking of the following as an ending. I used a similar twist thirty-six years ago in "Rapture in Space," but maybe I could get away with using it again.

"You are so sweet to me!" Jane said to Link. "We deserve each other. Also, you're pregnant with our daughter…"

"Me?" said Link.

"Trust me, honey. I'm a wetware engineer."

***

I'm bullshitting about this intelligent protean creature named Cee Cee, and saying she's a slime mold, although I don't know much about them. I've seen videos of slime mold colonies humping up and forming moving Zhabotinsky scrolls in a Petri dish. And the better-known type of slime mold is a colony of amoeba-like critters that have joined together into a single giant cell with a zillion nuclei inside it. That thing, sometimes called a grex, can crawl around or form a fruiting body and burst out with spores.

But I'm not really using any of this detail in the story. Slime mold is more like a magic, protean, supercomputing, do-anything substance here.

***

Instead of just using the craft of humors to get a clear idea of someone's personality—whatever that would mean in practice—two real world use cases for the craft of humors are as follows.

- You can use the craft to predict what someone will do.
- You can use the craft to find ways to manipulate someone into doing what you want.

I need to try and build u the uses of the craft of humors, given that this is supposedly the big Fibonacci theme of the tale. I might get more of this done when I finish it and do my rewrite.

***

What about the plot? Here's where I am.

- *Setup thus far.* Link, Jane, and Cee Cee the veebie. Jane sells Cee Cee buds. They live in an abandoned tools shop and pay rent/protection to Dickie Strunk. They're broke. Link agrees to help Strunk with a bogus cyber currency called BukBuk. Link's working on his Fibonacci Humors, and now Jane has put Cee Cee on the project, and she'll perfect the craft of humors.

- *Twist.* Cee Cee shows Jane how to see Link's personality in humors. Cee Cee befriends Homeless Barb and Ken.
- Link comes home with Knott. Knott sells out his BukBuk and leaves for Mexico. Link decides to wait overnight till BukBuk goes higher.
- *Uh Oh.* BukBuk is okay in the morning. Using the craft of humors, Link sees that Strunk is going to assassinate him. And he sees that Ken is the hit man. He's a bulber herdsman. Link makes his own deal with Ken. Calls Strunk to come over.
- *Saved.* Strunk captures Jane, kills Cee Cee. Ken and Link feed Strunk to a bulber. Link cashes in his Buk-Buk. It's worth $9.87 (987 is a Fibonacci number). He covers his tracks and pins the BukBuk scam on Strunk.
- *Epilog.* Revive Cee Cee from Barb's bud. Set up marketing Fibonacci's craft of humors.

June 3-4, 2020. Finishing "Fibonacci's Humors".

Bruce is clamoring to see my draft. "Truck it on over here."

I'm gonna fully finish it first. And then I'll roll back most of the cuts he'll make, and keep the good things he adds. I won't get into arguing with him about it. (I wish!) I'll just do what I have to do to get the collaboration done, and I'll send the story to Brolli.

And meanwhile, in my head, as I'm working on the story day after day, for hours every day, in the back of my mind I'm obsessively drafting peremptory cover letters to Bruce when I send my completed story to him. "Don't edit what I wrote. It's already impeccable. Just insert new material into cracks. Think in terms of collage, not overwriting." Such a waste of energy on my part, getting into these mind wars with a guy who is, basically, one of best and oldest friends. Yes, I know I'm crazy.

One upside to this tortuous process of composition is that I'm being careful to make the story as solid as possible. Making it harder for my devouring rat of a collaborator to gnaw his way in. I'm glad to be writing at all, but I'll be so glad when this collaboration is done. It was more pleasant when I was working alone of "Mary Mary."

***

To Do

- * Unity of place and time. Get the whole thing done during a day and a night.
- Drop the Fabio reference, or integrate it.
- Give Fibonacci more of a personality.
- * Personify the craft of humors as a sim of Fibonacci himself.
- * Jane and Cee Cee see the bulber Ghillie down by the creek.
- * Jane uses her craft of humors to manipulate Barb and Ken into saying she can come over to their barn and do some wetware programming on the bulbers
- * Knott comes home with Link. Gets zillion nucleus them a secure web connection.
- * Cee Cee puts Fibonacci on the squidskin screen for a minute.
- * Jane leaves to do the treatment on the bulbers
- * Link and Knott watch Fibonacci on the squidskin screen some more.
- * Knott sells off all of his BukBuks, and scores nearly five billion. Link stupidly insists on leaving his cut of 500 million in play to see it go higher.
- * The bulbers are on their way. Jane controls Ghillie and she's riding on him. Bawnie is under Strunk's command, and he's riding her.
- * Strunk shows up; he's captured Jane and has a knife at her throat. Fibonacci advises Link and Knott to flatter Strunk. Fibonacci chimes in.
- * Bawnie shoots a flare and sets Cee Cee on fire. In this moment of distraction, Jane gets Ghillie to snap off Strunk's head.
- * Jane has a seizure from back propagation of Cee Cee's death agony.
- * Ken and Barb restore Cee Cee from Barb's bud. Fibonacci is back
- * Jane revives. Fibonacci is back.
- * When Link goes to cash in, his net worth is $9.87.

Knott laughs, and gives Link five million bucks.
- * Jane gets Ghillie to inflate with helium, and to balloon-ride Knott down to Mexico. Jane and Link wave goodbye as dawn breaks.
- * They make love. Jane tells Link he's now pregnant with Fibonaccia.

***

Just about finished it on June 5. Another fuckin' masterpiece, as I like to say. I'll reread the whole thing for a day or two, and send it to Bruce on Monday.

June 7-9, 2020. Polished Fib, Showed to Bruce.

I printed out "Fibonacci's Humors" and reread it, marking it up pretty heavily, and entering the changes. Pretty much of a rewrite—it took four days. The story is quite solid now. I'll eventually give it another polish, but at this point, I might as well face the music and send it to Bruce. Cover letter below.

Here's "Fibonacci's Humors" Ver 6. I kept about 4,000 words of what we had from before, and I grew it into a tight, solid, finished story, with characters and plot, ready to publish, 9,300 words. It's the story I was wanting all along, enhanced by your inputs.

Of course to be a bona fide Rucker-Sterling tale, it needs more Bruce. I'm not looking for heavy revisions, overwriting, and deletions. I'm likely to revert that kind of thing. The story really is done. But it needs your presence. Embroidery, eyeball kicks, fresh lines, telling images, Austin atmosphere, second-unit takes.

You can collage stuff in where you see fit, or, if you don't want to bother doing the detail work, just read the story, get into the zone, crank out two or three thousand words of your primo prose, and I'll figure out how to work it in.

So get something back to me in a week or two. I'll do the final cut then, and I'll send it to Daniele Brolli. I think it's slated to be yet another masterpiece in our canon.

Bruce seemed to like the story, said he'll work on it now,

in fact said he was "amazed," which is a rare bit of praise. He was worried the story might end up too long, but I checked with Daniele Brolli, and he said that's no problem, and that he's very happy to have the story coming in soon.

***

Next Installment at June 15-26, 2020. Fibonacci Finale. Bruce Problems Again.

June 10-13, 2020. Now What. Losing Hope.

So, okay, back to, sigh, groping mode. This is when I miss writing novels as opposed to stories.

For lack of any better idea, I could work on "E is E, Part 2". Of course "E is E" was already rejected by *Asimov's*, *Lightspeed*, and *Analog*, and will probably be bounced by *Evergreen Review*.

Recall the Susan Protter dictum I mentioned last month, "Why would you write a sequel to a flop?" Possible answer? "Because I can't think of anything else I want to write."

***__

So okay, I'll do it. As it is "E is E" is under 4K words, so why not make it three times as long. Without going all "Donald [Duck] in Mathmagic Land" on the reader's ass, one hopes.

Went and found this video on YouTube and watched it. Pretty terrible, though with some nice bits on the conic sections.

***

Went back to look at "E is E" and now I'm like, why bother adding a new section. The only motive for this would be, basically, the hope of a novel. And I still can't face that. The hopelessness. Silbersack tells me Night Shade outright fired half their employees bevore the virus, and now they have the rest of the staff on "furlough." He says a royalty statement should be due soon, but he's not sure they'll send it.

I haven't had a pro-zine sale since January, 2019. "Surfers at the end of Time," Then three stories rejected in a row at *Asimov's* and *Lightspeed*. Effectively having no pro fiction markets makes writing stories feel pointless and hapless. Day before yesterday I wrote a letter to Sheila at *Asimov's* begging for a word on "Mary Mary."

Are the magazines are even reading submissions these

days? Checking up on this, it seems the pro-zines are functioning. I found an online site "The Grinder" where ink-stained-wretch writers pool their acceptance/rejection/wait info, and I found the Of course, average wait for acceptance in *Asimov's* is 66 days. Rejection averages 4 days. I sent my stories on March 18, so it's been, um, 87 days. Is that good sign? Or does it mean my novelette has fallen between the cracks? I see it listed in the *Asimov's* submission-bot page as received. Maybe I'll write Sheila again next week

Wheenk, wheenk, wheenk.

I should do a new story, and then I can at least send that to *Lightspeed.* A story about what? Another on that juicy-ghosts theme?

Figure 26: *With My Friends*

Sigh. Maybe I'll go out in the yard and try to fix my new painting—which I ruined in revisions yesterday. It's just a random collage of things I like to draw. I'm working on the crap at the bottom so it looks more 3D and more like stone.

June 15-26, 2020. Fibonacci Finale.

This follows my post June 7-9, 2020. Polished Fib, Showed
to Bruce.
***

So on June 14, 2020, I got Bruce's ver 7 of the Fibonacci
story. And, naturally, he'd gutted it, taking out most of the
material in my second half, including the character development and the plot. And he had Fibonacci giving megalomaniac,
rah-rah political speeches, with the audience fawning and
exclaiming over Fib's genius.

And he favored me with a long cover letter crowing that,
while he'd wanted to do what I asked (add touches to my
finished story), he just couldn't stand my new plot, but *now* it's
so amazing and masterful that I shouldn't even touch it again,
and I should just forward his new draft to Daniele Brolli.

I kept tight control on myself, and, instead of getting into a
fruitless, no-win, I-shouldn't-have-said-that email exchange
with this guy who is—remember, Rudy!—my friend, I sent this
brief note.

Thanks, Bruce. As I said I'd do, I'll revert most of
your changes to my material, and I'll fit in your tasty bits
that are new. And then I'll send it to Daniele Brolli. This
will probably take me a week. We need to be done with
this. R.

Then I went through his version 7 as quickly and coldly as
I could, rapidly excising the new things I didn't like, but
keeping any good new eyeball kicks or phrases that he'd put in,
amassing these into a separate "Version 7 Scraps" file. And
then I collaged the individual Version 7 Scraps into my Ver 6
to create a Ver 8. That took twenty hours over the course of
two days at the screen. And along the way, I made a variety of
changes to my Ver 6 material in response to Bruce's not-
always-mistaken criticisms of what I'd done.

And now I've made a print-out of my new Ver 8, and I'm
marking that up, and I'll put in the changes, and add a few
more tweaks—which are still coming to me. This process is
likely to take another twenty hours.

When I'm done, I'll send it straight to Daniele Brolli. And when/if I hear back from Brolli that it's okay, only then will I let Bruce know, and only then will I show him my Version 8—lest he seize the opportunity to do a zillion more peremptory cuts and edits on my ass, as well as sending me another email about how I'm a bumbler and he's a genius.

But all this while the story *has* been getting better. Hammered on the forge of woe. Re. working with Bruce, I recall the classic Woody Allen big from *Annie Hall*, and try to convince myself that I believe it.

It reminds me of that old joke—you know, a guy walks into a psychiatrist's office and says, hey doc, my brother's crazy! He thinks he's a chicken. Then the doc says, why don't you turn him in? Then the guy says, I would but I need the eggs. I guess that's how I feel about relationships. They're totally crazy, irrational, and absurd, but we keep going through it because we need the eggs.

And here's my remerging new *To Do* list for the Fibonacci story. Will I ever be finished?

To Do

- * Jane dials down Fib's choler levels after his last rant.
- * Clip out some Fib-rant material from the end, and insert it right before Jane goes out to the stream, as an early warning, and to provide a reason for her leaving the shop.
- * Use "rodomontade" instead of "bullshit" after Fib's last rant. Or pomp.
- * Mention that a Patrizia's system doesn't have the power to run a Fib sim.
- * Ghillie doesn't need new antennas to interface with Cee II instead of Cee Cee.
- * Instead of airplanes, they have flappy blimps.
- * Rewrite Luis's repeat of Jane's fantasia about geology. Give Jane a shorter rap.
- * "Fibonacci didn't fully understand smeel, Jane but

we *live* in age of smeel, Jane. It's made manifest in our new servants and partners, the slime molds." Kicker: smeel is slime mold.

- * Rafaella is planning to go back to Pisa.
- * Don't mention majoring in history of math twice.
- * When Jane has Fib guess her first conversation with have Link mention that it was at a math class.
- * Link uses the Fib craft of humors to understand their friends at the party. A sentence or two would be enough.

***

June 19, 2020. Finished it today. I made a bunch more changes to the ending, which is pretty cool now. I had my characters Link and Jane mock a certain bombastic speech that Fibonacci makes—and then, after Fibonacci gets sexist and tell Jane she isn't fit to be a laboratory bottle-washer—then I have Jane reprogram Fibonacci so he becomes a more pleasant character after all.

And, as I said, some of Bruce's' criticisms did strike home. I got rid of a "Wild West" living lasso and Colt .45 pistol scene. I made the depiction of a Mexican family more sympathetic. I put in more sops for the Italians (our clients). And I used Bruce's idea of smeel being an objective correlative for slime mold computation. It's good to pump up the *fifth* humor (smeel). Fibonacci hadn't ever realized quite what it was.

Good bit: Bruce's notion of Fibonacci musing that, given his status as a biocomputer emulation, he's now alive inside a "slime abacus." A slime abacus is a biotech slime mold brain.

A long struggle, but in the end, the story is better than if I'd written it alone.

One thing I forgot to do was to lean a bit more on the use of Fib's craft of humors towards the end. I added this to my To Do list. In case I revise it again.

For now, though, I sent it to Daniele like I told Bruce I would. And I don't plan to show it to Bruce for weeks or months. It's sort of a codependency issue. I absolutely cannot control what Bruce will do if I let him get hold of the manuscript again. But I don't have to enable him by *sending* him the manuscript too early.

The story is done. I'm glad. It was a very difficult process. But the story is quite good.

And now I can move on.

***

June 20, 2020. A few more tiny tweaks; finishing my *To Do* list. Bracing myself for the final showdown with Bruce. I'm still (annoyingly) composing emails to him in my head. Stop it, Rudy! Don't cringe! I'll stall Bruce for as long as possible. It'll help if I can get Daniele's formal acceptance of the story first. At some point Bruce *does* tend to give up.

I'm starting to wonder about selling it to an English-speaking zine as well. I still have "Mary, Mary" in the queue at *Asimov's*. Could I try "Fib" with *F&SF*? Generally that guy won't buy from me, but maybe the historical aspect would turn him on.

***

June 21, 2020. Did a few more tweaks on the story, for a smoother ending, so I have Ver 9. Sent that to Brolli too. I hope to god he responds quickly.

Still haven't showed it to Bruce. My instinct is to keep stalling, although sooner or later I'll snap. I'm trying to wait until I hear from Brolli first. It'll be more of a *fait accompli* if I can honestly say "Daniele likes it a lot."

Meanwhile Bruce is cheerfully sending me links for things he thinks might interest me, like about jellyfish or Wolfram or flickercladding. As if we're good friends. As I darkly brood.

***

June 22, 2020. Now I'm up to Ver 10 with my secret revisions. Keep thinking of little tweaks. Tempted to print it out for another buffing. I wrote Brolli again, begging for a "nihil obstat" that I can wave in Bruce's face.

***

June 24, 2020. So Brolli wrote me to say the story's wonderful. I sent his remark to Bruce with a conciliatory note, like, "We're old friends and I want to stay that way," attaching Ver 10. After a couple of days, he wrote back that it was fine with him, and that he didn't want to "go to the mattress" over it. Big relief for me to have this done, and the story's wonderful.

***

June 26, 2020. I did still more tweaks on the ending of "Fibonacci's Humors," and sent a Version 11 to Brolli. And now it's really done. Onward. I showed Ver 11 to Marc Laidlaw, and he thought it was good.

One last thought…working with Bruce, it's like I'm an oyster and he puts sand inside my shell, and I grow pearls around the irritants.

And, as I often say after a collab with him: "Never Again." But you never know.

***

Daniele Brolli translated our story into Italian and included it in his edited collection *Ipotesi per Fibonacci* from Comma22, which appeared in late fall of 2020. I sent the original English "Fibonacci's Humors" to Sheila Williams at *Asimov's* and she bought it almost right away. It appeared in the August, 2021, issue.

June 27, 2020. Presentism?

I've finished six stories since starting these notes, about twenty months ago. So that's about three months per story. Or a hundred days. I'd like to get into some fresh thing for my next story.

Let's feel around for some images.

The one where I'm standing in an open doorway near the back of the Fillmore in SF, it's around '66, a psychedelic band is playing, maybe Quicksilver Messenger Service doing "Who Do You Love." It's night, dark outside, I'm smoking a joint. Looking out at an alley. Peaceful, peaceful. The music echoing in the auditorium, the pleasant summer night outside. A woman walks up to me, starts sharing my joint. [She's from a UFO?]

Two hours later, I'm walking inside an underground wasp nest wielding a flame thrower, and I'm half an inch tall.

***

My brother Embry used this word "presentism," referring to people tearing down statues this month—applying present-day judgments to older events. SF possibilities in this.

July 1-4, 2020. "Teep," the Novel.

So I'm ready to try and make the stories grow together.

Ready to write a novel made of joined stories. What they call a fix-up. In this context, I'm inspired, and have been for years, by Charles Stross's wonderful *Accelerando*. And I know I was able to build a fix-up into a novel before—with *Turing & Burroughs*. The sum is more than the parts. Once I went from my three or four Turing/Burroughs stories to the novel, a lot of very cool stuff emerged. Another inspiration this week is Bob Dylan's new *Rough and Rowdy Ways* album…made at age 77. If you're an old master, why not just do what you like.

Bits to fill in: Curtis Winch being a dog after he kills Treadle. Ramona and Gee starting Skyhive. An afterworld ectoplasm ghost scene within God's Mind.

The overarching themes that roll from story to story? (a) What is Reality, and (b) Software Immortality (with and without psidots and lifeboxes). As I've mentioned before in these notes, there's a spectrum of immortality levels…shading into ectoplasm, hylozoism and heaven,

- *Lifebox in Cloud*. ["Juicy Ghost" and "Mary Mary."] Lifebox communicates with a psidot that sits on a body and controls the body, using its sensors and effectors. This is the kludgy Skyhive approach.
- *Local Lifebox*. ["Mary Mary"] Store a copy of the full lifebox in a powerful, localized system that doesn't require a wireless hookup. Probably a lifebox can't be strong enough. But I used an "ectoplasm" which is a self-contained dark-matter matrix. You can embed your ectoplasmic lifebox into a sufficiently rich and living peripheral. Maybe you still have a backup life-box in the cloud? But if the dark-matter matrix is inde-structible, why bother with the hassle of a backup, and the hassle of synching it with the active lifebox.
- *Natural Computations*. [Used in *Hylozoic*, and maybe in "Welcome Home."] Embed your lifebox into a natu-ral computation like a stream or a breeze. Cf. Wolf-ram's worms in a box.
- *Heaven*. [Used in *White Light*, "Jack and the Aktuals," and "Everything is Everything."] Put the ghost entities into a higher space or a subdimensional space or an absolutely continuous plenum.

***

I'll try to use the stories "Mean Carrot," "Juicy Ghost,'"' Mary Mary," and "Everything Is Everything." Rolling these up together, I've got about 30K words right now. Getting close to half of a novel, given that the existing stories will grow.

I'll be developing the characters and changing the stories from their present standalone form. This will definitely be a Procrustean process.

I'll also need some fill-in stories. If what I have is about halfway there, that means I'll need four more stories.

July 7-10, 2020. Sold "Mary Mary" to Asimov's.

So Sheila emailed me on July 7, 2020.:

"I enjoyed the story, but I had a major problem with the sex scene between Mary and Carson. It can be interpreted as a rape scene because Mary doesn't consent to it until afterward. This scene isn't going to work for my readers. Don't really buy that she can be good friend with Kayla and carry on with the affair with Carson, who is such an unlikable character. I'd be happy to take another look at the story if you don't mind rewriting their relationship."

D'oh!

Originally, I had thought it would be cool to have the reborn Mary be kind of amoral, as she's not a "real" human anymore. But Sheila's point is valid. And come to think of it, I was just making Mary act more like a man, which is boring. So I did as Sheila said. God knows *I need this sale.*

So I changed the scene to have Mary fend off Carson—and that's more fun for the reader. And then I went through the story to change the buildup and the consequences. And then I couldn't stop myself from printing out, rereading, and revising the whole story except for the first ten pages or so, which I'd already revised a zillion times. And now it's really, really great. I emailed that one to Sheila on the morning of July 8, and that afternoon she bought it.

***

Working note: For the *Asimov's* rewrite, I dropped three "linked story" hooks that relate to Gee's role in the assassination of President Treadle, dropped them as they would make the story not be self-contained. Also I was slightly worried they might bother Sheila although probably she wouldn't have noticed or cared. (But keep in mind that she *did* turn down "Juicy Ghost" assassination story last year, deeming it too confrontational for her readers.)

In any case I'll restore the hooks for the story-cycle version when I'm done with all the other changes. Just so I don't forget the hooks, here are the snipped bits, and presumably I can remember where they went.

* "…he might help move you into a dog. Like he did for his friend Curtis Winch, they guy who assassinated President Treadle."

* "And one of President Treadle's boys assassinated him. I've been hosting Bernardo…"

* "…Curtis Winch is in there. The man who killed President Treadle." "Him again?"

***

At the end of the story, I put in an Also, opening for a sequel. In her taut new clone body, Mary feels squeamish about the possibility of having sex with Gee the old man, although he wants to marry her, and they're in love. Mary persuades old Gee to create a new clone version of himself so they'll match. Gee says he wants to keep his old body too, which is bound to be trouble. I suggest that old Gee and the new rejuve clone Gee might not get along. And I end it there.

In the follow-up story, which for now I might call "Mary Mary II" or maybe "Welcome Home." We'd have Mary with the two Gees, the old and the young, and, there's a chance she might end up having sex with both of them, the old and the young. And this edges into a male-fantasy zone that I need to steer well clear of. It's too Robert Heinlein / Woody Allen for an old man like me to write about a young woman character having sex with an old man character.

In the proof edits for "Mary Mary" I might even add a line or two to forestall this possibility—but I won't tell Sheila yet. I know from past experience that if I send in edits while the story's still in copy-editing, they'll be annoyed. They don't want a moving target. But there's that last moment during page proofs where you can to a quick acupuncture fix.

And in "Welcome Home" old Gee can quickly bow out.

He's like, "With two of me in the flesh, I just get in my own way." And then Mary and new Gee can go on as a cute pair for "Welcome Home," with old Gee like a friendly ghost.

July 9-24, 2020. Starting the Novel.

I made a "Novel Notes" section, and put it up higher in this document. I'll have to do a lot. I used to hear about authors who took, like, four years to write a novel, and I'd think they were self-indulgent, wimpy losers. But now, hey, I'm 74, and I'm thinking maybe *I* could take a few years to do this new novel. Fairly sure it'll be my last one. So why rush it. Polish the hell out of it, right? But don't let it wither on the vine. I'll start be revising "Mean Carrot" and "Juicy Ghost.".

TO DO

- * Rewrite "Mean Carrot," so Molly and Leeta (formerly Ramona) are wacky scientists instead of party-girl demi-mondaines. Make Leeta more like a businesswoman than Ramona was.
- * Foreshadow Treadle in "Mean Carrot."
- * Change Helsinki to Copenhagen.
- * Teep gene.
- * Give psidot a name in "Juicy Ghost." Helen.

Doing a lot of this, kneading the dough. I need to think about the in-between stories. Possibly "Psidot," "Bad Dog," "Mary Mary II" a.k.a. "Welcome Home," and "Worms in a ?Box." (The question mark is a typo, but maybe it would in fact work.)

And, once some of the extra stories are done, I'll want to revise "Mary Mary" and "Everything is Everything."
***

My three new species who carry the teep gene.

- *Huffy* as a fungus you inhale
- *Stumble* is a fungus like a tree-ear on your head and it sends tendrils into your skull.
- *Psidot* is quite different. A mobile, intelligent nudibranch that uses wireless and doesn't physically probe

into you.

[I considered and then rejected having the first two be slime molds. I guess because I had a slime mold in "Fibonacci's Humors." "Slime mold" is kind of a misnomer, as it's not a fungus at all. They're also called social amoebas, but they aren't really amoebas. The individuals can be called myxamoebae. Classic is the *Dictyostelium* slime mold. Wandering amoebas that fuse together to make a slug, also known as a grex or a pseudo plasmodium. slime mold on August 9, 2020, and went to having huffy and stumble both be fungi.]
***

And I can't go down to *one* species, as I don't see huffy and stumble as being parasitic gastropods (snails / slugs / nudibranchs). Along these lines I'll mention in passing one parasitic sea slug family is the Eulimidea. One parasitizes sea cucumbers. How great is that? Thyonicola doglieli,

By the way, in the *Wares*, I had a fungal mold that could serve as a nervous system for a wad of imipolex.
***

During a recent rewrite, I had Anselm turn out to be a kind of physical hologram, basically because I didn't know what he's supposed to do—and because, on a recent hike with my friend Gunnar, he suddenly seemed to disappear (he'd clambered up a high damn when I wasn't watching). And I was thinking that would be a cool effect in a story, to have someone just evanesce. But I rolled that back. It would be one too many special effects. Also I'd like to keep Anselm around; surely I can find something cool for him to do. I don't absolutely have to hook him up with Molly in a romantic way; we'll see how that goes.

July 24-Aug 4, 2020. Chapter Two Plans

Slowly I'm starting the chapter that's in between "Mean Carrot" and "Juicy Ghost." Chapter Two. I might call it "Treadle Prions." I want the chapter to have a self-contained story arc, *Accelerando* style. Here are some potential plot points.

- Molly, Gee, Leeta, and Anselm perfect the nudibranch psidot.
- Gee is working on his first lifebox.
- Loftus's espionage gave some useful info to the Forever Treadle lab. Carson Pflug involved.
- Somehow the teep gene potentiates the creation of a "Treadle Prion Disease" or TPD that's making people want to vote for Treadle.
- Thanks to Treadle prion disease, Treadle's popularity is shooting up. The election's going to slip away.
- Carson Pflug comes over to Dansk Junkers with info on the Treadle Prion disease.
- Anselm finds a vaccine against Treadle disease, and then he mysteriously disappears. (He's joined the aliens who return in "Everything is Everything.").
- The Forever Treadle cabal is also hearing about the psidot and the lifebox.
- They hire Curtis Winch for their hit man.
- Leeta makes a deal with the U. S. Secret Service. Or thinks she does. But she's being entrapped, thanks to Carson Plug. But then Carson Pflug flips yet again, and scores a kill-permit from the Secret Service.
- Molly and Carson bail from the Dansk Junker group to start her Skyhive project.
- Gee doesn't approve.

***

POV

I like Molly's voice. I think it's easier for me and for the reader with her POV for Chap Two as well. And then I'll have two chapters of Curtis, and then two chapters of Mary.

Looking *way* ahead, "Everything is Everything" is alternating points of view, with Wick and Vi, so maybe two do chapters of *that*.

So we might have Mo Mo Cu Cu Ma Ma Wi-Vi Wi-Vi. And maybe a wriggling worm chapter at the end?

I'd considered changing Vi to Molly, but I think it's better to have them be separate. Vi isn't reallly much like Molly. I have Wick as a math prof, and Vi as a librarian, while Molly is a wetware engineer.

Possibly we see Wick and or Vi in some of the earlier chaps in background, and ditto for seeing Molly in a later chap, like coming in and saving the day in the Wi/Vi chaps. She's old. Maybe has a new body.

***

Back to the question of plot, I'm trying to get to the point of writing a first sentence for Chapter Two. I considered flinching away and switching to trying to start Chapter Four instead, but nah. Need to do Chap Two first. Keep pushing, Rudy. Eventually the stone wall with open. Really I just have to write any old sentence. Like that first brush mark on a blank canvas.

I was going to set chap Two in Helsinki, because I like the *idea* of Helsinki. I like the word. But, come on, I can't set a chapter in a town I've never visited. I'll set it in Copenhagen. I've been there. That Freetown Christiana district is cool, I have mental good images of that. The Dansk Junkers have their lab there. But Anselm can keep on being Finnish anyway. It's not all that odd for a Finn to be in Copenhagen.

Molly, Anselm, Gee and Leeta are in Christiana. They have a really large barn that's partly 3D printed. The printed matter is kind of alive, or programmable, like the Mean Carrot. Anselm has built a sauna with holograms in the steam.

I'll need to beef up the Treadle espionage issue.

If Skyhive commercializes the lifebox, who markets the psidots?

***

I've been thinking of ways for the Treadlers to deploy broadband teep propaganda. It can't just be wireless mind-control ads. It has to be somehow new. Otherwise it's a shopworn paranoid-schizophrenia trope like in my short-short "The Third Bomb."

Oh, I've got it, what if it's a virus akin to the Coronavirus. You catch it and you get sick with Treadlerism. There's no teep capability being communicated, just a set of beliefs—or, rather, personality traits—that are coded into the virus's RNA. People are just coming off the pandemic infection before the November Presidential election—just in time—which is why Treadle loses, at least on paper, even though he then manages to steal the election, leaving it up to the Freals to assassinate him.

So the story in Chap 2 could be called "Treadle Disease." Yeah!

Rephrased this in a happy email I sent to Marc Laidlaw just now.

> "I worked on publishing Terry Bisson's *Billy's Book* for him as a three-edition Transreal Books release all morning, then vacuumed the house. Laid around in a coma all afternoon, napped, and finally I saw the path for the new chapter 2. Like in the Lou Reed song, "Waitin' for the Man." "She's never early, she's always late, first thing you learn is that you always have to wait." And? A pandemic virus that makes people want to vote for Ross Treadle (= D. Trump). Tada! The good guys find an antidote in late October, but it's too late to score the anti-Treadle landslide that had been expected, only a slight majority, close enough so that Treadle manages to steal the election, and now direct action is required: Curtis Winch with the wasps in Chap 3: Juicy Ghosts.

***

If I'm going for a *Manchurian Candidate* kind of thing, I really need to put more about the looming Treadle into Chapter One. Morals cops. Like…*imagine* an eighth year of Trump!

***

I'll call the Treadle campaign organization TF for Treadle Forever.

How does that Treadle disease work? It's wetware propaganda. Degrades the empathy circuits of the brain. Makes it hard to focus. Degrades your color vision. Puts a steady ringing in your ears. You feel isolated. Treadle hones a pitch to suggest he'll heal these symptoms. Ad with your POV from a cradle and Treadle leaning over you, "It's gonna be all right." The disease makes you like the sound of Treadle's voice. Complete news blackout on the existence of the disease.

Easy to spread. And it might infect the cornea and the tympanum. If you get Treadle disease, you *literally* can't see or

hear properly
***

[*Unused idea:* If I wanted to go back to obsessing on slime molds, I might think Treadle Disease is akin to amoebic dysentery, given that slime mold cells are a bit like amoebas. *That* disease is technically called amoebiasis, and causes bloody diarrhea. Forget that. By the way, I read online that some poor laborer in India got a cellular slime mold infection in his cornea. Like I was talking about just now, that idea could work for Treadle disease.]
***

Loftus's session should have a consequence. Not just industrial espionage. Bascially I want Loftus to lead to the Treadle disease epidemic.

Go back to saying that Loftus was a rogue Treadler op who's a veep at One Wow, and that he was tasked to speed up the progress…but now add that he's a Treadler agent.

So…what did Loftus *gain* for the Treadlers? Well, now they know that they can use radically expendable agents as spore bombs. And they tweak stumble so it carries the wetware propaganda agent, Treadle disease. Send a tweaked Treadler stumblebum to a Finn Junkers meeting, and he's teeping out info and then he explodes like a biotech bomb
.***

We need a Dr. Evil type Treadler scientist who crafts the Treadle disease. But I don't want an extra character. And I don't want it to be Anselm. Let's enlist Carson Pflug. Of course later, in "Mary Mary," Carson is working with Leeta at Skyhive—but it's plausible that he would flip, and leave Forever Treadle, and come over to Leeta's side. He's a sleaze. In "Mary Mary" I present Carson as more of a manager than a techie, but he could be more of a techie in his earlier years. And he might bring an assistant tech with him. Bea Wormsley. Like the woman in that Heinlein novel (*Sixth Column* or *Revolt in 2100*) who tortures the hero with a long needle. And maybe giggles while she's doing it.

Would be nice, sooner or later, to make up a timeline—I won't reveal the year numbers in the novel itself, but *I'll* know them.

August 5, 2020. Prion Diseases.

Tempted to make the Treadle disease quite outré.

Getting away from bacteria, virus, fungus infections, we have prion infections. Rare. Mad cow disease leads to human. Creutzfeldt-Jacob disease. Kuru spread among New Guinea natives because they ate the brains of dead people. Fatal Family Insomnia seems to be genetic. All caused by the accumulation of misfolded prion proteins in the brain. Leads to spongy holes in the brain. Called transmissible spongiform encephalopathy. Sheep get scrapie.

A prion disease is a geometric thing, not a chemical thing. Prion proteins in the brain do something they don't fully understand...they live on the surfaces if nerve cells, in synapses. Prions are said to protect the fatty myelin sheaths around nerve cells and axons. The prion protein has two versions, the normal one and the so-called "scrapies" one. This name is taken from the prion sheep disease. If you get a scrapies version of a prion into your system, it might slowly convert regular prions into the scrapies form, and then your brain is fucked up. You tremble, stagger, can't understand things.

Best way to catch kuru is by eating a dead kuru sufferer's brain which, as I mentioned, they were doing for centuries in New Guinea. But it can take ten or twenty years for the symptoms to kick in.

Treadle Prion Disease? Well, nah, not this time around, too much trouble and too distracting. But maybe eventually, prion misfolding is a great idea for a story.

August 8, 2020. Psidot vs. Uvvy?

Using slime mold feels like a dumb distraction. Let's just have huffy and stumble be fungus like I originally wanted. A black mold and a tree-ear fungus with hyphae in the head.

***

It's cryptoamnesia on my part to act like the psidot is something new, and that it's different from my old uvvy. Did uvvies have any different kinds of properties than teepies? Maybe not so different. Can't think of any. One difference is that I never much worried before about how uvvies actually work. Or maybe I did worry about it, and I've frikkin' forgotten that too. Might be easier for reader of my full oeuvre if I stick to uvvy.

Did I ever say where the word uvvy came from? In a 2004 blog post about an interview called "Cyborgs, future of humanity," I say "uvvy" comes from "universal viewer." And I specifically talk about using it to be in touch with your lifebox in the cloud—which is exactly what you use a psidot for. I never made a big deal about uvvies being telepathy devices but, come to think of it, they always were.

(By the way, I found that blog post by using my "Search Rudy's Lifebox" web page. Kind of cool to have this prototype lifebox actually help me in planning a novel that includes lifeboxes!)

Snag—or opportunity. In that 2004 post, and in novels like *Freeware* and *Jim and the Flims*, I say the uvvy is made of computational smart plastic, rather than being a living organism. And I think *Freeware* is certainly later in my future history than is *Teep*. But maybe in the future they have both uvvies and psidots.

I am fond of the new word psidot. In my novel *Teep*, I could say psidots are better than uvvies. That was, come to think of it, my original intention. I'll have the stumble and the psidot and Column? mention that there already are the plastic uvvies around. [And, again, I later changed the name *Teep* to *Juicy Ghosts*, but I won't keep harping on this.]

***

I might at some point want an umbrella word for all teep devices whether plastic or biobot. Let's say "teepies," if it comes to that. Could be a spectrum of lower and higher fidelity teepies. We call an iPhone a *phone*, different as it is from the Bakelite black rotary dial phone that Mom and Pop had at 620 Rudy Lane, Louisville KY, in 1952. You can use the same word for some appliance even if its underlying tech changes.

August 6-9, 2020. Peep Versus Teep.

I need to get really specific about how my teep is going to work. I'd like a nuts-and-bolts, nerdy, real-tech explanation for the teep. And only then can I worry about possibilities relating to a teep gene or to a mental Treadle disease.

***

The rock bottom low level of "teep" is simply a silent phone call. My transducer reads my subvocal speech, converts it into an audio file, and sends that audio file to the auditory nerve of your brain, and you experience it like a signal that would have come off your eardrum. You hear my voice in their head. I can also use my ear as a mic for you to eavesdrop from.

Can I make it video call? Sure. Tap the feed off my optic never and send it to your optic nerve. What's harder is to get an image that I visualize and send *that* to your visualization center, whatever that is.

There's a whole history of the remote viewing trope. Living someone else's experiences. Like in that movie. *Strange Days*. Much easier to implement than full telepathy. You're using another person as a remote. I should have a word for it. Parateep, remote viewing, *peep*.

All that low-end uvvy does is peep. Doesn't initially get to teep at all. But the stumble is edging toward hi-fi teep? Is Anselm adding something? Maybe it's just know-how.

***

My original notion for my novel *Teep* was that it would be, to some extent, a near-future Silicon Valley thriller. In my 2019 public talks in Miami and Pisa, Italy, I grandly claimed that commercial teep isn't all that far off. My novel *Teep* can make good on that claim by showing a plausible path to commercial teep. But in terms of near-future tech, I was really only talking about peep. Bait and switch. The silent telephone.

Best way to make peep by a conceivable near-future tech is to relate it to existing wireless/cellular electromagnetic signals. Low-power biogenerated electric-eel-type wifi? But we have to amplify it and send it online. In my original "Mean Carrot" chapter, I imply that teep can reach at least fifty miles…all over the SF Bay Area. I'll piggyback my teep wifi onto the actual existing wifi/cellular network. Like video phone calls or photo attachments or mp3 files. Each teep message is like a text message with some kind of file attached. A teepcode file.

I don't need a separate teepcode server, as long as the teepcode is digital. Down the line, if teepcode is analog, we might need a special server. Eventually, analog teepcode gets into the juicy ghost thing, Supposedly the teepcodes are richer if they're analog. For analog, we'll need living servers like Gee's redwood tree or, for that matter, Skyhive's baguette.

The vexing problem is the input-output transducer, that is, the encoder / decoder interface between the client's brain states and the teepcode files being sent.

- A imagines saying a sentence or sees something (peep). Or has an emotion or a vision (teep).
- *Encoding.* A's teepie converts the pattern in A's optic nerve or A's speech center (peep) or A's full brain state (teep) into teepcode.
- Transmission. A's teepcode is sent by wireless to B's teepie.
- *Decoding.* B's teepie converts the teepcodes into a pattern on B's neurons
- B hears a sentence or sees something (peep), or has an emotion or a vision (teep).

Here is a key point about the coding or transducer process for teep, taken from my Miami and Pisa talks:

> A possible problem with full brain-link teep is that you might have trouble deciphering the intricate structures of someone else's thoughts—seen from the inside.
>
> Sharing lifeboxes could help make sense of another person's internal brain links.
>
> That is, as well as using ethereal brain-wave-type signals, you'll want to use hyperlinks into the other user's lifebox. The combination of the two channels can make the teep comprehensible.

I can totally work this in. I'll need to make a fresh tweak to the novel. You can do peep without a lifebox, but to get closer to teep you need a lifebox. So creating at least low-end lifeboxes *precedes* teep. Without lifeboxes, the stumble teep is, as I say, lo-fi.

In-between situation: The sensors for subvocal speech transmission are enhanced and multiplexed, so that you get a choir of A's internal voices. So B might hear a jumble of several tracks talking at once. It's an effect I've heard on, for instance, a Firesign Theater album, that is, near the end of *We're All Bozos on This Bus*. And probably it would be useful if B has some kind of lifebox context to be footnoting and annotating the speech threads in real time. Realtime lifebox lookup.

My point here is that you can segue from peep towards teep if you make the peep richer and add interactive lifebox context to the fugue-like chorus of A's many simultaneous voices.

Now we might suppose that One Wow is only shooting for peep, but they already know they will need something like a personal context for interpretation. Like the way that deep-learning voice-recognition works on smart phones.

But Anselm is going to do something to greatly enhance the peep that they're getting off stumble. Maybe he came prepared with really high-end lifeboxes for the women.

***

In going from peep to teep, do we need to use woo-woo quantum like in *Big Aha*? Real teep is so hard that at first it seems like you need rubber science. But maybe multiple tracks are enough. In reality you get the "I am" thing for free, as it's the same for everyone, modulo emotional coloring.

And I can chip away at shared emotions teep with something like a "Penfield mood organ," that is, a thing like P. K. Dick's notion of a device that plays your feelings. The "organ stops" could be emotion-generating hormones or, more indirectly, stimuli to regions like the adrenal gland, the thymus, and whatever else.

I looked at *Big Aha* again to refresh my memory of how teep worked in there. It had to do with the on-going one/many rhythm of consciousness, merging into the universal wave function (cosmic mode) and collapsing back down to specificity (robot mode), doing this about twenty times per second. And there a condition called qwet—for quantum wetware—whereby you gain access the pulsing mechanism and wedge your cosmic/robotic cycle onto fulltime the cosmic mode. Not a drug, exactly. More like an infection.

[I read some of this in my Nightshade paperback edition; sadly the 2016 Transreal ebook's text is formatted as justify instead of left-align; making it kind of unreadable. I need to fix that.]

ENCODING

Siphon off brain wave signals from the optic nerve and the auditory nerve and turn those into a digital file of low-fi teepcode. The fungus actually "wire taps' the nerves with its hyphae. The uvvy an and the nudibranchs just sense the brain waves from the outside. These tweaked nudibranchs have a little bit of an electric eel thing going on.

Kicking it up to full teep, the fungus or nudibranch converts the full brain patterns into teepcode. How? It's gotta be a quantum state. Many overlapping classical states in one. A vibe.

TRANSMISSION

I'd better suppose that the fungus and the nudibranchs both have can generate electric fields. They encode a sound, a sight, a thought as a teepcode current loop, and amplify the signal like a crowd doing "the wave" in a stadium. A faint electromagnetic wave. Or, if you want to go with proteins (probably too slow), sends out a set of signals representing the folded molecular bonds and atomic structure of an info-coding protein.

You have a teepcode sensor in form of an app on your smartphone. Like a barcode scanner or a QR code reader or an audio recorder. Your phone forwards this signal to your correspondent's phone.

RECEPTION

When pick up a teepcode signal on your phone, it sends a weak electromagnetic field to tickle your fungus or nudibranch. Like the way Google Play on my cell phone sends a song to your living-room speakers.

DECODING

For peep, your teep device patches signals into your optic nerve and auditory nerve. For full teep, it creates a quantum field that energizes your brain, replicating the state of your correspondent's brain.

August 11-12, 2020. Teep Gene? How Teep Feels. Chap 1.

I'd been vaguely supposing that the presence of a so-called teep somehow converts the human body into a kind of wirelessly connected, or quantum-entangled walkie-talkie. Not entirely clear if the teep gene just lives in the body of the biodevice or whether the teep gene migrates into the human body.

I'd initially written it so that the fungus activates a latent human teep ability, and it uses our teep for remote virtual mating. So what does the teep gene do? Is it generating a chemical that turns us on?

Fuck the teep gene.

****

I'm trying out the multitask version of teep plus organ-stop emotions.

Off and on I'm managing to focus on my flow of con-sciousness, thinking about how it would be to share that via true, deep telepathy. What's in my mind? A sample below.

***

I hear Sylvia doing dishes upstairs, and her footsteps. Machines in the distance outside. I regret clearing our hillside last week. Tightness in my chest, angina? The raspberry red of the quilt Sylvia made. Faint ringing in my ears. Memories of cicadas in Lynchburg and Louisville. The stacking of the dishes makes a two-step sound like walking. I see the shape of our house in three dimensions, the room with Sylvia is illuminated. The frames of my glasses constrict my vision. Take them off. Physical sense of myself typing, and the flesh of my body, and my crossed shinbones, and the sea-swell of my breaths. Some trivial device beeps nearby. I visualize my mind as a dark velvety zone inside my skull. Make a painting? With an R. Crumb oaf profile outline. What are the icons inside? A dog barking, a motor scooter, more footsteps. My skull is small. My tingling brain, the heart of it, my awareness, always there, does yours feel the same? Itch, scratch, hair. Phosphenes in my visual field. Get into the shower. Glorious symphony of tunable water sounds. Daily the same.

***

I don't like what I wrote for Chapter Two at all—and I really do feel I need get Chapter One in better shape first. And all of these recent notes have been about doing that. And working on the notes is starting to make me confused and unhappy. So instead of revising these last two posts yet again inside these notes, I, um, edited them a whole lot more *outside* of this document, and put that version into a blog post, "Peep and Teep."

And now I hope I get into the novel writing. I keep recalling this thing Bill Gibson says he does, which is to revise his novel-in-progress from the very start every time he goes to add something. Hard to believe that. Like Chapter One gets revised 100 times, and Chapter Twenty gets revised 5 times? But for the moment I'm doing like angel-voiced Bill, and I'll be revising Chapter One over and over for maybe a week or two. Go for that lambent high gloss. It's actually more fun than to be shivering naked on the nearly empty stage of Chapter Two, which is cluttered with the few awkward props I tossed out there.

August 14-19, 2020. Teep Mind. Treadle Disease.

Still working on *Teep*, pounding my head against a solid stone wall, waiting for the *open sesame* door. Positive sign: I'm tracking my word count, and it's steadily growing.

I finally got the Chapter One sci gimmicks straight, and the characters kind of consistent, and nearly-the-same things merged. I put in that thing about teep being a higher order of telepathy that uses more than just peep-level "audio" and "video". Still didn't exactly say how teep works. Holistic quantum states? I'm a bit loath to invoke quantum computation yet again, but what else is there?

I do need to remember that the readers don't care all that much about how something works. Just have a short, easy-to-remember, rubber-science name.

I've been thinking about various add-ons to the audio-video of uvvies. Brain-chem. You send descriptions of hormones maybe, or of transmitter chemicals…sending my specs from me to you, and then, in your head, some process assembles them or brings them forth. I don't want nanotech assemblers, and bio-processes feel a little off Maybe I'll use cytoskeletal quantum computations. Like the flickering computations I used to see along the teeth of a long, moving "rake" in the Brian's Brain rule.

I briefly checked back on the 1990s Penrose-Hameroff "Orchestrated Objective Reduction" theory of consciousness as a physical process that relates to quantum computations in the microtubules that form cytoskeletons in neurons. They're made of tubulin, which is a nice word. Someone chewing a wad of tubulin like gum.

Here's a note from a blog post by Hameroff, with three good buzz phrases lightly edited and numbered.

> Microtubules inside neurons provide exactly, pre-cisely, 100 percent what [our critics are] looking for.
>
> (1) Viewing neurons as computational primitives is an insult to neurons.
>
> (2) Brain mappers should look deeper, smaller, faster—*inside* the neurons.
>
> (3) Cytoskeletal circuits of ... microtubules (or *quantum resonators*) are key instruments of the quantum orchestra.

I do love the buzz of having quantum computations in your brain. Gotta just go with it. A good fit with my juicy ghost claim that organic computation is indeed richer to strict digital computation.

I met Hameroff years ago at the early Artificial Life conferences, and he's a good guy, and I might as well mention him and Penrose in passing, but wouldn't want to overdo it. One minus is that Penrose made the mistake of trying to resurrect the irrelevant and discredited Lucas argument, but that's neither here nor there. And Hameroff's writings can be a little too insistent, but, hey it works for SF and, in the end, he may be at least partly right.

We'll have a spin-off by Anselm, Molly, Gyr and Gee.

Reading up on tubulin today, protein that makes cytoskele-ton inside neurons...I want to use it for telepathy quantum resonator. Ribbon diagrams...what the heck IS a ribbon diagram...I always wondered.

　　　***

I'm roughing out ideas for the disease that the Treadler Forever election campaign spreads. It's an internet transmissible physical virus, teep-tech related. It makes you stupid and angry and resentful and partly deaf and blind, and it makes you want to vote for Treadle. It's Treadle Disease. Still can't quite figure out the full details of how it works. I suppose it's related to the cytoskeletal tubule-resonance field which the psidot uses for teep.

You know how certain movies or songs or internet memes can change your mood? And mood is equivalent to a (fleeting) state of brain chemicals. The *tubule* resonator changes the quantum fields, and changes those chemicals, and that changes the moods.

We might say that Treadle Disease tweaks the limbic system. That's a set of areas of your brain that relate to emotions. Hippocampus, amygdala, like that. Limbic has a good buzzy sound.

The Treadle pandemic breaks out in October, before the election, and my heroes come up with the cure, the antidote, and let's say the cure is a mental trick, not a bio virus but a simple old-school "meme" or "internet virus" and they set it loose and everyone sees it. Or it goes out like a mantra sound. Or a song by this musician I wrote about in *Postsingular*: Tawny Krush and the Kazakhstan guitar corps.

Both the disease and the cure might be the same kind of thing. A bit like faith-healing. "Lay your hand on the radio." The cure generates a herd immunity. "The Emperor's New Clothes" is a type of psychic herd immunity story. At some point they shrug off the barrage of lies. The mean, greedy man is jeered off stage. Best solution to his election-stealing plans? Landslide. But he wins anyway. So they have to assassinate him.

Re. the freedom meme, I think of the classic video of Jimi Hendrix playing "Star Spangled Banner" in 1969 at Woodstock. If you see that… your Treadle Disease infection is gone. Your limbic system is AOK!

August 21-24, 2020. Chap 2. Gossip Molecule.

I did a rewrite of my chunk of Chapter Two today. It's about 2,200 words and I'd like to get it up to 5K or 6K. I moved Molly over to Christiana, set her up in a love affair with Gyr, and introduced the psidot. Now she's about to wake up after a night of passion with Gyr—and I need for something abrupt to happen. We can't just go along with incremental product development. I need to turn a corner and start a new scene, and later there has to be a second corner and a third scene. Three scenes, and the first scene is done.

Given that I'm calling the chapter "Treadle Disease," it has to hit right now, as I begin scene 2. It strikes the Christiana freals. And in scene 3, Gee, Molly and Leeta will cure the plague.

In Scene 2, Gyr has Treadle Disease. How did she get it? Gyr got up early and was online and some malware got to her. The smarter-than-expected Treadler hackers followed the trail of Gee, Leeta, and Anselm. Let's suppose that thanks to the stumble party with Loftus, the Treadlers got some kind of tracker into them. What they call a gossip molecule— a long, skinny one that wags its toothy, chatty, simpering, country-telephone-operator "head" like the DNA molecule in the cartoon sequence in *Jurassic Park*. The gossip molecule can actually broadcast on wireless. It uses Van der Waals forces along with quantum coherence.

So when Molly gets up, she's in the mood of that dreamy Roy Lichtenstein Pop painting of the woman in bed, looking at her heart-throb's portrait in a frame by the bed, and she's saying *Good morning...darling*. She finds Gyr in the barn's common room, watching a Treadle video. Gyr might be echoing some catchy slogan that Loftus used—I need to think of a Treadler campaign slogan. Meanwhile Gee seems to have fled, which makes Molly suspicious of him, but we'll find he's in fact circling around, disposing of Vixen the gossip-molecule-amplifying Happy Sleigh. maybe he's even back in the U.S. and getting into position and waiting for Molly and Leeta to hack the Treadler Disease antidote.

For the shape of the book, I need for Anselm to die (or evanesce) in Scene 3. But it can't be a heroic kamikaze attack against the Pig—as we have Curtis Winch doing that in Chapter 3. I don't want Anselm to steal Curtis's thunder. This said, Anselm shouldn't just get snuffed in some futile, random, depressing way. He too is heroic, but in the context of a psi science thing. His lifebox is inflated to cover the entire worldwide web. He soul unfurls across the sky. Cool. I think of RFK's eulogy for JFK, where he quotes Shakespeare. The quote was also on the handbill for my father's funeral, sigh.

> As individuals we can't just look back, we must look forward. When I think of President Kennedy, I think of what Shakespeare said in *Romeo and Juliet:*
> "When he shall die take him and cut him out into stars and he shall make the face of heaven so fine that all the world will be in love with night and pay no worship to the garish sun."

Chokes me up.

So what about the Treadler campaign. Who and what does he hate? He wants to be a dictator. He opposes privacy. He wants full control of the uvvy channel.

He supports gig-slaves! Like Uber workers, but worse. You wear a shock-uvvy and some person or scheduling program sends orders to you via the uvvy, and if you obey you get cash credits, and if you disobey, you get a correction signal, which might be a twinge of pain.

Note that in "Mary Mary" I have an alternate take on this, where your cloud-based lifebox mind might to gig work by, say, driving those biobot cabs that I call thudhumpers.

Gig serf. Boss —> shock uvvy —> human brain —> human body.

Virtual gig serf. Boss —> lifebox —> psidot —> biobot remote.

I need that Treadler slogan. Free to Gig!
***

I had a great writing day on Aug 24, 2020, my best day in a couple of years. I wrote 2,300 words, where normally 1,000 is a good day. When did I finish *Return to the Hollow Earth* anyway? Let's see, it was around June, 2018, two years ago.

It's not like I was in an especially happy mood or anything, I'd been quarreling with Sylvia because we're cooped up, and the air's all smoky now from a 40-mile-long wildfire just over the ridge from San Jose. At the end of my rope. I needed the *escape* of writing, and once I sank my teeth into the story, I didn't want to let go.

So now I'm nearly done with Scene 2.

August 25-26, 2020. Metatron. Revise Gossip Molecule.

For curing Treadle Disease, I had an idea while cooking supper on the evening of my big day of writing, Aug 24, 2020.

What if Gee uses the Dansk Junker tools to enlarge and improve the lifebox of every single person in the US. And for each person, their lifebox starts talking to them like a Good Angel or a Jiminy Cricket or a Muse. Call him the recording angel Metatron, who's a real thing in Kaballah, sometimes viewed as a second JHVH (God). From the online Britannica: "Metatron is commonly described as a celestial scribe recording the sins and merits of men, as a guardian of heavenly secrets, as God's mediator with men, as the lesser Yahweh, and as the archetype of man."

Metatron wakens sufferers from their Treadle Disease stupor. He uses, let's say, a holonomic scroll unwrapping diffeomorphism to disassemble any gossip molecules that he finds within the user's mind.

And—this is where it gets tricky—the soul or spirit or essence or background mood of each expanded lifebox is this common Metatron force, and Metatron is in fact Anselm. Anselm is in some sense a part of the fabric of every single lifebox. He is "cut out into stars and he makes the face of heaven so fine that the world is in love with night and pays no worship to the garish sun." (The garish sun being Treadle.)

And Anselm can't come back from doing this. He's gone. He's Metatron for good. A perfect fade-out for my beloved dead friend and Mentor, the poet Anselm Hollo.

Backing up, let's say Molly wakes up Gyr and Anselm. And then Anselm does the cosmic inflation Metatron thing and saves Amerika. What about Gyr? Is she still down with Molly? Why not. Happy love ending for those two.

***

When do we introduce Curtis Winch? Does that go into the end of this chapter or maybe into the start of the "Juicy Ghost" chapter? But I like the balance of that chapter. So maybe I'll bring in Curtis at the end of Chap 2. Could even have it be a scene. Or maybe we don't even need to explicitly introduce Curtis, as he introduces imself.

All we need to do is to set up the spot where Curtis meets the freal lab people…which I'd said was a trashed Vic in Oakland. I should change this to Gee's cave above Santa Cruz; that would give the book more unity.

***

I need to tighten the relationship between teep and Treadle Disease. That gossip molecule which I use as a "Treadle Disease precursor" and a "matter-modem"—it ought to be a Dansk Junker discovery that they're using for hi-def teep. To transfer emotions.

For normal psidot teep, I want to rule out actual internal change to the users' brains. I'd want the gossip molecule to live in the nudibranch.

It *would* be nice if Molly discovered the gossip molecule, as I like for my heroines to have agency. *But*, in Chapter 1, the One Wow stumble tree-ears are derived from the huffy mold that Gee invented. And for consistency, we have to have gossip molecules in the huffy. In general, the gossip molecules are what makes the teeping *biobot thingies* work.

I had a word for "biobot thingie" in *The Big Aha*, look it up, oh yeah, it was — *nurb*. Maybe I'll do a search and replace in the novel right now and replace most of the "biobot" occurrences by "nurb"? Well, I tried that just now, and I think it's one too many new words for my long-suffering readers. Idea: I'll use *biot* instead of biobot. Biot is fresher. Done deal. Rephrasing what I just said: "The gossip molecules are what make the teeping *biots* work."

Back to my line of thought, if Gee invents the gossip molecule, what does Molly invent? I think I have to let her invent the psidot. At present, I have a scene in the evening with Gyr wearing a psidot; and she uses it to cure Molly's stumble addiction. If Molly's gonna have a role in the psidot, she has to work on it during her first day at the Dansk Junker lab. And *then* they're using it in the evening. Maybe they already had a sea slug teepie nurb ready, but it's not quite working, and it's Molly who makes it happen. She makes the psidot's gossip molecules send matter modem signals into the human brain. Without breaking the skin. They access brain only by quantum vortex fields, like the old uvvy does.

To Do

- * Have gossip molecules in the all the teep biots from the start.
- * Treadle Disease is a prion disease that includes a matter-modem gossip molecule.
- * Gyr shows Molly her psidot & Molly perfects it.
- * Gyr heals Molly with a cascade of a trillion Zhabotinsky vortex scrolls.

August 29-Sept 1, 2020. Chap 2. Cure Treadle Disease.

Chapter Two "Treadle Disease" is close to being done. Molly's in a lab with Gee, Leeta, Min, and Max. They have Anselm and Gyr in bubble-isolated beds next door. Molly's gonna put psidots on herself and on both the patients. And then she'll find the cure.

Earlier I had an idea of using customized individual lifeboxes to snap people out of their individual Treadle Disease fogs…but that's too unwieldy. But I'll keep *some* of that Metatron rap anyway.

For now let's say Molly starts by using a technique on Gyr that's similar to what Gyr did to cure Molly's stumble addiction. A customized Zhabotinsky scroll quantum vortex that slips inside your cytoskeleton microtubules. Make the vortex a fractal so it hits all eighty billion neurons at once. Or call it a trillion, as you may need about a dozen vortices per neuron. We can get to a trillion. Classical turbulence says vortices shrug off smaller vortices. In cascades. I've been this plenty of times, looking at whirlpools in creeks and swimming pools. And two to the fortieth power is order of a trillion. That's feasible; you can do it in a second.

But, wait, what are those vortices going to *do* in those microtubules? In the case of healing the stumble addiction, they scrubbed out the microtubules. Roto-rooter! But to get rid of Treadle Disease, they unkink the wrongly bent prions that hold the gossip molecules that are tuned to the Treadle Forever lab signals. And the vortices ought to snip in half the Treadler gossip molecules too.

So Molly cures Gyr with the kiss of a trillion vortices, like Prince Charming with Sleeping Beauty. And they make out, and then they get Anselm into the action. And Anselm says he can use Metatron to administer the kiss of a trillion vortices to each sufferer in the US!

And Molly comes along with Anselm to help. He's the flying Metatron add-on like a huge B-52 bomber (or, no, make it the old WW II B-29 with propeller engines), and he's the pilot and Molly is the bombardier. *Oh* yeah.

And it's all cool, and they're cleaning up the country, but then—oh fuck!!! Those bastard-ass Treadle Forever techs have hacked into Metatron, and they jam him into eternal lifebox-inflation mode, and Anselm and Molly start a cosmic-inflation mode, growing endlessly, swallowing all the lifeboxes in the world. "I contain multitudes," one of them later remarks. They merge with the Absolute Continuum, and won't reappear till the final chapters. For now they're gone. Or something like that.

At present I've written up to the point where Anselm and Molly are about to take off.
***
Things to do.

- * Treadle Disease is eliminated.
- * Molly and Anselm disappear.

Molly and Anselm physically disappear. They're swallowed by a being from the subdimensions, or perhaps they experience runaway lifebox inflation.

Molly has been the POV character for all of Chapter Two. I run her POV right up to the disappearance or, if I wanted to be coy, I could tell about that from somebody else's POV. Like have an "epilog" at the end of Chapter Two, from POV of either Gyr or Gee.

But, no, it's kind of cool to just end Chapter Two with a "blackout." Do that before talk Anselm and Molly take off? Or, fuck, just do your job Rudy, and have Molly tell the story right up to where the mothership saucer or giant subdimensional alef-two sea anemone abducts her and Anselm. It'll be the critic from the "Everything is Everything" chapter.

***

Okay, I'm writing the scene where Molly sends a quintillion vortices into the US, which is a dozen of them for every damn brain neuron in the country.

Catch: how exactly do the vortices get from Molly to the targeted people?

Backing up, how did she put the vortices into Gyr? Well, she teeped into Gyr's mind via psidot, and created the vortices in the teepspace of the Gyr's mind, and then shooed the vortices out to the far nooks and crannies of Gyr's brain. I'm thinking of a given cure-vortex running around the brain like a tiny superhero tornado until it reaches a certain neuron, and the vortices are sent in like junk mail.

I *love* this image of creating a horde of trillion vortices in one central place and then "sending them out" like paper voting ballots, one (or a dozen) to each neuron

But this final step needs to be physical. You want to *literally* placed quantum-mechanical energy vortices into the Treadle-Disease-bearing neurons of Gyr's brain. How does that happen? *Visualizing* the vortices moving around in Gyr's brain isn't going to *put* them there.

So—reset—we have to use the matter-modem aspect of Treadle Disease. We'll send a vortex blueprint *signals* to all of Gyr's neurons at once, and the signal makes the neurons build the curative vortices in place.

And the way to do this would be to simply "jam" or co-opt the Treadle Forever lab transmitter that is sending propaganda to the gossip molecules installed in people by the Treadle Disease. And sly, skeevy Gee will know how to do that.

***

So I implemented all this and more in a frantic three-day bloodlust-writing-frenzy with multiple rewrites, Sept 1-3, 2020, bulking Chap Two to 9,500 words.

September 3-7, 2020. Segue "Juicy Ghost." Revise the Rest.

I want to insert some segue material in the voice of Curtis Winch before the Lincoln Memorial scene on Treadle's

Inauguration Day in Chapter 3, which was the first part of *Teep* that I wrote, starting in January, 2019, as a story called "Juicy Ghost.

And now, circling back, I need to anneal "Juicy Ghost" to the "Mean Cucumber" + "Treadle Disease" chapters that come before.

I hesitate to write the segue because (a) I am emotionally attached to the drama of the beginning of "Juicy Ghost" as it stands in the short-story form where you're *in medias res* and you have to figure things out. And (b) it's extra work. And (b) is the real reason. Fear and sloth.

So, sigh, okay, I'll write the segue. Maybe not today. I need to take a walk or work on my painting: commercial title "Healing Angel," colloquial title, "Molly Zaps the Treadlers."

Figure 27: Healing Angel

Here's things I'd want to have in the segue.

- * Gee, Gyr, & Leeta move from Denmark to the

whipped Oakland flats house.
- * They recruit Curtis. He's a homeless UC Berkeley dropout.
- * Curtis helps burn down the Treadle Forever lab in SF.
- * Treadle wins the election.
- * They begin breeding special organisms. (Add a little more about this.)

Funny (to me) line when Gee sees Curtis burning the Treadle campaign headquarters to the ground: "Maybe *this* will make for a fair election."
***

I'm wrote really fast for about a week, not even thinking about it much or looking at notes, just diving in every day and writing like crazy. Revising without even marking up a printout. I did 1,500 words one day, then 600, and then finally, finally, I was ready to reread and mark up the rest of the original "Juicy Ghost" story, and polished and tweaked it a lot, adding another thousand words, and wrapped that up on Sept 8. I was in a bloodlust writing frenzy to paraphrase programmer John Walker's "bloodlust hacking frenzy." Very enjoyable.

Sept 8-13, 2020. Second Half of "Juicy Ghost"

And now I'd like to double the length of my Chapter 3, so it's about the same size as Chapters 1 and 2. The table is set, and there's more good dishes I can serve.

For sure I want Curtis, now using the body of a dog, to bite someone.

And it seems like we'd want to have Treadle come back so Curtis can kill him again. I had some ideas along these lines when I was just starting out, back in February, 2019. The motto I had then was that, as in the *Terminator* movie, "Killing him feels so good that you can't do it just once."

Here's a draft Scenario #1 coming out of that material. This would be the second half of the chapter. I'm not actually gonna use this one as is, but it's a start.

- Curtis's psidot Jilljill tells him that *Treadle was wearing a psidot.* Carson and the Treadlers ripped off the tech. Leeta finds that Ross Treadle's soul/personality is ensconced in a lifebox in a Pentagon cloud.

- Gyr figures out it was a Treadle *double* that Curtis kills. A meat puppet. Not a clone, but a tweaked biot manta ray, rolled up and stuffed into a suit. A manta ray in drag with its skin painted orange. Arms curiously flexible. Cthulhu-esque.
- The Treadlers and the Secret Service let Curtis assassinate Treadle as a trick on the Freals. The Treadlers orchestrated the stand-in (a) to nullify chances of a successful assassination, (b) to pave the way for Treadle able to return with the aura of a Risen Prophet, and (c) to demonize the Freals.
- The freals find and liquidate the real Treadle.
- The freals root out and erase the Treadle lifebox.

If I have Curtis kill the flesh Treadle with a knife or a gun or something it's too repetitive, and it makes Curtis look like a murderous psycho. I need a subtler kill, or I let one of Curtis's pals do the hit. As for the cyberspace Treadle lifebox kill, we'll probably let Gee handle that.

Re. Scenario # 1, it's too complicated to have Curtis be killing a fake, dummy Treadle. A let down.

But having a fake Treadle afterwards that's a good idea. Have him come back as a clone like Mary later does, but don't go into the clone process details with Treadle, as I'll be doing the details with Mary.

What is Curtis's dog-name? Topsy. Rags. Arf. Arfie. Vau. Woo. Woofy. Woofer.

Re. Curtis being a dog, Bruce Sterling happened to send me a review of a Soviet art movie <u>Space Dogs</u> about Laika the space dog, and the review and the movies web pages gave me some suggestive passages which I shuffled together for inspiration.

> The viewpoint follows these modern creatures low
> to the ground, with minimal narration, hewing closely
> to the dog's point of view, with wandering, move-
> ments, the strays navigate the urban environs. rendered

as a strange, alien environment. Pulsating sounds and
unidentified passerby take on an unfamiliar quality as
the dogs explore this strange world. They trot from city
sidewalks to leafy resting grounds, digging and barking
and snarling and playing. It's beautiful, almost dreamy,
but you become acutely aware of the gulf between
human and dog. In one jarringly long close-up the dog
fells the keeper of the fallen President Treadle's lifebox
and infects him with Freal Disease, putting him under
control of ultra-space-cadet hacker, Gee Willikers of
the freal rebels.

Now I'm looking for ways to speed up my new scenario.
Curtis is in Woofer. There are wild street celebrations about
President Treadle's death. Woofer's owner Loranda takes
Woofer to the park. At this point Jillljill warns Curtis that
Treadle had a psidot, so he might still be around. At the park, a
thud humper with violent Treadler agents comes after
Woofer/Curtis.

They've traced Jillljill with satellite eyes. Followed the
wasp to the dog. Followed the dog to the park. Curtis/Woofer
heads for some bushes, hops over to a stray.

When Woofer emerges, he *sob* gets shot? No, be nice. The
pigs search Woofer for a psidot and don't find it, and the crowd
drives them away.

To hide himself, Curtis retreats down to a spark of mind
deep inside the dogs he rides. Switches hosts several times. Do
the digging, barking, snarling, playing thing in a pack in some
vacant lots by the tracks.

Gee pops up. Tells Curtis the bad news: Treadle plans a
comeback. They're growing him a clone. Curtis has to go
"rabid," and bite Treadle and give the clone body a "Freal
Disease" to take over Treadle's body system so that Gee can
source back the lifebox's location and erase it.

How is it that Woofer attacks? I like the image of a Cujo-
type dog flying in through a window, breaking the glass,
slavering open jaws, locks onto the prey. One bite will do it.
But let's go against type. Curtis is in a dachshund, yes! A
sniffy, wiggly dachshund in the home Mrs. Earbore who's
hosting clone-Treadle as he recovers.

Okay, then, here's my scenario #2, and I'll write it now. I'm editing and re-editing these points as I go along.

Sept 12, 2020 Almost done now. I did 1,800 words yesterday and 1,900 today. Awesome. So great when the muse hits me this hard. Happily typing all day long, constantly in motion, doing quick corrections, fixes, returning to the growing edge.

For the last scene I think I'll bring in the cat and the maid. Her name, Candace. The cat's name? Yahzha. But maybe I don't bother giving them names. Change the outline again.

Sept 13, 2020. I finish the chapter. 1,600 words today. What a week. Up pas 51K total now. The novel is going to fly. Here's a drawing of the scene right before they blow up Ross Treadle's clone. On the couch are, left to right, Treadle's clone wearing Wladimir the psidot, the narrator Curtis Winch holding Friedl the dachshund with the psidot Jilljill it Friedl's mouth, and Treadle's lawyer's wife Lucy Popham. Standing up are Treadle's lawyer and former Attorney General Chuck Popham, and a bodyguard called Captain Burke.

Figure 28: Treadle's Clone

- * Gee tells Curtis that *Treadle was wearing a psidot.* Carson and the Treadlers ripped off the tech. It's a previous-gen psidot, named Wladimir, without Molly's upgrade.

- * Curtis makes friends with the little girl at the house. Loranda. They go to a park with Loranda's Mom to celebrate the death of Treadle.
- * Treadle goons show up at the park and try to snatch Woofer. Treadle's goons tracked Curtis's wasp by satellite. They saw the wasp land on Woofer. If they can physically get hold of Jilljill, they can backtrack their way Curtis's lifebox on Gee's server…and erase it.
- * Jilljill hops onto an alternate dog, a horny English-professor terrier. Curtis sinks into dog life for a time, switching Jilljill from dog to dog, till there's no chance the Treadlers know where he is.
- * Gee tells Curtis that Treadle has a lifebox stored by the Soviet KGB. Treacle's goons are growing a clone he can return. It's up to Curtis to take him down.
- * Curtis gets Jilljill onto Friedl, a cute dachshund belonging to Lucy Popham, the wife of Treadle's former attorney general Chuck Popham. A cat watches the transfer.
- * They're sitting on a couch with Treadle's clone, who's using a psidot called Wladimir. Curtis gets Jilljill into Friedl's mouth, and sits on the Pophams' laps.
- * The who's cat shows up, mewing. She was a watchcat, linked to the dead-ender still-loyal Treadle body guard, Captain Burke. He saw Shrill Yelp touch Friedl and he's suspicious. But Popham doesn't take him seriously, and Lucy protests, and by now Curtis has moved Jilljill to the inside of Friedl's mouth.
- * Friedl lunges and puts Jilljill on top of Wladimir on Treadle's neck. Curtis virtually goes through Jilljill and Wladimir to destroy Treadle lifebox in the KGB cloud, He meets Molly there. She helps him.
- * Meanwhile Jilljill eats Wladimir. She chameleon changes her color to that of Wladimir. Popham and the guard don't notice the change of psidots.
- * Curtis is running the Treadle clone. He says he's fine. Molly tells him she can explode Treadle's clone by turning part of him into antimatter. Turns out one microgram of antimatter makes an explosion equal to

eighty pounds of TNT.
- * Curtis in the Treadle clone sends Friedl, the maid and the Popham couple outside. For security. Secret meeting with his seven guards. Curtis explodes the TNT-laden clone like bomb, destroying Popham's house and killing Jilljill as well.
- * Jump cut.

September 14, 2020. Better Ending for "Juicy Ghosts."

So I finished the chapter yesterday, but now, having slept on it, I'm seeing some issues I want to fix.

And by the say I'm changing the chap title to the plural, "Juicy Ghosts," as we get T's juicy ghost into the chapter as well.

***

First of all, I really didn't mention teep at all during yesterday's scene in Chuck Popham's library. I guess I'd better say that Curtis is shielding himself from being visible. Call it "cloaking," and work that word back for earlier usage. If you're cloaked, can you pick up on the others' thoughts? Possibly the comm-channel has to be two-way, so if you're cloaking, then you're deaf. Like you've put a black velvet ba over your head. This would make it easier to write some of the scenes. Constraints always help.

***

I'm uneasy about yesterday's ending of "Juicy Ghosts," that is, the idea of using antimatter to explode Treadle. Supposedly Molly is a ghost, and she "flips" a microgram of T's matter to be anti, and that equals eighty pounds of TNT. But this adds on a whole extra antimatter tech beyond that of the psidots' etc. Also it promotes Molly as an all-powerful goddess, and then one would wonder why she wasn't helping out in the upcoming "Mary Mary" chapter. Although, yeah, Molly could show up near the end of that chap.

Re. the explosion, my initial idea had been that Gyr or Gee might use the matter modem to send TNT into the Treadle clones' cells and then have that explode. TNT is poison, so the clone would die of poisoning before it exploded, but I guess that would be okay Like he morphs into a man-shaped stick of dynamite, which is kind of cool. How does Curtis ignite it? With a brain-pulse flash of electricity, I guess. He's the fuse. That's cool.

"I'm feeling explosive. I'm dynamite!"

Backing up, I have to admit that I don't exactly remember how the matter modem things works, even though I just wrote a whole lot about it, a couple of weeks ago. Does the matter modem even make sense? Is it necessary? What's the difference between the gossip molecule, the matter modem, Treadle Disease, and the cure for Treadle Disease? Sheer bullshit, PhD, piled high and deep. Initially I invoked the matter modem as a way of teeping moods—in the form of neurochemicals that the receiver creates to match the brain chemistry of the sender. I want to skim over those passages and see if I can simplify them.

***

Another issue is that it might be more impressive if there were about thirty guys in Popham's basement. Somehow, by the way, I don't want it to be the vice-president's house. He's too boring.

So Popham has a platoon of putsch troops in his basement. How could they have dug out so much room? Let's say it was designated as an emergency bunker for Treadle. For the story, I'd need an advance hint from someone that there had been a lot of work here. Gee would know about it. Sure.

A whole dorm of shock troops down there. A good reveal. If Popham is in on this, he might as well die too. We might also suppose that he had some inchoate plans for installing *himself* as Prez. So at the end, Treadle's clone (with Curtis running him) and Popham and Captain Burke go down there.

I think leave out that corny Curtis-isn't-heartless routine about Curtis giving any non-loyalist soldiers a chance to escape.

***

Went to the beach for the afternoon. Wonderful. The smoke cleared up enough to show some sun. The waves, ah. Walked a couple of miles up and down Seabright & Boardwalk beach with Sylvia. Both of us very happy.

When I got home, before and after supper, I rewrote the

end of Chapter Three. Did a nitroglycerin thing instead of antimatter. Also removed all uses of the confusing phrase "matter-modem" and rechecked all the uses of "gossip molecule" to make it uniform.

Still need to add a sinister, surreal non-cartoony envisioning by Curtis of the gossip molecules as they load nitro into Treadle's clone. Not like hillbilly DNA this time, but rather like Swiss knives with a thousand flexible blades. The gossip molecule's head rushing up and down the lengths of its branching spines. Or maybe they're even a bit like anemones— prefiguring the creature at the math seminar in "Everything is Everything." The Molecule That Became God.

Got 900 words today. I'm fantasizing about asking Silbersack to send this new Chapter Three to the *New Yorker*. They *have* been running literary crypto-SF, that is, speculative or surreal fantastic literature.

And I'm itching to submit the as-yet-finished novel to some publishers, if only to find out whether it's going to be a Kickstarter Transreal self-pubber this time out. If it was the latter, and I knew that for sure, I'd almost be tempted to try and publish it by December. But no way I could make that schedule. I need at least two more months, and more likely four to finish writing it. Kickstarter takes a month. Pubbing and shipping takes a month. So likely I wouldn't be able to get it out till Feb or March.

September 15-18 2020. Big Picture. Fate of "E is E."

Probably I should reread and mark up Chap 3 "Juicy Ghosts,", but I don't feel like it this morning now. Or reread and mark up Chap 4 "Mary Mary" and get more of a segue connecting it to Chap 3. I have a sense that Chap 4 is several years or maybe even decades later than Chap 3. Mary could narrate some back story to convey that. Or just do the jump.

Possibly there could be an interstitial chapter, like the way I inserted Chap 2 "Treadle Disease." But I'd need to find a story for that.

Re. Chap 4 "Mary Mary" there's also the option of stretching out the real ghost stuff at the ending. I'd need to reread that to figure out what's possible there. If I bulk it enough, I could have Chap 4 bud off the later sections as a separate chapter. That might be a good way to go. Something with the thing about spirits of place? I did a little of that in *Hylozoic*.

And what about "Everything is Everything?" I'm not sure it belongs in the book at all. I like it as a story, and I like Wick and Vi. Don't know why I couldn't sell it yet. Maybe I just go and tweak it as a story one more time and stick it in *Big Echo*, and write something completely different for the later part of *Teep*, something that grows organically out of the earlier chapters, and which has the same characters and the same science.

Num	Title	Count
1	Mean Carrot	9,280
2	Treadle Disease	10,370
3	Juicy Ghosts	12,530
4	Mary Mary	15,734
5	Noise/Information	0
6	Everything is Everything	4,700
7	Party at the End	0
All	TEEP	52,614

I'm looking at my chapter word counts, with today's version shown above, if I include "E is E." I wonder if I should bud off some of "Mary Mary" into the first part of the hypothetical chapter "Noise/Information," and add on 7K words to complete *that* chapter? No, it's better to leave "May Mary" alone, as it's a nice, rounded novelette. Get a fresh idea for "Noise/Info."

Schedule? Write 12K new words for Noise / Information. Add 7K to "Everything is Everything". Do 10K for the hypothetical "Party at the End." That makes about30K more, bringing me up to 82K, which is enough for a novel.

Theoretically, and under ideal conditions, I *could* write 30K in ten weeks if I average 3K a week. So that's about 3 months. And then I'd revise for a month. So I could conceivably finish by mid-January, which is four months from today, that is, mid-September.

Meanwhile I printed out Chap 3 "Juicy Ghosts" and Chap 6 "Everything is Everything," and I will just fucking proof them.

And proof Chap 4 "Mary Mary" too. And then figure out how to fill in the missing puzzle pieces.

One factor worth mentioning is that Chapters 1-3 are a more or less cohesive arc that cumulates in the annihilation of Ross Treadle. So ideally, Chaps 4-6 might comprise a second arc with some specific goal. And then Chap 7 can be a fun *envoi*.

If I really wanted to bail, I could do 1-4 as a novella.
***

Now it's Sept 16, 2020, and I'm still waffling about "Everything is Everything." It really *doesn't* fit. And forcing Molly and Anselm is as the superspace aliens is absurd. So, *sigh*, I'll cut it, and roll it back to its story form, and send it to *Big Echo* like I said, although first I'll check that *Evergreen Review* isn't going to use it. (Highly unlikely they will.)

What pushed me over the edge on this decision was a passage about fix-up novels in Charles Platt, *An Accidental Life, Volume 3, 1970-1979*, self-pubbed. Platt just happened to send a paper copy to me yesterday, and I've been avidly tearing through it.

> "…merging my novellas into a single plot with continuing characters … would be a lot of work, and would violate a cardinal rule in fiction by imposing a new plot on existing characters. Plot should grow out of the characters, not the other way around."

Here's the new word count table.

#	Title	Count	POV
1	Mean Carrot	9,280	Molly
2	Treadle Disease	10,370	Molly
3	Juicy Ghosts	12,530	Curtis
4	Mary Mary	15,734	Mary
	TEEP	47,914	

And right now I'm going to work on finalizing "Everything is Everything" as a story. And in the background, I'll be mulling over what to add to *Teep*.
***

I checked with John Oakes at Evergreen, and no, they had no intention of pubbing "E is E." So I got my courage up and sent it to Charlie Finlay at F&SF. I did really heavy revision and upgrades on it—two rounds—wanting to bring my A game. Took about 3 or 4 days. It got really good, and I sent it off.

A week later Finlay sent me a rejection. That guy doesn't get me, and he never will. I sent it to *Big Echo*, the guy there Rob Penner, he loves it, but he isn't really planning any more issues, although maybe he can do a mini-issue with my story and one of his and an interview with someone. I told him I'd try *Clarkesworld* first (long-shot), and I sent it to them.

September 20-25, 2020. On Past "Mary Mary."

So now with "E is E" done, one way or another, I need to get something going after "Mary Mary." I reread the present ending of "M M" last night, and I can see there's room for some spirit and ghost stuff coming after that, which might be fun. I'm always wanting to write SF about the afterworld. As a young teen I was very excited to get my hero Robert Sheckley's *Immortality Incorporated*, but, although wonderful, it was a bit of a let-down in terms of depicting the afterlife. I did the afterworld it in *White Light* straight up. And *Jim and the Flims* was totally about the afterlife. And there was a little of it in *Hylozoic*. I guess I don't have all that many new ideas to write about. Oh well. What's that word I use about my repeating book ideas? Cryptoamnesia.

Actually it's more like plain old amnesia. In *Jim and the Flims*, I had this aethereal stuff called kessence that was kind of like dark energy. And the ghosts were made of that. I'll tip my hat to that and say (once only) that what Gee calls ectoplasm in called kessence by some physics guy.

There's already some weak, computer-software kind of afterlife in *Teep*, augmented by the "juicy ghost" move. And kick on up to ectoplasmic ghosts the end of "Mary Mary," and now I think it would be interesting to have even more. But I need an angle, and a problem.

Bascially chapters 1-3 are a rounded-out novella in three acts. And now with Chap 4 "Mary Mary," I'm starting a new half of the book, a new novella, and I'm going to need an arc.

Which I don't presently have.

So to start with, I'll type in my corrections to the end of "M M," and then see if that kicks something off. And I need to proof the first part of the story again and make it blend smoothly with the end of "Juicy Ghost." Like, I'm adding a few sentences about how Leeta stopped working with Gee and founded Skyhive on her own. And harking back to Carson being in on the Prez Treadle hit.

I'm saying there's a ten-year gap between "JG" and "MM."
***

I decided to split the Mary Mary chapter after all, and to call the 2nd half "Ectoplasm," as Mary gets an ectoplasm ghost there.

#	Title	Count	POV
1	Mean Carrot	9,280	Molly
2	Treadle Disease	10,370	Molly
3	Juicy Ghosts	12,530	Curtis
4	Mary Mary	12,097	Mary
5	Ectoplasm	4,985	Mary
6	?		Molly
7	?		?
	TEEP	49,262	

I got Mary an ectoplasm ghost, and her ghost goes inside her meat clone. She's sees some tattered old-school ghosts in the woods. Instead of having two Gees, I had him retrofit his old body. I wasn't liking the possible three-way-sex scenes with Mary and two Gees, and I don't think others would either.

But now I need a story arc for the even the "Ectoplasm" chapter, let alone an arch for the whole second half of the novel. Some threat or problem they have to solve? I want something kind of tech-like and manageable, not a giant war with the minions of all Hell or anything like that.
***

Curtis Winch is on ice in Gee's redwood tree, also a backup of Gyr, although presumably she's still alive. Maybe in the last chapter I bring back Curtis for the POV. He's a good character. Re. Cutis, even though he's said he's asexual, it would make for a happy end if I could pair him up with someone. Well, Gyr and Molly are a pair, and Anselm seems strongly hetero, so that leaves Leeta or Kayla. I see Kayla working for Curtis. She's more his age, and more likeable. If I really want to tie up all the loose ends, I could pair Anselm with Leeta that could kind of work, although Leeta would need to undergo a road-to-Damascus experience and come over to the Good.

You'd think the redwood tree would have lifeboxes of Molly and Anselm as well. But let's say those lifeboxes disappeared when Molly and Anselm evanesced into the Higher Beyond after the Treadle Disease cure. But let's say that toward the end of the "Ectoplasm" chapter, Mary talks to an ectoplasm ghost that is remnant of Molly. And the remnant points the way for Mary to head off after Molly and Anslem, off into the Beyond.

Before getting to that chapter-bang-at-the-end, I need ectoplasmic ghost stuff to fill out the chapter. I need to do a lot of work to clean the Augean Stables.

September 26, 2020. Clarify Teep and Gossip Molecules.

Let's start with teep connections and about gossip molecules. I made all this up as I went along, and it's a mess. Here's some changes I want to make.

- Stick to doing teep as faint brainwave signals. Don't use the word "wireless, don't use "quantum waves."
- The gossip molecules create the mood-altering neurochemicals in place. Psidots infuse gossip molecules into the user.
- The psidots communicate with the neurons and the gossip molecules via quantum vortices.
- Delete all the mentions of Zhabotinsky and Zhabo.

To fix these things I searched through the novel text twice, and adjusted each mention of "teep" or "gossip molecule" to fit in with my new way of thinking.

September 28, 2020. Ghosts: Real, Data, Juicy, Zhabo, Hylo.

I need vocabulary. I have several different kinds of ghost and components, closely related.

- *Juice.* An individual's I Am or White Light. The central essence of a mind. The core consciousness of an organism. It's a quantum state, a gestalt, an uncollapsed wave function. It's not ectoplasm. Not sure if Juice can be entangled with more than one other system at once. That is your Juice might be entangled with another person because you're doing teep with them, and it might be entangled with some lifebox ware that's backing you up.

- *Real Ghost.* Old-school ghost from a dead body. It only emerges when you die; until then it's latent, or rather, *potential*, and if the vibe is wong, you might not get a real ghost at all. It's made of dark matter, a.k.a. ectoplasm. The ectoplasm acts as a lifebox: it retains the dead person's memories and modes of thought. And the real ghost now hosts a copy of the Juice from the dead body as well. What's debatable is whether your real ghost can use your body's Juice if you're currently entangled with an artificial lifebox. If no, it's an interesting limitation. If yes, then the Juice in the real ghost remains entangled with the Juice of the lifebox—so people can keep talking to a your after you die—and that's interesting too.

- Lifebox. A lifebox. A code and data simulacrum of a personality. It has a square-root-of-not circuit that allows it to have a barebones Juice field that can be entangled with the Juice of a living being.

- Juicy ghost. A lifebox connected to a living organism. Two linkages: the psidot link of memories and thoughts. The Juice link consisting of entangling the lifebox Juice with the organism's Juice.

- Zhabo or Ecto ghost. A lifebox which takes the form of a 3D Zhabotinsky scroll of ectoplasm that's spawned by a toroidal vortex ring. It's not dependent on a server.

- *Hylo ghost.* A lifebox which takes the form of some complex, natural process, e.g., a flicker flame, a ripple in a stream, an ant hill, a colony of bacteria in the dirt. The process contains the data and procedures that emulate a person. The process has its own Juice, or quantum field, which may be entangled with the Juice of a person.

Here are some issues to deal with.

- What are the physics of the Juice? Go with uncollapsed wave function. A data lifebox is a bio computation (on the baguette or on Gee's redwood), and it has an uncollapsed wave function too, but it's pretty blank and computeresque. To get my Juice, the lifebox entangles its wave function with my Juice
- I was going to say a Juice-to-Juice link is an aspect of teep, but maybe that's too much to ask. For full teep, we have the data transfer, and the neurochemicals transfer—and maybe a fainter entanglement is the third level.
- What part of my brain or body facilitates entangling my Juice with some other system's Juice?
- Would be simplest if the gossip molecules did teep Juice link too. Like maybe they use the ensemble "wave"-cheer-in-a-stadium thing. On the other hand, a hylozoic lifebox isn't going to have gossip molecules, so maybe the Juice merge could happen via a mantra. In a recent revision I spoke of the Juice as being housed in the microtubules of the neurons, for whatever that's worth. Mantra = hum = resonance in an organ pipes of the microtubules
- The real ghost only comes into existence at your death. Your ectoplasm makes a form, and your Juice goes over to it. While you're alive, your ectoplasm is latent.
- It would be redundant to have Mary's hylo ghost go into clone Mary, because then, in effect, Mary is hosting her lifebox, and her lifebox is already in her brain,

so what's the point? Ditto with merging her body's Juice with the Juice of the hylo ghost, if the hylo ghost is inside her. The whole point of the lifebox is that it's not living inside you.

- So drop the scene of Mary's ecto ghost diving into clone Mary's bod. Clone Mary should get her psidot back almost as soon as Mary's lifebox goes over to Gee's tree.
- What about Mary's real ghost. It ought to be hanging around Kayla's back yard. And if it's entangled with Mary's Juice, maybe Mary can be in touch with it.
- What channel do lifeboxes use for talking to psidots? I've been saying brainwaves, using the user's skull as an antenna. Would be better to say the users' body as antenna, not just skull as, in particular, that wasp whom Curtis controls doesn't have a skull. So bioelectric field, sure. Or go to a quantum-entanglement channel…it's the future, so why not. And then that channel is open to natural computations as well.
- So we'll need to assume that hylo lifeboxes can pick up bioelectric signals just as well as the baguette and the redwood did. And these hylo lifeboxes have Juice fields that are entangled with the Juice of the user. So…why not just use the quantum entanglement for the communication channel instead of the bioelectricity. Seems like it would take a lot of crunch power to detect and process bioelectric fields. Easier to wave a hand and say it's quantum entanglement.
- There ought to me a moment when the redwood lifeboxes switch over to using quantum linked Juice fields instead of bioelectric "wireless" to talk to their hosts.
- Psidots are alive. Do they have Juice fields?
- Can you send your hylo ghost around at will? You can always communicate with it via Juice. Probably you don't even have a server-based lifebox anymore. Do you still have a psidot? Well maybe, but maybe now you just use it for teep? Or are you merging Juice all over the place, like even to order a pizza.

- What about that kludgy routine of Gee creating a hylo or ecto ghost creation via toroidal vortex ring, looped around the edge of the redwood's "cunt lips," the loop like the worldsnake swallows-its-own-tail toroidal tornado I invented for Bruce Sterling to use at the end of his novel *Heavy Weather*.
- There would be a nice twist if we limit the Juice. Like I have a juicy ghost of myself, and I die, my body's Juice is busy with my lifebox juicy ghost, and when the *real* ghost wants Juice, my body is like, "Sorry, this resource is currently in use." Maybe then *I don't get a real ghost*. If I want to run this routine, I'll need to drop the notion of multiply linked Juice, and drop the idea of using it all over the place, like for every teep conversation.
- But maybe only a real ghost can go to heaven, and those fake ones can't. And if you don't even get a real ghost because of your fake ghost, then you've sold your immortal soul for cheap, made-in-China, tech-glitz, gee-gaw baubles.

With the seeds of these inchoate thoughts in mind, I did an initial pass on the novel a couple of days ago, searching for "juice" and "juicy" and making changes. But I'll have to do it again. The biggest problem area is the "Ectoplasm" chapter.

- You don't constantly know you have a real ghost, but you know if you have a lifebox or a juicy ghost.
- Maybe the real ghost doesn't really exist (or emerge) until you die.
- A juicy ghost can help you by having the Skyhive lifebox doing online computing for you. Gee's redwood can do this too. But how about a natural computation lifebox?
- How does a hylo lifebox communicate with the user and with the want cloud? Maybe the user still needs a psidot? And we'll say the hylo lifebox has some psidot elements so it can get the hylo host to hear your QE signals

- A hylo lifebox might hop around, like the way a wizard has an astral version of himself that possesses people. Doesn't have to be in your body all the time. But it likes to be in there to get energy. You're playing the role of the server that houses your lifebox.
- A hylo ghost might just settle into a new host instead of you putting a psidot on the host.
- Like a psidot + lifebox combo, a hylo ghost can ensure your immortality. You can take possession of any person or animal, even without putting a psidot on them, and even with no lifebox on a server. You're indie.
- Where did Molly and Anselm go? What form were they in? I guess they were juicy ghosts, bodies lying on the beds, psidots on, and their lifeboxes generating images of a virtual space they were in. But when they disappeared their bodies went with them.

September 29, 2020. Tectonic Shift.

That September 28, 2020, entry is so unwieldy and rife with bulleted points that I can't even reread it. Too much for me to handle today. I'm desperate for a quick fix.

I'm at that point of the novel that I once heard my mentor Robert Sheckley call the "black point." You're lost. At sea. You can't see the shore you started from, nor the shore you wish to reach. I think I say this at some (black) point in my novel notes each time.

Today I went to the real ocean, walking on Panther Beach north of Santa Cruz with my old pal Jon Pearce. Off and on, I thought a about my *Teep* plans. Mainly it has to get a lot simpler.

Rather than tweaking on Sept 28 "Ghost Survey" entry anymore, I'll set that entry aside for now— a record of my groping toward the light, and a possibly reference to return to if I hit another dead end.

And now for some concise, non-bullet-pointed plans. I hope.

***

So, once again, what do I mean by a lifebox becoming a "juicy" ghost when it links to a living organism? And what is the enabling-of-this-transformation tweak that Gee has just made at the start of the story "Juicy Ghost"?

Step back. When I started using the phrase "juicy ghost" two or three years ago, I was thinking about how to remedy an ordinary dumb AI program that lacks, if you will, soul, or the inner White Light, that is, our numinous sense of the I Am. Every living organism has these things. If we can pass that feeling to a dull robotic AI data ghost of a person, then we can make it a *juicy ghost*.

My reasons for proposing this trope are simple. We humans like to feel that we're better than AI programs, and that we still *will* be even if the programs can beat us at chess. We like to suppose (correctly or not) that Ais without that inner Self cannot in fact write as well as us or create art that's as good.

And Gee Willikers found a way to have a program share in that juicy quality precisely when it's hooked up to a living organism.

So what exact quality of mine is Gee going to feed to my lifebox to make it have Soul?

Introspection time. I feel aglow from my two hours on the beach. Full of White Light. What *is* it, though? How could it be conveyed to an AI in the cloud?

Stream of consciousness rap:

> Sitting here at a table on the sidewalk in front of Zoccoli's in Santa Cruz after two hours on Panther Beach, I know exactly what the feeling is. The *Om*. The mirrorball inward reflection of my Self. The cool breeze on my bare legs, the murmur of voices, music practice sounds from an upper story of painted brick building behind me, the sun heavy on the asphalt street, the sour green light through the leaves and through the red cafe umbrella. The specks of not-very-good chocolate in my teeth. The slight wheeze in my chest. The Here, the Now. The radically contingent nature of life.

How to pass this to the Rudy lifebox?

I guess what I want to say is that the solitary lifebox AI program doesn't *have* a haptic stream of consciousness. That's stream the core of my consciousness: the ongoing time-bound stream of thoughts and sensation and emotive neurochemicals. My realtime stream. That's me.

And now I ask yet again, what is the *change* that Gee made to the lifebox architecture that makes it able to appreciate my stream. Slow-fade memory. Echoing. Overlaying. Time delay loop.

An inner narrative. Yourself watching yourself watching yourself, as Damasio says.

Butt simple fix: the lifebox runs the incoming organic host's stream around a loop three times.

***

Next topic. What about the communication channel? Quantum entanglement is a last resort. I'd like to use wireless but that seems like a heavy power demand. But keep in mind that we're twenty or more years into the future. So let's say we use "ultraweak" wireless. It can be very faint, and the smart filters can see it. And for our purposes it can be interchangeable with brainwaves or even bioenergy.

A living plant or leaf has bioenergy, so they could be in the game. But we'll leave out the ripples and flames and air currents that I sometimes like to include. I don't need full hylozoism in this novel; I had plenty of it in *Hylozoic*.

Butt simple fix: use ultraweak wireless and forget about non-organic hosts.

***

As for the feeling of merging with a teep partner, well, we'll just use the same process as passing your juice to a lifebox. A live stream of your full sensory experience with emotions added in, thanks to the gossip molecules. The lifeboxes don't actually generate the neurochemicals, but they emulate what they do.

KISS. Keep it simple, stupid.

Butt simple fix: Use the live stream for teep *and* for making a lifebox into a juicy ghost.

***

Too much confusion if I have so many kinds of ghosts. I *don't* want the traditional ghosts in there. They belong in a completely different novel. We don't want to fucking deal with that can of worms. Teep is about commercial teep, and we can have at most one woo woo thing, and that's going to be the disappearance of Molly and Anselm, whatever that eventually turns out to be.

Butt simple fix: Get rid of the real ghosts.
***

So on Sept 29 and 30, 2020, I did several "search" passes through the novel and implemented the four fixes mentioned above.

Along the way, I eliminated every mention of "wave function" and "entanglement" and "Juice" with a capital J. Checked every mention of "juicy." Checked every mention of "quantum" and kept only the quantum sensor vortices. Deleted some sections of the chapter formerly known as "Ectoplasm." Mary's new autonomous indie lifebox is now made of "quintessence," and I changed all references or "ectoplasm" to "quintessence."

October 1-3, 2020. Astral Bodies. Tokamak Snakes.

Go another step, and start calling Mary's quintessence body an astral body most of the time.
***

I added more discussion of why Gee made Mary convert her lifebox to an astral body before *he* did it to himself. He truly didn't know how to. Seems kind of mean and manipulative, though, Gee making her take the risk. Sexist. Not so different from Carson wanting to do experiments on Mary. So Mary has to call out Gee on this pretty strongly.
***

I wove in some sentences about Gee fixing the lifebox ware so that the Spork *emulates* the effects of the neurochemicals whose presence is flagged by gossip-molecule-templates in the user's stream of consciousness messaging.

Why emulate and not just assemble these neurochemicals? Aa biocomputer-hosted lifebox (as on the baguette or the redwood) *could* in fact create those chemicals, but these biocomputing systems aren't at all like human brains made of neurons, so the same chemicals wouldn't make sense. Therefore they are instantiated as platform-agnostic *virtual chemicals*.

And when you go to astral body, then you need to emulate

the neurochemicals in the astral body as well. They might be visible (to some) as color shadings.

***

What do you call a person who has an astral body? Wizard, mage, magician, sorcerer, adept, initiate, ascended master. It's needs to be readily seen as ungendered, so "wizard" would be pushing it, also that word is a bit SWIL (Swarthmore Warders of Imaginative Literature) and spit-talk (an expression that our daughter Georgia used as a girl to refer to boys talking about superheroes). "Adept" is kind of good.

***

I wanted to have the astral body be a 3D Zhabotinsky scroll shaped like a jellyfish, but that's a by-now-overdone blind reflex on my part. It would be cooler if it's simply a toroidal vortex ring. Like a smoke ring. Like the plasma in a tokamak fusion reactor. Actually I was already calling that a Zhabo ghost the other day.

***

Sooo…here comes a crazy-ass leap into the void: I'll have Gee's source of quintessence be "tokamak snakes" who bite their tails and turn into quintessence. And these become astral bodies.

If I were to do that, I'd want to prefigure and have a few hissing tokamak rattlesnakes around in Gee's cave from the start. How is it in a tokamak snake's best interest to transmute itself into quintessence? Well, it can be a type of reproduction. They spin off little mini eddy-like toroidal vortex rings that then congeal into baby tokamak snakes.

Where the fuck did Gee find the tokamak snakes? Did his menagerie perhaps start with a tokamak snake egg? Well, no, we don't want *eggs* if we have the spawning repro method.

It just started with a tokamak snake that showed up in a cranny of Gee's cave. And—*Molly and/or Anselm put it there.* Some years after they ascended into the Beyond. "Mary Mary" is happening ten years after the events of "Treadle Disease." So somewhere in there M & A made a move.

I'd want to go see the nest of tokamak snakes, deep in the large number of chambers and branchings of the cave in Gee's hillside. Like he's Hephaestus or Pluto or Fafnir tending his fire nest. Newts instead of snakes? No, snakes. Like in Escher's last engraving, the coat of mail, but the circles are snakes.

[I worked on this approach for two or three days, but then I abandoned it. See October 7, 2020.]

***

When the chapter starts settling down, make sure to have the ball walkers Glory and Miss Max around after Mary gets back into her clone body at Gee's. The ball walkers are good for comic relief and variety.

October 4, 2020. Scanner Darkly.

I'm rereading Phil Dick's novel, *A Scanner Darkly* once again. It's such a masterpiece, and I almost think a lot of the critics didn't notice that, because it's so language-with-a-flat-tire and low-brow, and academic critics are so achingly straight.

It's not necessarily the best idea for me to reading the novel just now, as it bleeds over into what I'm writing. I keep wanting to use Phil's expressions *slushed, gunjy,* and *like that.*

I just love his character Barris.

> Barris's eyes, behind his green shades, danced.
>
> "Your eyes dancing don't mean nothing to me," Charles Freck said. "What's wrong with the cephscope that you're working on it?" He moved in closer to look for himself.
>
> Tilting the central chassis on end, Barris said, "Tell me what you observe there with the wiring underneath."
>
> "I see cut wires," Charles Freck said. "And a bunch of what look like deliberate shorts. Who did it?"
>
> Still Barris's merry knowing eyes danced with special delight.
>
> "This crummy significant crud doesn't go down with me worth shit," Charles Freck said. "Who damaged this cephscope? When did it happen? You just find out recently? Arctor didn't say anything the last time I saw him, which was the day before yesterday."
>
> Barris said, "Perhaps he wasn't prepared to talk about it yet."

"Well," Charles Freck said, "as far as I'm concerned, you're talking in spaced-out riddles. I think I'll go over to one of the New-Path residences and turn myself in and go through withdrawal cold turkey and get therapy.... so I wouldn't have to go through this meaningful shit I don't dig day after day, if not with you then with some burned-out freak like you, equally spaced."

"... it's my theory that I did it," Barris [later told Bob Arctor]. "Under posthypnotic suggestion, evidently. With an amnesia block so I wouldn't remember." He began to laugh.

"Later," Arctor said, and snapped off his bedside lamp. "Much later."

My character Gee keeps getting more like Barris. And like the character Baxter in *Be Not Content*.

Scanner has a thing about the drug-damaged left brain, and thoughts leaking over from the right brain, and the person feels like the thoughts from another person or from an alien...so great. Maybe something like this could happen to my character Mary—thoughts from the tokamak snake.

"Are you getting any cross-chatter?" one of the deputies asked [Bob Arctor] suddenly.

"What?" he said uncertainly.

"Between hemispheres. If there's damage to the left hemisphere, where the linguistic skills are normally located, then sometimes the right hemisphere will fill in to the best of its ability."

"I don't know," he said. "Not that I'm aware of."

"Thoughts not your own. As if another person or mind were thinking. But different from the way you would think. Even foreign words that you don't know. That it's learned from peripheral perception sometime during your lifetime."

My favorite scene of all is Arctor's freakout, on a freeway, after he nearly dies because someone (Barris?) has fucked up his car under the hood so that his macerator sticks at full speed.

He felt, in his head, loud voices singing: terrible music, as if the reality around him had gone sour. Everything now—the fast-moving cars, the two men, his own car with its hood up, the smell of smog, the bright, hot light of midday—it all had a rancid quality, as if, throughout, his world had putrefied, rather than anything else. ... The smell of Barris still smiling overpowered Bob Arctor, and he heaved onto the dashboard of his own car. A thousand little voices tinkled up, shining at him, and the smell receded finally. A thousand little voices crying out their strangeness; he did not understand them, but at least he could see, and the smell was going away. He trembled, and reached for his handkerchief from his pocket.

Later Barris kind of instantiates that thing about a slushed freak somehow knowing foreign words for no reason.

"Easy, easy," Barris said. "As our German friends would say, *leise*. Which means be cool."

I used a Polish variation on that line in my novel *Mathematicians in Love*. My character Bela is waiting for his band's stand-in guitarist, Jutta Schreck.

"I talked to Siggy fifteen minutes ago, man," said Rubber Rick. He waggled his tongue. "Siggy's her himbo-slash-bodyguard." Rubber was an older guy, in his forties, with an odd, zigzag comb-over and a close-cropped devil beard. He claimed he got a lot of sex. "Siggy says, *opanować się*," continued Rubber. "Means 'be cool' in Polish. Jutta likes to get lifted before she comes on. You gotta know that." He was wearing a cell phone headset.

"In other words she's shooting up," said K-Jen in tart, California-girl tones. "How headbanger. I hope she remembers our songs. Do you have the playlist, Bela?"

October 5-6, 2020. Tokamak Snakes.

I started a big painting today of Mary with, left to right, Gee's tree, a ball walker, Mary and her torus-like astral body halo, a cave-pit full of tokamak snakes, and a UFO with a face in it, probably Molly. "Mary and the Tokamak Snakes."

What's the name of Mary's snake? Wilbur. Fred. Joe Btfsplk. Zuzzy. Zsuzsa.

The snakes don't *turn into* quintessence tori—the tori are emanations of their flesh bodies. A tokamak snake's innards are made of meat. The quintessence torus is the *snake's* astral body that can move in and out of its flesh body. The painting ended up like this.

Figure 29: *The Halo Card*

(I'll drop that that reproduction mode I described, that is, splitting vortices off their astral bodies. KISS. I had been thinking of those complicated lifecycles you see for, like, certain kinds of jellyfish. Tiny little shrimp things, then stacks of sessile disks, then disks float away on their own and become rhythmically pulsing adult j-fish.)

At some point pretty soon, Mary has to notice that Zsuzsa's

mind is present in her astral body. So, oh oh, maybe wasn't such a great move after all. Instead of being hosted by a corporation, she's being hosted by an alien's mind.

Thinking about the pit of snakes, and about all the extra lifeboxes in Gee's server tree, it occurs to me that maybe all the words, lifebox people in there will very rapidly be housed in astral bodies from the tokamak snakes. A shocking, unexpected cascade.

It happens fast. Although each of the lifebox people needs to undergo a port like Mary's, it was enough for Mary to do it once. Because the tokamak snakes were watching, and now they themselves can port human lifeboxes into their toroidal astral bodies.

Did Gee expect this?

(Some of these lifeboxes, in particular Curtis Winch, do not have living bodies. Others still do. For those with no host bodies, the tokamak snake can be, to some extent a host body, but they won't have control over it.)

The cascade can be a good ending for the chapter. All the snakes kind of collecting human minds. Not exactly an invasion. The snakes are more like tourists or, heh heh, soul collectors. Lepidopterists, in a way.

October 7, 2020. No Tokamak Snakes.

This week I keep waking up around 4 am, and then flashing on the remaining plot for my novel, and feeling that what I did yesterday doesn't work. Despair over the alien tokamak snakes arrived on schedule last night. Those guys have to go. Shit. So…reset.

What do I need from my plot?

- Interesting further moves relating to teep, lifeboxes, and immortality. Remember, I want to keep amping it up, over and over, like in Stross's *Accelerando*, one click at a time. Don't do it all at once in any given chapter.
- I need an arc for Chap 5 Astral Ghost so it feels like a short story…some kind of crisis that can be solved, or some curious phenomenon that can be investigated and perhaps even brought into the home.

- I'd like the chapter to be 10K words long.
- My gimmicks and critters can't be preposterous and kludgy.
- I need to be setting up for a novel arc, with a connection with Molly & Anselm's disappearance.

At present I'm fixated on the idea of finding a lifebox storage that doesn't depend on a server. I want this for emotional reasons that probably relate to me having been forced to self-publish many of my books. And I'm gonna find a way to do it.

But alien tokamak snakes are absurd.

I do like the halo move a lot, and I hope to keep that.

For a while I was thinking of the halo being made of some human-ghost-type substance I called *ectoplasm*. And that got so tangled with religion and spiritualism that I gave up on it.

Then I went for rubber-physics *quintessence* as a halo substance, and didn't see where to source it from, so invoked the alien snakes. I wrote some fun scenes with the snakes this week, but it just feels too utterly ridiculous. And, as a practical matter, being hosted in an alien's astral body is a lot worse than being hosted in Gee's tree. It's not indie at all.

So what to do?

If I back way, way up, I recall that, initially, I mean a few years ago, when I first imagined this novel, I wanted to use the spirt-of-place natural computations at the ultimate lifebox storage form. And more recently I was talking about hylo (short for hylozoic) ghosts. That's still a workable idea.

I almost came back to lifeboxes as natural computations, or *hylo ghosts*, on September 28, 2020, when I did a ghost survey about the various options I had in mind.

But the next day, I shied away from hylo ghosts and went for quintessence. I thought hylo ghosts were too close to *Hylozoic*, and I couldn't see how to work the communication between a hylo ghost and a human body.

But now, looking back at my ghost survey, I see some points I might take seriously, or that I might get into in the final chapter. For now, my astral body really can be a hylo ghost or what I've also called a zhabo ghost. But we'll include a touch of quintessence.

An astral body, whatever kind of "ghost" it is, is free to *leave* a given body, so it can ensure your immortality like a lifebox. When an astral body is floating around it's a pattern of quintessence like that halo vortex ring that I like to talk about Once you learn the astral body move, you're full indie, in that your lifebox needs no server. And if you can do the halo move, you're a "saint."

With these thoughts in mind, I spent the rest of the day rewriting the second half of Chapter 5, whose title is now "Astral Body" instead of "Tokamak Snakes." I put all the tokamak stuff into an "Unused" subsection of these *Notes*.

I didn't use the expression "hylo ghost" in my changes, I talked about a universal lifebox and about a quintessence vortex ring. Covered my ass (re. scientific inaccuracy) on quintessence by having Gee say he doesn't use the world "quintessence" in the same way that scientists to, and I took the trouble to make it sound more like a field (which I think it actually is) than like aethereal substance.

In order to keep a little of the snake stuff, I had Mary see a single snake in the clearing, and she does teep with it. It's a big rattlesnake, all mean, not an alien, not a tokamak ring. Gee put a psidot on it, and uses it as a watchdog. Gee has a number of other animals teeped up with psidots, and we can talk about this a little more at the end of the chapter and put some of that in earlier on as well.

At the end of the day, I felt I'd gotten over my latest big fix. And in the night, I had a dream that I went to a dentist and he reached into my mouth and very easily lifted out a lower molar that's been hurting me for months. Symbol for doing a fix?

October 8, 2020. Keep Psidots Till Last Chapter.

Maybe if you have an astral ghost for your lifebox, then you don't need a psidot in order to talk to it? To go this route, I'd need for the ghost to do what the psidot does, that is, have quantum vortex tendrils to read your nerve signals and your neurochemicals. And it would triple loop your stream of consciousness and emulate your neurochemical moods. But for the astral body to affect your moods it would still need to use your gossip molecules to instantiate the actual chemicals in your head.

But maybe it's better not to complicate things right way. We just now added astral bodies instead of lifeboxes, so it's too much upheaval to get rid of the psidot right away.

For now I'll characterize the psidot as an all-purpose psychic-phenomena channel. Like a USB plug is today.

My feeling is that, once you make something work one way, it's confusing to have it work a second way. Don't want two ways at the same time. Have one or the other, not both. When you want the change, then throw out the first way and use the second way exclusively. But with just one astral body in play just now (Mary's), we don't have the infrastructure ready for eliminating psidots across the board. Do don't throw them away yet.

I'll keep the elimination of psidots in reserve. Down the line, in the final chapter, I can get rid of psidots and have universal telepathy via astral bodies. But not just yet.

How about teeping with animals, or with people who don't have a psidot. Could that be possible? Well, if I want it, I can get it by, again, claiming the astral ghost can do those vortex threads.

I've always liked the phrase, "He understood the speech of birds and animals." For now, Gee and Mary only understand the speech of the animals who have psidots but ultimately—at the paradisiacal end of the book—psidots will no longer be needed and everyone will understand the speech of birds and animals via their astral bodies.

Post psidots, an astral body can just *settle into* a new flesh host instead of you putting a psidot on the host and linking it to an externally hosted lifebox. So I can restore that pleasant scene of Mary's ghost diving into her clone's yummy meat. But now I could have her settle into a body that isn't hers.

And we get the spirit familiar or astral body thing too. A hylo ghost can settle into (take possession of?) any person or animal or plant or even any physical process, perhaps with no psidot or lifebox server involved.

And ultimately, an astral body can settle into (take possession of?) any person or animal or *plant* or even any *physical process*. That's at the very end. The *nec plus ultra*. (Nothing more beyond.)

October 9-13, 2020. Skip Gap. Molly Fate. Top Party.

I can do much more about teeping with animals. Mentioned already in "Treadle Disease."

Have a bunch of animals under Gee's and Mary's control repel an attack on Gee's cave. Battle scene! That would be a good ending for the chapter. And I could come up with oddball ways to block even a missile or a plane-dropped bomb with the animals. I can invent that stuff pretty easily as I go along.

Who would be attacking them? I don't think *Leeta* would be attacking as Gee is likely to cut her in on the astral body action.

No, the obvious attackers would be the remnants or spiritual heirs of the Treadlers. The way I've structured the book at present is that Treadle is ten years gone by the time "Mary Mary" takes place. So it would not be Treadlers *per se* who attack Gee's cave. But their political party would be the best enemy by far. Would give the book unity. And would be a higher-level instance of the axiom, "You have to kill the Terminator more than once."

So look, I'll need to cut the gap between Chaps 4 and 5 down to just one year. Instead of it being ten years. What would I need to change?

***

To Do

- * I'd thought it might take more than a year for Skyhive to ramp up into a huge business. But, hell, our Leeta could do it in a year.
- * Mary's memories of the Treadle assassination are fairly fresh; bring them closer to the present.

***

Give the Treadler-type people a group name like Heritagists from the *Ware* series. I could even use that same name if I wanted to; it, would be kind of funny to me—although possibly confusing to readers who've read the *Wares*: "Wait, is *Teep* in the same Ruckeverse as the *Wares*?" Nah.

So okay, I want a right-wing, anti-citizen party with a name based on some high-flown (bogus) principle. Heritage. Honor.

Fairness. Straight. Elite. Faith. Tradition. How about the Tradition Party and the Tradders, which is comfortably close to Treadlers. Too close, maybe.

Better if it's *not* so close to Treadle. How about the Forever Party! Perfect. Or is it? Forever Party sounds like Party Forever, which is kind of a good thing, isn't it? But that fact could be viewed as bitterly ironic. Forever Party means Party Never. Would Never Party be a better name? No. Forever Party. But that's still not perfect. It's not stupid enough.

Free Party. Awfully close to freal. Quo Party. For status quo and QAnon. Quorum Party. Means nothing, but sounds obnox. Quality Party. Highline Party. Topper Party. Topsy Party. Topster Party. Top Party. Go with that.

"I contain multitudes—my mind is a focus group."
***

We'll give astral bodies or animal bodies to *some* of the lifeboxes inside Gee's server. Keep in mind that a most of the clients might are still alive, as Skyhive is only one year old. So most of them do have bodies, and those who are dead others might own biots or clones. So there would only be as small group of "orphan" lifeboxes, say a hundred. Also keep in mind that Skyhive is new, and expensive, so they don't have a really enormous customer base yet.

The orphan lifeboxes can be a platoon to fight for Gee in the battle of Gee's Cave. Unfortunately a couple of them might be traitors, and working for the Top Party.

To organize them, Gee might be using that super Junker-designed AI agent Metatron.
***

What about Molly and Anselm? At the end of "Treadle Disease" they were teeping into Metatron, a supercomputing AI. They had lifeboxes, presumably on Gee's server. And then they saw a bright light and their bodies disappeared. Let's say the bright light was an enemy force. Let's say it was the Top Party AI. Run by their own evil mad scientist. It's too soon for that to be Carson, also he's not smart enough

So I need an arch-enemy mad scientist. Default brainless move: Gee has an evil twin. Should I do that? Maybe. Judge. The Janitor. Can I say janitor? Turns out that word is now borderline un-PC—*sheesh*. Fixer. Mr. Tidy. Partch. Tighty.

Bink. Coggy. He's in a mental hospital. Shuffles around. Classic stereotype. I kind of like the sound of Coggy. Cogs like gears. Coggy Spinner.

Okay, I did this: Molly, Anselm, and Metatron were attacked by a giant Top Party AI thing like a spider. Does *that* fucking thing need a name, too? Well, I can just call it Coggy, same as the name of the human Top Party mad scientist. The online Coggy is the essence of human Coggy.

Coggy went through Molly and prefigured the Winch-Treadle nitroglycerin routine by poisoning Molly's body in the Junker barn. Let's say it gave her a heart attack—or, no, something worse, so it's gonna be hard to even clone a Molly from the remains. Coggy was going to wipe Molly's lifebox off Gee's server as well, but Molly moves her lifebox elsewhere.

So later Molly is somehow still in teep space. She's got an indie lifebox somewhere. And she gives Curtis the idea for the nitro trick.

***

TO DO

- * Introduce the *Top Party* early on They can be the enemy after Treadle himself is gone.
- * Have a few ball walkers in Chapters 1-4. The early models use uvvies instead of psidots.
- * Include Miss Max and Glory when Mary gets back into her body with the halo.

Oct 14-16, 2020. Setting Up the Chap 5 Ending.

I'm fumbling around trying to find a climax for Chapter Five: Astral Body. The obvious one would be an attack on Gee's server and cave, mounted by the Top Party, possibly with Skyhive joining in. The battle could run into Chap 6; they could lose; and in the final Chap 7 they emerge victorious.

Re. the Battle of Gee's Cave, I think that ultimately Leeta *would* be on Gee's side, so maybe she's been ousted by Skyhive. Suppose Carson has managed a last-minute end-run to take over Skyhive.

Molly comes back.

Where is Anselm?

***

Right now the end of Chap 5 is kind of shaggy. I couldn't resist having this long encounter between Mary and Zsuzsa, the rattlesnake who's psidotted to Gee. But the encounter is kind of pointless; it has no relation to the plot, and introduces no new gimmicks.

After much clamoring (by me) the ball walkers Glory and Miss Max also reappear in the latter part of Chapter 5 but, again, they advance no plot points nor any gimmicks.

I think I'd want to give the ball walkers psidots (which they don't have in the Oct 13, 2020, draft) and hook them to Gee. Gee is getting ready for the attack.

But first we have the love scene between Mary and Gee. And then the attack starts in.

***

Gee's Army: Rattlesnakes, the two ball walkers, a dozen bluejays, a pair of mountain lions, a thousand swarms of gnats (with each swarm itself being a telepathic AI). Maybe the fog, and the air currents, if Gee can put sentience into them. Smart fire! And Gee's friend who drives the thudhumper. Maybe a bunch of thudhumpers show up. And Metatron. And the orphan lifeboxes. Molly.

Top Party Army: Killer drones, helicopters with machine guns, napalm, a squadron of thugs with guns, satellite-mounted death-ray particle beams, mind-controlled Skyhive clients. And don't forget Coggy. And forced lifebox gig workers.

Uh oh.

But, wait, the Top Party is not in power, so they won't be able to get things like Army helicopters. Otherwise Gee might need to call in the now, legit troops of President Sudah Mareek's administration, but I don't want to go there. Want Gee and Mary to handle it themselves. With maybe Molly in the mix.

[*Side joke.* "We're saved! Here comes the cavalry." *Calvary is the hill where Jesus got crucified. The name means skull.* "We're lost! Here comes Calvary."]

So Gee's gang is getting their asses kicked, but then things get better due to some sneaky teep strategy another. A bounce We already had a bounce with Treadle Disease spreading and being cured, and a bounce with Treadle getting elected and assassinated. It's a typical pattern for this kind of action-adventure book.

To make the attack bounce worthwhile, we need for it to involve some new gimmick or strategy that we can exploit as a peacetime app in late Chap 6. And then we'll still need something else for Chapter 7, yet another twist, but I won't worry about that yet.

Re. bringing back Carson—I'm so sick of that guy. If he takes over Skyhive and comes back, let's just kill him really fast. A triple hit like Curtis did on Treadle: natural body / lifebox / clone.

I'm not at all up for killing Gee, not even for a little while. Killing and resurrecting is a move I've already used with Molly and with Curtis and with Mary, so if I do it with Gee it's too stale, unless the resurrection gets all hylozoic…but I'm kinda doing that with Molly already.

***

Yadda, yadda, yadda. Talk is cheap. How do I fucking finish Chapter 5?

Need a sense of foreboding about the attack. Gee knows it's coming, but he wants to be sure and fuck Mary before it comes down. So he's not talking about it.

Zsuzsa the snake spills the beans about the impending attack.

And the ball walkers know about it too. So, yeah, then they *are* doing something for the plot.

"I found Molly." She's inside Metatron. They make her a body; but how? Well, what if Molly saved the full map of her body into Metatron while she was alive. They "write" her with at 3D meat printer.

Gyr should show up.

***

Could we use teep / lifebox / clone tech for teleportation? Well, yeah, in a way. That would be a nice new present to unwrap.

Body + psidot $\rightarrow$ body + psidot + lifebox $\rightarrow$ (body + psidot) + lifebox + (clone + psidot)

Unlike the usual teleportation-booth scenario, you don't destroy your original body when you teleport. And you need to prepare the clone beforehand, and that takes a while, growing the clone in a tank. Although I guess we could really go apeshit and claim the clone body is created by, like, a 3D bioprinter. I guess we could have those by then.

And in that case, then we could perhaps be doing a destructive "read" of the body here while "writing" it over there. Just like in those trad teleportation-booth scenes.

But, no, don't do a digital 3D meat-printer build, it's so digital and voxel-based, and completely goes against the woven "juiciness" of analog living organisms. The new body *has to be grown in a tank*. This said, there's no reason I couldn't accelerate the growth to an insane blur, like a fast forward stop action video of maggots eating a dead animal, only played in reverse.

Tweet version:

> Teleportation for TEEP. Do mind with lifebox. Body with digital 3D meat-printer? Naw, want woven "juiciness" of analog life. Grow bod in tank. BUT accelerate growth to insane blur, like nauseating fast-forward stop-action video of maggots eating dead animal—played in reverse!

***

To Do

- * Give Gee psidot links to some animals early in Chap 5. Setting up his "army."
- * Early in Chap 5, prefigure the attack by Top Party + Skyhive.

***

Okay, as of Oct 16, 2020, I've done all the setup work for Chap 5. I integrated the snake and the halo, and now Gee and Mary are making love, Gee having retrofitted his body, but he didn't get a new one. Gee is using Metatron to be in psychic touch with all the animals in his neck of the woods. "Like Prospero in *The Tempest*," I say to myself, not that I actually remember he details of that play. A wizard with a host of spirits to command.

The attack looms.

Carson went over to the fat cats of the Top Party and got backing to buy out Skyhive and take it over. Which will be very bad for the Skyhive clients, I'm sure.

And "tonight" Carson and the combined forces of the Top Party and Skyhive security will show up at Gee's, wanting to kill him, and disable his redwood server, and blow up his cave.

Oct 17, 2020. Structure.

Is the battle scene a new chapter? I think it should be. Chapter 5 is presently 9.5K words, which is on the short side, but not overly so.

If I give the battle its own chapter, it can stretch out a bit. For the flow, I pretty much need to stick with Mary for the battle chapter, so that's three Mary chapters in a row. Oh well! I can, divide the book into three parts. Part I: Molly, Molly, Curtis. Part II: Mary, Mary, Mary. Part III: Molly. And possibly a word from Curtis.

I'll need to figure out the action for Part III, but, hey, *on s'engage, et puis on vois.* Re. the size of those future chaps, at present I've got 56,000 words on the novel, and, well, I'll see how long I can stretch out the battle Chap 6. If it's long enough, then Part III could just be a single Molly chapter, which could be a nice way to end. The Muse will tell me what to do. I have to believe that. I have no other option.

Re. overall structure, I just now noticed a disparity I'd overlooked—probably because the chaps gestated as unconnected short stories. Originally "Mean Cucumber" was third person, but I changed it to first person to match "Juicy Ghost." But the Mary chaps are still in 3rd person. I can leave them that way or not. I kind of like them in third person, as it gives Mary a feel of dignity. The Molly and Curtis chaps are more demotic and chattier—and first person works for them, especially for Curtis. And if I "fence off" the Mary chaps in a Part II, then the change from 1st to 3rd person feels a little less jarring. And I go back to 1st for Part III.

I'll revisit all this later on. Meanwhile…write the battle.

Oct 18-21, 2020. Battle.

Gee and Mary will win the fight, with Mary turning the tide.

What stops the bad guys from just hiring a helicopter and dropping a large bomb?

I'll say that Gee can constantly realtime tweak the sat-nav
and GPS so nobody can find his spot on a digital map. Gee
didn't yet know how to do this for Curtis Winch when he was a
dog, but now he does.

Did the sat-nav watch Gee, Mary, and the ball walkers
running home? Well, Gee tweaked their signals. A drone
search army? No, the drones get tricked too. How about an
army of insects. Gee tweaks the mining of their data. And you
can't satellite track Bernardo's thudhumper driving in because
of the ubiquitous Gee sat-nav tweak. Did taking in all those
Skyhive clients set up a beacon? Well, those locations can be
spoofed and shifted as well.

Could they use a paper map? Well Gee isn't ON any paper
maps.

An *optical* bomb-sight could spot Gee's cave—but suppose
I say that Gee keeps an air-based mirage warp over his spot,
like a lens of air refractivity. You'd need, maybe, a large,
buoyant ctenophore. An acre-sized flying jellyfish. What the
hell, in for a penny in for a pound, we'll use that.

Gee is spoofing all the searchers to a spot one and half
miles away. Fake Gee's cave. So they're bombing the wrong
place, a mile away. Good opener for this section; that's what
wakes up Mary and Gee.

   ***

The concealment measures are flimsy. If anyone with any
clout was *really* looking for Gee's cave, they'd find him. Let's
say that, up till the assassination, nobody cared enough about
Gee to look for him, and afterwords he got a deal with the
government, in gratitude for killing Treadle. Like witness
relocation. So the Top Party doesn't get him.

   ***

Gee has arranged for Carson to take a ride in Gee's
thudhumper friend Bernando to the airport. Carson imagines he
bullies Bernardo into driving him to Gee's cave. But actually
Bernardo takes Carson to the decoy site, and drives away really
fast. And Top Party is doing a bombing right then. I'll say
Carson escapes, and tells Top Party they're bombing a decoy.

Right when Carson escapes, he learns that Leeta has erased
his lifebox—but he gets on the horn with the actually, Top
Party and they restore it. And then Carson organizes a by-foot

search for Gee's cave.

For if you actually hike in, you can find the place. A human chain of people walking in a line, hundreds of them, combing for Gee's cave—that would work. Like "beaters" driving game. If you spaced the people thirty feet apart, then about 300 of them would make a line about two miles long. Once they see that the "Gee's cave" location is fake, they walk a two-mile long downhill. Somehow they know the cave is about the same altitude as the dummy, and that the cave is south of the dummy.

Rattlers bite them. They slip on slugs. Lions take out a few. And coyotes. Crows peck them. Gnat swarms choke them. Squirrels bite them, and drop heavy cones on them. The lifeboxes in Gee's tree—they emit halo toruses that zap the searchers with sparks.

Can they detect the signals from Gee's redwood? Well, maybe not, if the signals are subtly blended into ambient RF crackle.

The bad guys bring in a patented Skyhive blanket jammer that blocks ultraweak wireless in a whole general area. Making it hard or impossible for Gee or for the Gee redwood lifeboxes to contact any local remotes, in particular the army of bio remotes. But the zapper donuts are indie, and they continue their work.

To keep her flesh-connectivity with her halo in the absence of ultraweak wireless, Mary sinks her halo down into her chest. She physically crawls in through the hole in Gee's redwood and shoves her hand into the server goo, so as to serve as Metatron's physical body. Big scene.

Gee heads for the physical Top Party headquarters at Stanford, leaving Mary to hold the fort.

Metatron grows out from Mary, a weightless creature of quintessence and light, looking like a full-size B-29 bomber. Like a maxed version of a kid dressed up as "an airplane" for Halloween, Mary is walking Metatron along, and he's zapping every one of the Top Party pigs. A big B-29 bomber. There's a pilot whom Mary can't quite make out, a figure in one of those earflap pilot hats, and with goggles

Here comes Coggy, a giant fire tarantula, perhaps setting the trees alight. The pilot gestures to Mary not to worry, and steps out of the plane. It's Molly.

Molly conjures Metatron into the giant, living mandelglob (3D Mandelbrot set) from my story "As Above, So Below." She douses the flames and she kills Coggy by weaving his legs into re-entrant loops. Go back to Molly POV?

With Mary as host, Molly wipes out all the attackers on the scene and even destroys the Top Party servers and their honchos. Like the "Blue Wave" on November 3, 2020, I hope.

And then Gyr shows up with a scrap of Molly meat. Gee grows the clone, and we do the backwards-in-time version of grubs eating a dead fox scenario go grows Molly's body.

Then what does Molly do? Well, maybe that's the book's final chapter. She's into these networked lifebox mind things like Metatron and Coggy. They're like brains whose neurons are lifeboxes. Metabrains. Maye there's a fad for them. A Machines of Loving Grace scenario, a foolish belief in big tech. But the architecture poops out. No juice.

Eventually go back to basics, future Eden, with everything a mind. Yawn.

***

TO DO

- * Don't repeat ball walkers bonking heads and modulating the sound.
- * Mention tracking when the ball walkers reach the top of the ridge.
- * Mention Mary's heavy shoes.
- * Bernardo's lifebox in Gee's redwood.
- * Mention banana slug butler again. What's his name? Bunter, like Lord Peter Wimsey's man in the Dorothy Sayers novels.

October 22, 2020. Reset. Do a Carson Chap.

I started writing the battle as a third Mary chapter, and it's flat, as Gee is just telling Mary about all the exciting things that happened to Carson just now, including dying off-camera, and that's totally dull. Show don't tell!

I ought to do the battle chap from *Carson's* point of view. Let him be a person, and *not* just a pesky evil stereotype. Give the man some pathos. Let him chew the scenery. Let the POV character be evil for a change.

Writing Carson's POV opens up some good possibilities, including inside views of the Top Party conspiracy to take over Skyhive and do mind control like never before.

I'll hop back a few hours in time and start up Carson's narrative that afternoon when he went over to the Top Party.

Opening line for Carson's chapter ☺

People think I'm an asshole, but I'm not.

It would help to know a little about Carson's background. I'll say he grew up in Illinois. Like my friend CS. I have Carson's last name as Pflug, which is odd, but I'll keep that. He's short and wiry, about 5'4". How did he get in with connecting the Oakland assassins with the Secret Service? He was a business/tech major at UC Berkeley, and he met Leeta there. Started out as a liberal, but joined the Top Party for job contacts and to "work from inside." Organized some IT work for them, though he himself wasn't a programmer.

He met a Top Party guy called Ben Kraal, who knew people in the Secret Service. The Secret Service were curious about Leeta, so Ben arranged for Carson to put Leeta in touch with the SS. It wasn't clear to Ben what was going down, he thought the SS was out to entrap Leeta. But Carson learned they wanted to help her. The SS got some money to Leeta, and Carson got a cut.

The Top Party urged Carson to work with Leeta's Skyhive, to some extent as a mole. They dream of taking over all those lifebox minds.

Carson met Kayla at Berkeley and honestly loved her, but they drifted apart. He was hooked on stim drug and porn, and thought about business deals all the time. He dreams of making a big financial score and thereby getting Kayla back—not realizing this path would never work.

Oct 27-Nov 10, 2020. "Carson Pflug" Chapter.

I'm writing some really funny/sad stuff on the new Chapter 6: "Carson Pflug." In the end, its often the best when I give up on planning or thinking and just start writing. Fabulating, making things up, writing to amuse myself. I took off from that start line: "People say I'm an asshole, but I'm not."

Going good, although tomorrow we're driving up to Fort

Bragg, CA, to welcome Isabel, who's moving from Wyoming to California with U-Haul. So I might not write as much this week, which is fine.

I have Carson about to graduate from UC Berkeley as an undergrad biz major now. He's just now met Kayla, so I'll kind of nail that down. They're happy and in love, but soon he'll have to drift.

***

Nov 4, 2020.

Back at work again. I'm writing a lot of dialog. Carson with Leeta, Kayla, and this new villain, Jerr Boom.

After the fact, I realize that I subconsciously got that new name from the name of maintenance manager at the visiting-faculty-housing apartments in Neckargemünd by Heidelberg when Sylvia, the kids and I were there on my two-year grant at the University, that would have been 1978-1980. The manager was called Herr Bohm, and he was pretty much the enemy of the lodgers, especially of our kids, especially of Georgia, who got caught for drawing a mocking caricature of the man, which she deliberately left where he'd find it. Herr Bohm's biggest enemies of all were the members of this one American family from the Midwest, hicks, they could never learn to pronounce the guy's name the German way; they called him "Herr Boom."

Thus: Jerr Boom. First I had "Jerr," just as a groovy nickname, and then the Boom popped to the surface, and, as I say, I didn't initially know where it came from.

Jerr Boom is a Steve Bannon type guy, in tight with the Treadlers and the Top Parry, but not unintelligent. A double or triple agent, ruthless, always out for himself.

I love writing dialog; the word count just piles up. Might want to fill in a few more visuals and interruptions for these passages.

I'm about 4K words into the chapter now. And I'm finding some new plot connections involving Carson. Looking ahead, I need the segue to the freals, the assassination, and Skyhive. Then the sellout of Skyhive and, finally, the Battle of Gee's Cave. It' feels like I still have plenty of room for that if I'm shooting for 11K or 12K.

To Do

- * Describe Carson meeting Leeta at Berkeley. Let's say it was undergrad.
- * Carson's contact at the Top Party. A Bannon-type guy. Ben Hoove, or, no, Jerr Boom.
- * Does Leeta have a last name? Patel.
- * Leeta has unrequited crush on Carson.
- * Carson is go-between between Leeta and Secret Service, via Jerr Boom & the Torks.
- * Carson goes to work with Leeta at Skyhive.
- * Carson gets Top Party to do a hostile takeover of Skyhive.
- * During the drive to dummy Gee's cave, Carson notices that his lifebox is gone.
- * Mention cave's sliding door several times.

I need to figure out exactly how it is that Carson becomes alienated from Kayla and then spends so much time in his pupa. Is it another woman? Possibly it's a virtual avatar of Leela, and Carson doesn't realize that's who it is? That would be rich. Or maybe he *does* know who it is, but pretends he doesn't because he wants to gain status at Skyhive. Or, simpler, he and Leeta both know. Of course.

Nov 9, 2020.

I've got the chapter up to 9,600. Phenomenal progress today; I wrote 2K, pretty much typing as fast as I can for hours, the scenes and dialog and eyeball kicks just flowing out. In the zone. I was calling the chapter "The Showdown" at first, and then "The Plot," but now it's "Carson Pflug." The last chapter will be who knows what. Depends on what ends up happening.

I sold the "Treadle Disease" chapter to a subscription ezine called Black Cat today. Edited by Paul Di Filippo. $50. It's exposure.

Nov 10, 2020

The chapter's up to 11.5K. Carson is about to go to the dummy cave, nearly get bombed, set up a line of beaters, and have the showdown with Gee and Mary. I think I'd like to wrap all that up in this chapter and have Carson die at the end. Is there enough room? Well, the most recent chapters were 11.5K in length. But the old "Juicy Ghost" chapter—which is, in a way, similar to this one, being the memoir of a killer—that one ran 13.7K. So let's say I could run out to that length or even a little more if I want to. Let's say 14K if I wanted to, giving me 2.5K more words to play with. Or longer. Whatever it takes.

In terms of making Chapter 6 manageable, I can also print it out and edit it down a bit...I'm sure there's some repetitive or otiose passages in there, as lately I've been having so much fun typing that I'm not doing my usual work-flow schtick of write/print-out-the-new-stuft/mark-it-up/type-in-changes/think-of-what's-next— and repeat.

Nov 11-13, 2020. Bomb Carson. End of Chap 6.

I had 12K on the chapter on Nov 11, and they *still* weren't doing the Battle of Gee's Cave. Carson and Jerr Boom were in the thudhumper on the way to the dummy cave and are about to get bombed.

I went ahead and bombed them dead in a thousand words more, and never even got to the Battle of Gee's Cave. It's like I vamped my way out of ever writing that scene. I often inveigh against repetitious vamping—if it's like in a crummy country music ballad where they keep raising the pitch by a few notes, and playing the whole fucking verse again, with louder chorus. But I suppose I can permit vamping when it's surreal and off topic.

So, yeah, killed off Carson and Jerr at the end of Chap 6, the guy's hoist by their own petard, bombed by the flappy. And they aren't there to urge the raid anymore, so it doesn't have to happen, at least not yet.

The bomb comes twice at 7 pm, matching when Mary and Gee heard it at the end of Chap 5.

I sent the *Teep* doc thus far to John Silbersack to see what he thinks

Nov 14-30, 2020. Revising Chaps 1 & 2.

I decided to print out the six chapters I have, to mark that up, and type in the changes. Get it all straight before I write the finale.

It can take a week to do a chapter—seems I'm looking at close to twenty corrections a page, and I've got 191 pages, nearly 200, so I'm talking about 4,000 corrections. Sheesh. Don't think about it that way, Rudy. Think in terms of pages and chapters. Take your time and enjoy it. Knead the dough.

I printed out the Nov 14, 2020, manuscript, double-sided, and three-hole-punched it and put it into a binder. I have a manila folder where I carry around about six or seven pages, and work on those with my standard-for-many-years Pilot P-700 Fine (0.7) black-ink gel pen, though this I bought a Uniball Power Tank pen that can write at an angle or even upside down if I'm lying on my back, and we'll see if that can work for me too.

I did a first correction session on November 14, 2020, and another on Monday, Nov 16, 2020—when I took my slim folder-sheaf up into the woods above the Jesuit center and the so-called St. Josephs Hill up the streets from us. Nice to be outside while working—it was a beautiful sunny fall day—though a little sad not to be *seeing* the day, and eventually my ass got tired from sitting on the ground and I had to stop.

The process is really astoundingly slow. I have to think about everything so much, and fix so many things. After I wheenked about this to fellow-writer Marc Laidlaw, he said something good.

I like the revising part of a novel but it is very overwhelming when you step back from it. But it's good to know you're improving it—you're the only one who can do that, it's your job, you get to discover these things in your draft that you didn't really notice when you were writing it. For some reason I always think about when I was revising *The 37h Mandala*, sitting in the library at 24th and Mission with my big fat print-out, feeling like there was so much work to do and I was only one person... You have done this so many times, you have the routine down way beyond any amount of experience I'll ever get to...but even then, it doesn't get any easier, does it?

Nov 21, 2020

I think I'm almost done with Chapter Two now. Really having to do a lot of rewriting, to make things work. Rounded out Liva character a little. Made Molly's two mind-edit sessions different from each other. Making the rubber science a little more uniform and internally consistent.

With the end of Trump's reign now on the horizon, the novel has a different feel. More like history instead of frantic, fearful prophecy. Fine with me! I think it'll go own better this way—that is, I think it has more mass appeal if Trump/Treadle really *has* been thrown out. If he was still in, the sting of my story would be too great.

Nov 27, 2020

Still not quite done revising Chapter Two. It really *is* taking me a week per chapter. The chapters are long, and there's a lot of tidying up to do.

I decided to have the Treadle Disease and its cure be focused on corrupt Treadlerized gossip molecules—instead of infected neurons—and this required dozens of changes. Now I wonder if it wouldn't be a *lot* easier for the reader if I just stick to talking about infected neurons. Possibly the gossip molecules are *attached* to the neurons, like waving pennants or tails or flagellae. I'll take care of this.

Right now I'm at the end of Chapter Two where something bad happens to Molly, destroying her physical body and leaving her mind stranded in teep space. I didn't want to totally kill her, as I'd like her to return in the final chapter and have a happily-ever-after with Gyr. But I'm vague on what actually happens, and I would like to know before I get back to Chapter Seven—unless, sigh, I don't actually figure it out until I blindly, gropingly write my first draft of Chapter Seven.

The thing that attacks her—I'd kind forgotten this— is Coggy, a Treadler version of the freals' Metatron. Makes sense, makes symmetry, but if I keep Coggy, I need to weave in Coggy into the earlier and later chapters. Currently I've gendered Metatron as male, but female would be better, and Coggy could be male, which is, at least these days, the default gender for villains. Coggy is a big wad of gears, like a stupid-ass giant Transformer robot.

Maybe Metatron has a painting on her fuselage showing a crocodile in a 1940s pinup pose. And in way it might be a self-portrait of Metreon. Is there any connection between this crocodile, and the crocodiles who ate Carson Plug's father? Or would that constitute faux virtuosity, as in overelaboration, as in trying too hard, as in getting desperate, as in jumping the shark? Yes, it would. Don't use a crocodile. Use a math dragon that's a Gosper fractal.

Nov 28, 2020

Okay, I prefigured Coggy.

And I integrated the gossip molecules into the neurons as flagellae, and made a variant form of Treadle gossip molecules themselves "be" the Treadle Disease virus.

And I clarified the scene at the chapter end. Coggy kills Molly's body, but Metatron helps her hide her soul/lifebox/mind from her nemesis Coggy, with Molly becoming something like a supernatural being, at least for the nonce.

Nov 29, 2020

Thinking it over, I realize have five "curing" scenes in the chapter and they go on for too long, and this is totally overkill. I need to simplify and condense. I have three types of cures.

- Molly cures her addiction by singing to each of her neurons.
- Molly cures her Treadle disease by internally making a turbulent cascade of a trillion cleaner tornadoes that go to each of her neurons.
- Molly cures Gyr and then Anselm and then everyone in the US by sending cleaner tornado templates to each neuron in each person involved.

In the third type of cure, I said she had to send a separate message to each neuron, and that therefore she needed Metatron to help with the messaging, as Molly alone wouldn't be able to send so many messages.

But, really a *single* message to a person would be enough. We can assume that, just as with sending neurochemical template messages, the one message can be simultaneously deciphered by each of the gossip molecules in that target person's brain.

And if we do it this way, then (a) describing the cures of Molly and of Anselm is simpler, and (b) Molly would only need to bring in Metatron for the final case, the case where she messages hundreds of millions of people at once and I do want Metatron to be needed for that.

Note also that, if we're not messaging the individual neurons, then we don't get into needing a quintillion messages. We can just suppose that sending hundreds of millions of messages is already difficult enough to make Molly need Metatron's help.

***

So I did all that today, adding about a thousand more words, even though I thought I'd be shortening it. Well, I fleshed out the ending a bit more. Chap Two is now the longest in the book, but probably some of the later chaps will grow as well.

Nov 30, 2020

Geeze. In the night I rethought the details of Molly's eradication of Treadle Disease and decided to fine tune it a bit more. I wanted to handle any free-floating Treadle Disease viruses as well as the installed Treadle gossip molecules, and to make sure she nails the (majority of) people who don't have psidots.

One thing that still bothers me is that, wanting to simplify things, I more or less said that the Treadle Disease virus is exactly the same thing as a Treadle gossip molecule. That might not be true, but maybe it could be. It would be nicer if I had one and the same name for these two things. A "Treadle gossip molecule virus" instead of a "Treadle Disease virus."

So now I fixed that too.

And I moved about 2K words from the start of Chap 2 to the end of Chap1, so as to balance the chapters' sizes. They're both from Molly's POV, so it's smooth enough either way.

And now I'll finally start proofing Chapter 3.

To Do

- * Almost nobody has a psidot yet, so don't act as if Molly can subdistribute cleaner tornadoes through peoples' psidots. Could I maybe say she can route them through people's uvvies? But street uvvies aren't geared for transmitting emotions; that new emo add0on was only in the *experimental* huffy and stumble. So Molly *does* need to go for quintillion or sextillion fold direct access.

Dec 2-12, 2020. Revising Chaps 3-4.

Dec 2, 2020.

Getting on with it. With Chap. 3, I again saw the clean blank manuscript printout pages, and thought, well, there won't be many corrections. But there are. Although less than before. This is, after all, a chapter I've revised over and over, starting in February, 2019, as the story "Juicy Ghosts."

I figured out how to save Gee from being guilty of a mass killing when he collapses the Washington Monument. I had him teep all the people on the ground near it, giving them instructions on which way to run. The mass killing would have been a problem, as it would undercut my general presentation of Gee as a good guy.

Working on the chapter today at a table on the street outside the Fleur de Cacao Cafe, it felt really cool to be writing SF that's so skintight close to the real world. Pynchon's routine about "dt," rapping about when you're writing something that's a lambent glow overlay upon your somatic life at that very moment.

Dec 4, 2020.

Finished Chap 3 today. Some great stuff in there. And I went back and further simplified some of the Treadle-Disease-cure stuff in Chapter 2.

Dec 5, 2020.

Into Chap 4 now. Marked up about a third of it, typing in the changes now. It's dull, but at the same time it's fun. My body gets tired from the keyboarding.

Dec 7. 2020.

Today I finished correcting Chap 4, and then when I went to copy the file from my desktop to my laptop, I copied the file in the wrong direction, and overwrote today's file with yesterday's file, and lost the typed-in corrections on eight pages that I did today over about six hours. I was tired, and in a rush, and I unaccountably ignored a warning sign on the screen that I ordinarily would react to. Fatigue, I guess. I've really been pushing hard and it's taking forever.

And there's no fix for this particular kind of overwrite

goof, at least not that I can find. So exhausting. And the edits I made today were really good. It's not just a matter of copying the hand corrections I made on the printed pages, it's also a matter of rearranging things and doing light edits, and checking for consistency, and hopping around and adjusting earlier premonitions or the later back-references. Problem solving. I solved a lot of problems today, and now I have to redo those solutions tomorrow.

I just have to live through it. Happy news, we got an Xmas tree today, we've never gotten one so early, normally we'd consider that tacky and declassé, but this year we're dying for any scrap of glitter or fun. Put on some new colored mini-lights, two 70-bulb chains that S fond for $7 total at CVS. What a great deal. Ditto on normal disdain for COLORED lights on our tree, instead of white, but I begged Sylvia and she relented. In theory we each get our pick on alternate years, but she's stonewalled me last year. Looking at the light from them in the corner of the living room now. Almost as good as being drunk and stoned.

Dec 8, 2020.

In the morning, turned out there were only six pages to retype, and I got it done pretty quickly. I think I remembered all, or most of, the side-fixes I made as well.

I notice that I've broken 75 K words. On to Chap 5!

Dec 12, 2020

Had another file disaster with Chap 4, my second in a week. And it was already completely done.

Maybe I'm getting too senile to manage my documents. Today I put the novel into Outline mode, with just the chapter headers showing, and the chapters' texts collapsed into the headers. I do this so I can click on each header and then read off the word count for that chapter from the info bar at the bottom of the Word window. I click on each header and copy that chap's word count over to my Word Count table in these Notes. And today I suddenly noticed that my whole Chapter 4: Mary Mary was fucking gone. So I must have accidentally pressed Delete while that chapter header was selected in Outline mode.

So then I did a really serious and desperate effort to find an earlier version of the book file somewhere eon my computer, and there happened to be a recent automatic backup made Dec 6, 2020, and I could get that day's version of the Mary Mary chapter out of there and copy it into my novel file. But, I'd done revisions on the Mary Mary section on Dec 7- 8. In fact these were the same fucking revisions I'd lost and redone earlier this week.

But, thank god the revisions and their dates are in the marked up draft I'm saving in a 3-ring binder. So, by consulting the binder, I was "lucky" enough to be able to type in those motherfucking changes for the *third* time. Does the Muse have something against these pages? They seem okay to me. But what do I know?

I didn't have the heart to tell Sylvia what I'd done—I already wheenked to her when I lost that material earlier this week—but she kind of noticed my dejection. "You're working really hard on this revision, aren't you?"

Yes, I am. Too hard. And now I woke up at 2:30 am and couldn't stop fretting about finishing my third-time data entry. So I got up and did it and now it's 3:30 am and I'm going back to bed.

December 9-20, 2020. Cryptoamnesia. Psidot? Quintessence?

Revising Chaps 5 & 6 now.

Rather than writing daily blow-by-blow progress reports, I'll summarize some of the issues, and my eventual solutions. The "Astral Body" chapter took more work to revise than the previous ones. It felt like I had more problems to solve this time, and that's probably true, as this more recent chapter, hasn't been worked on as much as the earlier chaps. And by the time I was done, I'd tried out three or four different ways of making Mary's astral body.

WARES CRYPTOAMNESIA.

It found it useful to take a fresh look at the fact that I've been using some of the Chaps *Teep* tropes for forty years— ever since I started up the *Wares* around 1980.

(Put lifebox into psidot.) In *Wetware* I had a happy cloak (~ psidot) that holds Wendy Mooney's mind, and it settles onto a clone of her body and runs her. Note that in *Wetware* I didn't

bother having the software off in a lifebox; it was effectively inside the happy cloak. So now I'll have Mary's lifebox in her astral body, and she'll simply put her astral body (= lifebox + psidot) onto her clone,

(Skip the psidot.) In *Software* they flash-loaded personality software directly onto a kind of android. So why not flash-download lifebox software directly onto a clone's brain without a psidot or an astral body involved? The possibility needs to be clearly raised, initially dismissed ("You need an astral body"), and perhaps later on implemented.

MERGE PSIDOT WITH LIFEBOX.

I was already thinking that *eventually* I'd transcend the psidot—but why vamp? Get it over with; do it in Chap 5. Have the "astral body" take over the functions of the psidot as well as the functions of the lifebox. What functions would I need to replicate?

- *Read/write the body's thoughts, and moods.* Initially an astral body uses quantum vortex threads to connect to the neurons and gossip molecules and nerves of the peripheral body's brain. Just like the psidot did. But if we stay with this, then the astral body is stuck to your body like a psidot. And I want it to roam. And I don't want a cumbersome pigtail or umbilical bundle of quantum threads. So I claim that the quantum thread business is simply an *installation* process that sets up quantum entangled hyperlinks between, for instance, the peripheral's neurons and the processing notes in the astral body. The write works the same as the read, but in the other direction.
- *Reading moods can be an issue.* Note that writing neurochemical templates to the brain's gossip molecules generates moods—and that the astral body needs mood emulation code to decipher the mood templates from the body. To make a temporary complication, Mary's astral body initially lacks the mood emulation code, and she's cold and heartless, but then Gee fixes that.
- *Installing gossip molecules.* The astral body will be

using gossip molecules just like the psidot did. In order for an astral body to work, the subject needs to be inoculated with gossip molecules. This isn't an immediate issue, as the psidot Miu Miu's already installed gossip molecules in Mary. (I need to mention this.) Down the road, I don't know, maybe future clones will automatically come equipped with gossip molecules.

- *Do teep.* This is ultraweak wireless, the same as with a psidot. I think the uvvy and the psidot used people's skulls as antennas—but I need to check this. In any case, the astral body, being a body of ionized gas, can act an antenna on its own.

- *Back up to your lifebox.* Your astral body is your lifebox *as well as* your psidot, so this backup will be taking place continually. But Mary says she'd like to have a backup lifebox that's far away and stored somewhere. She *could* use an old-school server-based lifebox as a backup, like using an external hard drive. But Gee didn't bother making one, and Mary doesn't get around to it, so this might be an issue. It's possible that Mary could in fact be fully destroyed by the looming Top Party raid. I don't think she *will*—as I lean toward happy endings—but it's good to have something for readers to worry about.)

It would be cool if Mary organizes all this in a single brainstorm flash. A good way to give her some extra agency.

So now, the astral body has the whole lifebox inside it, and it hangs out near the body. When you need to exchange signals with person or a lifebox that's further away you use ultra-weak wireless signals, which either the astral body or the peripheral organism can provide. (*Which?*)

Get rid of quintessence.

Quintessence seems confusing and extraneous and bogus. I had quintessence as being a life-and-mind-force that lives in objects or even in empty space. I wanted it so I could push onto full hylozoism and have a mind live in a rock—but I already published that novel *Hylozoic*. Let's drop it.

Instead, I'll say the astral body is alive because it has human mind software in it. It's very close to being a traditional ghost. And if, later, I want a human astral body to adopt some animal or plant or maybe even some physical object or process, we *could* do that.

So...okay. Mary's amped up, rearranged, and her psidot-including lifebox hops out of Gee's redwood. Initially I wanted it to land in/on a pre-existing vortex ring of air. I have a thing for those vortex rings—ever since my toroidal spacetime in my *G, R, & the 4th D*. But here again—*simplify*. Mary's lifebox/psidot creates the hosting aeroform itself.

- *Where did Mary's astral body come from?* The lifebox code exudes the astral body right out of the tree's portal.
- *How does Mary keep the astral body going?* The astral body needs energy both for sending ultraweak wireless and quantum entangled signals—and for staving off dissipation. Where does it get the energy? It does a solar-powered-car kind of thing, converting photons into energy. This also works in the "dark," as the astral body can also eat ambient heat, that is, infrared radiation.
- *Should an astral body be a vortex ring?* No. I was writing it this way before. A torus is such a cool shape. It's like a comic strip a halo. But the spinning is so frenetic. It would be nice if it was a jellyfish that I could plop onto the clone's head. Also, the jellyfish could pulse to move. And, actually, a "halo" can look like a disk.

A month or two ago I was talking about vortex-ring beings who I called <u>tokamak snakes</u>. Maybe there's some descriptive stuff in there I can use.

Instead of eating light, I *could* do a Maxwell's Demon thing, but, nah, too distracting to explain. I'm so far into the book that we've maybe used up the reader's "willing suspension of disbelief." I want something that's almost possible.

If Mary's astral body eats light/heat, her location can be sensed as a coldish spot.

***

I started revising Chap one on November 14, and finished revising Chapter 6 on December 20. Thirty-six days, just over five weeks. Six days per chapter.

It looks good. Now to start thinking about Chapter 7.

Dec 20, 2020 - Jan 5, 2021. Planning Chap 7.

I keep not wanting to write the battle scene. Bored with it in advance. I might skip it, and just have people talking about it later but—*show don't tell*—if they're gonna talk about it, I gotta stage it. The issue is to make it new.

And to make things easier for me, it doesn't have to be the first thing in the chapter. I can happen the next day. Yeah. So I went and shifted some of the prefiguring that was saying the battle would be that night after Carson's blown up. Move the battle to the next morning, and then Kayla has some time to establish herself as a character.

> I'm rereading *Gravity's Rainbow* yet again, and he has sections that roll on and on. I would be nice to get into a fabulating mood like that—like I was in when I wrote the first part of "Chap 6: Carson Pflug." Just be writing for the hell of it, and not necessarily even worrying about plot hooks all the time.

I'll have three or maybe four scenes in this chapter. Hefty. I considered rotating through a different POV for each scene, but I decided to stick with Kayla's POV throughout.

I'm looking forward to Kayla's fresh voice. An antidote to Carson's testosterone poisoning. Kayla is an artist, a smart woman, a mother, and I love her. And I'll do her in 1st person, to match the Carson chapter.

We'll have scenes about defeating the Top Party and advancing juicy ghosts towards the astral and the hylozoic. I think of "Chap 3: Juicy Ghost," where Curtis Winch kills Treadle three different ways. We'll defeat the Top Party on several fronts, and then go for the hylozoic finale. Over the course of the chapter, I'll want to tidy up and indicate the So, fates of the other main characters. Curtis, Molly, Mary, Gee, Gyr, Anselm, Jerr Boom.

Here's some possible events.

- Win the battle of Gee's cave, decimating the Top Party paramilitary.
- Liberate the lifeboxes from Skyhive into astral bodies.
- Metatron kills or assimilates Coggy.
- Convert some astral bodies into hylozoic "spirits of place."
- Meet heretofore unknown spirits who were here all along. Ghosts? Aliens? Higher beings?

I think I'll have these scenes happen over a fairly short timeline, maybe one a day. Don't mound them up and don't separate them too much. Like graduation week, or a wedding weekend. Doesn't have to be the mass of bursts closing a fireworks show.

* To Do: Kayla's Business

It will be interesting in Kayla can provide a bunch of biots to fight on Gee's side during the battle of Gee's Cave. Also, it will be good if Kayla has done some strong action on her own.

So we'll build up a thread that Kayla Stux, Max Prank, and Sergeant Bilko have set up a little business together, producing mass editions of their biots. Jeannie Jone of Mixed Bag is backing them. Like selling art prints. Their fabricator is north of San Jose in Milpitas. Mixed Bag Editions.

Opening Scene

Kayla notices Carson's death. She's talked to Gee and agreed to help in the battle, and she's ordered a hundred Bunter kritters. She calls Phil Bilko and gets him to come down and spend the night with her. Phil orders a hundred Miss Maxes. The next morning they all go to Gee's cave. How does Kayla a keep Daia safe?

*To Do: Top Party *Can* Find Gee's Cave.

This issue became a festering sore. I painted myself into a corner with my grandiose bullshit insistence that nobody can find the cave because Gee is such a good hacker. I knew it wasn't logical, but I pig-headedly kept doubling down.

And I said people *might* find the cave via a tracker device in the ball walker Miss Max. Jerr Boom got her Miss Max's link from Carson Pflug before Carson died or, no, he got it from the guy who built Miss Max. I liked this idea because it connected to the fact that Carson owned Miss Max for a few hours, some years ago. But I don't absolutely *have* to invent an outcome of that past connection.

So come on, get real, the Top Party will have known the location of Gee's cave all along. They've just been pretending they don't know. Waiting for the right moment to attack. Jerr Boom knows this, but Carson doesn't. Jerr Boom goes along with having Bernardo drive him and Carson to a bogus Gee cave spot—because it gives Jerr a change to have flappy bomb Carson when he gets there. A weird execution, that's all. I integrated this view on Jan 4 and 5, 2021

* To Do: Curtis Winch *Wants* To Stay In Teepspace.

Another sore point. I don't really want to write about Curtis Winch anymore. He's done his job. But his lifebox is in Gee's redwood, and I don't like to just walk away from him. I was thinking he needs to reappear and do *something*. But he's maybe gotten enough glory already, so I'm not necessarily looking for him to do a big save.

***

A week ago, a bad idea popped into my head: Have Curtis excise Top Party—and himself—from our spacetime with a superpowered broadsword! And instead of it being Metatron and Molly who wipe out Coggy— Curtis Winch joins in and excises the tainted part of Reality that includes Coggy!

Like the way my dermatologist used a flexed razor blade to remove a circular crater of cancered flesh from the back of my left hand a few weeks back. Like cutting out a brown, rotten spot on a peach.

And then, I was rashly thinking I might as well have Curtis excise not just Coggy but all the Top Party members and the Treadlers and all memories of these movements and maybe even—oh no!—Curtis Winch himself. He wins the war, but loses the battle in the sense that all traces of him are erased from spacetime. Perhaps as a lagniappe, he becomes an archetype, that is, racial memories of him live on as legends.

But this excision is too different from the rubber science that's in the rest of the book. I need to dial it down.

***

The simplest fix is that Curtis *likes* it in teepspace and doesn't want to come back into full physical embodiment. It's not that Gee is ignoring Curtis.

So on Jan 5, 2021, I went over the novel and had Curtis be saying he wants to live in teepspace, saying this near the end of the "Juicy Ghost" chapter, and had Gee confirm this in conversation with Mary in the "Astral Body" chapter.

And later, at the very end, I'll have a bit about Curtis liking being hylozoic. Because this way he's got juice, and he's been missing that.

TOP PARTY LIFEBOX CONTROL

Top-Party-controlled lifeboxes that are still in Skyhive. These lifeboxes are screwing things up all over the peninsula. Stealing things. Sabotage. Poison in food.

BATTLE OF GEE'S CAVE: PERSONNEL

The long-threatened raid on Gee's cave. Everyone is getting ready all night and the fight is at dawn.

Top Party Team. A panic-in-Duckburg situation. The attack on Gee's cave is staffed by humans and biots controlled by Skyhive lifeboxes!

Transreally, this echoes Trump's increasingly maddened incitements of his Trampers in early January, 2021. I keep thinking I'm done with our foul, nearly-gone Prez, and yet his ongoing realworld antis keep filtering into *Teep*.

Why doesn't Top Party just bomb Gee? They want his lifebox and his physical brain.

Gee's Team.

Kayla has a company in Milpitas growing her kritters. So she can bring in at least a hundred of them. Kayla gets Phil

Bilko to provide a bunch of Miss Maxes. Their friend Max Prank shows up with giant squids.

Molly.

To bring back Molly for the battle, Gyr sends Gee some DNA from a scrap of Molly meat. And Gyr is flying in herself. Gee grows the clone, and Kayla sees it—like a time-reversed clip of maggots eating a dead animal.

METATRON VS. COGGY

I've been wondering if I could delete Metatron and Coggy. They seem a bit fannish and added-on. But, on doing a search through the novel, I see that Megatron in particular is used quite a lot. So, okay, I'll let Metatron have it out with Coggy.

A big Marvel-Comics-type bout between two super-beings is a cliché. But hell, I'm trying to wrap up a genre novel, and people like to see what Bruce calls a "double-page-spread"—as in a comic. I did a cosmic beatdown at the end of *Million Mile Road Trip*, and it was satisfying. As I keep saying, I need to make all these things new. How can a battle between two gods possibly interesting?

***

Molly + Kayla + Metatron vs. Jerr Boom + Coggy.

Kayla sees Molly start fighting, and she sees Molly fall, and then Kayla steps forward to help, and she's imbued with the spirit of Metatron— who is a hylozoic Gaia goddess.

Their opponent is Jerr Boom, who *did* escape the bombing at the fake Gee's cave.

Big electrical storm of battling lightning bolts, sizzles down, Molly is alive and is now aglow with Metatron. Jerr Boom rides in on his flappy, gets energized by Coggy in midair, takes on a heroic stance. So Metatron and Coggy become energy fields around the human's forms—the combatants are like, if memory serves, the "champions" Hector and Achilles in the *Iliad*.

***

My peeps have to do something about this. Kayla and Mary coach the Skyhive lifeboxes on how to migrate to astral bodes. The Top Party forces are co-opted.

HYLOZOIC

This scene begins at dawn.

Some astral bodies, but not all, go hylozoic. That is, they instantiate themselves as organic nature-based animist ambient computations embedded in the chaotic natural process-es…maybe not even using halos this time around.

This the climax I planned since I even started writing the book, so why not just fucking use it. Yes, it overlaps with my novel *Hylozoic*, but not entirely. And it's not cryptomnesia because I do know I'm repeating myself, I'm *drumming in* the idea of hylozoism as it's so outre and hard for people to believe in. Also, in *Hylozoic* we didn't have people actually porting themselves into natural processes, so far as I recall.

And…once everyone is a wiggling leaf or a current in a stream, then what? They learn there were ubiquitous other beings all along, and we leave it at that. The hoary transcend-ence move, another of Bruce Sterling's notions: Merge with the minds of the universe. Say hello to the hylozoic gnomes.

OUTCOME

Molly + Gyr

Mary + Gee. Mary is mostly living with Gee, sometimes in his cave, sometimes in Mary's old house.

Anselm, Leeta, Kayla : alone, or with unknown partners.

Jerr Boom, Curtis Winch, Carson Pflug: dead

EPILOG

I was wondering if I might tack on a closing fugue that shows, or alludes to, author/narrator Rudy's own eventual death. Like at the end of that movie *Big Fish*, where all of a certain storyteller's characters show up at his funeral. No, don't to this, it's self-aggrandizing wheenk, and extra work, and would do nothing for the novel.

January 6-7, 2021. Kayla's Kritters.

To help get going on Chapter 7, I might make a list of actions, in order—like a shooting script. Yawn. How to die of boredom.

Would be more fun to just fucking *write* something on the novel. Postpone the planning Make it up as I along. And *then* make an outline…if I want…and at that point I can figure out and heal whatever key steps I omitted.

Let's start by inserting some backstory for Kayla. Prefigure her product line called maybe Kayla Kritters. I used the word "kritter" in *Frek and the Elixir*, and in *The Big Aha*, so why not use it again. It's more engaging than "biot."

I want her to be a more successful, more commercial, and pushier artist than I was depicting before.

I see her products not as single units, but as editions of multiple copies. Like print runs. A hundred of the Nippy dog and the Cawckle hen. On the border between fine art and mass art. Zubzub the snake. Hchnay, like how our one or two-year-old Rudolf used to say it. A glottal hiss at the start. And Thweepea the rabbit.

***

Note that we have the Carson and Kayla first-person chaps side by side. If I like, I can have Kayla give us a bit of a history of her life, squeezing in a short past-tense section, the way that Carson did. But the first sentence ought to be her realizing that Carson is dead. Here's a kick-off draft.

I feel it when Carson dies. It's not that I'm in direct contact with him. But I know.

I'm in Mary's house when it happens, staying busy, trying not to obsess on the breakup. I saw Carson ride off in Gee's thudhumper limo a couple of hours ago, at dusk. Carson and a sleazy Top Party pal of his, a guy named Jerr Boom.

The fact that Carson takes Jerr along makes me doubt he's really going to the airport, but I hold myself back from checking online. And I hold off on calling Leeta or Gee. And for sure I'm not teeping with Carson. I've permanently blocked all signals from him, and I need to keep it that way or I'll lose my fucking mind.

How did I get here?

So what am I doing instead? I'm teeping with my gallery rep, Jeannie Jone, who's on site at the Phunny Pharm in Milpitas, north of San Jose. We're producing a two-hundred unit edition of my latest kritter, a silly-ass rabbit called Thweepea, my stupidest Kritter yet —

growing Thweepeas in a funky vat in the clanking, industrial, wilderness of random biotech labs along the ever-grotty eastern shores of the south San Francisco Bay.

. Spending most of my days with baby Daia is getting to me. Everything I'm making wants to be soft and cute. Even though, on the inside, I'm full of hatred and rage. Nippy dog is out, Cawckle chickens in. And Thweepea rabbit is *all* in.

January 11-21, 2021. Issues For Chap 7.

So I worked in the Kayla's Kritters thing, and I set up a dinner date with Phil Bilko at Kayla's house. Kayla orders 100 Bunter slugs from Phunny Pharm in Milpitas, and Bilko orders a 100 Miss Maxes. The *yawn, slobber* "battle" is supposed to be at dawn the next day. And at this thought, my imagination comes to a screeching halt. "There must be some way out of here, said the joker to the thief."

Here's some issues. I'll asterisk them as I get them resolved.

* TIMELINE?

This chapter starts on Monday, April 17, 2062, and I expect it run for maybe three days.

* THE TOP PARTY TAKEOVER OF SKYHIVE WAS JERR BOOM'S SUGGESTION.

Write the Monday Carson scenes almost the same, but this time, it's Jerr who calls up Carson. He knows about Carson's expulsion and he sees the opportunity. Mainly he's in it to get Top Party control of Skyhive and, as a bonus, to execute Carson in a weird way. He'll use Bernardo's report about the bombing to intimidate Gee.

* HOW DO KAYLA AND PHIL THEY GET THEIR LARGE PHUNNY PHARM KRITTERS TO GEE'S CAVE?

They go to Gee's before dawn on Tuesday, leaving Kayla's at 2 am, and bringing along small *sprouts*, the size of action figures, and they plant them in wet banks of the stream by

Gee's at 4 am, working by the light of intense tweaked fireflies, and in an hour or so, the sprouts grow into full form. They get in an hour's nap. Rise at dawn. Beautiful scene in the mountain mist, the new-grown critters by the stream. Like Cadmus growing soldiers from dragon's teeth. Marshall McLuhan said the dragon's teeth were a metaphor for inventing the jagged letters of the first alphabets.

* WHEN DO THE TOP-PARTY-SKYHIVE CONTROLLED KRITTERS BEGIN ACTING UP?

This one is important. Would be logical to assume it's soon after Carson and Jerr orchestrate the Top Party takeover of Skyhive, on Monday afternoon. And it ought to be strongly evident by Monday evening.

This means that Phil Bilko may have some issues while riding in a thudhumper cab to Kayla's from Phunny Pharm. If Coggy/Top Part are swift enough, they might grasp that Bilko is bringing supplies for Gee, and they'd want to interfere. And if Bilko has a Skyhive cabbie, then the cab might be taking him to some kind of death trap.

So we'd need for Gee or Metatron to have the idea of giving Bilko a driver from Gee's server. Bernardo is busy at this point doing his thing with Jerr Boom and Carson Pflug. So I'd rather not use him. And in any case *three* rides with Bernardo would be too many. Get a fresh driver for Bilko. Let's call in Curtis Winch! He's in Gee's server, and I've been looking for something for him to do.

* WHO WATCHES BABY DAIA?

What about baby Daia? Seems reckless for Kayla to bring her to the battle scene, but unloving to leave her with a sitter when the Top Party Skyhive-gigger raids are rampant. ?And Kayla can't miss the scene, as she's our POV, also I want her to be a hero. Tough choice. Making a protective suit for the baby wouldn't be nice. I guess leave the baby with Sue Ellen, but then I'll have to build up Sue Ellen as being very safe and motherly. Maybe don't use that last name Sue Ellen Graffiti, or if I use it explain that she's nice anyway. A tattooed crone. Like Blank Reg.

* WHAT DO THE TOP-PARTY RAIDERS WANT?

"Eat Gee's brain." That is, they want to take control of Gee's redwood and of the lifebox minds inside it. And they literally *do* want Gee's brain. Imaging a Frankenstein type kritter with a lid on the top of his head, and he wants to put Gee's brain inside there. He's called a Frankenstein Brain Fetcher. Also there's a Bride of Frankenstein Brian Fetcher angling for Mary's brain. Love it! *Software*'s Little Kidders ride again.

WHAT ABOUT METATRON AND COGGY?

I'm still torn. Basically I think Metatron and Coggy are in fact quite different kinds of beings.

I might depersonify them. That is, think of them more like web services. Parallel processing protocols. Network architectures. Not Marvel Comics gods. In any case, struggles between them need to be visualized in a novel ways, so as to not be stale and fannish. Not a two-page spread. More like a mold or a yin-yang that becomes Zhabotinsky scroll. Or a scene that totally changes, depending on your point of view. Like Hilbert space renormalization. Like an airport's departures sign where all the little flapper signs change all over it and you're looking at something different, and there's that click-click-click of the signs flipping.

What do I use them for? Here's a few things I can think of. I'll keep them, but I'll slant more toward the Hilbert Space "you see what you expect" angle.

- * The B-26 bomber.
- * Molly's multiplexer for the anti-Treadle-Disease blast.
- A fight in teepspace that kills Molly.
- Hosting Molly.
- The final cosmic beatdown.

* WHO'S THE LEAD MAD SCIENTIST FOR THE TOP PARTY?

What if "Coggy" is the Top Party mad scientist? I've been needing this figure, and I can't just bring him in at the end, like to program the fucked-up the behaviors of the puppeteered

Skyhive lifebox remotes. And Coggy should have been around to design the Treadle Disease virus—I never really talked about who did that.

I've got it: Coggy is six brains in an aquarium tank with wires. And this sets us up for Top Party wanting to excise Gee's brain and put it in as brain #7. Coggy wants company. A new colleague. A fresh office-mate.

* HOW DOES CURTIS KNOW TO TAKE OVER PHIL'S CAR?

To get this in line, I need to work out the temporal sequence of events on that fateful Monday in April.

3 pm. Gee calls Kayla and orders some kritters. Warns about Carson and about the raid,

5 pm. Carson leaves. Kayla calls Phil. Gee goes to bed with Mary.

7 pm. Carson dies. Gee wakes up. Kayla knows Carson's dead. Phil is at Phunny Pharm. Gee sends Curtis Winch to take over the driving of Phil's thudhumper.

9 pm. Phil arrives at Kayla's. They chat and eat supper.

10 pm. They want to fuck, but Curtis Winch tells them the cops are coming. They have to go to Gee's cave now.

Who tells Curtis to take over Phil Bilko's car? Gee.

HOW MANY PEOPLE IN THE RAID SCENE AT GEE'S CAVE?

In.

2. Gee and Mary. Gee is rejuvenated, Mary has a new body and her lifebox halo.

2. Kayla and Phil Bilko show up, with

1. Curtis Winch drives Kayla and Phil, merges with Utila, buds off Curtis Glass.

1. Jerr Boom shows up in morning, Kayla quickly kills him. His psidot Tweaky Bird stays.

Maybe.

1. Leeta shows up at the end of the raid—she has a conversion experience, sees the light.

2, Gyr and Anselm might fly in from Denmark? Let's not do that, it makes it too crowded.

1. Molly has been inside Metatron and she could get a clone body with a lifebox halo. Then she could have a happy

reunion with Gyr. That could be in the extra chapter with the hylozoic stuff. Maybe Anselm was into hylozoism all along.

I could think of some subset of this group (other than Jerr) as the high tribal council of the freals. But why bother with that. I don't like ruling bodies.

January 13-23, 2021. To Dos for the Ending.

To Dos

- * Develop the character of Sue Ellen Graffiti, babysitter, old punk woman, like Bank Reg in *Max Headroom*. Have her be Mrs. Yahootie's wife.
- * Who tells Curtis to take over Phil Bilko's car? Gee does.
- * Tighten up Molly and Anselm as personas of Metatron. Except Molly got stuck up there in teepspace.
- * How do I handle the Kayla POV in Chap 7 if I want to show the scene of Curtis driving Phil Bilko's car? Kayla sees it like a lucid dream or like VR—because she's teeped into Phil, helping him and Curtis guide the car.
- * Issue of Top Party potentially controlling anyone who has Skyhive lifebox. This would be as bad as Treadle Disease. I don't want this. I need to explicitly rule it out. The lifeboxes might make suggestions to their owners. Like political ads. But the owners can ignore them.
- * Set it up so that Kayla got her lifebox moved to Gee's redwood during the raid. Mary's idea.
- * Phil Bilko also has a lifebox with Gee. The Mixed Bag gallerist arranges this for her artists. Like using Monkeybrains ISP instead of Comcast ISP.
- * Gee owns his own pelikaan flappy, and that's what they're using to fly transatlantic all through the book, and it's lurking near Gee's cave during the battle and comes in to help at the climax.
- * Can you copy a lifebox onto a new clone's blank brain? During most of the book, I of need to say no—otherwise there's no point to controlling a body with a

lifebox + psidot combo. Put in an early rap that programming a computation is "easy" but the brain's computation is so deeply tweaked you can't just blast the code and data in there. And don't bother activating spraypainting later on, as it's adds nothing.

- * They rebuilt the Top Party headquarters like fortress with a Treadle statue and still the Top Party bunker lab, where they store their lifeboxes as well. Mention that it's odd for right-wingers havin headquarters in SF, but don't bother saying why they did it.
- * Don't use a KGB lab is Moscow for Treadle's lifebox. It's in the bunker in San Francisco.
- * While Curtis is constantly using Metatron, we have teepspace Molly in the background, she's kind of the "gunner" with Metatron.
- * What about *guns*? I don't have guns anywhere in the book, and I'd like to not have them at all, as guns would ruin some of my fight scenes, such as the raid on Gee's cave. I do have guns in the helicopters at the Inauguration, and I'll keep those. The the Trump chopper guns are an anomaly, a shock, people didn't even know guns existed anymore. As for the Secret Service agents, they could be using something a little different. Long-distance shock sticks.
- * Molly ought to have brown hair since her last name is Santos

January 14-25, 2021. Sequence for Chap 7 Ending.

I have a lot of scenes to fit into Chapter 7. But I think I can bring it in at 15,000 words. If there's spill over, I might have an Epilog for the hylozoic spirits. Unless I fit them into the chapter rather concisely and leave certain things open for a hypothetical but not necessarily to-be-written **eeek** sequel.

Re. ducking a sequel, recall the crazy four-page summary of future story at the end of my 2009 *Hylozoic*, delivered by my author-character Thuy Ngyuen, with this summary obviating my need to write a possibly-to-be-orphaned-by-Tor sequel. Having recalled this, I now went and read that passage and it's very close the sheer gibberish and, by dint of its inaccessibility, rather dull. Not a good idea to publish a passage like that, but I think I thought it was a funny dada thing to do.

Well, I can't really dictate the length, not even now, with the end so near. That's the old corollary to Turing's Halting Problem, that is Computational Unpredictability, that is, you can't predict in advance the time that an arbitrary complex computation might take. (Wolfram calls it Computational Incompressibility instead of Unpredictability.)

I just have to let 'er rip and see whar she blows.

So here are ideas for scenes, with an asterisk after I finish the scene. I won't always bother to update the outline here to precisely match what I actually did.

* I: MONDAY EVENING

Kayla senses that Carson is dead. She and Phil Bilko purchase sprouts for a hundred Bunter Butler Thuggees, and a hundred-fold assortment, Miss Max Explosion. Or maybe Experience is better. Like the name of Jimi Hendrix's band. Or, no, just Miss Max Mix. Get them from Phunny Pharm north of San Jose. Bilko picks them up in a rented thudhumper, but the driver is corrupted by Top Party control of the gig-worker lifebox driver. Curtis Winch steps in, and drives to Kayla's via old logging roads. Soon after this, and before they can fuck, Phil and Kayla have to leave Kayla's, as Top-Party-possessed kritters are coming. Curtis drives to Gee's place like a maniac, dodging roadblocks through the woods, and zapping a Top-Party kritter attacker with a Metatron rays. Arrive at Gee's around midnight.

* II: TUESDAY WEE AM AND DAWN

About midnight, Phil and Kayla plant the sprouts in the wet dirt along the raging stream by Phil's clearing. Takes a few hours. Meanwhile they go to bed and finally fuck, and fall asleep. Molly shows up. Gee has grown her a clone. Gyr and Anselm fly in from Denmark on Gee's Pelikaan flappy during the night.

At 6 am they get up and see the intimidating Bunter X models and the perky Miss Max Mix kritters in the mist.

* III: TUESDAY MORN

Jerr Boom glides in on his flappy. Jerr wants to make a

deal with Gee. Tells Gee they need a Gee brain for their Coggy set-up, but it can be a copy. Gee can grow a clone of his brain and give them that with a copy of his lifebox. Gee says no way.

"Then we'll do the raid, and you'll die," says Jerr Boom.

And then Kayla kills Jerr. One of her Bunter X kritters splits the upper part of his body into an enormous pair of crocodile jaws and bites off Jerr's head. "That's for Carson," says Kayla. "Are you scared of crocodiles now, Jerr?"

Gee has the idea of fetching Jerr's psidot Tweaky Bird out of the Bunter X's gut. Curtis and Molly can use that to backtrack to Jerr's lifebox which is (now) in the Top Party bunker Treadle's lifebox was too.

IV: TUESDAY MORN. THE RAID.

The invaders appear.

Top Party troops come in. They might have some free agent mercenaries for officers, *Hee-Haw* studio audience types. Or human clones run by Skyhive lifeboxes of dead people. For troops they have kritters run by Top Party controlled Skyhive lifeboxes. Our freals put up a good fight, using Gee's animals, Phil's Bunters, Kayla's Miss Maxes, Curtis's Utila, and lightning blasts from Metatron. But they're losing. Maybe some tanks and heavy flappies are coming in. Pelikaan flappy to help, or no she's flying the others to SF. The Top Party guys are after Gee's head. Coggy threatens the redwood.

The bunker raiders leave in Pelikaan. Molly and Kayla decide to kill Coggy off. They use Gee's Pelikaan flappy to get to San Francisco fast. Bomb some Top Party raiders on the way.

V: TUESDAY NOON. RAID THE BUNKER.

To set up for this, i expanded the scene where they killed Treadle's lifebox back in the "Juicy Ghost" chapter. But given that i now wrote that scene, I can't have the same scene again for killing everything in the bunker. That is, don't show it in teepspace, show it in physical space.

The raiders in Pelikaan. Who goes on the raid ? Curtis in a glass-man body of psidot amoeba flesh. He can't get in purely through teepspace, not even withh Tweaky Bird helping, and we've also got Molly in the flesh ready to blast with with

Metatron to really clean the place out, burn it out to the core. If we want to bring Molly. Like the time I poured gasoline into the wasps' nest on our hill and lit it up.

We leave Phil Bilko at Gee's to handle the kustom kritters. Also I don't want Kayla to be dependent on him. Send her off to SF alone or, no, with Curtis and Molly.

Don't bring in Anselm and Gyr at all…but maybe I mention them in a Chap 8.

So this time say the Top Party security is really good and they can't get in via teep. Kayla gets them in. Her sparrow does the thing on the physical plane. One peck on the pavement. We could send her up there fast in Pelikaan.

Kayla walks into the square where the Top Part headquarters used to be. Now there's a statue of Treadle. And a heavy door in the ground that leads to the bunker. Kayla drops a tiny sparrow on the ground. It pecks the door once. The ground collapses, and Molly sets Metatron bolts to frying the Coggy tank brains, also all the Top Party lifeboxes stored down there. Curtis comes along for this too.

January 27-28, 2021. Done with Chap 7. Add Short Chap 8.

Finished Chap 7 in a huge burst yesterday and this morning. Bloodlust writing frenzy, as John Walker would say. Wrote 2,900 words in two days, thus bulking Chap 7 to over 12K words, the third longest in the book. A lot happens in the chap!

With the brain tank gone, Coggy is gone, so I was able to skip the Coggy vs. Metatron cosmic beatdown, thank you very much. Turns out that Molly and Metatron wiping out the Top Party bunker pit was the *real* cosmic beatdown, and a very satisfying one at that. Dynamite.

Oh, *hmm*, come to think of it, I can have Kayla explicitly face down Coggy right before her birdie pecks. So I put that in, drawing on Kayla kritter-building expertise. As long as I'm empowering Kayla, I'll give her a hypnotic teep power to stop that dog man from charging at her too early.

Along the way I managed to kill Ross Treadle a *fourth* time. His body, his lifebox, his clone, and now his memorial statue.

***

Still some loose ends, so I need the extra chapter, but it might just be 3K or 6K words. Not starting any new rabbits to running, just tidying up.

Whose POV for Chap 8? I think Molly—we started out with her in Chaps 1 & 2. Good to circle back.

I went light on the battle around Gee's cave in Chap 7, so I'll fill in some more from Molly's POV. Let's say she and the others get back to cave just in the nick of time, and the remaining dead-ender Top Party troops are trying to torch Gee's server redwood. And we open Chapter 8 with Molly experiencing that.

The near loss of Gee's server helps motivate the the mass indie lifeboxes thing. They do that in the afternoon or maybe on the next day. Halos for everyone. Leeta comes in on it, and they do astral bodies for the Skyhive lifeboxes too. Leeta has a new angle for money anyway. She's start up astral body barns.

So, yeah, Mary, Kayla, Gee, Leeta, and Phil Bilko design the better, easier-to-use halos. They port most or all of Gee's and Skyhive's lifeboxes to astral bodies. A few people don't want to change, and that's okay too.

What about remote bodies for indie lifeboxes? Well that's up to them; those who already owned remotes still own them. Some just skim around like small saucers.

Near the very end, we'll need to bring Gyr over and reunite her with Molly. Possibly bring along Anselm. Gee + Mary. Molly + Gyr. Kayla + Phil. Curtis, Anselm, and Leeta will live alone. And Jerr Boom is dead.

***

Drop these extra ideas:

- Ghost minds who've been there all along. Or, at very *most*, teasingly allude to the possibility at the very end.
- "Spraypainting" lifeboxes onto brains, as that serves on purpose and undercuts lifeboxes.
- People going hylozoic and becoming spirits of place or trivial processes wobbling leaves. Although I *did* originally want Mary Mary to end up as the waterfall in Big Basin.

I'd prefer to finish the book with what we have. No more new ideas. If I ever want to write about those extra ideas, I can do that in a story or a novella.

And I do *not* want to commit to or even hint at a sequel. At this point I might truly be done with novels. Round this one out and quite writing novels for good. (Maybe.)

January 30-Feb 1, 2021. Almost Done First Draft. Tweaks.

On the evening of January 29, 2021, I ran Chapter 8 out to 2,400 words, did a hasty half-page wrap-up and typed:
–The End--.

Went outside, came back in, and tweeted, "I finished writing TEEP, and went outside, the moon was full, and the sky was striped."

Hallelujah. I'll polish the last couple of chapters and send it off to Silbersack, and he'll try it on Oren Eades and Night Shade, and we'll see what's next. As an inveterate optimist, I imagine the book being a hugely popular anti-Trump political novel, as well as a revelatory envisioning of current and near-future developments in biotech, commercial telepathy, and digital immortality.

Weirdly, this week Microsoft patented my 1980 *Software* vision of digital immortality via amassing data bases of people's writings, emails, audio, video, actions, etc. Really they should at least have me up there for a nice speaking event. But probably scared to lend any traction to a possible intellectual-property-infringement lawsuit on my part—if it's not too grandiose for me to say that. But me publishing *The Lifebox, the Seashell, and the Soul* ought to count for something. It's close to being a "how-to book" on digital immortality.
***

* DOES ASTRAL BODY LIFEBOX USER NEED A PSIDOT?

Let's say yes. The transition from old lifeboxes to new ones is smoother this way. I'd considered having the new lifeboxes be like psidots and plug into your brain with quantum threads, and maintain these threads over physical open-air distances of tens of meters or more, but that's a hassle. As before, your psidot acts like a wireless hub and teep gateway for you. And it installs and manages your gossip molecules.

* "HALO," NOT "ASTRAL BODY"

I was thinking of calling them soul disks, and I was remembering of the ubiquitous AOL free DVD disks you used to see all around, shiny and silvery. Don't like "soul disk" though. How about soul jellies. Or thinking caps. In *Freeware*, thinking caps were parasitic brain interfaces placed in your head by a moldie, but so what. I can use a phrase in different ways in different fictional universes. But nah.

Just plain *halo* will be the best name for it. At one time it was going to be a toroidal vortex ring, but then that seemed too hyperactive, and I settled for a simple disk, slightly thick in the middle. Slight drawback is that the world "halo" is somewhat corrupted by association with the military Microsoft videogame Halo.

How to spell the plural of halo? Googled and found 300 million instances of "halos" and only 900 thousand uses of "haloes." Go with no e.

(A side issue. The thing is shaped like a *disk*. Or should I write it *disc*? Supposedly disc is used for optically-read computer storage and for (why?) Frisbees. Disk is used for magnetically read hard drives. Or for records. And in math you use disk. I'll go for disk as I don't want to promote the idea that thing is at all like an optical DVD or computer disk.)

* WHAT IS UTILA MADE OF?

I called her an amoeba, but she seems to be doing some-what muscular things, cf. her budded off body for Curtis. Wouldn't the bud Curtis need a psidot? Would Utila need psidots, perhaps lots of them? I considered finessing by saying Utila "is" a very large psidot. If I do this, then I need to think of her as not being an amoeba, but rather being a very large and lighter-than-air sea slug. Which is doable, but I would need to visualize and to implement it. Having a sea slug that split into buds is a bit iffy, but I could have it be a *gelatinous* sea slug. Maybe in some ways like a transparent sea cucumber, to bring in one of my favorite old animals. Or jellyfish? Well, amoeba is more fun, I'll stick with that.

* NAMES

Reading and even writing, I found myself mixing up the named Carson and Curtis. Too similar. I considered changing Curtis to Kurtis, but that overlaps Kayla. So I looked up some lists of popular Black boy names and hit on Maurice. I like that name, and it does sound kind of Black. So I changed it throughout. (In *Gravity's Rainbow* there's a cool, jiving Black guy called Maximilian, but I think Maurice works better for me here.)

I kind of wanted Molly to have carroty blondish hair, but on the other hand I thought it would be nice to have her be Latino, with the last name Santos, which make sense in that, over time, she becomes something of a divinity. But then her hair has to be dark. Unless I have her using dye of dome type. She could've tweaker her genes. But dark hair is ok.

* TOP PARTY PAID LEETA

Who *got* the money that the Top Party paid to own Skyhive? Let's say it was Leeta? She fully owns Skyhive. Owes to some investors, but paid them off. Maybe Leeta sold because she saw the halo tech coming. Feels that Carson did her a favor.

Top Party will want some control over Skyhive, and will be furious that "Carson" calls off the gigworking lifeboxes who are controlling the raiders. Of course they won't be able to find Carson or Jerr Boom. Have the Bunter X in fact eat the rest of Jerr Boom. And Leeta will hollow out Skyhive fast, be porting all the clients to halo discs.

February 2-4, 2021. 8½.

I want to add a little more to Chapter 8, bringing it closer to half the length of a chapter. So I name this writing journal entry after the cool Fellini movie **8½** — although I admit it would be more logical to call it **7½,** given that I'm working on a short chapter that follows seven long chapters.

Am I sure I want to stick to Molly's POV? Doesn't seem like she's central to the switch to halo lifeboxes. I could have sections in the chapter, and rotate to—who? Leeta would be a surprise, but I'm not that fond of her. Going back to Kayla might be good. Or Mary. But if I *can* stick to Molly and make it work, that's easier for the reader. I'll find ways to put Molly in all the scenes. And some angle that makes her important. Eventually I'll want to reread Chaps 1 & 2 so I get the same Molly voice in Chaps 7 & 8.

To Do

- * Problem with Jerr's lifebox. I have them retrieving the all-important CEO glyph from Jerr Boom's life-box—*after* Molly has completely destroyed all the Top Party lifeboxes stored in the Top Party bunker lab. Oops! So...obviously Jerr Boom stored his lifebox on some *different* server. He, quite reasonably in retrospect, didn't trust the Top Party server. He wouldn't have been on Gee's server, and probably not on Skyhive. So okay, I'll say he was on the Soviet KGB t server. Done.
- * What is the name of the little XC racer car? Call him Scuttler.
- * Use the name Citadel Club for the in-group of big-money Top Party donors. I made up this name back in 1968 in Highland Park, New Jersey, when Greg Gibson was visiting our honeymooner apartment. In the afternoon, I smoked pot with Greg and we walked around the leafy residential streets of Highland Park, and I pointed out a classical tower to Greg, and told him that was the headquarters of the local right-wing "Citadel Club," and that they were watching us through telescopes. Greg went for it, or pretended to, and he began acting paranoid, which made me laugh and laugh. A happy memory.
- Show the Frankenstein Brain Fetcher and his Bride.
- The Miss Minis aren't currently active in the battle. They should be like balloon animals who kill people by getting inside them, and then expanding.
- * Mention Molly's halo a few more times.
- * They need to erase Jerr's KGB lifebox.
- Mention that Gee's cave has a lot of rooms.

- * Who told Bernardo to take Jerr and Carson to a random location? Bernardo decided on his own, but Gee knew that would happen.
- Glory and Miss Max should be in on the happy dance scene at the end.
- Gee's thudhumper van should have its own name (distinct from the driver's name Bernardo).

Here's some scenes.

* TELEPORT

Molly and Kayla plan to ride that sports thudhumper to San Lorenzo to fetch baby Daia and some of Kayla's stuff. But at this point it's a little boring to have yet another car ride in the mountains, this will be the *fourth*; already had Mary & Gee, Carson & Jerr, Phil & Kayla. So skip the ride, and don't need Maurice as driver.

Go through Hilbert Space instead. Molly knows how. Renormalize. Potentially a big, bomb-drop-level, plot-changing event, but I want to damp that down a bit. For now, Anselm and Molly are the only two who can do it. And let's say Maurice can hop as well. You have to spend a lot of time in teepspace to get the hang of it. So at the end of the noble, teleportation is on the horizon, but not coming really soon.

* KIDNAP

In San Lorenzo, someone is about to kidnap baby Daia, or has already done so. Molly has to teleport to catch them, and she blasts them. The kidnapper is a rep for a Top Party backer who imagines Carson is still alive, and wants to set the Skyhive gigworkers back to attacking Gee.

The kidnapper is Jerr Boom. Perfect. And now the scene comes to me like I'm taking dictation or overhearing a conversation. Used it almost as is-is, printing the first take.

> "You can't be here, Jerr," says Kaya. "My Bunter X bit off your head and chewed you up."
> "Ever heard of clones?" goes Jerr Boom.
> "What about Tweaky Bird?" I [Molly] say.
> "Ever heard of copying a psidot?"

"You stood by and let me take Skyhive back from the Citadel Club?" says Kayla.

"Couldn't resist the chance to fuck those guys over," says Jerr Boom. "They're assholes."

"Give me the baby," I say to Jerr Boom.

"This where the bargaining begins," says Jerr. "I know what you want. But do you know what I want?"

I feel the gathering force of a fresh renormalization. This is a tricky one. But I can do it.

"I never will know," I say to Jerr Boom. "And I don't care."

In the blink of an eye, the envelope of space containing Jerr Boom flies off to—well, for lack of a better idea, I put him in thousand-foot-deep water beneath what's left Antarctica's ice shelf. Most of him. I kept his hands and forearms here, as I didn't want to risk nicking Daia.

Moving on autopilot, Kayla swoops forward and catches Daia before she can fall. Jerr Boom's forearms drop to the ground. Like with his clone's body earlier today.

"You can never kill a real villain just once," says Kayla, her voice shaking.

"But now I think we're done," I say. "Let get back in Scuttler for the hop back."

* REUNION

Gyr and Anselm show up. Good old Anselm has come along with Gyr the ride. Anselm can do Hilbert space renormalization as a travel method too—that is, he and Molly can teleport. They're the only ones who can do it for now, and it's hard to learn (by logging years in teepspace) so it won't be spreading like wildfire before my novel ends.

. Molly spends the night with Gyr. Anselm stays up talking with Gee and Mary.

* MAGIC FOREST

In the morning Leeta shows up. She and Kayla make peace. Gee, Anselm, Mary and Leeta do the big port. From now on everyone is going to use those halo lifeboxes like Mary and Molly have. Nice design for them by Kayla and Phil.

Molly and Anselm use renormalization to crumble the empires of the Citadel Club members.

A flock of halo disks swooping around like a flock of seagulls. They'll perch in trees. The Magic Forest.

They do a happy dance beneath the trees.

Pairs: Molly and Gyr, Gee and Mary, Kayla and Phil.

Plus Maurice, Anselm, and Leeta, in no particular order.

All is calm, the tension is gone. We don't explicitly announce our long day's victories in the media, but the rumors filter out. No more Top Party to worry about. And no more Treadle legacy. None of that is coming back. We're on a better path.

February 4-5, 2021. Grateful. It's (Almost) Done.

I've been writing some really funny and elegant stuff these last few weeks. To my fond eye, each page is like a tray of gems. It makes the long labor of rolling the heavy stone uphill worthwhile, and it's been about two years. It's work, being a writer. So glad to have made my way into in the heights again.

About three years ago Sylvia and I went hiking in the Sierras with some people our age, or younger, and we were loafing along at the end of line, but even so making our way up a really spectacular slope, with giant boulders and peaks beyond, and my heart leapt up.

"I didn't think I'd ever get to do this again," I told Sylvia. "I thought it was over." (What with my age, and my heart, and my legs.)

That's how the writing feels this month. And I really don't know if I'll ever get this high into the hills again. This could be it. Every year: words harder to remember, less energy, more need for naps, oh-fuck-it-ism. But I'm glad right now, and grateful.

***

Really is done, now, on Friday, Feb 5, 2021, 5:08 pm. At least that's what I'm saying right now. Huge push over the last few days. Writing constantly, with little effort.

February 8, 2021. In San Francisco

Sylvia's birthday. We came up to SF for two nights, old Campton Place hotel, now with Taj added to the front of the name, almost empty, due to the plague, and they upgraded us to a really nice corner room on the 15th floor, 1501, overlooking Union Square, with a wood floor and two windows. Isabel was in town, and we had a few joyous family meals with her and with Rudy Jr.'s family of five, eating outside in the cold. I wore a lot of layers.

This morning at dawn I dreamed I was rewriting the last pages of *Teep*…the dream went on for a very long time, maybe an hour, and I kept revising the rewrite, moving things around, gloating over its high quality. I've been writing so much that I really do dream about revising, with my keyboard, the whole thing. I haven't been on the laptop the last three days, a nice break. We're driving home via coastal Route 1 today, should be fun.

About all I can remember about the dream of the expanded ending is that it involved a wise older man, perhaps my character Anselm, who is indeed underutilized in the current ending. I'll print out the last chapter and look things over tonight or tomorrow.

February 9-17, 2021. Fix 7 & 8. Write the Ending.

Now to reprint and read the last two chaps, 7 & 8, which I haven't revised yet. And then I can email out a few copies, mainly to Silbersack and to March Laidlaw.

But meanwhile. I noticed an inconsistency.

Kayla learns about the Top Party takeover of Skyhive from Gee in Chapter 7, and she's mentioning it in her commentary on the Top Party raid. And she says a thing about the head of a snake and its body, referring to the fact that the Skyhive controlled raid will still happen after the bunker lab is gone.

And I have a reveal scene in the middle of Chap 8 where the Top Party rioters are setting fire to Gee's redwood, and they teep Leeta for help, and only *then* does Maurice learn, from Leeta that Top Party now runs Skyhive.

So I change the reveal scene to jibe with Maurice already knowing.

I should stipulate that the Top Party raid was well "baked in" before they attacked the bunker lab. I mean, clearly this is true, but pound it home an clarify why the raid would keep on going even if the bunker lab minds were gone.

***

Feb 12, 20211

I rewrote the ending pages three or four times by now, and, will do more. The prob is that I want to be done, so I was shorting on those last scenes, not wanting to visualize them, or complicate them, or work out consequences thereof. "Leave that to the next guy." The next guy being nobody, or the reader's imagination, or (barely possible) a future me who writes a sequel to *Teep.*

Looking back at some years-old writing notes last week, I came upon a passage where I talked about how I do not in fact normally write sequels, and I end the book like a musician who brings the final number to a frenzy, with fierce feedback and all the amps dialed up to 11, and he lays down his reverberant guitar on an amp and walks off stage as the feedback (feebdack) pulses and rolls.

Should I quit now and maybe later add an afterword "In Place of a Sequel." *Don't* do that, you doddering slacker! Finish it all now.

***

Feb 13, 2021.

Did maybe the final take on the ending. I had an issue about how the lifeboxes port themselves into halos; it needs to autonomous and autocatalytic and sustainable, that is, it can't depend of some external agent doing the port *for* the lifeboxes. The lifeboxes need to be a self-perpetuating ecosystem of their own, with no need for active human supervision.

So to get ready for that I needed to go back and redo Mary's first-ever port from lifebox to halo. And the kicker I thought of is that—the system become more and more and more self-perpetuating because the existing halos help the old lifeboxes do their port.

I have not yet explicitly resolved the issue of how new users with no lifebox at all will get into the system. I need at least to say something in passing on this. Can be as simple as existing halos simply recruiting humans to get a halo. Yes, do that, allow the halos even subdivide to reproduce.

***

Feb 14, 2021.

Another full day of work on *Teep*—"really" fixing the ending, or almost. Will reread tomorrow. Writing the ending of a novel is hard because I tend to rush it on first second third or fourth version as I'm so eager to be Done. Can't slow down and actually *think it out* it ill about fifth or seventh or whatever try.

***

Feb 15, 2021.

At some point the psidots might be dispensed with, but can I do that in this novel? I'm inclined to stonewall and stick with the belief that it won't work without psidots. Psidot teep is one thing. It came first. Lifebox immortality is something different, it builds on psidot teep. I think I already had Gee holding forth upon and drumming in this belief. But—maybe he's wrong?

I am already pushing the idea that the halo lifeboxes become an independent life form that is symbiotic with us.

So then, as a final step, I could say that, by way of promoting our partnership, the halo lifeboxes *themselves* begin culturing and distributing the psidots. Like ants who farm edible fungus in their nests. Love it.

Might work some of that in today while I mark up and type in yesterday's ending's printout. Still here typing in bed. My butt hurts, I've been doing this every day.

Also I'm doing more work on revising my passages bout the port from trad server lifebox to new halo lifebox. Making a completely do-it-yourself thing for the increasingly autonomous lifeboxes. A new race a-borning.

***

Feb 17, 2021.

I more or less finished it on Feb 15, 2021, and mailed copies to Marc Laidlaw, John Silbersack, John Walker, and my younger writer friend Robert Penner who edited *Big Echo* ezine.

Drove to Carmel yesterday with Sylvia, a nice day off. At home in the evening, I dropped the DOC into InDesign, exported as an EPUB, converted into a MOBI with Kindle Previewer, and emailed that to my Kindle via Amazon. Read the last chapter, lying on the couch with my Kindle, highlighting problems.

Today I scrolled through Chap 8 on the Kindle, spotting the highlights, and typing fixes into the DOC on my desktop PC, and fully rewriting the last page or two. Printed that last bit just now, and if it's okay, I'm done. Again.

Go outside, Rudy. Fix the sprinklers. No, wait, finish fixing the ending. And that's what I did.

February 19, 2021. Marc's Remarks. Penner on Title.

Marc Laidlaw read the book pretty quickly. I know it's borderline vain, but I'll copy two of his nice remarks here. I need all the encouragement I can get at this early stage. The way my career has been going—and with Night Shade on the skids—Kickstarter + self-publication is at this point very much a possible fate for *Teep*!

> This is some of your best stuff, it just flows wonderfully, the characters are great—especially Anselm. He's a wonderful mouthpiece for quirky observations. It's cool, especially having seen the separate pieces of these over the past couple years, to see the way you've put them together and developed something larger out of them.

And he liked how quickly the book moves. He posted a nice tweet about this when he was done reading it.;

> TEEP, is a thing of absolutely breakneck pace, high energy throughout. It feels like it was written in one sustained breath, though I know he's been working on it for a couple years, breathing periodically. Hope it finds a home.

Marc had some suggestions that I'm thinking over.

- *Goal.* Make it clear from the start that universal free lifeboxes are the goal.
- *Top Party Menace.* Since the book concludes with a final (?) defeat of the Top Party and the Citadel Club, I ought to make clear soon after the end of the "Juicy

Ghost" chapter that the revolution still isn't over. It would be interesting to have an actual scene at a literal Citadel Club headquarters, at, say, the Pacific Club on the hill near the Fairmont in SF.

- *Why Mary?* Need a clear reason why Mary is so important. Why is Gee so sure that she's the "One?" Just having him see her band is unconvincing on its own, although he *could* see her and at that point be tipped into action—and, by the way, this should be live and not online. I could add a scene at the start of her chapter of her having an experience where (a) she learns the threat of Top Party is still on and (b) she has a psychic experience of teepspace in which she displays her untapped psychic power. Her little music band might be playing in the lounge at the Citadel Club and someone is threatening her and takes her to the Top Party bunker lab, and she's saved by the discorporate Molly, and Gee notices. And then he loses track of her and later he sees her at the Pot O' Gold and get goes all in, having Carson recruit her.

Another input was that Robert Penner of Big Aha really liked to novel, he was very encouraging, and he urged on my suggestion that I change the novel's title from *Teep* to *Juicy Ghosts*.

February 20-23, 2021. Mary Segue.

If I can get a good Mary segue, that might do it. Crude approach would be to have an evil Citadel Club guy about to tie her to a table and torture her in the bunker lab, and Molly saves her. The guy could even be Jerr Boom. How would Molly know of this?

It might be akin to a black magic ceremony, and they're trying to summon up a spirit from teep space. Coggy could be involved. Maybe they were trying to steal Mary's brain, not for any special reason, but because she was handy. Or Coggy "saw" something about her. In fact, 'Coggy' could relate to 'precog,' and he somehow sensed that Mary would give birth to the halo lifeboxes.

A closed causal loop there. Molly and Gee save Mary who

is being hassled because she's going to invent the halo lifebox—and because of this meeting, Gee does help Mary invent the halo lifebox.

***

But, no, I don't want to have an extreme, baroque, grotesque scene like that at the start of Chapter 4. Just something simple, a scene from during the year and a half passage of time between Jan, 2061 and April, 2062. The Treadlers were decisively defeated in January, 2061, but they've been machinating for a year and a half and are coming back in April, 2062.The Top Party / Citadel Club are planning for.

- Mid-term election in Fall, 2062, and the chance to flip the House and Senate.
- Getting control of the gigworking lifeboxes.
- Destroy Gee Willikers and the Finn Junkers.

Mary's somewhat apolitical, but someone could talk to her about this. Maybe Gee himself. could overhear talk about this. I could combine this conversation with the decisive concert, when Mary and Kayla are performing at the Pot O' Gold and Gee gets the notion that Mary might be able to port herself to a halo lifebox. Thanks to her voice. The voice thing—Gee can hold forth on that a bit. It's a move I've used before, having a voice express a soul. In fact, I already have a bit of that in the earlier sections of *Juicy Ghosts*, don't I?

Who else plays with Mary and Kayla, by the way? Think of them as a bluegrass quartet. Squash Plant. We have fiddle (Kayla) and mandolin (Mary), and could use bass (Dick Cheeks), and banjo (Joe Moon).

By the way, it's not necessarily the case that Mary's talent is magically unique. It's enough that she's a good, self-expressive singer, and that Gee sees her *in person*. And he falls in love with her. At present that scene happens off stage, and with Gee perhaps even seeing the show online, and, as Marc Laidlaw pointed out, it needs to be in the book

***

Timeline for Mary's life.
She's 80 in *Juicy Ghosts*. So...
1982 Born in San Francisco. A Millennial.

2000-2010 Bums around US and Mexico with hipsters. Weed and fireworks.

2010 Settles into music scene in San Jose. Works in a fabric store.

2020 Lives with a fisherman Kip in Scott's Valley. Sells fish at farmers' markets.

2030 Kip dies in freak storm. Moves to San Lorenzo, buys tiny house seed, derived from squash.

2030-2060 Works at Lorenzo Country Store, has her band the Squash Plants.

2061 Meets Gee while she plays with Squash Plant at Pot O' Gold, August, 2061.

2062 April. Dies. Gets psidot-lifebox-clone body. Divorces Carson, moves in with Gee. Learns to port her server lifebox to a halo lifebox

***

Mary was born in San Francisco near the turn of the century, an only child. She didn't like home life, school, or politics. She preferred walking around the city looking at people. And seeing live music. And fireworks. When Mary declined to enroll at a community college, her mother told her she had to get a job. Mary left home, hooked up with some traveling hipsters, and changed her last name to match her first. Mary Mary.

For the next few years Mary drifted around the US and Mexico, getting by with casual labor, joining up with roving buses of hipsters, couch-surfing in university towns—and hitting music shows. And fireworks festivals—most notably the big one in Tultepec, where hundreds of people run around pushing fireworks-laden constructs called toritos, or little bulls, a bit like explosive piñatas on wheels, furiously spouting sparks, spewing firecrackers, spinning pinwheels of flame, firing exploding rockets—not into the sky, but across the market square. Amelia, Mary's best friend at that time, caught a fierce blast in her face and had to go the hospital in Mexico City. Mary stayed with her for a week, and then Amelia died.

Back in the Bay Area, Mary drifted down to Santa Cruz and got into the music scene. She'd learned to play the mandolin, and she had a beautiful singing voice. She had a day job in a fabric store, selling cloth to quilters and dress-makers.

And then she met Kip, the love of her life—well, first she met Kip's wife, and then Kip, and she took him.

Kip worked on a fishing boat out of Santa Cruz harbor, catching squid and snapper, and running crab pots during the season. Kip's wife never gave him a divorce, but she left town, so Kip and Mary had Kip's tiny cottage to live in. They never had children, but they were together for nearly ten years. And then Kip was lost at sea during one of those crazy climate-driven storms.

Kip's wife got the house and moved back into it, not that Kip would have wanted it that way, but what could Mary do. At least she managed to empty out her and Kip's bank accounts. She used her money to buy a small lot in crumbling San Lorenzo, and one of the new biotech house seeds that were derived from squash plants.

And thus Mary found her mountain home. And she spent the next thirty years of her life working at the San Lorenzo Country store. She never found another man to live with. But she had her little band, who she called the Squash Plant. Mary sang and played the mandolin, with a changing cast of disreputable mountain types filling in on fiddle, banjo, bass, or whatever.

***

Maybe instead of having Amelia die, have her papers be lost, and there's a hassle getting back into the States, and the hassle pops into prominence the fact that Top Party is bouncing back. If I do this, then the Tultepec trip has to happen in 2061, though, and that doesn't really fit.

Most of that life story isn't working. Really I just want the Mary-meets-Gee scene. I'll think about it for a few more days. But meanwhile…

February 24-25, 2021. John Walker Chimes In.

John sent me a great set of comments and a long list of proofing corrections. Wonderfully thorough and attentive. And he even noticed all the cross-references to my earlier books. What a mind on that guy.

I typed in John's proofing corrections today, and I'm working on the comments. Patching together the necessary BS and rubber science fixes. I'll asterisk them as I get them done.

* Teep & Psidot Bandwidth.

The teep and psidot bandwith problem…yes, as you suggest the way out would seem to be something along the lines of entangled quantum vortices and the dark matter (dark energy? quintessence?) Hilbert space channel of, as you say Spaceland 4D channel. I went for the big lie and wrote this:

> "At the risk of boring the shit out of you, I'll say a word about ultraweak wireless. It's quite distinct from the wireless signals that were used for old-school smart phones. The giggle is that *ultraweak* wireless is in fact much *stronger*. It's not a standard electromagnetic-wave-type signal at all. Ultraweak wireless uses new physics. It wriggles out of our workaday four-dimensional spacetime continuum, out into the raw Hilbert space of quantum mechanics, and wings through those dark caverns, free as a bird, unfettered by such mundane niggling factors such as distance or signal power. You teep someone via ultraweak wireless, and, baby, you're *there*. And even so feeble an organ as a human brain as the *oomph* to pull it off."

* Treadle Disease Propagation Speed.

John made the point that at first it was hard to give Anselm the Treadle Disease; Loftus had to inoculate him with a thorn. And then suddenly a day or two later, almost everyone in the US has it. To me this fits with the insane upward rush of the Corona virus. But for it to be this fast, you need a tweak.

I went for sleek, wriggly, hyperactive viruses. They are in contact with Top Party labs via their bristle antennae, and those guys are crunching and improving the design and downloading the fixes to the viruses in realtime.

* How Utila the Giant Amoeba Flies.

John says that I'm saying it's levitation, then the chunks should levitate too. Membrane-enclosed "balloons of" hydrogen, created quickly and discarded casually. Created by photocatalytic water splitting, a type of artificial photosynthesis that produces hydrogen from water and light. Carried out by our tweaked amoeba. 100 hydrogen balloons of 8 ft diameter can lift 2,000 pounds, or a ton. Enough mass for about 30 of our blob guys. One balloon can lift 20 pounds. So a humanoid kritter chunk of the flying amoeba would need about four balloons.

I say the amoeba is forty meters (120 feet) across and, say, a meter thick, which gives it a volume of about 1,500 cubic meters, which is about 1,500 tons (water weighs a ton per cubic meter), which means 150,000 of those 8 ft diameter balloons, a 400 x 400 grid of them, 3,200 feet on an edge, so if I want to fit them over an amoeba that's 120 feet across, I'll have to stack the 8-ft-diameter balloons about 20 balloons high, or 160 feet high, call it a hundred feet. Make the ameboma a little less so we get can be with a bubble that's a hundred feet high, or 30 or forty meters high.

Drop the "paratroopers" lumps down and they walk back to camp our they ascend a handy dangling slime tendril.

* *Juice*

The juice was a big thing to me when I started the novel, and then I forget to keep pushing on it later on, but supposedly a lifebox needs it to be hip. So you'd wonder how, for instance, Molly's raw teepspace lifebox was makin' it. John also points out that any Skyhive lifebox ought to be able to draw in juice from the living server dough. And Gee's guest lifeboxes could draw "elan vital" from the redwood server tree. I want no for Skyhive, and yes for the redwood. Can I *use* the phrase "élan vital?" Sure. And run some jive about it being holistic ensemble quantum state function. And admit you can draw a bit of juice off a biocomputing server, but it's feeble.

* *Renormalization Is Too Powerful.*

If everyone learns to renormalize, they greedily or angrily destroy the world in short order. Limit the power to rare god-like figures like Molly and Anselm. I had this issue at the end of *Realware*, and in that case, it was called the alla, and in fact you alerted me to that some plot-killer aspect, and in Realware I ended up suspending the allas' power. But here's I'll say it's a power for godlike beings who will use it properly, like Moly and Anselm.

* *What* is *a Halo Lifebox?*

What the hell is it made of? I initially wanted to say quintessence, then for some reason backed off, seemed like too much extra BS to feed the reader. So I said charged ions, but I forgot to say they're in some odd quantum-computing linkage. But I loaded up on that. Play the quantum card.

Teepspace is Real

An additional late-breaking comment by the sage John Walker:

> As to the issue of where the halo lifeboxes are hosted, the reason it didn't bother me and I didn't say anything about it is based upon an assumption I made about the ontological status of teepspace which, as I think back on it, is never made explicit in the novel. The discussion of teepspace as a Hilbert space and the ability to renormalize things in consensus reality gave me the impression that teepspace is an actual, real space of some kind, which users of psidots are able to access. It is not, for example, a simulation like a massively multiplayer game running on a server like Skyhive or Gee's in the redwood tree. If it were a hosted simulation, then people hosted on Skyhive wouldn't be able to communication with those hosted elsewhere, and I don't think that's consistent with Gee's re-hosting some people without their knowledge: if they were suddenly cut off from those still on Skyhive, they'd immediately know what was up. But if teepspace is *real*, wherever it is and however it works, there's no reason one shouldn't be able to host a server there instead of externally. It's kind of like replacing Gmail with hosting your own mail server on your own machine. You can do it (heck, I did it for more than 25 years), and it's just a matter of performance, maintenance effort, and security. So, people with halo lifeboxes have just migrated from the cloud to their own hosting in teepspace.

Frankly, the point he's making is a little confusing to me, especially at the end. And even if it was hosted VR, there'd be no reason why the various servers' VRs can't connect (via messaging) into a seemingly seamless whole. I need to discuss this with him some more.

But I like how he puts his finger on the fact that I'm

viewing teepspace as "real." And maybe that makes ports more feasible.

I guess the "cyberspace" of the internet isn't quite as real as teepspace? I mean, if all our computers died, there wouldn't be any web cyberspace left. But as long as living organisms are around, I guess teepspace *is* real, and maybe it's real when they're gone as well. To me teepspace is similar to what I call the mindscape in *Infinity and the Mind*. The class of all possible thoughts.

I ought to say this explicitly in *Juicy Ghosts* as soon as someone starts using the word teepspace."

February 26, 2021. The Mary Fix.

That sketch of Mary's life a few days ago was fun to write, but that itself shouldn't go into the novel. Or I use at most a two-paragraph version. I need stuff that's right to point. Specifically I want a scene set in August, 2061.

(a) Gee sees Mary's band Squash Plant play in pot O' Gold. Kayla is 7 months pregnant, but she plays the fiddle anyway.

(b) Gee talks to Mary, and he's in love with her. [This makes it less weird for Gee to be offering her a psidot-lifebox-clone immortality set-up through Carson in 2062.]

(c) Gee speculates that Mary's voice is her soul.

(d) Gee tells Mary about the return of the far right. Mid-term election is coming, Top Party wants gigworker control, and they eventually want to kill Gee, but for now they're just watching him.

***

Another draft.

Mary is born in San Francisco in the late 1900s, an only child. She doesn't like her parents, her school—or politics or drugs. She enjoys walking around the city looking at people, and seeing live music. She likes the botanical garden too.

After high school, Mary's mother tells her she has to get a job. Instead, Mary hooks up with nomadic hipster scene, drifting around the US and Mexico for nearly twenty years, hitting tribal gatherings and music shows. The fireworks festival in Tultepec is a recurring high point, with thousands of people bringing fireworks-laden constructs called *toritos*, or little bulls—explosive piñatas on wheels, spouting sparks, vomiting firecrackers, and firing rockets horizontally across the market square.

Mary ends up in the funky Bay Area beach down of Santa Cruz, where she gets into the roots music scene. She plays mandolin, and sings. For a while she lives with a fisherman, but he's lost at sea during a crazy climate storm. Turns out he leaves her the deed to a small lot in tiny San Lorenzo, in the Santa Cruz Mountains. Mary gets hold of a biotech house seed—a relative of the squash plant—and she grows herself a domed, green home on her lot.

She never does find another man to live with, not she especially wants to. She spends the next thirty years working at the San Lorenzo Country store. She starts a bluegrass band, called Squash Plant, with a changing cast of colorful mountain types backing her on fiddle, banjo, and bass.

On the night Mary meets Gee Willikers, she's close to eighty, which is kind of insane, and Squash Plant is playing at the Pot O' Gold, a funky San Lorenzo road-house. It's August, seven months after Treadle's assassination. Mary's fiddle player is her neighbor Kayla Stux, ten months pregnant.

"You up for it?" Mary asks Kayla as they set up.

March 3-5, 2021. Finishing the Fix.

I finally got the Mary fix going today. I'm adding the new scene at the start of Chapter 4, alternating between working on that, and going through and changing how Mary talks about Gee in the rest of the chapter, given that now she will have met him before. I also need to change Jose Luna and Dmitri Cheeks into members of her Squash Plant band.

Almost every night I have intricate dreams about writing new material into the book. Like the novel-writing subsystem in my brain doesn't know it's time to stop. Maybe if I can lay the Mary fix to rest, I'll calm down.

Finished this fix on March 5. I ended up rewriting it three or four times—I always imagine I can just type some extra bit and it's done without me having to revise like I do on the main text, but first draft is never as clean as I want. Partly because when I'm writing the first draft of any scene, I never fully know how the scene will go. I have to animate the characters and watch what they do, and how they interact.

Anyway I got it, along with the twenty or thirty adjustments that were then necessary in the following material, to take into account that Mary would of course remember this meeting with Gee.

I made Dick Cheeks and Joe Moon be in Mary's band Squash Plant all along. I got too cute with their names and have, like, two or three versions of each, I need to just pick one and stay with it. I am torn as I love Cheeks and Moon, because those were names my pal Niles Schoening and I used to call each other when we were planning to get drunk in high school, '62-'63, but I'm tempted to get authentic and have Dick Chechen and Jose Luna, maybe even with an accent on Jose. Oh, I'll just go with Cheeks and Moon, and mention those are stage names that they like to use, and drop in one sentence about those "real" names.

Dear Sylvia kindly read the manuscript, finishing just now, and she liked it quite a bit, which is so nice. She even allows that the women characters are fairly reasonable. And she likes that sweet ending too.

She marked a few dozen changes, and I'm almost done putting those in.

July 16, 2021. Self-Pub

So meanwhile, John Silbersack and I sent the *Juicy Ghosts* manuscript to Oren Eades at Night Shade, to Liz Gorinsky at Erewhon, and to Jacob Weisman at Tachyon. The first two never answered. And Weisman said no, he thought the political assassination stuff was too much.

Silbersack told me the real problem is that the sales of *Million Mile Road Trip* were terrible. It got some great reviews, but it didn't catch on at all. Maybe the COVID plague hurt our sales, with all the bookstores closed. But even so, *MMRT* only sold about 500 ebooks so far. Weak.

I could have dipped down to smaller and smaller presses for *Juicy Ghosts*, but, as with my other recent "late style" novels *Turing & Burroughs*, *The Big Aha*, and *Return to the Hollow Earth*, I decided I'd rather self-publish it with good old Transreal Books. And get some decent money with a Kickstarter. And not have to beg.

So I launched my Kickstarter for *Juicy Ghosts*, and in a couple of days I'd blown past 200 backers and $13K, and still climbing. A pleasant surprise. Happy days here at Rucktronics World Headquarters.

I think people are *hungry* for a novel that features the killing of an evil President. Pent up demand!

I've drafted a cover design for the novel and for these *Notes*. Designer daughter Georgia R. will polish them up a bit. I'm getting my old proofreader Michael Troutman to go over the novel; he has a very good eye.

So now it's just a matter of wrapping up a bunch of details. Silbersack may yet sell it as an audiobook, or in Europe. And some publisher might reprint it in a few years. Main thing is to put it out there. *Finis coronat opus*, y'all.

NOVEL OUTTAKES

One Wow Rogue Exec

"We already guessed that," I tell him. "But he won't say who he works for."

"Ay, there's the rub," goes Chex. He was an English major, and he appreciates that I took a Shakespeare seminar before settling into Wetware E. "He's a black op for One Wow. The top execs want him to accelerate your work. And he's cozy with the Top Party cabal."

Anselm Warning

"I happen to think there's a second reason for why the stumbles infect human brains," puts in Anselm. "Not such a nice one. But I'll tell you later. For now I'm here to observe."

Loftus Offers

"I'm a researcher too," says Loftus. "I find things out, and I make introductions. How would you feel about an off-the-books sublicense deal for your new product?"

"How do you *think* I'd feel," I snap. "I happen to like having a job."

Anselm Disappears

"I *am* Anselm," says Gee. "Anselm is an illusion."

"Wait," I interrupt. "How do you mean?"

"My hacks are vast," goes Gee. He makes an odd gesture— like a wizard's mystic pass. Anselm vibrates into a dense compact mass like a bologna sausage with two eyes on one end.

Uvvy Rap

And there's apps for tingles and smells and tastes, too. And of course porn, and spam, and ads, and blockers, and filters, and firewalls. Yadda, yadda, yadda.

That low, grasping stuff isn't my bag.

Trolls

"Trolls are cute," said Leeta, reaching down to pet the bristly tip of the closest giant carrot. And then her expression changes. She's just noticed the three-foot-tall figure stalking out from the underbrush and onto the gravel path. He's ugly and he stinks from far away. He wears no pants. Nasty. His feet have purple toenails.

"*Hej*, Ørni," Anselm says to the troll. "This is Molly and Leeta. Scientists. Friends."

Ørni seems not to want to understand. He runs straight at Molly, eyes goggling, green tongue dangling, snaggle teeth bared. Waving a gnarly little wooden club. Molly rocks back on one foot and kicks Ørni very hard in the chest, sending him rolling across the gravel path to collide with one of the big carrots.

"That troll hates me," says Molly. "His name's Ernie?"

"Ørni," replies Anselm. "He helps fend off mass tourism. It was bad for a while. Dansk Junkers were considered cute and transgressive. Ørni is regressive and anti-cute."

Stumble Drug

"I'll get Gee," says Gyr. "We'll be able to fix it."

And now here's Gee, lanky and odd, holding a little plate with a prawn-cucumber smørrebrød. Clearly he's glad to be back with the Junkers. Vixen pauses her chord progressions, like a band dropping down behind a vocalist.

"Are you ready to rock and roll?" screeches Gee. His voice is, high, cracking, and only approximately musical.

"Be sensible," Gyr tells Gee. "You have to help Molly."

"Got it," says Gee. "I already checked on Leeta, but she wasn't hooked." Gee makes a magician's gesture with his hand, as if casting a hex on me. I feel a tingling in the uvvy on the back of my neck.

"What's happening?" I ask

"I put a new app on your uvvy. BrainChem. It uses the uvvy vortex fields to herd your brain's fatty tissues into synthesizing pretty much any requested brain drug."

"What is the stumble drug, exactly?"

"Well, it's new," says Gee. "The stumble fungus invented it. An odd chemical. It's a zwitterionic tryptamine with a set of benzene rings. BrainChem is assembling a dose for you. Feel it yet? I've asked the app to wean you off it this week. Less every day. Unless you object. It's yours to control. But we need Molly in high gear—if we're going to eradicate the Treadle Disease."

"Sure! You bet! No problem!" I'm not sure what he's talking about, but I feel very good.

Hegel

"I find this a little bit exhilarating," remarks Anselm. "Do you realize that in order to get here, we walked the exact same route that Søren Kierkegaard used to take in the 1840s, wandering around Christiania? This is the very same philosopher who called himself a fly on Hegel's nose. And you're Hegel's great-great-great-great-great-granddaughter, are you not, Molly?"

"Is that true?" asks Gyr. Her eyes narrow, as she delves into the net.

"I heard it from my grandfather, yeah. He's three greats, and I'm five. But I never think about it. How would you even know a thing like that, Anselm?"

Molly Cures Her Stumble Addiction with Quantum Scrolls

[I decided to use a version of this for curing the Treadle

Disease, so I wrote something else for curing stumble addiction.]

Guided by Gyr's psidot teep, I set some of my gossip molecules to beating their tails. They swirl energy into scroll vortices. Quantum scrolls. Physical entities I've created within my brain. They're concentrated in a little cranny that I think of as my attic, between the hemispheres, towards the front.

"Subdivide the scrolls," says Gyr. "Let vortex them clean your brain."

"How?"

"Big eddies can decay into smaller ones. It works for quantum scrolls too. Straight quantum hydrodynamics. Drink from my fount of knowledge."

"Impressive," I say. I stream the facts and methods from Gyr's mind.

"Spawn," goes Gyr.

Each of my attic vortices shudders and splits in two, with the smaller vortices splitting again, down through as many levels as I like. It's something I've seen in creeks or in sunlit swimming pools. One becomes two becomes four becomes eight. Eddies dissolving into eddies—all the way down. The cascades of classic turbulence.

"Keep going," says Gyr in my head. "A vortex population explosion. Split the vortices forty-seven times. Two to the forty-seventh power is over a hundred trillion. And that's how many neurons you have in your brain. The point is to end up with one tiny nano vortex for each neuron. Like individual case workers."

This insane dodecaduplication sounds more than a little risky, but I'm in a reckless mood, here in the rainy Danish night with this enticing new woman. I press ahead, doubling and redoubling, on and on.

"Perfuse the vortices to your neurons," says Gee. "A fresh analogy. It's like you're running a hotel, and the attic is filled with a host of wee housekeepers, and you tell them to each go clean a room. And they sort it out themselves."

I feel swirly and bemused. "Come again?"

"It's like you took a shot of heroin, and each neuron in your brain gets an opiate molecule."

"I don't take heroin."

"Stumble is just as bad. Stop stalling."

So now—and I'm definitely reluctant—I nudge those furiously spinning vortices out of my attic—and they're off! Dusting out the cores of my neurons' internal microtubules—banishing the vortex fog and creating a mellow, relaxed mood that reaches all the way down to the bottom of my medulla.

Hell, I don't need drugs at all. The White Light is always here. All hail the One. And like that. My withdrawal pains are gone—and they won't be coming back.

Gossip Molecules of Treadle Disease

Min picks up Gee's thread. "Once installed in an organism, the gossip molecules replicate and mass together. They writhe in unison, flourishing their van der Waals forces. A synchronized wave." I see a crowd in a stadium. Min sways back and forth; she raises her hands and spreads her fingers. "The gossip molecules form a coherent macrostate. They manipulate vortical quantum fields."

Molly Cures Herself

We press ahead, chanting faster, some of us improvising solos.

"This is good," says Gee, watching me through a glass window at the side of this…recording studio. "Now go out caroling. Sing to each of your neurons. Beguile them. You and your host of wee choristers. You'll sing each neuron into health."

"All of them?" I teep to Gyr while I'm still chanting.

"It's doable," says Gyr. "It's like you took a shot of heroin, and each neuron in your brain gets an opiate molecule."

"I don't take heroin."

"Stumble was just as bad. Stop stalling. You know what you're supposed to do."

So okay—the process sounds risky, but I'm in a reckless mood, here in the rainy Danish night with this enticing new woman. And maybe I'm reluctant, too, maybe I love my addiction that much, but—go for it, Molly.

I nudge my hazy cloud of trillion Molly selves out of the studio, and we're off! Our multifarious voices cheer my individual neurons to their cores—banishing all remnants of the stumble fog; ushering in a mellow, relaxed, homeostatic balance of neurotransmitters that reaches all the way down to the bottom of my medulla.

Yah, mon.

I don't need drugs at all. The White Light is always here. All hail the One. And good stuff like that. My withdrawal pains are gone—and they won't be coming back.

"Ta da!" I tell Gyr. "I'm cured. Easy as pie. Thanks for the magic spell."

"We Junkers need you to be in fine fettle," says Gyr. "You're our star. Bombardier Molly of the Metatron A-team. Today you revamped our psidots and made yourself well—and tomorrow you go after Treadle Disease."

Not sure what that last part is about—but I'm brimming with joy and optimism. "Sure! You bet! No problem!" It's been a hella long time since I felt this good.

Metatron Quintillion

You already saw her do a trillion things at once, and now she'll do—a few hundred million times as many things. That would be few hundred quintillion Treadle gossip molecules in all."

I do the math. A million is 1,000,000, which is two sets of triple zeroes, which means multiplying by a million moves you two steps higher on the "-illion" scale. So we got from trillion to quadrillion to quintillion.

Carpet Bombing USA with Zhabotinsky Scrolls

Fixing Anselm.

Quickly and efficiently, I spawn a fresh crop of one trillion Zhabotinsky vortices. They vibrate around us like infinitesimal gnats.

"You have learned well, grasshopper," goes Gyr.

"Help me herd them, Master. They'll unsnarl the prions on Anselm's neurons."

"Got it," she says.

The virtual Gyr executes an elegant pirouette. With a graceful sweep of her arm, she sends half the twirling Zhabotinsky scrolls out to the horizon and, I assume, into the recesses of Anselm's body. I send off the others. Far and wee.

We hear a high, thin hum.

***

Fixing US.

"Shed shed shed," I say. I'm stockpiling those quintillion Zhabotinsky scrolls in the bomb bay of the B-29. Looking down through my window on the floor, I see North America like a shape on a map. Metatron edges back and forth, positioning us above the center, somewhere in Kansas, and zooming in so that the country just fills my field of view.

"Single out the afflicted," says Anselm.

Pinpricks of light appear across our nation's spreadness. Each point marks a sufferer of Treadle Disease. Many in the Midwest, and even more on coasts, which is where the Treadle campaign needs the most help. If someone's going to vote for Treadle anyway, no need to infect them.

"Shed shed shed," I'm saying. This is taking a lot out of me. I'm up to a quadrillion Zhabotinsky scrolls now. I have a dark murmuring cloud of them in the back of Megaton's fuselage. Ten more steps. "Shed shed shed,"

"We'll send them down there all at once," says Anselm. "Catch the Treadle Disease by surprise."

"Shed shed shed."

"Aren't you ready yet, Molly?"

"Shed!" I cry. "That's one quintillion! A trillion vortices for every man woman and child in the homeland." I pull the lever for the bomb-bay door.

What's Real?

But wait—how come the spectators and the politicians were still here even though the Washington Monument had fallen down? Had I really seen that happen? Maybe no. My new mods did that to me more often than I liked. They overlaid false realities on top of what my sensory inputs were really gleaning. It's like my post processing faculties were amped up to schizoid levels—by way of preparing for when my body was gone. And, um, had we inaugurated Manka Ranka? Yeah, I thought so, but that her name? And had we converted the troops? Possibly. And the Russian palace guards machine-gunning us? Too pat. That's why Leeta had been laughing like that part was a movie, and saying the symbolism was—what was her considered phrase? *Pretty corny.*

How the Chatbot Works

They use quantum entanglement, or molecular wireless signals, or Martian homeless-person schizophrenia rays, or whatever.

***

How does Gee's chatbot tech work? Basically, you paste this tingly shiny patch on the back of your neck, and that's a communication channel, and you can efficiently, hear and see your toy ghost in your head, which can be useful. You update it with feeds of your daily life so it gets better at being you.

But a toy ghost isn't what you'd call conscious or alive, and it's no substitute for immortality. But our man Gee Willikers has a plan for making the ghosts funkier. Something about mixing in biocomputation. I doubt he'll finish the project in time to save me. Given that I only have a couple of hours to go.

Old Assassin Origin Story

I'd been a worker in the secret lab that created the wasps. Originally, I'd been a copy-writer for the group's social media jamming. But now as the final crisis arrived, I'd been shifted into lab work, even though I knew little about science. More of a literary man. A dissenter.

For the last six months I'd been, effectively, a janitor in the wasp lab. And then Treadle won, or stole, the election. It was time to act. I volunteered to be seeded with wasp eggs, to grow the larvae to term within my flesh, and to carry them to the Inauguration for the moment of the hatch.

Kurtis and Leeta, of the transbio faction, thought it was a great idea. I was old. No great loss. Kurtis our faction's leader promised me I'd get life after death—and Leeta, our chief tech, said it was true.

How Jilljill Saves Curtis's Emotions

This was initially in Chapter 3, but now it's a repeat, as I already have it in detail in the first two chapters.

"How about my emotions?" I ask Jilljill.

"We've got that covered too," she says. "I sent these

special molecules into you. Gee calls them gossip molecules. They detect your neurotransmitters, and send templates of the chemicals to the lifebox computation. It has special code for emulating emotions."

"Can it send emotions back to me?" I ask.

"Perfect question," says Jill. "It sends neurochemical template to your gossip molecules, and they build the actual chemicals on the spot. In your brain."

"That's messed up," I say.

Kill Scene Draft

I wish I could see Treadle's face—but he's flat on his back on the on the Inauguration dias. And my vision is growing dark. I'm on the ground too. My torso is slick with pulsing sheets of blood. Those wasp larvae had burrowed deep.

Leeta was distancing herself, doing her crowd-surfing trick again. As she faded from my view, she threw back her head and chirped from the back of her throat. A cyberbio trigger code. The killer wasps subdivide into swarms of cyberbio gnats who whirred away.

Segue from Death

At this point my narrative has a glitch. It's that jump cut thing I was talking about? Well, turns out that for me there *is* action on the other side. The all-meat Curtis Winch is gone, but a chintzy, temporary, paper-doll version of me is encoded in my toy ghost. Fairly worthless, right? Like living on as memorial web page, or as a Speak & Spell toy. BFD. But wait.

Thanks to the wasps and the freaky Gee Willikers, my toy ghost gets ported over to the living meat of Ross Treadle's nasty, fat bod. I'm not a toy ghost now. I'm a *juicy* ghost. And that makes all the difference.

Implanted into Treadle's body by one of the two wasps that survived to reach its target, that is, the nasty, fat bulk of President Treadle's bod.

In a sense, it's my toy ghost that's telling you this story now. But there's a kicker. Nourished by the nasty warmth of the Chief Hog's flesh, my toy ghost bloomed into a juicy ghost. So I woke up inside the Treadle bisimulation, not knowing where the fuck I was.

Soviet Lifebox for Treadle

"Once you and Friedl are in the house, you get hold of Treadle's psidot. The psidot is called Wladimir. He looks like a gray ladybug. He's linked to Treadle's lifebox in the Soviet KGB cloud."

***

"I'll crush Wladimir," puts in Jilljill, sounding tough, graceful, and confident. "I'll run a vortex thread through Wladimir and all the way to Treadle's lifebox in the KGB lab."

***

But I'm not really clear on what happens then. Follow a thread? What kind of thread? To me, Gee's concepts are like ghosts in a dark room. I'd like to think he said that when Jilljill touches Wladimir, she'll send a zap through him that erases Treadle's lifebox in KGB cloud-cuckoo-land.

***

I slip inside the shrieking whirlwind's vortex thread. It carries me through a hail of Treadle memories, and outward to the psidot Wladimir's source of power—which is a dowdy, concrete cube at the University of Moscow. No title on the building, no windows, only one door. A KGB research lab. I'm inside it now, looking at a twinkling box of lights. Treadle's lifebox. Someone hands me a heavy fire axe. Who?

Antimatter Explosion for Treadle Clone

In my head I see that glowing woman again. Molly. The one who healed us from Treadle Disease and disappeared. And now she's—what? A friendly ghost? Friendly to me, anyway. Not friendly to Treadle.

"I'm going to make him explode," Molly tells me. "I can reach under space now. I'll flip half of him into antimatter. It'll be like pulling the rug out from under his feet. The blast will take out the So, whole house, and everything in it. You'll need to get the innocents to go outside. Get started."

...

"Don't even try!" I yell, jumping to my feet. I go into the kitchen and holler down the stairs. "Men! I need you up here. All of you. Right now!"

So the boys storm up the staircase, guns in hand, ready to

kick ass. These are Treadle's true loyalists, the rottenest apples in the barrel.

"You stick with me," I tell them. "We're about to make a move. And the rest of you, out of the house! Now! Push them out, men!"

Shouting and protesting, Chuck and Lucy are bundled out. Lucy carries Friedl.

"I don't need this," said the housekeeper. "I quit." She goes down the stairs and off down the block.

"Stay on the other side of the street!" I warn Lucy and Chuck once more. I shake my fist for good measure. Lucy gives me the finger, but she goes across the street. And Chuck follows her.

Back in the house I eye my seven stalwarts. "Are you boys with me all the way?" I ask them. "Anyone have doubts? Because if you do, you should leave right now."

"Hell with it," says one of the younger guys. "This has no point, Mr. President. Or whatever I'm talking to. Everyone knows you're dead."

"Go on, then!" I holler at him. "To hell with you."

Two more of them leave as well. And then we're down to Jilljill, Ross Treadle's clone, and Treadle's four most hardcore, devoted backers.

"Light us up," I tell Molly.

Clone for Curtis Winch

And when that's ready, you'll coach me on Mary's musical latex death-mask Morph Move. And we'll do Curtis, too. I owe him. He's been in the freezer for about ten years. Ever since he blew up President Treadle's clone."

"Poor guy. Why did you wait so long?"

"Oh, things pile up. And he wasn't in that big of a rush. He's kind of, I don't know, misanthropic. He likes being zoned out. Also, I think you must have noticed that when you're a non-juiced lifebox, you don't have much idea about the passage of time."

"Well, do him too. He deserves it," says Mary. "Juicy ectoplasmic ghosts all around!".

Flying Ball Walkers

"Right," says Gee. "And I want those two ball walker pals of yours to carry us. Glory and Miss Max."

"They're not really strong enough," objects Mary. "And they can't run all that fast, or all that far."

"I'm gonna give them wings," says Gee, creaking open the barn's back door.

Instantly on the alert, Miss Max stalks over, six feet tall and ready to kick ass or, if necessary, to disembowel one of them with a clawed foot.

"It's me," Mary tells her. "Mary from before."

"You molted?" says Miss Max, her voice still doing that *parp-parp* thing.

"Sure," says Mary. "You're not remote controlled yet, are you?"

"Mrs. Yahootie doesn't want to rent me a lifebox brain," parps Miss Max. "I'm glad. I'm doing fine."

"No you're not," says Glory, picking his way over to them, avoiding the piles of ball-walker poop. "You still don't understand about straw." Glory's tiny focus of attention shifts to Mary and Gee. The ball of his head gapes. A grin.

"Yes, it's me!" says Mary. "And my friend Gee.".

"We need you guys to carry us a couple of hundred miles," Gee tells the two ball walkers.

"Go away," says Miss Max. "Too far." She turns her back and begins scratching at the ground, sending tufts of straw and manure their way.

"You'll *fly*," Gee calls to the big ball walker. "I've got the fixings to transform you shitkickers into transport drones."

"I want to fly," says Glory. "I want to fly."

"I'll fly higher than you," says Miss Max. "I'm bigger and smarter."

"You're not smarter," Mary tells Miss Max. "And that's a fact."

"Grow us our wings," says Glory, dancing around in excitement.

"Let me call my elephruk," says Gee. "He's nearby."

"But will you be stealing us?" asks Miss Max.

"I'll give Mrs. Yahootie the elephruk in place of you two,"

says Gee. She'd like that. "Mary, can you go inside and talk to her about it? I'll wait in the elephruk. He points into a dark vacant lot. In there."

Gee's Army of Local Animals

Above the clearing some crows flap and caw. A lot of them, maybe a hundred.

"My guardians," says Gee.

"How do you mean?"

"In case anyone ever does get close, I've got my army. Most of the animals around my cave—they're linked into me with teep. For the last year, I've been putting psidots on every one of them I can get my hands on."

"You're teeping the crows? You hear cawing all the time?"

"I don't usually listen," Gee says, laughing. "But at least once a day I So, merge with my full legion. Staying in touch. This emergent network agent named Metatron who helps me with my biome view. Birds, snakes, squirrels, slugs—even gnats."

"You're totallly bullshitting me," says Mary.

"It's for real," says Gee. "I'm all over my little Eden. In the plants, in the air, n the animals, in the ground." He holds up his hands, madly wriggling his fingers.

"I want to see," says Mary.

"Come on in."

Mary teeps into Gee's head. A marvelous, articulated feeling, with minds on every side, and bodies to match. Including the calmly idling Utila aeroform overhead.

The gnat swarms are especially odd—hive minds of a few hundred gnats at once. Somehow very similar to the scattered, distracted thoughts that Mary used to get when driving a car. Not that anyone drives anymore. But now, with her new body and her lifebox brain, if she did drive, she'd be better at it. But, um, wait, she's losing the thread—

Gee does something in his head, and the surrounding minds synch into a schematic pattern that resembles Christmsas lights scattered across the surface of an old, very large airplane.

"That's Metatron," goes Gee. "That sysadmin creature I was talking about," goes Gee. "Metatron. He likes to imitate a World War II bomber. My friend Anselm got him to start doing that. Who knows why. Other times he's a zigzag dragon. About a thousand times as smart as we are. That woman Molly Sanos I mentioned, she lives inside Metatron now. She's his bombardier, not that I ever see her anymore. But tomorrow, after you're an indie lifebox, Molly and Metatron will—"

"Can we talk about one thing at a time?" interrupts Mary, withdrawing from the visions in Gee's mind. "Let's do our ball walker run to the cosmic blimp works. That's what I'm up for. Not a slobber-session about your imaginary airplane dragon and her unseen bombardier Molly."

"Fine, fine, fine," says Gee.

***

"We have a good army," says Glory. "Rattlesnakes, crows, jays, squirrels, a pair of mountain lions, swarms of gnats—and some very big banana slugs. As big as Bunter.

"And don't forget Gee's flying jellyfish, Utila," adds Miss Max. "Our umbrella. She hides us.

Kayla At Work

She's in her studio in her house, peacefully crafting a clawed replacement foot for somebody's ball walker.

Cloaked Mode Delay

"Cloaked mode is when you fox the Skyhive surveillance channel by feeding it spoofed conversations about nothing."

"Doesn't Skyhive hear you asking you psidot for *cloaked mode*?" asks Mary.

"No," goes Carson. "Psidots keep their public channel on a three second delay. So they have time to hide the cloaking requests."

Oscar the Ghost

The closest one of them approaches her. Could it be Oscar? Has he been tracking her for all these years? She seems to hear his voice.

"Long wait, Mary. Long wait. I'm fading down."

"I can find you a body," teeps Mary. "Give you some juice."

"Too late." The Oscar ghost—if that's who he is—drifts away.

***

"Autonomous lifebox souls are like old-school ghosts," muses Mary—and goes off on a tangent. "I wonder if I'll find my old boyfriend Oscar. He's been dead a long time, and now I'm dead too. Oscar didn't have a lifebox or anything, but maybe he's a regular ghost—if there's any such thing."

"I doubt it," says Gee. "Ghosts are a metaphor for where we're heading. But you're right to remember the folklore of it all. I like that."

"I think I told you not patronize me."

"Never!"

Mary's Ghost

Does she have a real ghost, too? She did die, after all, lying there in the yard beside Kayla and Carson's house. Did she have an immortal soul that went off—somewhere. On her own, not worrying about all of Mary's modern tricks with her live psidot, and her cloud-based lifebox, and her tank-grown clone, and now her ectoplasmic lifebox in the mix as well.

Indie Lifebox Connect to Clone Without Psidot

For starters, she drapes the disk of her halo onto Mary's head like a skull cap or a wig. Clone Mary breathes on unperturbed. No signals from her.

"You have to plug in the quantum vortex threads," says Gee aloud. "Like Miu Miu did."

"I have absolutely no idea what you're talking about," says Mary.

"Come on," says Gee. "Deep down you remember. Sprout a bunch of quantum threads."

So Mary relaxes, and by some unaccountable inner process, she grows prickles all over her underside. Invisibly fine tendrils, zillions of them.

"One thread per neuron, and one thread per gossip mole-cule," says Gee.

***

Also, I'd also like to mention that I don't like my halo being glued to the top of my head. It'd be much better if it could float around—so the Top Party thugs can't immediately kill the halo at the same time as me. Like hit me on the top of my head with a machete.

Vortex Ring Soul

As Mary moves through the portal, she spots the new home that Gee had promised: a vortex ring of air, a transparent torus that's endlessly spinning on itself. Its currents draw in the annular disk that codes Mary's soul

The inner edge of the disk rises into the throat of the torus, continues on through, and slides down along the torus's outside, meeting up with the trailing outer edge of the disk. The edges fuse, covering the vortex-ring torus like a skin.

The lifebox pattern merges into the vortex-ring flow. Like cream threading into stirred coffee. Mary's lifebox is a subtle weave of flow-lines within the toroidal current of air.

Mary has survived the port. She's an ascended adept in an astral body.

The vortex-ring floats free of the redwood, continually turning within itself. It drifts across the dappled glade, emulating Mary's mind with its churning. The ring's yubba-vine dose of quintessence keeps the air current from dissipating or slowing down.

***

The circlet of ionized, naturally computing air is endlessly spinning.

A swarm of gnats hovers in the ring's core, ascending and descending on the micro-breezes. It's as if the gnats are talking to the ring, and maybe they are, given that, as Gee showed her, the swarms are tiny minds. Mary can gnat's feel the swarm as an articulated web of moving dots, and with circuits of logic chasing around the web. If *twitch*, then *dart* and/or *zoom*.

Description of Indie Lifebox

"The server doesn't have to be some big corporate thing. Skyhive's server is dough, and mine is a tree. Naturally occurring computations. But any natural process will do. At the lowest level, everything's a natural computation. A human, an animal, a plant, a flame, an ocean wave, a current of air. Your lifebox can be a hosted anywhere you like. And it can move around. No Skyhive to charge you rent or make you do gig work."

Ectoplasm

"Hold on," says Gee. "I'm getting there. Ectoplasm can hold an info pattern for quite some time. It's saves patterns as quantum loops. And it needs to draws a little bit of energy. In that sense, it's like a lifebox."

"But at the same time it's different," says Mary, her voice flat and weary. "I hate you, Gee. You're the most boring person I've ever met."

"Hold on!" repeats Gee. "The big upside is that an ecto ghost doesn't need to be stored on a server. And if people don't need lifebox servers, the corrupt, exploitative scam of Leeta's Skyhive is of business."

"But you just said an ectoplasmic ghost needs energy to stay in action," says Mary.

"But their needs are very low. To start with, an ectoplasmic ghost scores a burst of energy from the dead body it comes from. And then it's good for a couple of years. And even while your body is rotting, you can sip a little energy off it. So it figures that people see ghosts in graveyards. In time, the ghost grows tattered and torn. But they can recharge. Maybe by taking possession of person or an animal or a plant or even a ripple in a stream. Or by scaring people and feeding off their shudders and screams."

"Okay, what's ectoplasm?"

"It's an old-school notion," says Gee. "A joke word, really. Ballyhooed by psychics and spiritualists in days of yore. Most of them were hoaxers. In the darkness of a séance, a medium might pull a greasy strip of gauze out of her mouth and say it was ectoplasm. Maybe with a cut-out paper picture of a face at one end. Grandma Lulabelle, here to tell you where she hid her diamonds."

***

She hovers there for quite some time, maybe an hour, enjoyably pulsing, content to alive, settling in.

She notices a pair of kindred forms peeping out from behind the trees, old-school ghosts, lost and unconvivial, like tattered flags of surrender. Mary has two advantages over them. First, she's brand new, and with a full energy bank. Second, she knows Fweedle.

Not that Mary *consciously* knows Fweedle, god forbid. but it's built into her mental architecture. And this means that she can link directly to a human body, with no intermediary psidot. *Score!* Ah, to luxuriate in the supple warmth of a carnal form. And the sooner the better.

***

"What if I find the ghost of my old beau Oscar?" says Mary, playing with Gee. "Maybe you could get him a meat body."

"Like I'd help you do that," says Gee. "And don't forget you'd have to teach him Fweedle so he could take possession of whatever random new clone you got for him. And even if you did all that, it probably wouldn't work. Dude's been dead for, what, twenty-five years with no living body's feed? He's a faded prom corsage by now. A sad toy in the attic. Forget about him."

***

She carries a chair outside the cave and sits in the clearing, watching for ectoplasmic ghosts. She sees four of them over the course of a half hour. They cross he clearing at odd angles. She tends to see them only from the corner of her eye. Or as shapes peeking out from behind something else.

Mary has the feeling that they're local, that is, that their decayed remains are quite nearby. And it could be they're drawn by Mary's presence. She's a fellow ectoplasmic ghost, fully energized, and with a bitchin flesh bod. Maybe they're admiring how Mary's ectoplasm shines through her skin.

She finds she can pick up some thoughts from the ghosts. The channel feels something like brainwave-based teep, but it's—wispier. Unmediated by modern biotech, and with a spooky, atavistic feel. She's never noticed ghosts before. Her sensitivity to them comes from being in an ectoplasmic body herself.

Turns out the four wraiths come from bodies interred right around here, in the wilderness, far from the tame graveyards of the towns. Who are they? A woman slain by a cruel lover. A crackpot hermit who starved to death. A depressive teen who shot himself. A baby abandoned by a desperate young mother.

Quintessence

"Quintessence?"

Gee turns sneaky. "Well, I don't like to make this sound too complicated. But we need a way for an indie lifebox to send and receive ultraweak wireless signals. And I think it'll help to add this esoteric yet ubiquitous substance to the mix."

"Quintessence," says Mary once again. With a bit of a sinking feeling.

"The Greeks talked about it. It's the element that's beyond earth, air, fire and water. The fifth thing. Quint + Essence. Modern physicists have talked about it too. For them, quintessence is beyond the four modern basics: atoms, neutrinos, photons, and dark matter. But the physicists don't have it exactly right. Truth be told, I'm using the word quintessence in my own peculiar and idiosyncratic way."

"Why am I not surprised?" says Mary. "So my all-new, server-free lifebox will be a pattern of quintessence that can settle into pretty much any natural process or object at all. And—stop me if I'm wrong—you have no idea whatsoever how to do this, but I'm supposed to figure it out. Me, Mary, all on my own."

Gee beams. "Exactly. And I know you can do it. In a few minutes, your indie lifebox will float out of my server tree in its default state: a vortex-ring of ionized air, like a smoke-ring, and veined with quintessence. It'll power up some ultraweak wireless and hook up with your juicy clone body. Goodbye to rapacious lifebox server farms! All hail Mary the liberator!"

"I do like that last part," allows Mary. "This quintessence is real?"

"Oh, yeah," Gee's sim says to Mary's sim. While they're having this big discussion, the two of them are still inside Gee's redwood server tree. "The quintessence will keep the airflow going. Like a lubricant. Erases the friction."

"How much?" asks Mary.

"How much what?"

"How much quintessence do you have for me to use. A pound? A ton? A trillionth of a gram?"

Gee turns shifty again. "Quintessence isn't something that I *have*. It's a field. It's everywhere."

"So I won't be made of quintessence?"

"Are ripples made of *water*?" goes Gee. "Not really. They're patterns in the flow of a stream. Is a hairdo made of *hair*? Not really. It's—"

"Shit," goes Mary. "You almost had me for a minute. I thought you had a real, actual, no-bullshit method for getting my lifebox off your server. But no. I think we're done. I'm flipping my focus into my meat body."

"Wait!" implores Gee. "Please? Don't even think about quintessence. You're going to port your soul into a vortex ring of air."

Tokamak Snake, Take 1

"This is the part that's wild and spooky," says Gee. "This is where quintessence comes in. When a tokamak snake grows to a certain size, it swallows its tail, and its gut becomes a toroidal vortex ring of—quintessence. The vortex ring is like a tornado bent around in a circle. Or like a smoke ring, right. Twisted strands of energy, and you don't see the skin anymore at all. That's how I got that sample of quintessence that I was talking about."

"I though you made it with some kind of lab equipment."

"I'm a biohacker, Mary. Organisms *are* my lab equipment. Anyway, when a tokamak snake turns into a whirling 3D Zhabotinsky vortex, it sheds baby vortex rings, and then those little guys stop biting their tails, and they turn into newborn tokamak snakes. Cute little fellers. With diamond-back-rattler skin."

***

As Mary moves through the circle of the tokamak snake—*aha!*—the snake sheds its skin, unveiling a spinning, gnarly, toroidal ring of quintessence within. The skin dissolves into scales of crystalline quintessence that settle upon the rectangular tapestry of Mary's soul—like sequins on a mummy in a pharaoh's tomb. The scales fuse together and firm up, capturing an eidetic image of Mary's lifebox mind—like a Shroud of Turin, if you will. And immediately Mary's original and now-unneeded lifebox retreats into the server's archival core.

Tokamak Snake, Take 2

"Go for it," says Gee, who's channeling her thoughts. "Astral body sounds perfect. Meanwhile I'll put a tokamak snake in place. They resemble diamondback rattlesnakes. But that's not what they are at all. Not regular snakes by any means. I think they're from another planet. Or another dimension. They're aliens. Tokamak snakes. I call them that because of their—their astral bodies."

"Jesus, Gee, you're such a screwball. Do the tokamak snakes talk to you?"

"They teep. One of them, Zsuzsa, she told me that they rode to our upper atmosphere in a giant glowing orb. Their mothership. Ten years ago, I found Zsuzsa and her mate Ond in a way-back cranny of my cave."

"If it's been here ten years, why aren't you talking about them all the time?"

"Well, I've got a lot of irons in the fire," says Gee. "And those snakes—they do a thing sort of like going into cloaked mode teep? I totally forget about them for months and years at a time. And then I'll notice that they're still in my cave. Living off lizards, mice, gophers, like that. They have a nest in one of the way, way back chambers of my cavern. Very weird vibe in there. About a hundred tokamak snakes in there now. A snake pit. Full of funky teep that I can't understand. And they project these—I'll use your word—astral bodies. Like glowing donuts you can hardly see. Floating around over the pit. Vortex rings. Like smoke rings, but they're twisted strands of quintessence. Zsuzsa let me crush one of the astral bodies of one of her great-grandchildren, and that's how I got that sample of quintessence that I was talking about."

"I thought you made it with some kind of lab equipment."

"I'm a biohacker, Mary. Organisms are my lab equipment. Anyway, last month Zsuzsa and Zsolt told me—" Gee pauses and looks at Mary. "Guess," he says. "Guess what they told me." His eyes are dancing.

"If you think I'm in on the secret, you're sadly wrong, Gee. It must be lonely, being so utterly and completely slushed."

"Zsuzsa and Zsolt told me to bring you here. They said you'll do the port that launches the cascade."

Mary's sim voice rises to a wail. "How am I supposed to—
"

But now Gee is gone.

***

As Mary moves through the circle of the tail-biting tokamak snake—aha!—the snake projects a toroidal ring of quintessence. It's a vortex ring, spinning on itself, and it vacuums up the tapestry disk, the rearranged lifebox that was Mary's soul, the disk like her personal Shroud of Turin.

The inner edge of the disk goes up inside the throat of the torus, through the throat, and down along the torus's outside, meeting up with the outer edge of Mary's disk. The edges fuse, covering the tokamak torus like a skin, or like a glove covering a hand.

And now the next step. As soon as the eidetic replica of Mary's lifebox has covered the torus's surface—it soaks in like ink on blotting paper. Her mind-pattern blends into the steady vortex-ring flow. Mary is veined all through it.

***

She pauses and doubles her point of view, checking on the tokamak snake's astral body. It's still out there in the clearing. A quintessence circlet, hanging there, forever twirling in on itself, with its shifting surface like mother of pearl. A small swarm of gnats hovers in the ring's core.

"You did a great port," says Gee, dropping his suit. By now he knows Mary better than to press her. "That song of yours. So great."

"And your tokamak snake Zsuzsa," says Mary. "Radical. To say the least."

"Like I said, I've got a whole pit of them," says Gee. "In the nether reaches of my mad scientist cave. Did I mention that Zsuzsa and Ond arrived on the night that Molly and Anselm disappeared?"

"I don't even know who Molly and Anselm are," says Mary. "So let's not go off on another bullshit tangent. What I want to know is how I take care of my astral body. I mean— I'm sharing it with an alien snake? Is that really better than having my lifebox in a redwood tree server run by you?"

"I hope so," says Gee. "Maybe you have full control of it."

"I think still belongs to Zsuzsa!" says Mary.

"Can you hear Zsuzsa in your head?"

Mary pauses, thinking. Tuning in on the signals from her lifebox mind—the lifebox that now lives inside Zsuzsa's astral body. And—yeah, there's definitely something off. A lurching sporadic hiss—tokamak-snake voices. Flashing images of delicious baby mice. The back-wrenching pleasure of twisting her body around Zsolt. The joy of sinking her fangs into—

"Shit, Gee. Can I go back to my old lifebox?"

"We, um, we'd have to make a new one. Just now the old one got erased. As part of the port. Try and live with it for now. Settle in. Maybe you'll like it."

"But you didn't want to try it on yourself," says Mary acidly.

"To tell you the truth, I hadn't thought this far ahead," says Gee. "Maybe you'd have more power over the astral body if it lived inside *your* meat body—like a spirit familiar. Instead of living in Zsuzsa. And I'm guessing the astral body wouldn't mind drawing energy from you."

"She could be my spirit familiar," says Mary. "And I'd be an adept." She focuses on her and Zsuzsa's astral body and summons it. With no sign of effort, the smoke-ring-like form glides into Gee's cave. Mary finds herself able to tweak the astral body's size. Should she really make it small and stash it in her body? Fees way creepy.

She hits on a has a better idea. She matches her astral body's diameter to that of her head, and sets the ring to hovering just above her. Like a halo! Saint Mary of the Tokamak Snake.

Gee stares at her in a strange way. "What?" says Mary. "Can you see it?"

"I always have trouble," says Gee. "Is—is there a glow?"

"My aura," says Mary. "My tokamak serpent. My soul."

"Very fine," says Gee. "Maybe that's what haloes always were."

"The saints and angels didn't have psidots," says Mary.

"If we work on it, maybe we can probably bypass the psidot," says Gee. "But that's enough hard stuff for today." He pauses, still looking at her. "A few minutes ago, I asked you to marry me. What happened to that?

***

We'll table that issue," says Gee. He seems to enjoy the back and forth. "I still want to know how you did that port. Overlaying your lifebox onto an alien tokamak snake's astral body. No mean feat."

"Like anyone is going to want to live this way," says Mary. She finds that she's unconsciously swaying her shoulders as if slithering across the ground. "You know what I'm imagining right now?" she asks Gee. "Writhing through a damp burrow that runs from the back of the snake pit to a bramble thicket by a stream. Curling up and waiting, motionless as stone—and then striking at a wee titmouse bird, feeding on seeds on the ground. The joyous peristalsis of forcing the bird down her long, long throat, feather, bones, beak and all. *Aaah*."

***

She carries a chair outside and sits in the clearing between the cave and the redwood. And then she notices the rattlesnake lying near the base of the redwood tree. A big one; the size of an arm. The snake's eyes glitter; it raises his diamond-shaped head and hisses. Flickers its tongue.

"Zsuzsa?" says Mary, her throat dry. Slowly, slowly, she rises to her feet. Getting the chair between her and that ginormous snake.

The snake twitches, and the motion moves down her long body like a wave. She's bigger than an arm. More like a leg.

Mary does her best to send images of friendship. Hearts, smiles, flowers—does any of that work for a snake? She goes into the kitchen, finds some a steak and tosses it across the clearing to Zsuzsa—who gulps it down. Just darts her head, and the stake is a lump about a foot down behind Zsuzsa's head.

"Live and let live," says Mary, gesturing with her hands. She moves the toroidal astral body into view. Slides he hands around the outer surface. "I live out here." Then she sticks her hands down inside the torus. Slight tingle. "You live in there." She sends hearts, smiles, flowers, and a raw stake.

Zsuzsa emits a long wavering hiss that just might be a friendly laugh. And then she disappears into a hole beside the tree that Mary hadn't noticed. Whew. She sits back down on the chair—with her somewhat compromised halo floating over her head.

Despite all the weird interpersonal—can she use that word relative to an alien snake? Despite all the weird back and forth, Zsuzsa's astral body is a great storage medium, and a great platform for her emulated mind's Fweedle code. Mary feels more like her real self all the time. Especially with that giant rattlesnake out of sight. Maybe this is turning into a happy ending.

***

And now, at last, they make love. It's great. Although at one point Mary wraps her legs around Gee's abdomen and squeezes so hard that he nearly suffocates.

"Easier to swallow my prey when its unconscious," she tells him when he protests.

"We might just want you to roll back to a regular lifebox on the redwood server tree," says Gee as he catches his breath.

***

[Tweet version]

Mary: "My lifebox mind—I share it with an alien snake?"

Gee: "It's OK."

Later Mary and Gee make love. And Mary scissors her legs around Gee's chest and squeezes so hard that he nearly suffocates.

Mary: "Easier to swallow my prey if its unconscious."

Gee: "Maybe you go back to a solo lifebox."

Server-Aided Port from Lifebox to Halo

This is almost right, but I rewrote it yet again to make it totally indie and do-it-yourself. Something a lifebox can do on its own. Had to do this so the giant mass migration at the end of the book works.

"Halo is great," says Gee, who's channeling her thoughts. "A lifebox that floats around on its own. A mind outside your body."

"So give me a nudge."

"My server will arrange your info into an optimal pattern for this. And I'm draping a yubba vine around the redwood's exit hole. It's alive with electromagnetic fields that will help you be assemble your halo."

"No dials and wires?"

"Organisms are my lab equipment."

"I still doubt if I can—"

But now Gee is offline.

Mary senses a bright spot in the ambient green light. It's that warped triangular door at the base of the redwood tree. She's seeing it from inside. That's her assembling exit. The thick, rounded lip around the door glows a pale shade of magenta. Yubba vine energy.

Mary recalls a remark by her high-school math teacher, from sixty years ago. The teacher was wonderful lady, calm and smart, and she liked to quote the sayings of French Mathematicians like: *Allez en avant—la foi vous viendra*. Press forward—and faith will come.

Mary raises her voice in song, although what she's singing, she couldn't say. She emulates the lyrical chanting of a reggae deejay, an aria from a Mozart opera, a grrl-punk rant, a soaring gospel descant, a country-honk yowl. Singing her soul. Projecting herself.

Like a fluttery mother, the redwood server is grooming her, using energy tendrils to comb out Mary's tangled lifebox links, and arranging Mary—or the idea of Mary—into a virtual shape that resembles, well, it looks like a moon jellyfish that's steadily pulsing. A surreal, iridescent dome within the server's teepspace.

As Mary moves through the yubba-vine-wreathed portal, still singing, she feels her halo taking physical shape. She's undergoing an alchemical transformation into stable patterns of ionized air.

Two Bodies for Gee

I'll get the new Gee clone up and running, and then have old Gee immolate himself in some noble kamikaze save-the-souls or exploring-heaven gesture. Despite his prior reservations, his reached a state of enlightenment wherein he doesn't really mind scuttling his old form. He's quietly realized there's no point in having two bodies.

Don't call Me "Partner"

"Look, Mary, when the balloon goes up, your instincts are as good as mine. You're a partner."

"The word *partner* is for conning suckers. Store owners tell their checkers and baggers that they're partners."

"More than a partner.

Lifebox Control

Gee talking to Kayla.

"If a lifebox happens to be making money by running some kind of kritter as a gigworker, then it *can* control what that particular kritter does."

"What if you're dead?"

"If you're dead, and you're rich, your lifebox is controlling a clone with a blank brain—and the Top Party could be puppeteering that body. Assuming you were stupid enough to have your lifebox on Skyhive."

Gee Previewing Carson's Actions.

Gee: "Well, naturally Carson isn't going to China like we told him too. Half an hour ago he went to some big money Top Party guys, and organized a hostile takeover of Skyhive, with Carson as the new CEO, and now it's Leeta who's getting fired. Carson thinks he's leading the raid against us tonight. He plans to corner me, and take me alive right before they bomb my assembling redwood server and my compound."

Battle of Gee's Cave Draft (Mary POV)

I want to rewrite some of this to be from Carson's point of view, and include it at the end of the "Carson Pflug" chapter. Or I might still fit some of it into the end of the "Astral Body" chapter.

An explosion wakes Mary. Shit! It's already night. What were they thinking? The attack is on. Or is it? All is still. Did she dream the explosion? A faint, warm glow fills the cave. Mary's halo. And the ball walkers are in here too. They seem scared. But Mary doesn't bother to teep with them yet.

"Gee!"

He opens his eyes and smiles. "Whoah. You sent me on a dream ride, Mary. Best I've slept in months."

Another explosion. It echoes off the cliffs and hills. But it's not very near.

***

"They're hitting the dummy Gee's cave site," says Gee.

"The location that the navigation systems paste in whenever any kind of mapping device thinks its tracked me down. My malware hack. Unfortunately I couldn't divert it by much more than mile."

"I don't hear a helicopter," says Mary.

"Flappy biots," says Gee. "Launched by the Top Party. Like I told you, Carson teamed up with them."

"So where is he now?"

Gee sits up, naked and stern. He does his thin-lipped smile. Mimes an explosion with his hands flying apart.

"I'm thinking that Carson got there early. He asked my thudhumper Bernardo take him to the cave instead of the airport. He figured he'd take me hostage before the bomb." Gee raises his eyebrows. "Couple of slip-ups. Bernardo took Carson to the fake Gee's cave, dumped him there, and took off. And the bombing came earlier than Carson had heard it would. Hoist by his own petard"

"Carson got blown up?" says Mary.

Gee nods. "And Leeta erased his lifebox. Right before the Top Party fired her from Skyhive."

"So you and I are free and clear?"

"Not exactly."

Leeta hears voices from afar—some rough, some shrill. Men and women picking their way through the woods.

"Can't spoof direct human vision," says Gee. "When the Top Party realized their target was off by at least a mile, they got about three hundred old Treadlers to volunteers. A line of them, two miles long. They know we're *somewhere* in this ass-end scrap of wilderness. And within mile of the bombing. They're like beaters flushing game. They'll know it when the reach our clearing. The smells. The ultraweak wireless. The ambient teep."

"Time to get dressed," says Mary, pulling on her clothes. Good thing she has heavy shoes. "Let's ambush them. I'll tell my halo not to glow."

"You, me, and my animal friends," says Gee.

"You don't have a machine gun?"

Carson Proposes Skyhive Takeover

Later I decided it would make the plot work better if the

takeover is Jerr Boom's idea.
***

It's me that should be running Skyhive, and not Leeta. Yes. And suddenly I see the way. Hostile takeover! I'll call Jerr Boom. He'll get some Top Party donors to buy out Skyhive.

But, um, why would those fat cats listen to me? Well, look, by now, being out of power has got to be chapping their asses. And they can't go all killer cowboy on Sudah Mareek. The public, the hackers, and the Secret Service—they love Sudah, and pay-back assassination isn't in the cards. The Top Party needs elegant lateral moves. Such as taking over Skyhive, the largest immortality-rental company in the world.

The win for the Top Party? They'll control the tens of thousands of lifebox souls inside the Skyhive server. They can set these souls to screwing up our society in a zillion different ways. Before long, people will want the grand old Top Party back. Make our country great again.

The win for me? I'll be the Skyhive CEO. And Leeta will be out on her ass. And I'll have our security staff and the One Party thugs do a terminal hit on Gee Willikers and his dumb-ass cave. And, who knows, who knows, eventually I might still get Kayla back.

By now it's two in the afternoon. I put in a teep call to my Jerr Boom, with my psidot in crypto cloaked mode.

"Leeta fired me and I want to get even," I tell him. "Big time."

"Big is good," says Jerr. "The Top Party is feeling small."

"I'm thinking of a one-two-three," I say. "We take control of Skyhive. I become CEO. We raid Gee Willikers."

Sergeant Bilko

I was going to use the name Sergeant Bilko for my charac-ter Phil Bilko, because I loved the Phil Silvers comedy show about Sgt. Bilko in the late 1950s. But then I decided this would bore or repel or baffle my readers younger than 70—so I just changed the name to Phil throughout. I briefly considered making the name change "on stage," but then decided that would be a pointless distraction. But here it is, with Kayla talking.
***

All my life I've had trouble finding the right man. My two art-fab pals Max Prank and Sergeant Bilko could be prospects. Well, no, Max is gay, so not him. And Sergeant—why does he insist on that stupid first name? It's some 20th Century cultural referent, but who cares. A twelve-year-old's idea of wit. But I do like the tweaky kritters he makes, also he's funny, and he smells good, and he wants me.

I teep Sergeant Bilko as Carson's thudhumper disappears through the trees.

"Hey," I tell Sergeant Bilko. "It's me. I can date you, but you have to change your first name."

"My trademark," he says.

"I don't ever want to say that name again," I tell him. "It's stupid. I need for somebody to consider my feelings for once in my motherfucking life."

"A little wound up, are we?"

"Pick a new name or I'm hanging up and I'm never talking to you again."

"Never again!" he's amused, but slightly worried. "Okay, fine, you can call me Phil. The actor who played Sergeant Bilko on TV in the late 1950s was called Phil, so—"

"No explanation needed," I interrupt. "Phil is fine. Do you want to come over?"

Danes Show Up

And my old partners in crime Gyr and Anselm are showing up around three am

***

In the night I hear some stupid yelling out in Gee's living-room. People with accents so extreme they sound fake. A comedy act? Oh, right, it's Gee's friends from Denmark. Fine.

***

Now that we're actually getting up, it's finally quiet in the living-room. Two women lie entangled on a couch beneath a blanket—Gyr and Molly? A troll-like older man with a beard snores on a pile of cushions. Surely that's Anselm.

Leeta Tells About Top Party Takeover

I liked this scene, but it became obsolete, as Maurice would already know about the takeover by the time this scene would

happen.

"Teep Leeta!" Kayla tells him. She gestures at the hooting mob below. "The kritters and clones, are powered by gigworking Skyhive lifeboxes, right? Leeta can take those lifeboxes off the job. Left on their own, the kritters and clones won't hate us. And we can put out the fire in time.'

Yes!" yells Maurice. "Yes, yes, yes!"

A moment later he's teeping with Leeta—but he's so excited that he's also yelling out loud. "Leeta, baby, it's your old running bud Maurice Winch. *Yeah*, I'm back. Who else could have utterly destroyed the Top Party bunker lab? Me and Molly Santos and this wild new talent called Kayla Stux. Teaming up like old freal times. You're still one of us, right?"

Leeta teeps some acts version of "No."

"Listen to me, will you? There's a few hundred asshole rioters here by Gee's cave. Mostly kritters and clones, run by Skyhive lifeboxes. And you're the Skydive CEO, right? So do us a favor and turn them the fuck off."

A longer pause, while Leeta teeps some intricate demurral.

"How do you mean, sold the company?" cries Maurice. "Who? Carson *Pflug* is CEO? Well, listen, Leeta, I've been zoned out in teepspace for a year and a half so how the fuck am I supposed to know every detail of whatever shady shit that you and Jerr Boom and the Top Party and the Citadel Club have been—"

Another pause. Leeta is still explaining. I have the impression she's annoyed. But Maurice is on a trip of his own. He's having an inspiration. His face turns sly, and his expression takes on a hopeful cast. Like a death-row prisoner overhearing a call about his reprieve.

"Never mind all that, Leeta. I didn't mean to hurt your feelings. And no, I don't think you're shady. Wait! Don't hang up. It took me a minute to understand that Carson Pflug and Jerr Boom are in charge of Skyhive. Fine. So now all I need to do is to ask one of them to turn the rioters off. No problem. I'll do that. Thanks for helping me."

Kayla gives Maurice a very odd look, but he keeps piling on the bullshit.

"And listen, Leeta, while I'm talking to Carson and Jerr, I'll make sure they get you hired back at Skyhive. They went too far. And you're my old friend. I'll that see you come back in as Skyhive brass, okay? Senior strategist. *Yeah*, I can do that. I'm the Man."

What Do the New Halo Lifeboxes Do Now?

I was going to map it out in detail, but that's too boring.

If a given halo lifebox's owner is still alive, the default choice is to fly to the owners' side, wherever they are, and to move in with them. But if the owner is very far away, then the halos also have the option of perching on a tree in Gee's grove or, for that matter, settling anywhere at all.

The lifebox's whose owners are dead fall into two categories. In the cases where a halo is associated with a kritter or clone remote, it may suit the owner to keep the halo near the remote. And in the cases where the halo has no associated body at all, the halo again might live in Gee's grove, or anywhere else at all.

NOVEL DESIGN

SUMMARY

Juicy Ghosts is about politics, telepathy, and immortality. I started it in 2019, as a reaction to Donald Trump's repeated remarks that he planned to be a *three*-term president. That pushed me over the edge.

I started with a short story called "Juicy Ghosts." Rebels bring down an insane, evil President who's stolen an election. They sting him with a lethally tweaked wasp, erase the online backup of his mind, and explode his clone. Too much? It's hard to stop, when you're having this much fun! Over the next two years, my story grew into a novel. I had to write it. I had to stand and be counted.

So, yes, *Juicy Ghosts* is a tale of political struggle—but it's more than that. It's hip and literary, with romance and tragedy. Plus gnarly science, and lots of funny scenes. I used a loose, say-anything style. The point-of-view characters are outsiders and slackers. The majority of them are women, and they give the tale a grounded tone.

We'll see commercial telepathy, or *teep*, before long. And

we'll want a channel that's richer than text and images. Users might transmit templates for the neurochemicals that are affecting their current mood. Your friends feel your pheromones! In *Juicy Ghosts,* people do this with *gossip molecules*, which are nano-assemblers with tiny antennas.

I've been writing about digital immortality since my early cyberpunk novel *Software.* The idea is to represent a soul by a digital program and a data-base, calling the construct a *lifebox.* But in *Juicy Ghosts* a lifebox needs to be linked to a physical body. It's not enough to be a ghost—you want to be a *juicy ghost.* The linked body might be an insect or an animal or a biotweaked bot—but high-end users will have tank-grown clones.

Lifeboxes and clones will be expensive, so most people will settle for free lifebox storage provided by tech giants. The catch is that if you accept this free service, you're obligated to do gig-work for the company—as a bodyguard, a chauffeur, a maid, of a factory worker. Typical of our times!

I like happy endings. I'd rather laugh than cry. My characters destroy the evil President's political party, topple the pay-to-play immortality racket, and provide everyone with free lifeboxes and physical bodies. Ta-da!

TIMELINE

I think of the start year as 2060, an election year. A forty-year jump from now—analogous to how I wrote *Software* in 1980 and set it in 2020. But this time I won't actually mention the year date in the book.

Date in US	Event
2060	
May - June	Carson works with Leeta. Joins Top Party and marries Kayla.
Oct 27, Wed	Jerr Boom hires Carson to send Loftus to spy on Molly.
Oct 27, Wed	Molly, Leeta Anselm, Gee at apartment in SF. Get high on stumble
Oct 28, Thu	Come down off high Kill Loftus. Fly to Copenhagen.

Oct 29, Fri	Arrive Copenhagen, morning local time. Cure Molly, sleep with Gyr.
Oct 30, Sat	Gyr and Anselm have Treadle Disease. Molly starts work.
Oct 31, Sun, 9 pm	Molly cures Treadle Disease. It's Nov 1, 6 am, in Denmark, Molly's body dies and she puts her lifebox into distributed storage.
Nov 1, Mon,	Gee, Gyr, Leeta leave Nov 1, noon, DK time, arrive SF Nov 1, 3 pm, CA time. Maurice burns Top Party offices 9 pm. Meets Gee, Leeta, and Gyr team.
Nov 2, Tue	Treadle Election Day.
2061	
Jan 20, Thu	Triple hit on Treadle. Kayla becomes pregnant with Daia.
August	Mary plays with Squash Plant at Pot O' Gold and meets Gee. He tells her the Top Party is coming back strong.
October 10, Mon	Baby Daia is born.
2062	
April 2, Sun – April 15, Sat,	"Mary sick for 2 weeks, dies. Daia 6 months old. Mary in Skyhive for 2 days. Then in clone. Argues with Carson.
April 16, Sun,	Mary tells Kayla about Carson hitting on her. They go to the bar, meet Gee, Mary rides thudhumper to Gee's house, sleeps in separate bed.
April 17, Mon	Mary & Gee raid skyhive, liberate Mary's lifebox. Mary ports to halo lifebox. She fucks Gee. Meanwhile Carson and Jerr Boom take over Skyhive. Carson is killed by Jerr Boom trying to attack Gee's cave. Maurice Winch drives Phil Bilko to Kayla's house, and they drive to Gee's.
April 18, Tue morn.	In the wee hours, Phil and Kayla plant their kritter sprouts at Gee's and they fuck. And Molly gets a halo lifebox and a clone body. At dawn, Molly kills Jerr Boom's clone. Kayla,

	Molly, and Maurice Winch destroy Coggy and Top Party bunker lab in SF. Top Party Skyhive remotes raid Gee cave. Bunters & Miss Minis and Maurice/Utila defend.
April 18, Tue later.	Kayla takes over Skyhive, turns off remote raiders. Victory. Turns out Molly can teleport or "renormalize." She hops Kayla to San Lorenzo. Jerr Boom kidnaps Daia. Molly kills him for good. And Maurice wipes out his lifebox at the KGB. Gyr & Anselm arrive by teleport at midnight.
April 19, Wed	All at Gee's. Everyone gets a halo lifebox. They port all the Gee and Skyhive lifeboxes into halo lifeboxes. The world is back on track.

TITLE

I was originally going to call the novel *Juicy Ghosts*, but then for a while I switched to what seemed like a simpler, more commercial name: *Teep*. But after I finished the novel, I decided it really *should* be *Juicy Ghosts*, as that's a more intriguing title, and teep is really just a small part of the book. So as you look through these notes, keep in mind that when I talk about my novel *Teep*, I'm talking about *Juicy Ghosts*.

CHARACTERS

It's better not to have more characters than necessary. So I try to have each of them play parts in more than one chapter. But even so, I ended up with maybe eleven of them. For some of them, I put the name of their psidot after their name.

- *Molly Santos*. Bibi. She's in "Mean Carrot" and "Treadle Disease. She starts a romance with Gyr, and disappears while curing Treadle Disease. I think she'll return from living in the net-mind AI Metatron, and get a new body—but maybe she'll prefer to remain discorporate.
- *Leeta Patel*. Leeta is in "Mean Carrot," "Juicy Ghost," and "Mary Mary." Leeta's family is from India. She's

a mixture of good and bad. She and Carson Pflug went to UC Berkeley biotech biz management school together and both got expelled.

- *Gee Willikers.* In the foreground or background of every chapter. The old mad scientist genius bio & teep hacker who invents everything. He ends up in a rejuvenated body with Mary.
- *Mary Mary.* Miu Miu. Old woman who gets new body. Kayla's neighbor. Invents the astral body. Gee's lover.
- *Anselm Saarikoski.* Finnish biohacker friend of Gee's in "Mean Carrot." Works with Molly in curing "Treadle Disease." Settles back at the Dansk Junkers in Copenhagen. Possibly he returns in the final chapter to do something with Kayla. Last name is taken from the name of a poet whom my friend Anselm Hollo translated.
- *Signe Jensen.* Molly's girlfriend in Denmark. Excellent wetware engineer. Works with Anselm. Changed from Gyr to Signe to avoid confusion with Gee.
- *Liva.* Signe's older friend.
- *Maurice Winch.* Jilljill. The star of "Juicy Ghost." Goes into storage afterwords, but possibly comes back for a late chapter. I don't see him hooking up with anyone, unless it's Leeta.
- *Carson Pflug.* Trony. He's in "Juicy Ghosts" in a minor role. Marries Kayla and gets a job with Leeta. Plays a villain in "Mary Mary," and "Showdown" is from his POV, and he turns out to be a bit more sympathetic a character than expected. Possibly he saves the day.
- *Kayla Stux.* Younger character in "Mary Mary." An artist, biobot sculptor and repairwoman. Married to Carson, divorces him. Possibly she's back in the final chapter."
- *Phil Bilko.* Fellow kritter artist. Friend of Kayla's.
- *Jerr Boom.* Tweaky Bird. Shitweasel triple agent, works for Top Party, Skyhive, and Gee. Employs Carson Pflug.

CHAPTER SKETCHES

These are very informal and scrappy outlines that I did not in fact use much, nor did I update them afterwards to make them accurate. Nor does the outline run to the end of the book.

1. Mean Carrot

POV Molly, San Francisco. Includes Leeta, Anselm, Gee Willikers

I should resolve a sexism #metoo issue. Molly and Leeta are, in effect, prostitutes. And the resolution consists of each of them "finding a man." The women are strong and tough, but even so, the basic set-up is what they call "problematic" these days. Perhaps I can position them as being drug dealers rather than party girls? That's not enough. Make them be scientists. Give them equal footing. *Big* rewrite for this.

2. Treadle Disease

POV Molly. Copenhagen. Includes Gee Willikers. Anselm, Molly, and Curtis Winch

I need several things in this story.

(1) The backstory of the Treadle dictatorship—and the Freal liberation movement. Gee, Leeta, Curtis, Anselm and Molly are involved with the Freals. Anselm is a hardcore anarchist. Should have some groundwork for this in "Mean Carrot." Street demos. Troubles with cops and passports. Growing sense of doom,

(An alternate chapter title: "The Stone Pillow." That's the name of an unwritten story by Robert Heinlein, which was meant to lay the ground for the rebellion against a religious autocrat in his story "If This Goes On—" which appears in his collection, *Revolt in 2100*. But that's too derivative, remote, and not really focused on the main point, which is the dawn of workable teep.)

(2) The transition from the stumble fungus to the psidot slug, which I saw as being like a nudibranch. What if we keep the fungus, but have it living inside the slug—instead of inside a human host's brain. Cf. the fungus that lives inside an ant's head.

(3) The development of the online lifebox. Much of this is

in "Juicy Ghost," and in "Mary Mary," so I'd only need to lay groundwork...don't want to beat the trope to death, as by now it's rather familiar. I'd like to lift a move or two from Cory Doctorow's *Walkaway*, particularly the notion that you can test your lifebox ware to destruction, and if it crashes, you tweak and reboot.

3. Juicy Ghosts

POV Curtis Winch. Washington DC. Includes Leeta, Slammy, Gee Willikers.

First half, Curtis Winch becomes a wasp and kills Treadle.

Second half is Curtis Winch as a dog. From the point of view of a kid in the family that "owns" the Arfie-type dog whom Curtis Winch is now using as a biobot remote, via the psidot that Curtis put onto the skin on the underside of the dog's earflap. Have the kid be a girl...naturally I think of Georgia and Isabel. Call her Emma? It, would be nice to have her be Black, without making a thing of it.

Maybe Curtis bites someone and infects them with himself.

I feel this passage ought to be in there, but I don't remember if it is.

"Only by linking with a living being did the psidot lifebox personality (somewhat magically) become living. It gets quantum aha from the organism. A lifebox on its own in the cloud—it's more like a really good chatbot. It has no *soul*, in the bluesy sense of the word. It's robotic. Even though it might *say* that it's alive, it's isn't *funky*. It's a Spork-language cloud-based data-base-mining computational architecture with no real mind."

4. Mary Mary

POV Mary. Carson, Gee Willikers, Kayla

Maybe I split this chapter in two, and stretch out the second half just one or two more scenes worth. Rather than writing a whole extra "noise" chapter? We'll see if I want that "noise" chapter or not when we get there.

Those tattered ectoplasm ghosts I have floating around near the end—I almost wonder if it was a mistake to bring them in.

5. Astral Body

POV Mary.

Mary gets a quintessence vortex ring for her lifebox storage, and she has her clone meat body. Gee retrofits his meat body.

6. Carson Pflug

Run back through the events from Carson's point of view, clarifying what was going on behind the scenes. Kill Carson at the end.

7. Kayla Stux

Kayla and her friend Phil Bilko grow some kritters to help Gee. They become lovers. Curtis is back. Curtis, Molly, and Kayla go to SF and burn out the Top Party bunker lab.

8. Molly Santos

The raiders have surrounded Gee's cave, he's under siege in side with Mary and Phil. They figure out way to get Skyhive to decommission the gigworker AI of the rioters. Gyr comes over to be with Molly. Lots of astral body lifeboxes. Happy ending.

More?

Two extra things. (1) A distinction between the dark matter ectoplasm astral body ghosts and the old school ghosts. (2) Embodying your soul as a hylozoic natural computation, a spirit of place.

A shift or double-deal on the concept of heaven. Our physical world could be heaven just as it is, and we're the ghosts in it.

But there's something else living here as well. At first we think it's noise in the universal computation. But it's more than that.

The Author peers at his pages, unsure of his latest revisions. A vessel bursts in his brain.

Jump cut.

SOURCE MATERIAL

THE ABSOLUTE CONTINUUM

From the first draft of *"Preface for the 2019 Edition of Infinity and the Mind."* Some of this material made its way into my story "Everything Is Everything."

***

I propose that our physical space is an absolute continuum, and that Cantor's transfinites are all around.

These days people are prone to thinking digitally. The internet and the smart phone dominate intellectual life. There's a numbing tendency to equate our world with a simulation on a dinky grid. Is your mind a wind-up toy? Space a heap of blocks? Time a scrapbook of stills? The cosmos a puny integer?

Some people don't want the world to be infinite. And they invent theories to decree the world to be finite. But there's no reason to believe them. Georg Cantor argued for infinity in 1885:

> The fear of infinity is a form of myopia that destroys the possibility of seeing the actual infinite, even though it in its highest form has created and sustains us, and in its secondary transfinite forms occurs all around us and even inhabits our minds.

When Cantor speaks of "infinity in its highest form," he means something like the Cosmic One, the Big Aha, or the White Light. It doesn't have to be a traditional religious thing. I'm thinking of an all-suffusing glow, or a feeling that all is one—an experience which many of us have, however briefly. Thereby we get a numinous sense of the absolute infinite.

And when Cantor speaks of transfinite forms being all around us and in our minds, he's expressing another aspect of our perceptions. When you're in a relaxed mood, the physical world feels smooth, sensual, rich, and endless. Note, however, that if you're feeling stressed, the world seems cramped, shoddy, and all too finite.

Cantor was inspired by his wonderful 1873 theorem that

the countable infinity of the integers is smaller than the infinity of decimal values on the real number line, which is often called mathematical space, or the continuum.

Our world would be less interesting if all infinities were the same. Cantor showed that there's a tower of infinities: starting with alef-null and alef-one, also written as $\aleph_0$ and $\aleph_1$. The scale runs ever upward, with the absolute infinity Ω at the top, like the vanishing point in a perspective painting. Ω is somewhat ineffable. If you reach out to grab it, you always find you're holding some smaller cardinal κ. This phenomenon is known as the Reflection Principle. You can't ever manage to grasp Ω tightly enough to say, "What about $\Omega + 1$?"

In *Juicy Ghost*, I'm going to focus on an additional type of absolute infinity: the *absolute continuum*, also known as the class of surreal numbers, or *No*. It's much larger than the garden-variety space continuum of decimal numbers. In an absolute continuum, every gap is filled.

By a "gap" we mean any two sets of points L and R, with every member of L being less than every member of R. In an absolute continuum, there's always a point in between. And we're allowed to have L or R be an empty set. So if L is {1, 2, 3, 4, …} and R is empty, then the simplest number in the "gap" will be alef-null.

The construction principle doesn't sound like much, but it produces a lot. You end up with all the familiar real numbers, plus all of Cantor's transfinite alefs, plus the infinitesimal *reciprocals* of all the alefs, not to mention crazy things like "the alef-seventh root of pi divided by alef-one."

John Conway worked out the theory of the absolute continuum in his ground-breaking book, *On Numbers and Games*, and his system was elegantly popularized in Donald Knuth's *Surreal Numbers*. The famous computer pioneer Bill Gosper once remarked: "Conway is approximately the smartest man in the world."

The absolute continuum *No* is a type of absolute infinity that's quite distinct from the "largest number" Ω.

No is at least as big as its subclass Ω, and it may be bigger. There's a sense in which the class No is *wider* than the class Ω. In fact *No* is as rich as V, the class of all sets. We don't know the exact size of *No*, and maybe it can't even be measured on a linear size scale like the alefs. I'll touch on this issue in my fifth chapter, "The One and the Many." By the way, asking whether the absolute continuum *No* has size Ω is akin to Cantor's Continuum Problem, which asks if the decimal real number line has size $\aleph_1$.

I'm claiming that we live in an absolute continuum like *No*. A four-dimensional absolute continuum of space and time. How might we imagine perceiving this?

Discrete infinities aren't very natural to think about—consider the stars in an endless universe or the ticks of an eternal clock. Imagining them requires you to partition seamless reality into chunks, and to enumerate the pieces, and to find room for them all.

It's easier to think of infinity in terms of continua. An interval of time, a gradation of color, a nuance of feeling, a puff of air—these range along infinitely subtle continua that are compact enough to keep in your room.

And what of Cantor's transfinites, that is, alef-one, alef-two, and the rest of his prankster band? Keep in mind that if physical space is an *absolute* continuum, it extends all the way out to Ω. And, as I mention in my "All the Numbers" chapter, one can think of alternate universes as being located at transfinite removes. You can stash an absolutely infinite supply of alternate worlds on the road to Ω.

But, again, it's more satisfying to think about infinities that are within our immediate purview. And this can be done with the transfinites. Given that, say, alef-three is on the absolute continuum, then the reciprocal of alef-three exists, and it's very nearby. And—if there are alternate universes out there, we can fit them in right here. Like reflections in the mirrored surface of a glass ornament. Within the infinitesimal subdimensions of our bodies.

As Jorge-Luis Borges might put it, alef-seven dreams in the petal of a rose.

At this point I need to interrupt my agreeable fantasia and mention the tedious difficulties posed by quantum mechanics. One hears that it's meaningless to speak of space at levels smaller than at lengths below, say, 10^{-35} meters. And some

even say that space itself is tessellated into indivisible lumps.
Ah, the myopic fear of infinity! First comes a call for
finitistic austerity, then a grudging admission that granular
space doesn't quite make sense, and then comes the lilting
injunction: "Be happy! The universe is incomprehensible! How
wonderful!"

To me, incoherence isn't wonderful. It means your theory
isn't done. Reality comes first. Theories come second. In this
vein, I'll quote a few lines from a 1926 poem by e e cummings,
entitled "voices to voices, lip to lip."

> While you and i have lips and voices which
> are for kissing and to sing with
> who cares if some oneeyed son of a bitch
> invents an instrument to measure Spring with?
> ...since the thing perhaps is
> to eat flowers and not to be afraid.

Great. The world arises on its own, and it exists independently of our theories about it. Our ever-changing opinions
can't limit what the world can do.

Brave words, but how am I going to preserve our absolute
continuum in the face of quantum mechanics? Well, let's
suppose that the quantum level is like an interzone, or a glitch,
or a rumble-strip. We can trundle right over it.

And beyond, or beneath, or beside, this layer we enter what
I like to call the subdimensions. According to the viewpoint
I'm describing, our physical space has sub-quantum,
subdimensional levels that allow space to be an absolute
continuum.

I think of an 1877 work, *Die Philosophie des Als Ob*, by
Hans Vaihinger. In English the title would be *The Philosophy
of As If*. I like those two words *Als Ob*. Vaihinger proposes that
you might, if only for pleasure, choose to believe certain kinds
of metaphysical doctrines, even if there seems to be no hope of
proving them.

Right now I'm fascinated by the notion that our physical
space is an absolute Conway continuum. I've always felt it's
sad to stare out at the stars and yearn for distant vastness. We
can have humongous infinities right here.

Thinking this way makes the world seem more interesting, and provides a sense of peace. And there's an extra bonus to having our space be an absolute continuum. You yourself are absolutely infinite!

Any bounded region of a continuum can be put into a point-to-point correspondence with the whole of that continuum. This holds for the absolute continuum as well.

So if your world is an absolute continuum, then your body comprises an absolute continuum. And therefore, yes, you're absolutely infinite, just as you are. Your endlessly various gnarliness threads down past the alef-seventh level, and ever deeper towards the ineffable $1/\Omega$. You're a higher being, friend.

One more bonus: There is a popular quantized-space argument for the claim that, if you are only a finite pattern, and if space is infinite, then your pattern is likely to repeat. There will be endlessly many yous. How dull. And what a waste of infinity. Happily, this argument doesn't go through if you and the cosmos are both the same size continua. If you're absolutely infinite, you have enough wiggle room to be terminally unique.

***

Okay, now it's time for my fervent peroration.

Here in 2018, my wife Sylvia and I drove to the seaside town of Santa Cruz the other day. While she scavenger-hunted the shops for buttons for two children's sweaters she'd knit, I sat on the 3rd Avenue Beach in the sun for a couple of hours, enjoying the long smooth waves, and pondering this preface.

As I say, I'm trying to think that the space around us really *is* transfinite—not only with all the usual real numbers, but with even more points dusted into the infinitesimal gaps. I'm saying space is an absolute continuum, jam-packed with surreal numbers. And never mind about atoms or quantum mechanics—you can go on down and down. And sure, there might even be alternate universes down there—why not! There's room for everything amid the cascading levels of alefs.

Dream with me. Let our full native space be a glittering absolute continuum, running up and down the size scales, with no end in sight. We've been safe in heaven all along, with stars twinkling within and without, our absolute continuum like a phosphorescent sea, like a spangled scarf of light, as above so below.

If only I could ever remember that for more than a minute at a time!

ON *HYLOZOIC*

I started rereading *Hylozoic* in February 7, 2019, looking for insights on telepathy and embodied minds.

I'd forgotten how many things I put in there. I have to admit this book is a daunting read for many, or even most people, or even me. I'd forgotten how hardcore SF I decided to go on this one. It would help of course if you've recently read its prequel, *Postsingular*—which I haven't read in a long time.

Such a blizzard of made-up words and outré science at the start. Silps, teep, teek. Quantum this and quantum that. Octillions of atoms. Eighth-dimensional memory. The Big Pig soul of Gaia.

Maybe, *sob*, my SF novels aren't as readable and accessible as I imagine them to be. At least not *Hylozoic*. Even the *title* requires an initial note to explain.

Anyway, in this post, I'll compile a list of specific things I might want to reuse in the *Juicy Ghost* stories. And while I'm at it, I'll mention any glitches I notice.

***

GLITCHES

That wall they build in Chapter 1, I got a feeling that the foundation row's top wasn't flat enough to be balancing those shale stones on to make a sill. I say the foundation row is disk-like stones lined up like books on a shelf, which suggests the top will be kind of domed, like you have a cylinder lying on its side. I should have said those stones were like triangles, with the points down.

***

THINGS TO REUSE

Projecting your mind into a bluejay is good.

The idea of each waterfall having a little soul, or "silp" is good. I can sense that in the St. Joseph's Hill woods these days, hiking along that seasonal creek, off the bend on the path to the old nunnery. Each cataract has its own soul

I used the Latin phrase *genius locus* for *spirit of place*.

Telepathy is fine, but having teleportation and telekinesis is a little much. They're essential to *Postsingular/Hylozoic*, but I won't use them in *Juicy Ghost*. But you totally need telepathy if you want to talk to the silps and juicy ghosts. Re. telepathy, we do it via quantum entanglement?

JOURNAL NOTE ON FREETOWN CHRISTIANA

From my published *Journals 1990-2014*
June 19, 2000. København. Freetown Christiana

Mogens, Morten and I took a water taxi across the harbor, and entered Christiania from a marshy area that felt like the countryside—ponds, reeds, trees, a barn or two, gravel roads. Before long we were seeing small, hand-built houses, brightly colored, some with fanciful roofs.

We passed two kids who were gently and sympathetically leading a staggering-drunk woman away from the roadside where she'd passed out. They were taking her towards the village center, presumably to her room. It wasn't like the U.S. at all. Back home, you hardly ever see individuals helping or even touching a drunk street person. Instead we call in the authorities.

The gravel roads and pathways of Christiania were immaculately clean—no litter, and none of the broken glass you'd see back home. I marveled at this, and Mogens said, "We maintain a certain level of order on our own."

"That's something we're unable to do in America," I said ruefully.

There's some friction with the Danish police in any case. The Christiania Cafe had a sign saying something like, "This is the safest cafe in Copenhagen. We've had six thousand police raids since 1974."

§

A sudden rainstorm hit, and we stood under some eaves. A guy near us was smoking a blunt. Nearby someone was playing an AC/DC album. The band was in fact slated to give a concert at a Copenhagen soccer stadium that night.

"Are you ready to rock and roll?" I screeched in my Angus and Brian voice.

"I find this a little bit exhilarating," remarked Morten, looking around. "Do you realize that we've just walked the exact same route that Søren Kierkegaard used to take in the 1840s, wandering through Christiania? This is the very same philosopher who called himself a fly on Hegel's nose. And you're Hegel's great-great-great-grandson, no?"

STORY INFO

STORY IDEAS

I might be working on some short stories as well as a novel, so I'm keeping sketches of possible story ideas in this leading section—where they're easy to find. Note that there's more thoughts on these stories scattered though the individual Writing Notes entries further below.

I also added in a few items from my older "Story Ideas" document that has been kicking around for several years.

And as time went by, I put an asterisk in front of the names of the stories I actually wrote.

* Mary Falls Sketch

Later I changed this title to "Mary Mary."

I think I first wrote this up around March 15, 2019.

Mary is a nice old woman. She dies and migrates into the digital afterworld under the auspices of a company called Juicy Ghost.

They equip her with a physical world peripheral, a tank-grown human body. Mary-2. From the cloud, Mary can see through Mary-2's eyes. And she can control what Mary-2 does.

Mary gets evicted from Mary-2 by a pushy juicy ghost that poses as her.

Juicy Ghost Incorporated acknowledges the error, but the only available peripheral is a biotech ranger-drone in a National Forest, electrically zapping dogs who misbehave.

Even in this body, the unfortunate Mary is evicted by a fake Mary. The Juicy Ghost company blames Mary for losing her body, they sever her contract, but as a consolation, they link Mary to a natural chaotic computation. That is, she becomes the spirit of place in a cascade in the forest's creek.

In the summer, the falls dry up. Mary has learned about natural computations. She mutates into the slow computation of the shifting of the crystals in the sedimentary stone.

I could merge "Mary Falls" / "Mary Mary" with my inside-Silicon-Valley-business "Teep" idea, have Mary become commercial teep crystals. A pattern in a stone. Have that be her tombstone, and call it "Mary's Stone"?

For a final twist. She does a repo on the squatter.

* *Everything is Everything*

I wrote on the topic of the Absolute Continuum a few years ago as "Jack and the Aktuals," and then in August, 2019, I put a taste of absolute continuum into "Everything Is Everything," which was initially named "Dream Work," and then "The Egg."

* *The Mean Carrot*

Hanging around with my five-years-older brother in Maine made me think again about that story But I don't have a kicker. I have the eight-year-old boy character and the overbearing carrot, and the carrot in some fashion abusing or oppressing the boy, although I'm not clear on how to frame this. The carrot whispering to the innocent boy, lying next to him in bed, the tip of the carrot twitching and producing a sticky drop of smeel.

This might be an upsetting story to work on. But maybe worth doing. Now that I did the upsetting Presidential assassination story, "Juicy Ghost," maybe do another upsetting story. Dig deep and do a string of upsetting stories? Oh, come on, Rudy, are you nuts? Write things that make you happy.

Push the Mean Carrot further. Oh I know, the Mean Carrot can be in the CIA dope story described just below. The Mean Carrot could be a controller alien. And I could write that without getting all emotional. It could even be funny.

So now I'm segueing into this story I wanted to write with Richard Kadrey, a story which somehow takes off on the early 1960s San Francisco party girls who, in the employ of the CIA, would administer LSD to their Johns so that male CIA agents could watch the effect though two-way mirrors in the apartment walls. The kicker would be that one of the women is an alien agent who is preserving classic new types. And then at the climax she preserves the CIA narrator guy.

The alien looks like a Mean Carrot. The Mean Carrot in bed with the CIA op guy. A languorous tryst. The tip of the carrot twitching and producing a sticky drop of homosex smeel.

I used the entrapment trope in the "pop-up restaurant = alien lobster-trap" story I wrote with Paul Di Filippo, "Yubba Vines." But this will be very different.

Not quite sure this is relevant, but I remember seeing a kinda-porn video in the early 1980s about the transsexual Sulka, and most of it was a guy on a psychedelic trip with Sulka and he doesn't know what he's doing. Very soft-core, lots of silhouettes and Da-Glo color washes. It's not even clear what the guy does with Sulka, nor clear whether she's pre-op or post-op. Maybe it was called "Sulka's Wedding?" I can't imagine now where I saw this video. They didn't have internet then. Did I see in in a Times Square peep house? Was there a porn video rental place in Lynchburg skeevy enough to have this video as a VHS? Doesn't seem likely. Maybe I got it at the Chinese liquor story in Los Gatos who rented porn? Would they have had this title? Would I have bothered to watch it? Evidently my memories of this episode have been selectively erased. Anyway it's fodder for the story.

Here are some more notes for story, made I made a couple of years ago.

Write about the CIA's 60s practice of dosing investigative targets with acid administered by hookers in San Francisco bars. And bringin aliens. See this 1979 book, John Marks, *The Search for the Manchurian Candidate*, and this link to a 2012 article in *SF Weekly*.

https://archives.sfweekly.com/sanfrancisco/operation-midnight-climax-how-the-cia-dosed-sf-citizens-with-lsd/Content?oid=2184385&showFullText=true

I'm thinking don't have it be in the 60s—although the nostalgia is tempting—have it be now.

Pynchon in *GR* wrote of a drug called (maybe) New Stuff, one of whose effects was to make you forget how and where you scored it, so the only way to score it is to happen on someone who is in the act of taking it. Somehow this reminds me of one of Richard Kadrey's his fakebook pulp cover. *The Day Mom Took Molly.* "First she lost her inhibitions, Then the lost her clothes, and then she lost her mind,"

I see there being a secret lodging where the incomprehensibly advanced alien Mean Carrot is controlling things. A shed in a concrete "back yard" behind a train car apartment on Oak or Fell St. That can be where some of the characters meet, maybe at an author's birthday BBQ party. Maybe there's a stripper/comfort-woman named Molly and she's a main narrator. Possibly two alternating main narrators, Molly and the CIA researcher. That might work for a transreal approach if I co-write with Richard.

The CIA research guy is, of course, a nerdy perv. Highly sublimated.

* Surfers at the End of Time

My initial idea was for story involving branching time. Taking off on a Gibson idea from *The Peripheral.* Character could be like me in grad school. That way I could write about having toddlers—I think about that age group a lot these days from seeing my grandchildren.

Suppose there really is only one truly existing path through the branching thicket of possible worlds. The others are only juiceless abstractions. Fine.

My gimmick is that I'll suppose that our branch is not quite a pure jagged line. It *does* very commonly grow a stub out a few seconds (or longer?) past a given branch point, then back up and got to the other branch. There's a continuous line of time but it sometimes loops back a bit and then starts forward on a new tack.

Most people don't notice this, as when time backs up, events run backwards and memories get erased. But our hero or heroine *does* learn to notice. (I'll figure out the gimmick later.)

The backups are very common, in fact they're all but ubiquitous.

How to make this into a fresh and true metaphor for some transreal concern of mine? I would like to argue (by example) against the ignorant and defeatist notion that all possible universes exist. The story should hinge on there being only one or a few really existing worlds.

But the time-stub thing is rife with contradictions and paradoxes. I'm now reading Annalee Newitz, "Future of an Alternate Timeline." In this book, there's only one time line, but people can time travel, and they're continually editing the timeline.

I don't think Annalee has thought it through, but in this situation we actually have a second dimension of time. And as the time travelers act and make their edits, the timeline is changing in the second dimension of time.

So in effect there are a continuum of timelines, and you are in fact going into parallel timelines when you go into the past.

And the same is also true for a growing and shrinking stubs cosmos. Here, we are also editing our timeline and there is a second dimension of time in which the edits take place.

In my novel *Mathematicians in Love*, I had a series of parallel times, with a new one appearing each "week," having been edited and rewritten by the giant Jellyfish God of La Hampa.

***

In the end, I did my time travel story with only one timeline and no stubs. You need to take a holistic spacetime view and have only one dimension of time. That's my story with Marc Laidlaw: "Surfers at the End of Time."

STORY PUBLICATIONS

"Juicy Ghost," Posted on Rudy's Blog, June, 2019. Appeared in *Big Echo*, October, 2019.

"Surfers at the End of Time," with Marc Laidlaw, *Isaac Asimov's SF*, December, 2019.

"The Mean Carrot," *Big Echo*, March, 2020.

"Everything Is Everything," *Big Echo*, October 2020.

"Mary Mary," *Isaac Asimov's SF*, March, 2021.

"Fibonacci's Humors," with Bruce Sterling, in Italian in *Ipotesi per Fibonacci*, edited by Daniele Brolli, Comma22, 2020. And in English in *Isaac Asimov's SF*, August, 2021.

The stories that didn't end up as chapters of the novel can be found in the 2021 edition of my Complete Stories, and the original 2019 "Juicy Ghost" story—which sparked this all—is in there as well.

FAREWELL!

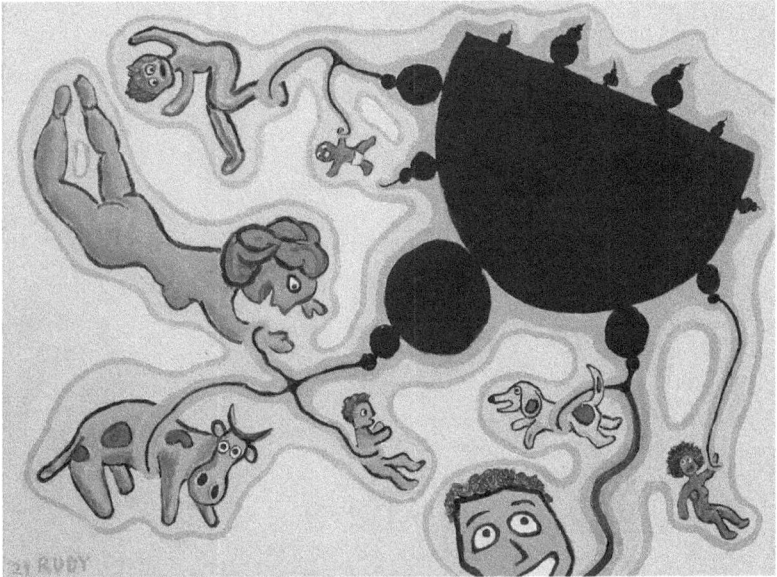

Figure 30: *Self-Portrait with Cubic Mandelbrot UFO*

Here's a last illo. Says it all. A painting I did in July, 2021, where a complex cubic Mandelbrot fractal is connected to a bunch of critters. Kind of like a multibody juicy ghost! The divine Oversoul. With me at the bottom of the frame there, smiling.

—Rudy Rucker, August 2, 2021